Adlard Coles'
HEAVY WEATHER SAILING

Adlard Coles'
HEAVY WEATHER SAILING

Thirtieth Anniversary Edition

Peter Bruce

INTERNATIONAL MARINE • CAMDEN, MAINE

Contents

Part 2
STORM EXPERIENCES

Foreword

SIR PETER BLAKE

In 600 000 ocean miles to date, I have been in many gales – in small and large yachts, and in a wing-masted multihull, the latter being probably the most worrying time of them all.

My first major gale at sea was in the south-west Pacific in 1969 with my parents in our 34ft (10m) ketch *Ladybird*. It was my first time in really heavy weather with screaming winds and seas that came crashing over the decks. The yacht was hove-to under storm jib and fully reefed mizzen. Each big wave sounded like an express train approaching, followed by a couple of seconds of quiet; then a crash that threw the yacht over on her side, at the same moment as the light coming through the ports went frothy green when the crest submerged the decks. We stayed below, playing cards and eating corned beef hash and soup. The sails shuddered violently even though they were very small and sheeted tight, as the sailmaker had not installed large enough leech cords. Although we were relatively safe in a well-found vessel, we were distinctly relieved when conditions eased.

A more recent and equally memorable experience took place early in 1980, when we were caught in the Tasman Sea by the tropical Cyclone David as we headed towards Auckland in the maxi-yacht *Condor*. We had plenty of warning, were well away from land, and took precautions very early on.

Despite much criticism from one of the crew, who thought we should still be sailing, the yacht was hove-to under trysail and storm jib as the wind rose above 30 knots. Then, with the wind going off the clock for long periods, the jib was soon down. The surface of the sea was smoking as though it was on fire. All the small waves had disappeared – just blown away – and we felt that being hove-to was the best way of riding out this storm. As conditions worsened we discussed, but did not employ, what we felt was our only other option, which was to run before the seas, trailing warps. We felt that lying a'hull would have been very dangerous. Sitting harnessed on the cockpit floor we took note of the time taken to go from trough to crest of each sea – between 5 and 6 seconds – and they were the most enormous waves imaginable. When the wind eased 18 hours later – which it did very quickly, leaving us with a towering and confused cross-sea – the feeling of relief was immense. We were lucky and came through unscathed.

Even more recently, aboard the 92ft (28m) *Enza (New Zealand)*, while setting a new round-the-world non-stop record in 1994, we nearly came to grief on a number of occasions. We had near misses with icebergs, and times when we nearly went end-over-end.

We had sailed across the Pacific Ocean at between 60° and 63° south due to light head winds to the north. However, trying to make to the north as we approached the passage between Cape Horn and the Antarctic Peninsula proved very difficult as winds were between north and north-east at gale force or more. Two hundred miles south of Cape Horn the wind was peaking at 60 knots with the sea white in large patches from the fully breaking 'greybeards'. Conditions were extreme with very cold temperatures and seas that we conservatively estimated to be over 60ft (18m) high. It was a time when I wanted to be somewhere else ... anywhere else. The seas were breaking right across the yacht which, by this time, had no sail set but was being driven forward at right angles to the seas at around

10 knots. It was mid-afternoon and we were very concerned about what to do next. We tried running dead downwind with the seas behind us – but the big cat took off at 20–25 knots and would have pitch-poled before long; besides, the islands of the Antarctic Peninsula were only 250 miles away downwind, and at 20–25 knots it was not going to take long to reach them. We started work on making a drogue, the only thing we thought might save us. It was going to consist of the anchor chain and various warps strung out in a bight behind the yacht, but the wind decreased slightly and swung north-west just before dark so we were able to claw to the north and into the relative safety of the south Atlantic.

Only a few weeks later, 300 miles from the finish at Ushant in some of the worst weather I have ever encountered, we were again close to flipping. The full south-westerly storm was from behind and huge, very steep and dangerously breaking cross-seas created great holes in the ocean. *Enza* was a runaway. Twice the yacht went 'down the mine', meaning that the bows dipped, she buried right back to the mast, and both the rudders came out of the water. As the cat stopped dead from high speed one of the crew was thrown horizontally out of his bunk through a gap in the bulkhead into the galley. He was very sore, and there was chaos down below. We came down to bare poles but were still going too fast, so we quickly reassembled the drogue. In atrocious conditions the heavy chain was flaked and the anchor warp bound round it to add some area. Then, operating from both hulls, halyards and sheets of 328ft (100m) were tied at each end using sailmaker's twine to seize every knot.

We were not a moment too soon in getting the drogue streamed as the wind rose to 67 knots and the sea went totally white, but the yacht felt under control and safe again, even though she teetered at times right on the tops of vertical-looking sea faces. Boat speed peaked at 14 knots, but we were able to adjust the speed by altering the length of the lines. Closer in – higher boat speed. Further out – more drag. The drogue had turned a life-threatening situation into one over which we had some control.

Heavy weather, such as gales and the occasional storm, is a part of sailing across an ocean. One must give with the weather, as one cannot beat it. When coastal cruising, a prudent eye on the weather forecast will generally see one in harbour in time to avoid the worst. If not, then conditions on board can quickly become worse than in mid-ocean. The blasé coastal sailor may end up on a lee shore, ill prepared, and it is under these conditions that most tragedies occur. To be well clear of land removes one level of anxiety and danger. Whenever I am at sea and the weather is deteriorating I begin to get a rather hollow feeling in my stomach. Questions spin round in my head. What will the next 24 hours or so bring? Is the yacht properly prepared? Will the forecast (if there is one) be right? Have we enough sea room? Should we have a hot meal now before the seas get up? Is everything properly stowed on deck? And so on.

No two situations at sea are ever going to be the same. No two boats handle in the same way. For example, some heave-to well, some do not. Sometimes the heavy weather has been forecast, sometimes not. Weather forecasts must not be relied upon 100 per cent; it is important to look out of the window and make one's own assessment of the situation. But what is most important, whatever vessel one is in, is to be prepared. It is much easier to have thought about the consequences of heavy weather before leaving the comfort of the marina, mooring or quiet anchorage. One must add that being able to rely upon the structural integrity of one's yacht – her rig, sails, engine, hatches, general mechanical equipment and the ability of the crew – is equally important.

This book should be read and re-read by all yachtsmen and yachtswomen, whether they have aspirations to cross an ocean or simply potter about the coastline, whether they are skipper or crew. Not every idea examined will apply to every situation, but the knowledge gained may one day be invaluable. To put it in a nutshell, there is no substitute for forward planning and knowledge of what to do in heavy weather.

Preface

Adlard Coles OBE died in 1985. He left behind him a multitude of friends and admirers, many of whom knew him only through his books. Apart from his ability to write vividly and clearly, Adlard was an extraordinary man. In spite of being a diabetic, a quiet and very gentle person with something of a poet's eye, he was incredibly tough, courageous and determined. Thus it was very often that Adlard's *Cohoes* appeared at the top of the lists after a really stormy race. When reading Adlard's enchanting prose one also needs to take into account that he was supremely modest, and his scant reference to some major achievement belies the effort that must have been required. It is clear that Adlard minimized everything, which does him credit. As an example, the wind strengths he gave in his own accounts in the earlier editions of *Heavy Weather Sailing* were manifestly objective and warrant no risk of being accused of exaggeration for narrative effect.

Revision of this important book is a task that should have been carried out by Adlard himself had this been possible. With the support of Adlard's widow, Mamie, and son Ross, my father Erroll Bruce, a lifelong friend of Adlard, and the publishers, I have done my best to do what I believe Adlard would have liked to have done himself.

The fourth edition of *Heavy Weather Sailing* was a great success and somehow managed to lead on from where Adlard Coles had left off into more recent times. Adlard had perceived in his later editions that specialist expert advice was important, and this philosophy was extended in the fourth edition with contributions from authors representing responsible and experienced views that were likely to stand the test of time.

In this thirtieth anniversary edition, expert advice precedes the anecdotal text to bring theory before the practice. Moreover, as Adlard Coles' own collection of heavy weather experiences is so widely known and occupies a treasured position upon so many bookshelves worldwide, it was felt that the time had come to drop the majority of this material. Though storms at sea have not changed, the situation on board has. For example, yachtsmen usually know exactly where they are these days, removing one great difficulty experienced in bad weather in the past. There are numerous other ways in which heavy weather may affect modern craft differently, and there are many more options open to their captains. The new heavy weather experiences in this edition have been chosen not only because the storm may have been breathtakingly fierce, but also because ordinary sailors of the present will be able to relate easily to the situation.

When the fourth edition was being prepared there was some doubt in Europe as to whether some of the claims made for parachute sea anchors were valid, and a cautious line was adopted. Nearly ten years on the picture is clearer. Parachute anchors and other drag devices can be a valuable asset in survival conditions provided appropriate attention has been paid to the techniques of their use.

Out of the 27 chapters in the current edition, $1\frac{1}{2}$ chapters have been retained from the original Adlard Coles editions of *Heavy Weather Sailing*, $6\frac{1}{2}$ have been retained from the fourth edition, and there are 19 new chapters.

The earlier editions of *Heavy Weather Sailing* were more about prevention than cure and the same theme is maintained in this edition. Thus I have not gone into detail on matters such as rescue and survival, which are covered by other books. I should also mention that, as we are in an age where some have learnt Imperial units and some metric, in most places both systems have been used.

PART **1**

EXPERT ADVICE

1 Yacht design and construction for heavy weather

OLIN J STEPHENS II

Heavy weather has taken its toll among vessels of all the shapes and sizes that one can imagine, and the survivors have been just as varied. Is it worthwhile, then, to consider the design characteristics of yachts that should best survive the worst that weather can offer; or is handling the only factor? It seems clear that the boat counts too, and could be decisive, although once at sea the action of the crew is what counts.

To declare the obvious, to survive means to stay afloat, to keep water out of the hull; and further to remain in, or at worst return to, an upright condition. Strength and range of positive stability are first requirements. In the course of this study we shall try to determine how these essentials can best be refined and combined with other characteristics to provide for the safety and comfort of the offshore crew.

A lifetime around the water has shown me the many types of yacht that have come through the extremes of weather on long cruises. I think it must have been in 1926 when my brother Rod and I spotted Harry Pigeon's *Islander* lying in New Rochelle harbour, not far from our home. We were quick to greet him from a borrowed dinghy and to take him for a tour of the nearby countryside after inspecting the home-built 34ft (10.4m) yawl that he had sailed singlehanded around the world. Neither *Islander*'s light displacement nor the simple V bottom form made for survival difficulties. One was most impressed by the simplicity of the construction and equipment: no engine or electrics of any kind, no speedometer, nor even a patent log. We admired the man who made it all seem so easy. Soon we heard that Alain Gerbault and his *Firebird* were at City Island, so we went there. The contrast was in every way disappointing, but the older, heavier boat had made it through some very bad weather.

I had, and retain, a great deal of respect for the work of Dr Claud Worth, the owner, during the 1920s, of several yachts called *Tern*. He must have been a thorough and meticulous student, as well as a practitioner, of offshore sailing. He advocated moderate beam, plenty of displacement and a long keel. I read and re-read his books: *Yacht Cruising* and *Yacht Navigation and Voyaging*.

This background, reinforced over the years, had led me to believe that size and shape can vary widely, though I like to avoid extremes. If structure and handling are sound, then the larger the better; but the bigger vessel demands more of the builder and crew as the loads increase geometrically with size. Big sails supported by great stability require strength and skill to control; small sails can be manhandled. Similar observations apply to hull, spars and rigging.

Analytical studies, such as those carried out in the course of the joint United States Yacht Racing Union (USYRU) and the Society of Naval Architects and Marine Engineers (SNAME) study on Safety from Capsizing, and by the Wolfson Unit of the University of Southampton, have noted two characteristic conditions of capsize that have a bearing on design, ie those that occur due to the force of the wind on the rig, and those resulting from the jet-like force of a breaking sea. In the first condition the light structure of a small boat may not be over-loaded, but in the second the hull or deck may be smashed, destroying its ability to float like a bottle.

As the terms are often used, size and displacement mean about the same thing, although the terms 'light' or 'heavy' displacement usually refer to the displacement/length ratio, often expressed as tons of displacement divided by the cube of 1 per cent of waterline length in feet. Though extreme, one can accept a range of 500 to 50 in that ratio over a range of 20–80ft (6–24m) in waterline length. In geometrically similar hulls the righting moments increase in proportion to the fourth power of length, while the heeling moment grows only as length cubed. Because of this, small boat designs need more inherent power, ie beam and displacement, while big yachts with similar proportions need very large rigs. Thus smaller boats should avoid the bottom of this range and the larger boats should avoid the top. Figs 1.1 and 1.2 show a possibly over-liberal suggested range. I say 'possibly over-liberal' with the personal feeling that the area just below the middle of the suggested range, say 125 to 250 in the same length range, is best of all.

Displacement is determined primarily by the requirements of strength and stability and, further, for comfort in the sense of motion and of roominess. The yacht's total weight must

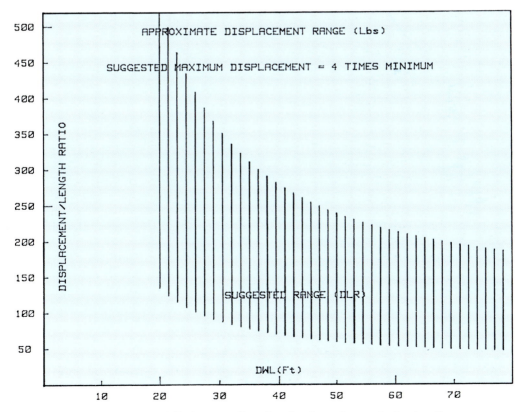

Figure 1.1 Suggested range of displacement/length ratios for a given waterline length.

provide for an adequate structure together with the weight of crew, stores and equipment, and for sufficient ballast to ensure stability for sail carrying power and a good range of positive stability. Truly efficient use of the best materials can give a light hull and rig and, with enough ballast, appropriate designs can provide stability, adding up to a lower limit on safe displacement. Though structural materials are not the subject of this study it should be said that, in the hands of a competent builder, sound light hulls can be built of many different materials including wood, GRP and aluminium alloy. The high-strength, high-modulus materials often used as composites, such as carbon fibre, offer – when used with care and experience – strength and light weight. Steel and concrete are inherently heavier, especially the latter. Boats with light displacement must have light hulls so as to carry a reasonable amount of ballast for the sake of stability. In heavier boats material selection is less critical.

The vertical centre of gravity and hull geometry combine to establish the range of positive stability. A good range, for illustration's sake, over 120° at least, will virtually assure that a capsized boat will right herself in conditions that have caused a capsize. Much lower values may ensure the reverse. The determination of range depends on a calculation that may be more or less complete in its application to deck structures, cockpits and allowance for some flooding. It also depends on the existing centre of gravity as affected by sails such as those that are roller furled. This suggests the need for some allowance over a stated minimum. It seems unfortunate that racing influences, earlier on the IOR, and still, although to a lesser degree, the IMS, have led to wide beam, and a shoal body: the conditions for a poor range. Ballasted narrow, deep hulls of the older International Rule type like a decked-over 12 metre could go to 180°, representing the full 360° roll-over. In beam and hull depth

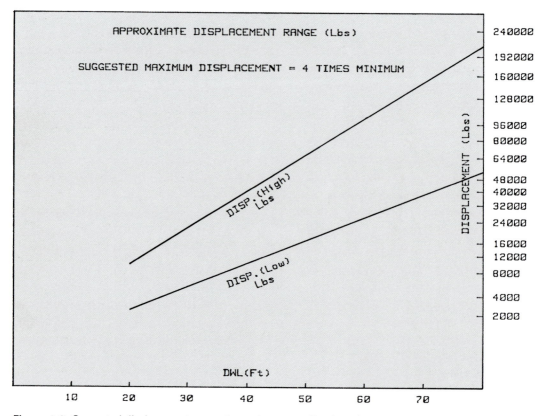

Figure 1.2 Suggested displacement range for a given waterline length.

moderation is the best course. Beam offers initial stability and roominess, but too much of it reduces the range of positive stability and results in quick motion. Depth provides easier motion, headroom, structural continuity and space for some bilge water; all desirable, but less conducive to high speed. Heavy ballast contributes to range of stability, but also gives quick motion.

A moderate ratio of beam to hull depth seems ideal; say, a beam of not more than three to four times the hull body depth, with the centre of gravity low enough to give a positive stability range of at least 130°. Here one may note that Adlard Coles' three *Cohoes* fall within the range of proportions that I have recommended. Also, that the damage to *Vertue XXXV*, described in earlier versions of *Heavy Weather Sailing*, was caused by a breaking sea that threw her over and down, smashing the lee side of her cabin trunk (coachroof), a vulnerable structure at best, due to structural discontinuity. The *Vertue's* small size probably did not permit the incorporation of the material needed for greater strength. A similar occurrence was the damage to *Puffin*, one of my own designs and not quite so small, but hit hard at a weak point. *Sayula's* survival, after a severe knockdown in the Whitbread Race of 1973, with great discomfort but minimal damage, contributes to confidence in the larger boat.

The danger of weakness should not be seen as condemnation of the coachroof, which is often needed to provide headroom and can also contribute usefully to range of stability by virtue of its volume if the hull is free of water. It is simply a reminder that all corners or abrupt discontinuities of area in a structure can be sources of weakness, and should be carefully designed and built.

It must be clear to many observers that the trend to keels that are very thin or narrow at the hull juncture weakens an already highly loaded spot by raising even higher the loads in that area, and in turn the stress in keelbolts, the keel and the associated hull structure. Whenever a narrow base is used, the structure must be most carefully considered.

The power to carry sail is quite different from stability range. A naval architect evaluates both at small heel angles by measuring the vertical span between the centre of gravity and the metacentre where, at a small heel angle, a vertical line through the centre of buoyancy cuts the heeled centre plane. The product of this height and the tangent (a trigonometrical function) of the heel angle gives the righting arm at small angles which, multiplied by the displacement, gives the righting moment. The displacement is constant, but with increasing heel the righting moment is strongly dependent on hull shape, varying with the heel angle and the ratio of beam-to-hull body depth. A beamy shoal-bodied boat will have great upright metacentric height without implying a large heeled righting moment which will have been lost with increasing heel when the righting arm shrinks and becomes negative. Good proportions between beam and hull depth will hold that factor almost constant up to angles of 35–40°, while assuring a safe range of positive stability. The first example will feel stiff, but must be kept upright to use the power of the rig, while the deeper boat can benefit from plenty of sail power up to a large heel angle. The beamy, light type depends greatly on crew weight to minimize heel so as to maintain sail power and speed.

Comfort is another characteristic related to beam. Over-generous beam contributes to roomy space below, but tends to quicken the vessel's motion and reduce the stability range. While this is not the place to discuss arrangement plans, reference to the importance of air without water in the cabin does relate to safety through the crew's ability to perform. I should like to refer favourably to the Dorade ventilator. Despite its appearance and the many efforts to design something better, it still leads the way in supplying maximum air and minimum water.

Like other vents, the Dorade can admit solid water if fully immersed as in a capsize. Preparation for the most extreme conditions should include replacement of the cowl with a deck plate. Similar positive closure for vents of any kind should always be available. In this vein it is well to avoid companionways and other deck openings that are away from the centreline where they are better protected from down-flooding.

Touching briefly on other aspects of safety and comfort we should consider strong, well-located hand rails and we should be sure that sharp corners are eliminated by generous rounding. Galleys should be arranged so that cooks can wedge or strap themselves in place and, if possible, out of the path of spilled hot food. The water supply must be divided between several tanks, each with its individual shut-off valve. This will save the supply in the event of leakage, and also provides control of weight distribution and reduces the large free surface effect of water surging about within the tank. Engine exhaust systems may admit water in bad weather, though careful design can minimize that problem.

Rigs must be designed for the high but uncertain loads of heavy weather. It seems evident that many racing rigs lack the strength to stay in place. Improved analytical methods such as finite element design have not replaced basic calculations based on the righting moment and the consequent rigging loads that apply tension at the chain plates and compression in the mast. Most designers use Euler column methods, often with assumptions on end fixity and safety factors based on their experience. According to such assumptions the safety factors will vary, but they must be generous so as to be ready for the unexpectedly severe conditions of heavy weather sailing.

Rig geometry and sail shape seem to be a matter of personal preference. Under severe conditions, however, the presence of two independently supported masts can be recommended. Strong storm sails and the rigging to set them quickly and easily are essential to a

A typical broach by a modern racing yacht, in this case a Mumm 36. If the balance between spinnaker and mainsail is lost, the boat will heel over and forces may be generated that are more than the rudder can correct. The yacht will adopt the angle shown, and due to the buoyancy of the wide stern the rudder may be partly out of the water, making recovery difficult. Although this is a frequent occurrence with modern racing yachts, and unnerving for those who are not accustomed to it, damage to the yacht or injury to the crew is rare. *Photo: PPL*

well-found offshore yacht. The storm sails should not be too large. No more than one-third of mainsail area is suggested for the storm trysail and about 5 per cent of forestay length squared for the storm jib. Sail area relative to stability can well be considered in the light of the home port and cruising grounds, and primarily as it relates to comfort more than to safety. Sail can always be shortened, but too large a working rig means frequent reefing or sailing at an uncomfortable angle of heel.

The areas of storm sails given above are very close to those defined in the Special Regulations Governing Equipment and Accommodation Standards of the Offshore Racing Council. Although drawn up for racing yachts there is a great deal of good material in these regulations. I recommend a review of this booklet to anyone preparing to sail offshore.

On the subject of hull geometry I have stressed the ratio of beam-to-hull depth. There are other considerations, less important but still meaningful. Positive and easy steering control is one such. In this day of analytical yacht design there is still no subject more deserving of intensive study than that of balance and steering control. Possibly the lack of understanding explains why there are few subjects that stir greater differences of opinion than the shape of the lateral plane, including keel and rudder. Let me outline some of the problems and some partial answers.

Course stability is often characterized as that condition in which, without the adjustment of the steering mechanism, a boat sailing a given course when diverted by an external force will return to the initial course. This could be a definition of self-steering ability. Many boats can be trimmed to steer themselves under the right conditions, but few will do so on all courses and wind strengths. The forces involved and the direction of their application and the tendency of the hull to turn one way or another at different heel angles and speeds form a very complex system, and one that is difficult to balance. We can accept these difficulties and yet ask for steering that is light and responsive. Even that can be hard for the designer to assure, but I believe that there are a few helpful steps.

A long keel is frequently cited as the best solution. Probably it is, if light weather speed is less important than good manners on the helm, and if the length extends well aft. The disadvantage is the great wetted area that goes with the long keel. Such a keel seems to do two things: turning is necessarily less abrupt and, second, a large part of the lateral plane is abaft the centre of gravity. Think of this the other way around, keel area forward, and visualize a sea turning the boat. It is as though the boat were being towed from a point abaft the pivot point so that the further the new course departs from the original, the further the inertial direction departs from the course, thus causing the boat to turn continually further from the intended direction. Conversely, if the tow point, the CG (centre of gravity), where the force is applied, is forward of the pivot, the CLR (centre of lateral resistance), then the more the course changes the more the direction of the inertial, or tow, force is directed back towards the original course. I should add that this principle of sailing balance is not universally accepted, though to some it seems evident. This principle was first brought to my attention by Dr John Letcher.

Small wetted area carries with it advantages that have resulted in the almost universal adoption of the short keel and separate rudder. Comparatively it means equal performance with less sail area, especially in light weather, or to windward when speeds are low. Using a short keel the required position of the ballast dictates the location of the keel which further dictates the location of the CLR. This disadvantage can be lessened by locating disposable weights as far forward as possible, permitting ballast keel to come aft, but such gains are limited and the best available strategy to move the CLR aft seems to be to use a large skeg and rudder. These serve the function of feathers on an arrow. Most new boats follow this pattern and, if the ends are balanced, they can behave well, exhibiting no loss of steering control, ability to heave-to or other good seagoing characteristics.

Other characteristics that seem to contribute to good manners are reasonably balanced yet buoyant ends, and moderate to light displacement. Both minimize trim change with increasing heel so that the unavoidable changes in the yacht's tendency to alter course occur gradually and the abrupt application of helm is seldom needed. Easy and positive control is valuable in a big sea.

For the sake of an easy and steady helm the pressure of the water on the hull must be evenly distributed and constant over the range of speed and heel. Long lines, minimally rounded, with relatively constant curvature, make for constant water velocity, and thus constant pressure, over the hull surface. Any short quick curve in the path of the water implies a quick change in pressure on the hull surface and, very likely, a quick change on the helm. Again, a light displacement hull with moderate beam and rather straight lines in the ends best meets these conditions.

The motion of a yacht in rough water is probably better understood than is balance under sail. It depends a great deal on the weight and the way it is distributed. Weight distribution may be considered in any desired plane, usually in longitudinal and transverse senses. It is measured by the moment of inertia and is usually expressed as the gyradius which relates the moment of inertia to displacement. The former is the sum of the products of all weight elements and the squares of their distances from a chosen axis. The radius of gyration, or gyradius, is the square root of the quantity, moment of inertia divided by the total mass. It serves as a measure of the yacht's resistance to acceleration around the chosen axis. Thus a large gyradius, either longitudinal or transverse, tends towards easy motion and is desirable in terms of comfort. In passing, it might be observed that the need for a very minimum longitudinal gyradius has become an article of faith among racing sailors. One suspects that they are right more often than not, though studies of resistance in waves show mainly that the weight distribution that results in synchronism with wave encounter is clearly bad; otherwise the effect is small.

Weight itself, or – more correctly – mass, also slows acceleration so that the motion of a heavily built boat tends to be comfortable. Being heavily built, elements of mass such as framing and planking increase the moment of inertia. In this calculation the rig, due to its distance from the centre, makes a major contribution. Anyone who has experienced the loss of a mast in rough water will confirm the quickened motion that follows. Thus, by resisting sudden roll, a heavy rig contributes to both comfort and safety, as studies have shown that, by increasing the transverse gyradius, resistance to capsize in a breaking sea, like that of the 1979 Fastnet Race, is greatly enhanced.

Variations in hull shape are most significant as they relate to displacement and stability, but some other effects of shape are worth noting. I have referred above to balance between the ends. This does not mean anything like true symmetry. My approach was by eye, which spells guesswork, possibly judgement, though today it is easy to check heeled static trim with a computer, a step towards eliminating excessive trim change.

It is well to avoid flat areas in the hull. These can easily develop in the ends, especially in a light displacement design where the fore-and-aft lines become pretty straight. If sections have a moderate U shape, rather than a V, the flat area that occurs where straight lines cross in a surface will be avoided. Even some slight rounding on a long radius extends the period of impact, reducing the tendency to slam.

Freeboard is another characteristic on which moderation is a good guide. High sides increase stability range but present a large area exposed to the impact of a breaking sea, while a high point of impact increases the overturning moment. Low freeboard leads to the early flooding of the lee deck with its sheet leads and fittings. Related to freeboard is sheer. It can be argued that this has more to do with appearance than seaworthiness, but I think a good sea boat should keep her ends above water without excessive freeboard amidships.

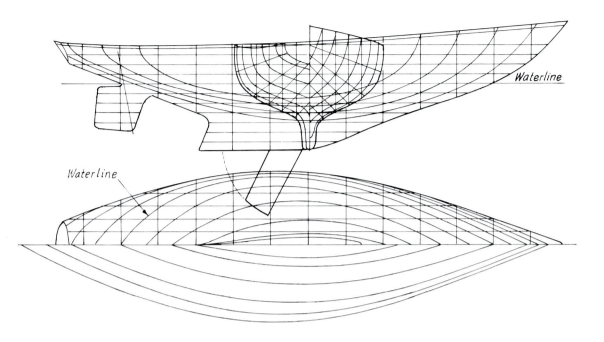

Waterline

Waterline

Figure 1.3 The lines plan of *Sunstone*, previously named *Deb*. Her present owners, Tom and Vicki Jackson, live aboard throughout the year and have achieved outstanding success in RORC races.

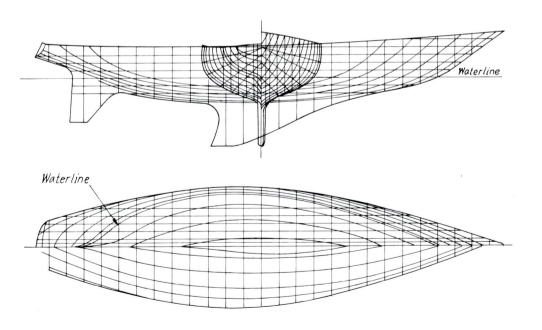

Waterline

Waterline

Figure 1.4 The lines plan of *War Baby*, previously named *Tenacious*, winner of the 1979 Fastnet Race. Her present owner, Warren Brown, has cruised extensively in her.

Let us agree that the beauty of the Watson and Fyfe boats of the early part of the century was also functional.

Cockpits that can hold a great deal of water can be dangerous, but may be considered in relation to the size and reserve buoyancy of the hull. It is essential that all cockpits will be self-draining through scuppers, which should be large. Deep cockpits offer protection and comfort, but their effect on buoyancy must always be considered. One's priorities may play a part in cockpit dimensions, but the smaller cockpit must be the safest in the end.

The conditions we are considering are less than ideal for centreboarders. They have their supporters and I have been responsible for many centreboard designs. I always tried to advise the owners that capsize was possible (although I hoped very unlikely), but in many cases the stability range was less than I should have liked. In other cases where draft was not too restricted so that the ratio of beam to depth was not too great, and other details such as freeboard and deck structures were appropriate, the stability range seemed fully acceptable. Among S&S-designed centreboarders, *Sunstone*, previously named *Deb*, due to her rather deep hull, seems a good example of a centreboarder suited to heavy weather sailing (Fig 1.3).

I hope it has been useful to consider, one by one, a number of specific characteristics. While each has an influence on the ultimate ability of a yacht, it is always the combination that counts. No individual dimension means too much on its own. Good performance can be reached by different paths and, finally, the good combinations are the ones that work (Fig 1.4).

When I think of the boat in which I should be happiest in meeting heavy weather I visualize one that is moderate in every way, but as strong as possible. I should avoid extremes of beam to depth or depth to beam, either very light or very heavy displacement, or a very high rig. I should like the ends to be buoyant, but neither very sharp nor full, and neither long nor chopped right off. Though I have stressed resistance to capsize, in my own seagoing experience I have never been worried on that score, but I have occasionally been concerned about leaks or the strength of the hull or rig. In the final analysis, I recommend moderate proportions and lots of strength.

2 The stability of yachts in large breaking waves

ANDREW CLAUGHTON

CAUSES OF CAPSIZE

What causes a yacht to capsize? Sailing dinghies and lightly ballasted daysailers such as a J24 can be laid flat and capsized solely by the pressure of wind in the sails. In larger yachts the nearest equivalent of this is the broach while under spinnaker. In a bad broach the mast can be pressed down as far as the water, but once the heeling influence of the spinnaker is removed the yacht recovers to an upright position. Experience shows us that, in flat water, gusts alone cannot capsize a yacht. Even when encountering high and steep waves, the story remains the same. The action of wave slope in heeling a dinghy or daysailer may assist the wind in producing a capsize, but a conventional yacht's stability is such that it cannot be capsized by even the combined action of wind and waves, no matter how high or steep.

It is breaking waves that cause capsize; if the yacht is caught beam-on to breaking waves of sufficient size, then the exaggerated steepness of the breaking wave front, coupled with the impact of the jet-like torrent of the breaking crest, will knock the yacht down to a point where the mast is well immersed. At this point the yacht's fate is decided by its stability characteristics; it will either return to an upright position or carry on to an inverted position, where the boat may remain for some time until another wave disturbs it sufficiently to flip itself upright. If the wave is high enough or the encounter with it is timed appropriately, then a full 360° roll will be executed.

How big do breaking waves need to be to cause this type of behaviour? Unfortunately, the answer is 'not very big'. During the model tests that were carried out to investigate the problem, when the breaking wave was 30% of the hull length high, from trough to crest, it could capsize some of the yachts, while waves to a height of 60% of the hull length would comfortably overwhelm all of the boats we tested. In real terms this means that for a 10m (33ft) boat, caught in the wrong place, when the *breaking* wave is 3m (10ft) high, this presents a capsize risk; and when the *breaking* wave is 6m (20ft) high, this appears to be a capsize certainty in any shape of boat. The word *breaking* is in italic to stress that it is breaking waves that present the danger, while big waves in themselves are not a problem.

As shown in the photo below, the model tests were done in waves that broke all along their crest at the same time, unlike the waves at sea where short lengths of crest break as the wave systems interact. Once the breaking crest at the point of impact is as wide as the boat is long, then its full effect will be felt.

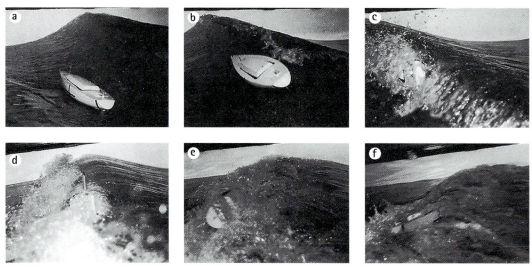

Above A fin keel parent model under test showing beam-on capsize.

a Beam-on to a large wave.

b Crest begins to break.

c 90° heel angle (transom visible).

d Upside down (keel and rudder pointing to the sky).

e Nearly upright again.

f Returned to normal!

HOW CAN CAPSIZE BE AVOIDED?

The simple answer to avoid capsizing is to avoid breaking waves. This does not necessarily mean staying tied to a mooring, but rather in avoiding certain sea areas in wind or tide conditions where breaking seas may be thrown up. For example, to help their small-boat fishermen avoid breaking waves, the Norwegian authorities define certain no-go areas as part of their weather forecasts.

Taken a step further, even if caught out in extreme conditions of wind and wave, a technique of avoiding the breakers can be employed, but on a more local scale. During the 1979 Fastnet Race many yachts were able to keep sailing, and actively pick their way through the waves, avoiding the breaking part of the seas, much as a surfer keeps to the unbroken part of the wave by tracking across its face. Once the boat is to one side of the breaking part of the crest the danger is over, and even delaying the moment of impact until the breaking wave has dissipated some of its energy will reduce the capsize risk. The wave is at its most destructive at the point of breaking and immediately afterwards. Active sailing also keeps the boat from being caught beam-on to the seas, which is its most vulnerable position. The risk is that a mistake in steering might cause a broach which results in the boat being left beam-on to the waves. This technique does, however, need a strong and competent crew to execute it for long periods of time. It is nevertheless a well-established and successful technique for dealing with heavy weather.

As was demonstrated by crews' experiences during the 1979 Fastnet, it is not always possible to avoid capsize situations. Due to crew fatigue, or plain bad luck, a yacht, especially if shorthanded, may encounter a capsize or knockdown incident. The research carried out in the wake of the 1979 Fastnet Race has been aimed at evaluating what features of hull design contribute to a safer yacht in survival conditions.

So far I have written in general terms about stability, but we cannot go much further without explaining in more detail the physical mechanisms that keep a sailing yacht the right way up, and how things behave once the mast is below the horizontal.

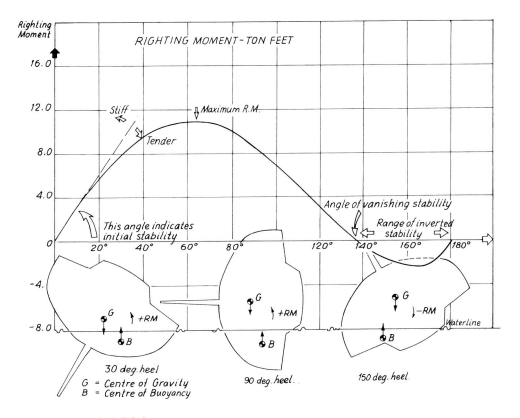

Figure 2.1 A typical righting moment curve.

Fig 2.1 shows a typical righting moment curve; this describes the variation of righting moment as heel angle increases. All of the yacht's weight can be assumed to act vertically down through the centre of gravity, while the buoyancy force opposes this through the centre of buoyancy. The righting moment is the torque generated by the increasing misalignment of the yacht's centre of gravity, which remains fixed on the hull centreline – unless the crew sit out – and the centre of buoyancy which shifts to leeward as the yacht heels. Intuitively one can see that in the normal sailing range of up to an angle of, say, 45°, an adequate righting moment to resist the heeling moment of the sails can be achieved either by a wide beam, so that the centre of buoyancy shifts outboard more, or by a low centre of gravity, so that it is further away from the centre of buoyancy. Whichever way the designer does it, a yacht has to have an adequate righting moment at 30–40° of heel to carry its sail properly. Some boats are stiff, ie the righting moment rises quickly with increasing heel angle, while others are more tender, ie with a slower rise of righting moment. In the latter case, such boats very often require the crew to sit out to produce an adequate righting moment, by shifting the centre of gravity outboard.

At the point of maximum righting moment, the centre of buoyancy is as far to leeward as it is going to get. It then starts to move back to the centre as heel angle increases further. This means that at 90° the righting moment can be quite low, hence the ease with which the broached yacht can be held with its mast close to the water by the flogging spinnaker. A few more degrees past this point and the centre of gravity and centre of buoyancy are in line again, but the wrong way up. This is the angle of vanishing stability (AVS). At this point the boat is balanced in unstable equilibrium like a pencil on its end and can fall either way, ie back to upright or to end up floating upside down. At 180° heel – ie upside

Part of the Atlantic Ocean viewed from a Westerley Konsort (29ft (8.8m)) in April while on passage from the Azores to Scotland. If this kind of sea breaks just to weather of a small yacht she is certain to capsize. *Photo: Douglas Thomson*

down – the two centres are in line, and this is another stable position unless the boat is fully self-righting. Before the hydrostatic forces can act to turn the boat the right way up some external force must push the boat back past its angle of vanishing stability.

To calculate the righting moment curve for a yacht, the position of the centre of buoyancy is calculated from the hull drawings, using a computer. The position of the centre of gravity is determined by physically inclining the yacht a few degrees and measuring the heeling moment required.

The ability of a yacht to recover from a breaking wave encounter depends on the hull and coachroof shape. This is not only for its influence on how the breaking wave affects it, but also for its influence on the shape of the stability curve.

The conclusions about capsizing are based on the results of model tests carried out by the Wolfson Unit at Southampton University, UK. The tests were carried out using free-running models in a towing tank 60m (197ft) long x 3.7m (12ft) wide x 1.8m (6ft) deep. The breaking waves were generated by using computer-controlled wave makers, and fans provided a full-scale 40 knot wind over the test area. The behaviour of different hull shapes will be described in the context of the models tested at Southampton. The results from these tests were complementary to those obtained from the parallel Sailboat Committee of the Society of Naval Architects and Marine Engineers/United States Yacht Racing Union study carried out in the USA.

The three basic hulls tested were a traditional yacht form, a typical modern 'fin and skeg' yacht, and a derivative of the 'fin and skeg' yacht modified to give it higher freeboard with no coachroof. From these three parent hulls a further six forms were derived, each identical in all respects to its parent with the exception of beam, one narrower and one wider for each type. Models were then constructed from these lines plans to represent 9.75m (32ft) yachts at 1:13 scale. The lines plans of the 9 models are shown in Fig 2.2.

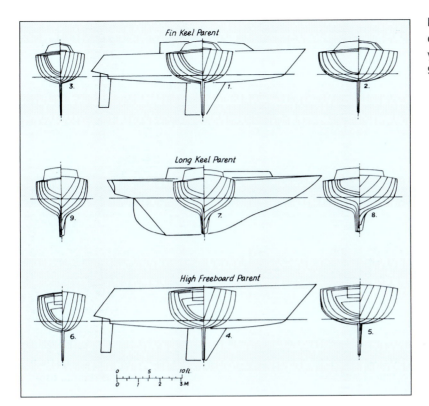

Figure 2.2 Body plans of standard series yachts. Length overall 9.75m (32ft).

The different characteristics of the hulls allowed individual design features to be evaluated in relation to three aspects of behaviour:

1 Hydrostatic performance, angle of vanishing stability and stiffness.
2 Response to the impact of a breaking wave.
3 Influence on controllability, ie how design features can help an active sailing approach in avoiding a capsize.

BEAM

The beam variation tests were done on the wide and narrow versions of the fin keel parent hull. The righting moment curves for the three hulls shown in Fig 2.3 are calculated with the centre of gravity at the same distance above the hull bottom and demonstrate the strong influence of beam on stability and stiffness. The widest yacht is the stiffest and has the highest maximum righting moment, but it also has a very large range of inverted stability. By contrast, the narrow yacht has virtual self-righting ability but would be hopelessly tender because of the flatter slope of the early part of the curve.

In the capsize tests both the parent and wide hull forms could be inverted by a breaking wave of a height of 40% of the hull's overall length (LOA) while the narrow hull form suffered only a 120° knockdown and recovered. However, a 55% LOA wave caused all the models to execute 360° rolls when caught beam-on to the wave. One of the factors influencing the behaviour of the wider-beam boats was the immersion of the lee deck edge as the boat was pushed sideways by the breaking crest. This dipping of the sidedeck appeared to produce a tripping action that the narrow boat was able to avoid.

Running before the seas, the wide hull proved quite difficult to control and did not show any more willingness to surf ahead of the wave than its narrower sisters.

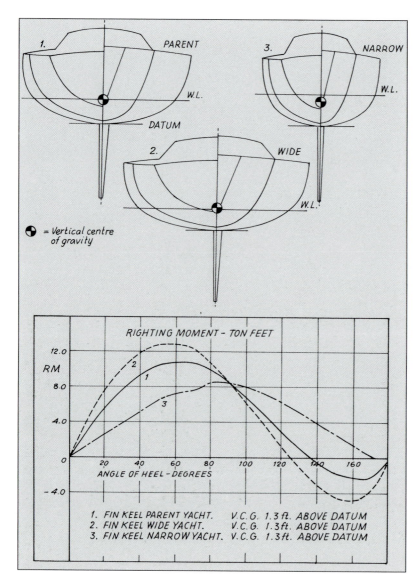

Figure 2.3 Righting moment for fin keel yacht beam series; the displacement is 4.5 tons.

FREEBOARD

A comparison was made between the behaviour of the low freeboard with a typical coachroof, and the high freeboard model with a flush deck. Both models exhibited the same propensity to capsize, showing that high freeboard does not increase capsize risk. Once capsized, the yacht with the lower freeboard and coachroof had a greater ability to self-right.

On studying the righting moment curves of the two forms it became apparent that it is the contribution to buoyancy of the coachroof that reduces the area of inverted stability. This is illustrated in Fig 2.4 which shows the righting moment curves for the two hulls. Also of interest is Fig 2.5 where the righting moment curve of the traditional yacht is shown with and without its coachroof, demonstrating how the buoyancy of a coachroof can increase the angle of vanishing stability.

The static stability analysis indicated that a further increase in coachroof size could eliminate the range of inverted stability completely (a concept used with great success in the RNLI lifeboats), thus rendering even a very light and beamy craft self-righting.

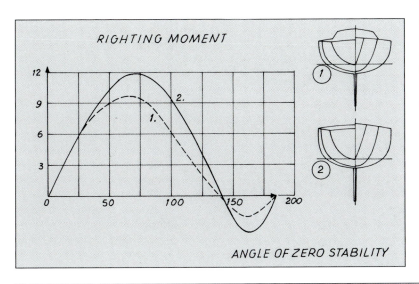

Figure 2.4 (left)
Righting moment curves for the freeboard variation:
1) fin keel parent with coachroof.
2) high freeboard without coachroof.

Figure 2.5 (below)
Righting moment for the long keel parent yacht; the displacement is 4.5 and 6.5 tons.

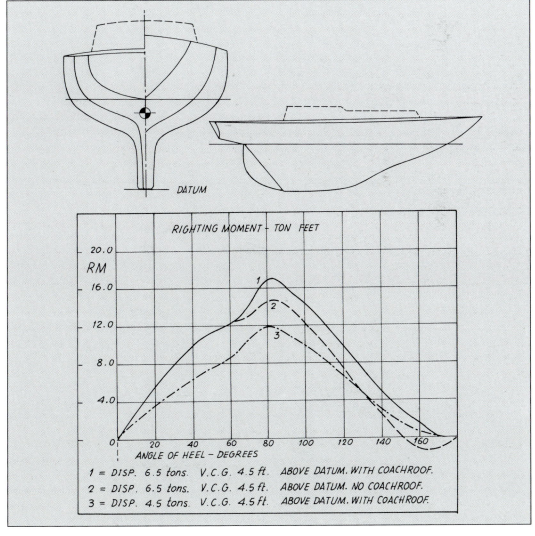

1 = DISP. 6.5 tons. V.C.G. 4.5 ft. ABOVE DATUM. WITH COACHROOF.
2 = DISP. 6.5 tons. V.C.G. 4.5 ft. ABOVE DATUM. NO COACHROOF.
3 = DISP. 4.5 tons. V.C.G. 4.5 ft. ABOVE DATUM. WITH COACHROOF.

FIN OR LONG KEEL?

One of the most obvious design developments in the last 20 years has been the substantial reduction in the lateral area of the keel. This aspect of design was evaluated not only by comparing the traditional and modern designs, but also by fitting extension pieces fore-and-aft to the fin keel so that the keel area was approximately trebled as shown in Fig 2.6. This produced no discernible improvement in capsize resistance and, more surprisingly, only a marginal improvement in controllability when sailing downwind. A similar result, at least as far as capsize resistance goes, was found when the fin keel and traditional design were compared at the same weight and position of the centre of gravity. Neither design showed a discernible superiority, although of course the traditional design with its narrow beam and larger coachroof had a higher angle of vanishing stability, and therefore recovered more readily from the knockdown.

When it came to downwave controllability, however, the traditional design model was far easier to control and, despite its greater weight, it surfed very readily. The more modern design, by contrast, was hard to keep stern-on to the seas, and once the hull was slightly pushed off course it broached beam-on to the breaking wave and, in this vulnerable position, was prone to capsize. These tests indicated that lateral area, *per se*, does not improve capsize resistance, and downwave control is not influenced only by keel area. It was the more balanced ends of the traditional design that helped its controllability as much as the larger lateral area of the keel, because, as a wave approached from behind, the stern was lifted less and, consequently, the bow was less immersed.

The wider-sterned modern design suffers because the passing wave lifts the stern and buries the bow deeply where it can exert a large turning moment on the hull. This will cause the yacht to broach unless the rudder can be used quickly to counter the turning moment.

The different behaviour of the three models – traditional long keel, fin keel, and increased area fin keel – gave a glimpse of the complex interaction of hull design features on controllability when running before large waves. The easy surfing and control of the traditional design model was a surprise. The results, however, should not be extended to a generalized conclusion about all traditional and modern boats. While a lighter hull will be carried forward more readily by an advancing wave, to benefit from the effect of the wave, the hull shape must be such that it can be held on course easily. In strong winds, as opposed to survival conditions, the light wide-stern boats can be propelled to high speed by the sails, and any lack of buoyancy forward is compensated for by the dynamic lift generated by the forward part of the hull. This will keep the bow up and will allow the rudder to control the boat with ease. However, once the driving force of the sails is removed and the boat speed falls – the situation modelled in the tests – it was apparent that balanced ends become an important part of the control equation. As with many aspects of sailing boat performance, it is the complete combination of design characteristics that is important, and herein lies the designer's skill to blend hull shape, keel area and weight successfully into a harmonious whole.

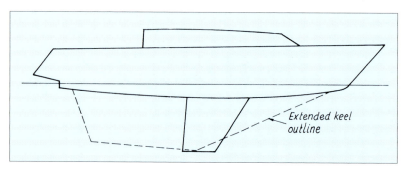

Figure 2.6 The keel extension.

DISPLACEMENT, VERTICAL CENTRE OF GRAVITY AND ROLL INERTIA

These three parameters differ from those discussed so far because they can be altered fairly easily on existing yachts, whereas the other parameters are fixed at the design stage and cannot be changed so readily.

Increasing the displacement of the fin keel yacht by 60% while keeping all other factors constant made very little difference to its propensity to capsize; however, the increased displacement did improve the course-keeping qualities of the yacht and its resistance to broaching. This result is not unexpected when viewed in the context of static stability, since an increase in displacement increases the righting moment in approximately direct proportion, as shown in Fig 2.5.

Changes in the vertical location of the centre of gravity (VCG) lead to some intriguing results. The effect of large movements of the VCG on the propensity to capsize was surprisingly small; indeed in some cases the high VCG configuration actually offered more resistance to a knockdown. When considering recovery from a capsize, however, then the

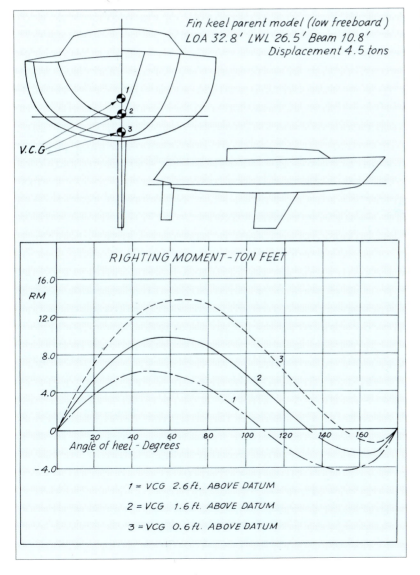

Figure 2.7 Stability curves of models with centre of gravity above and below that of the parent model.

Fin keel parent model (low freeboard)
LOA 32.8' LWL 26.5' Beam 10.8'
Displacement 4.5 tons

V.C.G

RIGHTING MOMENT - TON FEET

RM

Angle of heel - Degrees

1 = VCG 2.6 ft. ABOVE DATUM

2 = VCG 1.6 ft. ABOVE DATUM

3 = VCG 0.6 ft. ABOVE DATUM

high VCG should be discounted as it greatly increases the range of inverted stability. Again, as with increasing displacement, a lower VCG would be beneficial to the control of the craft as it increases stiffness at normal angles of heel. Fig 2.7 demonstrates the influence of the position of the centre of gravity on the shape of the righting moment curve.

Another feature linked to weight and VCG is the roll inertia or radius of gyration. Inertia is increased by moving the component weights of the yacht further from the centre of gravity, and by so doing the yacht is made less easily disturbed by roll-inducing forces, in much the same way as a skater can control the speed of a spin by bringing his arms in and out from his body. In a yacht a high inertia can be induced by using a heavy mast and keeping the ballast as low as possible, preferably on the end of a deep keel. The capsizing tests do indicate that inertia is one of the important influences on capsize resistance. As a rough guide, increasing the inertia of the boat by 50% increases the wave height needed to cause capsize by 10–15%. This is discernible experimentally, but its effect on the overall risk of capsize would not appear to be very great. Beware, however, of increasing inertia by use of heavy spars without a corresponding addition of ballast, otherwise the boat's VCG will rise and the angle of vanishing stability will be reduced.

SUMMARY

The model tests and hydrostatic calculations allowed us to discern the influence of several basic design parameters on a yacht's ability to resist capsize, or recover from severe breaking wave knockdowns. Fig 2.8 summarizes the results of the tests and calculations. Fig 2.8 describes how the fundamental design parameters influence capsize- and stability-related characteristics.

Two of the strongest influences on the vulnerability to capsize are both differences in form. First, a narrow craft appears to have improved resistance to capsize when beam-on to the seas, being able to slip away from the breaking wave. Also, the narrow beam leads to an increase in angle of vanishing stability. Second, the full lateral plane and *more balanced ends* of the long keel design make it less liable to broach and capsize in following seas. From the tests it was apparent that those yachts having angles of vanishing stability of less than 140° can be left floating upside down for a period after encountering a breaking wave. At the other end of the heel angle range, a high value of initial stability, which makes the yacht 'stiff' in sailing terms, does not provide resistance to the capsizing forces of a breaking wave, and it appears that it is the righting moment values in the range 100–130° of heel that determine the hydrostatic resistance to complete inversion and capsize.

The angle of vanishing stability represents a fundamental measure of the boat's ability to recover quickly from the impact of a breaking wave, and is the design parameter that determines whether knockdown and recovery, or full capsize, results from the impact. The angle of vanishing stability features strongly in the certification requirements for sail training vessels and yachts, and may be estimated from the formula below:

$$SV = \frac{B^2}{R \times T \times V^{\frac{1}{3}}} \text{ where}$$

SV = screening value
B = maximum beam (m)
R = ballast ratio: $\dfrac{\text{keel weight}}{\text{total weight}}$
T = hull draft @ B/8 from centreline (m)
V = displacement volume (m³)
AVS = (angle of vanishing stability) $\simeq 110 + 400 / (SV-10)$

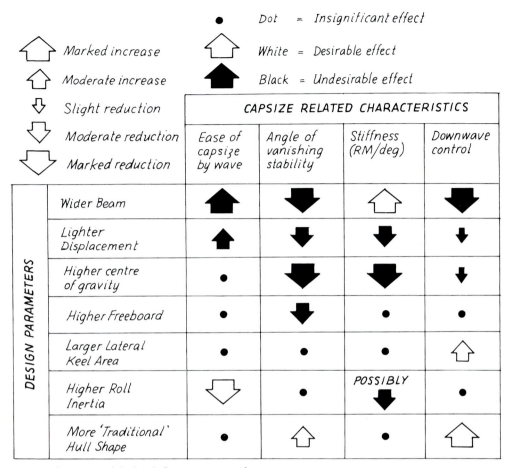

Figure 2.8 Summary of design influences on capsize.

Examination of the formula shows that beam acts to reduce the range – ie reduces the AVS – while a high ballast ratio, deeper canoe body and higher displacement increase the range.

It must be stressed that the formula is only an approximation based on the actual results of inclining tests and calculations on a number of typical sailing yachts. This means two things. First, it may over- or under-estimate the AVS by up to 10–15° in some cases, and second, it will not work for unusual vessels. Nevertheless, it offers a good guide. If required, the true value of AVS and a complete righting moment curve can be calculated using a well-established procedure of measurements and computer calculations.

The beneficial influences of increased displacement and inertia are also apparent from the tests, but these results highlight the difficulty of designing to minimize capsizability. Many of the design features one might adopt to resist capsize actually mitigate against desirable sailing and living characteristics, which are, after all, the boat's prime function for, hopefully, all of its life. For instance, narrow beam reduces both internal volume and the power to carry sail; high inertia leads to excessive pitching in a seaway, and so on. Finally, even when all the precautions are taken in our models tests, although discernible trends in resistance to capsize have been determined, no hull form or ballasting combination consistently resisted capsize in a breaking wave with a height of 55% of the yacht's length. Moreover, all the yachts could be rolled to 130° of heel by an appropriately timed encounter with the 35% LOA high breaking wave. This suggests that alterations in form that improve capsize resistance may be rendered ineffective by a relatively small increase in breaking wave height.

Small craft will probably be capsized if unlucky enough to be caught beam-on to an isolated breaking wave such as this South Pacific roller. *Photo: Rick Tomlinson*

So what is the answer to avoiding capsize? The best and most effective way is to avoid breaking waves by avoiding sea conditions where breaking waves are prone to occur. If caught out in extreme conditions, then by keeping sailing, the boat can be kept away from the breaking crests, or positioned to surf ahead or clear of them. This avoids the dangerous beam-on condition, and delays the encounter with the breaking crest until much of its energy has been dissipated. As discussed earlier, this strategy requires active rudder control and some skill to carry out. Ultimately, the technique may well prove beyond even an experienced racing crew, let alone a shorthanded cruising complement. Once the conditions are so severe that the crew are not able to remain on deck, then the vessel must look after herself. Unfortunately all yachts have a natural tendency to lie beam-on to wind and wave when left to their own devices. This is the most vulnerable position, and it is in this situation that the influence of hull design features on capsize resistance and recovery come into play, realizing, of course, that no conventional yacht design can offer complete immunity from capsize under these conditions. Naturally, increasing the size of the yacht will decrease the chances of encountering a wave capable of capsizing the boat.

After our tests and calculations examining all these different design features, one must admit to a sense of disappointment that no combination of hull form or ballasting arrangement offered a substantial improvement in capsize resistance. Something, say, that if the breaking wave height doubled, a boat could withstand.

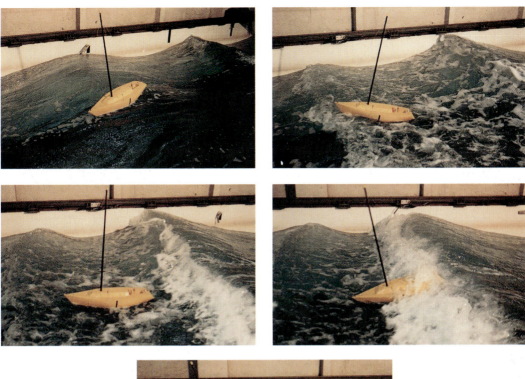

Yacht capsize and drogue research: the wide fin keel model being held stern to a breaking wave by a drogue.

It is worth mentioning that in recent years the Wolfson Unit has continued its experiments, supported by the Royal Ocean Racing Club, to evaluate the influence of a drogue or sea anchor on a yacht's behaviour in breaking waves. This research again complemented similar studies in the USA by Donald Jordan. These studies showed that use of a *suitable* drogue, deployed from the stern of the yacht, will cause it to lie steadily downwind and downwave, so that any breaking wave will see only the transom of the yacht and will not be able to exert any capsizing force. Using an appropriately sized drogue, even the lightest, widest fin keel yacht could safely survive the 55% LOA wave with no assistance from the helmsman, whereas lying beam-on it would be easily rolled over by the 35% LOA breaking wave. Indeed, it was only our inability to make higher waves in the tank that prevented us from moving further up the safe wave height range. As will be seen from the sequence of photographs above, the yacht moves steadily downwave with little or no disturbance from the foaming crest.

Thus it may well be that the drogue is the simplest and most reliable way of substantially reducing the risk of capsize.

3 Design trends of yachts in respect of heavy weather

PETER BRUCE

After so many years of evolution it might be thought that the optimum yacht shape would have been established but, for one reason or another, this appears not to be the case. New yachts appear continuously, none of them quite like their predecessors. As yacht design progresses, some desirable design features can be left behind as others evolve. Generally speaking, the boat industry gives people exactly what they want, and clearly people want boat speed, space, grace, comfort, lots of electronics, effortless handling and shallow draft. However, less obvious features, such as seaworthiness – particularly stability – and structural strength, tend to be taken for granted by the buyer.

Unlike cruising yachts, racing yachts are subject to a handicap rule, which could be used to pressurize designers towards seaworthiness but, through the influence of owners, the handicap rules are predominantly applied to achieve equality between competitors. It was not always thus. Up to the mid 1970s, certainly in the USA and UK, seaworthiness and strength were paramount considerations for racing yachts. Until then, yachts had a reputation of looking after their crews when it came on to blow; furthermore, it was rare for any yacht to give up a race due to her design or construction, or as a result of gear failure.

DESIGNS OF THE 1950S AND 1960S

Some comparisons illustrate the point. For example, a recent letter from John McDonell describes a storm that *Cavalier* encountered on the return home from the Sydney–Hobart race in 1963, after coming second. The 31ft (9.4m) yacht was built of wood by Swanson Brothers in Sydney, and by modern-day standards would probably be judged as extremely heavy and lacking some desirable accommodation features. Having suffered no damage after being rolled she might also be judged extremely seaworthy. *Cavalier* appears to have stood up to the storm much as one would expect of her traditional design and John McDonell could have had more complaints than he did. His first criticism was that the cockpit did not drain fast enough. The other problem in the storm was that she did not have the speed necessary to keep out of trouble. Yachts which do have such speed need to be steered constantly and with some skill, and this situation is satisfactory as long as there are sufficient willing and able helmsmen. Racing boats, such as those that do the Whitbread Round the World Race, will have enough such helmsmen, but cruising boats seldom do.

Many old-fashioned designs, such as that of *Cavalier*, were extremely strongly built of wood, having very severe conditions in mind. Notice her coachroof, which looks unlikely to be damaged by a breaking sea, and her small window which, if broken, can readily be blocked. *Photo: John McDonell*

One of the interesting aspects of John McDonell's account is how different it is from more recent storm reports where the aim is usually to slow down to achieve a 'comfortable speed'. A possible suggestion, which might have improved *Cavalier*'s handling, would have been to use her engine. This would have prevented her from 'stopping dead in the troughs' and would have given water flow over the rudder in the right direction at all times.

The fact is that many traditional yachts are renowned for their sea-keeping qualities, especially those yachts designed by Olin Stephens. Here is an account of one of his designs, *Half Pint*, a Swan 36, in an Atlantic storm, written by her owner Christopher Price, which reinforces the seaworthiness of this hull:

My partner and I left Gibraltar on 13 December 1968 for Lanzarote in the Canaries, with a favourable weather forecast of light to moderate north-easterlies. On 24 December 1968 we were due north of Casablanca, about 25 miles offshore. The wind had been building steadily through the night and by 0630 hours was steady at 40 knots from the SW, so I decided to heave-to under a backed storm jib, which made the motion more bearable.

By 1000 the wind had increased to 45–50 knots and we started to run off under storm jib alone, sailing parallel to the coast with a general heading of NE. The seas were very short and even with the storm jib alone the boat was punching into the backs of waves. At about 1530 in the afternoon the boat broached and was knocked flat with the mast in the water.

The boat righted herself immediately. We then put out two warps about 20 fathoms each, tied at the ends so as to form a bight, and made off at first the primary and then the secondary winches. The wind was now gusting over the maximum of 60 knots shown by our Brookes & Gatehouse wind speed indicator. By this stage I had no choice but to bring in the headsail and run under bare poles. In these conditions the boat was still making 5 to 6 knots, but the motion was relatively comfortable and the Hydrovane self-steering was able to keep our course with the wind 15 to 20° off our port quarter. The wind remained over 60 knots for most of the night, and at about 0130 the boat was knocked down a second time. We had to pump the bilges at least every half-hour because the boat was being continually swept by green water. Radio reports claimed that this was the lowest depression in the area in the past fourteen years. Throughout the storm the boat behaved very well. We continued cruising for another three years (Brazil, Caribbean, Bahamas, US), but never experienced anything approaching those conditions again.

In this example the Swan 36 ran at a comfortable speed using warps whereas *Cavalier* used none. Not being quite so heavy for her size as *Cavalier*, *Half Pint* might have surfed uncontrollably had she not been restrained. Different methods are appropriate for different boats. More importantly the two accounts suggest that there was not much wrong with the seaworthiness qualities of these two yacht designs of the 1960s, which were genuine cruiser-racers. From the 1960s onwards, racing yacht design evolved according to performance considerations. Yachts became progressively lighter and beamier, freeboard increased; and fin keels and spade rudders became the norm. They became faster and more exciting to sail.

Round-the-world race yachts tend to have a good stock of helmsmen. *Photo: Philippe Schiller/PPL*

1979 FASTNET RACE

The story of the 1979 Fastnet storm, albeit an exceptionally ferocious storm for summer, has been written up elsewhere in this book, but it put a big question on the stability of yachts designed in that era. In one noted capsize, the angle of vanishing stability was 118° and the boat had remained inverted for some minutes. It is memorable that at this period keels did not break off.

1984 VASCO DA GAMA RACE

After all the tremendous publicity that anything to do with the race had generated, many people felt that the lessons of 1979 must surely have been learned. However on 26 April 1984 an unforecast storm brought havoc to the 29 entries in the Durban to East London Vasco Da Gama Race. Winds of at least 60 knots over a period of 6 hours blowing in the opposite direction to the Aghulas Current created seas which caused three yachts to sink and the Lavranos 2-tonner *Sensation* to be wrecked on the coast. One of the yachts that sank, *Rubicon*, was lost without trace. Three yachts experienced 360° rolls. For example, in the case of *Spiffero*, a Dufour 34, the 360° roll dismasted the boat, and the deck-stowed liferaft, the engine and battery became detached from their mountings. The liferaft was lost and when the wreckage had been cleared away the yacht was rolled through 360° for a second time.

The official report, which there is no reason to doubt, said that the yachts were competently crewed and that safety regulations had been properly applied. The question that remained is whether modern performance yachts are sufficiently optimized for extreme weather.

1991 JAPAN–GUAM RACE

No further offshore races were to run into serious trouble until 1991, but then the matter of stability, coupled now with the strength of racing yacht structure, raised its head again. The Japan–Guam Race tragedy did not receive much publicity in the western world yet fourteen yachtsmen lost their lives. I am grateful to Barry Deakin from the Wolfson Unit who, in 1992, wrote the following description:

The 7th Japan–Guam Yacht Race began at midday on 26 December 1991 off the Miura Peninsula just south of Tokyo. Nine yachts crossed the start line in wintry conditions, heading for the tropical island of Guam over 1300 nautical miles to the south.

On the afternoon of the following day, with winds of 30 knots and waves of up to 6m (20ft), two yachts retired from the race. One, a Van de Stadt 71, was dismasted and the other, a Frers 48, had a torn mainsail. At 1540 a crew member, who was not wearing a harness, was lost overboard from the yacht *Marine Marine*, a Yokoyama 39, while trying to untangle a running backstay. He could not be found.

At midday on 28 December a female crew member of *Marine Marine*, exhausted and incapacitated by severe seasickness, was transferred to a patrol boat that had attended to assist with the search.

Twenty-four hours later with the rough conditions persisting, *Marine Marine*'s engine was started but a rope was around the propeller and the engine stalled. A tow was requested from a second patrol boat which made five unsuccessful attempts to pass a line to the yacht. That evening one of the crew became aware that the rolling motion of the yacht felt unusual and transfer of the crew to the patrol boat was requested. It was decided however that it would be too dangerous in the dark and rough conditions. The crew put on lifejackets and a liferaft was prepared.

The loss of *Exide Challenger's* keel led to an epic Southern Ocean rescue. To optimize performance, modern keels have become extremely narrow and thin at the root, and require very careful design and construction. Even then they are vulnerable to running aground. *Photo: Richard Bennett/PPL*

At around 0530 on 30 December the keel parted from the hull, which rolled upside down and filled rapidly with water. One crew member escaped through the hatch on his second attempt, finding it difficult to dive through it with the lifejacket on, and was joined a little later by two others. The incident was not seen by the patrol boat which had lost visual and radio contact with the yacht, although the empty liferaft was found at 0700. At 1020 an aircraft, which had joined the search, located the yacht with one surviving crew member. There was a hole in the hull roughly the same size as the root of the keel. A transverse frame was seen to have remained intact inside the hull. Seven members of the crew were drowned: four of their bodies were found inside the yacht.

On 29 December at 2030, while the crew of *Marine Marine* were beginning to worry about the motion of their yacht, *Taka*, a Liberty 47 about 230nm to the south, was capsized by a breaking wave while sailing under storm jib in a quartering wind of 32 knots. The maximum wave height in that area was in excess of 6m (20ft). The yacht remained upside down and after more than half an hour, the four crew inside the yacht made their way out through the hatch. Their EPIRB, which did not appear to be functioning correctly, was lost at this time. They found that one of the three crew on watch had drowned. After a further 15 minutes the yacht rolled upright. The upper washboard was lost and, as the yacht was half submerged, water continued to flow in. The mast was broken and the bilge pump tangled with ropes. The liferaft was inflated but capsized soon after with the loss of some of the gear. The six remaining crew boarded the raft and drifted. Despite the mobilization of 11 patrol boats and 52 aircraft, the raft was not found until 25 January when it was spotted by a British cargo vessel. Only one crew member remained alive, the others having died between 10 and 16 January.

The remaining five yachts finished the race between 1 and 3 January. *Marishiten*, a Nelson/Marek 68, broke the race record with an average speed of 10.1 knots.

An analysis of weather records for this and previous races reveals that, with mean winds of more than 30 knots and gusts of up to 50 knots during the first two days, this race was subjected to more severe weather than before. The margins are small however, with mean winds of 30 knots or more experienced during every race except one. Furthermore, such weather is typical at that time of year and so crews should anticipate that they might encounter very rough conditions.

The race is classified as ORC Category 1, and all yachts must meet the appropriate ORC special regulations in addition to a series of Nippon Ocean Racing Club Regulations. All yachts must be at least 10m (32.8ft) overall.

The NORC wasted no time in forming a research committee to investigate the casualties, it being officially approved on the same day that *Taka*'s liferaft was found. The man over-board was caused by human error, demonstrating the value of safety harnesses and lines, but the keel failure and the inability of *Taka* to return upright after a capsize suggest design deficiencies which were the subject of extensive research in Japan. Two lines of investigation were followed. In the first, the detailed arrangement of *Marine Marine*'s keel attachment and local GRP structure was studied from drawings, and calculations were carried out to assess the strength. It is not clear from the report on the investigation whether the keel was attached to a fair canoe body or a laminated stub, but detailed drawings of the local laminate configurations and the attachment of transverse floors show features that the Wolfson Unit considers bad practice.

The laminate thickness met the requirements of the ABS rules and the calculations indicate a safety factor of 2.71 when the laminate shear strength is compared with the static load of the keel with the yacht at 90° of heel. This load is chosen in the absence of any information on actual keel loadings caused by a yacht rolling in a seaway, and it is therefore difficult to draw firm conclusions from the value for fatigue considerations.

Disturbingly, the report suggests that the hull failed in shear around the outline of the keel and at the keel bolt washers, probably as a result of fatigue, implying that other well used yachts may lose their keels. The hull's shell had become detached from the transverse frame. The yacht was built in 1983 and had competed in many offshore races. She had run aground five years before the failure and required some repair to the hull-keel joint but details of the damage were not included in the report. The authors assumed that delamination between the shell and the frame may have occurred at that time and gone unnoticed by the repairers.

To take this study further, destructive tests were conducted on full size samples of yacht hulls with fin keels attached in various configurations. Hulls with and without stubs were used and a range of laminate thickness was tested. The samples represented a yacht of only 7.5m (24.6ft) compared with *Marine Marine*'s 11.9m (39ft), and the sample keel weight was only 20% that of the failed yacht's, so use of the data must be made with caution. The tests revealed that the breaking load in bending increases in proportion to the square of the laminate thickness, so any deficiency in the laminate will reduce the strength significantly. A safety factor of 3.3, similar to the calculated value for *Marine Marine*, was obtained with a local hull laminate thickness of 14mm which is also the same as *Marine Marine*'s, but the keel moment at 90° for *Marine Marine* was over eight times greater than that for the sample yacht.

Although there are insufficient details published in the report for a direct comparison, these figures suggest an inadequacy either in the structural design or in the assumptions used to calculate the keel loadings and hence the safety factors.

In the other avenue of research, the capsize of *Taka* prompted the Japanese to investigate its range of stability as derived from the hull measurements as part of the IMS rating process, and from drawings of the complete hull, keel, coachroof and cockpit arrangement. The IMS stability curve indicates a positive range of 108° (the angle beyond which the yacht would capsize in calm water) and when the cockpit and coachroof were taken into account in the independent calculation a range of 114° was derived. This range is below average for the fleet of 56 IMS yachts used for comparison, but seven yachts had lower values. The IMS rating system uses a 'Stability Index', which comprises the range adjusted by the size of boat and its displacement/maximum beam ratio, and *Taka's* value was only marginally below average for the fleet.

The effects of flooding of the yacht were investigated, and it was concluded that when upside down the stability gradually reduces as the amount of flooding increases. Thus the yacht remained inverted for a considerable time despite some flooding, but after the main hatch was opened the rate of flooding increased and the yacht righted herself, albeit in a seriously swamped condition.

These calculations and conclusions will be familiar to those who have studied the 1979 Fastnet Race Inquiry Report, which contains precisely the same results as computed by the Wolfson Unit in response to that disaster. At that time the Wolfson Unit was also commissioned to conduct a series of model tests to examine the behaviour of yachts of various forms, both traditional and contemporary, in large breaking waves (see Chapter 2). This work has been published and discussed at length at various times and has been complemented by parallel work conducted in the USA and the Netherlands. None of this work is referenced in the report however, and the Japanese researchers have undertaken their own experimental study of breaking wave capsize. Their experimental technique was very similar to that used by the Wolfson Unit, and their results and conclusions reinforce the findings of the work done previously.

At a scale of 1:10, they modelled two basic hull forms: a typical IOR form of 9.3m (30.5ft) overall, and a traditional long-keeled cruising yacht of 9m (29ft 6in). The first had a range of stability of 120° and the latter a range of 165°, both of which are typical for such types. The IOR yacht was capsized and remained inverted after the impact of a 3m (10ft) wave. That is a wave height equal to the beam of the yacht. The traditional yacht could not be capsized though, it should be noted, the maximum wave height available was only 3.4m (11ft). With the masts removed the IOR yacht capsized in waves of over 2.2m (7.2ft) and the traditional yacht was rolled through 360° by waves in excess of 3m (10ft). Because of its large range of stability it would not remain inverted.

The yachts modelled were 9m (29.5ft) long and, if it is assumed that the principal characteristics of a yacht remain in proportion as size increases, we may infer that a wave of more than 4m (13.1ft) high would be required to capsize *Taka*. The maximum wave height was well in excess of that at the time.

It did not require an extreme wave therefore to cause the capsize, but rather the combination of being caught beam-on to, or broached by, a wave of above average height which happened to be breaking at the time of the encounter. Perhaps the other competitors were fortunate enough not to have been caught in such a situation since the fleet stability statistics do not imply that they would have fared any better.

At the Wolfson Unit we would consider a range of stability of 114° to be insufficient for a yacht of this size undertaking an offshore passage. Indeed the yacht would not comply with the Department of Transport's Code of Practice for sail training vessels that would require a minimum range of 125°.

Some items covered by the ORC Special Regulations, which have been introduced to minimize the effects of failures such as these, were also inadequate. For example, washboards must be secured to the boat, but those on *Taka* were swept away. Bilge pumping arrangements on *Taka* were inadequate because one pump was disabled. Two pumps are required by the regulations but the other was presumably submerged in the cabin.

It is important to note that neither *Marine Marine* nor *Taka* were anything other than typical offshore racing yachts, and the force 7 to 8 conditions in which they failed were not particularly extreme. They were to be expected in this race.

It is unfortunate that the lessons learned since the Fastnet disaster do not seem to have changed design trends significantly and, furthermore, they appear to have to be re-proven when a fresh incident occurs.

1993 SYDNEY–HOBART RACE

The points made above are clear, but did not appear to have had much effect on yacht design. Perhaps there would have been an effect had there been loss of life in the windy and rough Sydney–Hobart race of 1993 but happily there was not. One of the smaller class winners and third overall was the 20-year-old S&S 34 *Marara*, a close relation of *Half Pint*. After a brief period of tail winds on leaving Sydney, most yachts were on the wind for three and a half days in gale or storm force winds. The 2 knot south-going current met the north-going wind causing steep breaking seas. Hulls delaminated, yachts sank, yachts were dis-masted, yachts lost their keels, and the skipper of one yacht spent five and a half hours in the water before being rescued. The New Zealand yacht *Swuzzlebubble VIII*, a Davidson 40, when under storm jib and trysail was rolled through 360° by a breaking wave, dismasted, damaged and swamped. Her doughty crew, by the way, cleared away the mast wreckage, put a No 3 genoa out as a sea anchor whilst bailing, managed to start the engine, and put into harbour unaided. Another yacht, a Farr 40, was doing 7.2 knots boat speed in 46 knots of wind when she fell off a wave. Next moment the starboard side of the main bulkhead, to which the chain plates were attached, appeared through the deck and then disappeared over the side complete with mast and rigging. There were no casualties in spite of all this.

Some instructive comments came from the winners and losers. Winners commented on strong crew teamwork, on strongly built boats and the necessity of having three slabs in the main rather than 'the two sailmakers try to persuade you to have'. Clearly storm trysails proved their worth as well. Comments made by those not so lucky were that the average modern racing yacht is more suited to inshore 'round the buoys' racing. The latest handi-cap rule (IMS) was encouraging light, shallow rocker craft which were very difficult to steer and would slam badly in a sea. Keels were not strongly enough attached, rigs were too light, and cockpits gave little protection in severe conditions. It was said by some that they were impossible to slow down too.

1998 SYDNEY–HOBART RACE

Conditions were more severe in the 1998 Sydney–Hobart Race and, sadly, there was loss of life. After the race had started a low formed suddenly in the Bass Strait, bringing winds of more than 70 knots for a period of 10 hours from a westerly direction. At Wilson's Promontory, at the north end of the Bass Strait, average wind was 79 knots, gusting 92 knots, a phenomenal strength for summer time and rather more than had been predict-ed. The south-going coastal current had been running strongly, but by the Bass Strait it had largely dissipated and its influence was probably small. Only yachts which were close to the Australian shore might have been affected.

Six people died, something like 55 people were rescued out of a total of 1135, six yachts were rolled, and seven yachts were abandoned, some of which sank due to structural fail-ure. One of these was the 1942-built 52ft (15.8m) wooden cutter *Winston Churchill*. When she was thrown into a trough it seems that her hull was opened up as part of her port side bulwark was torn off by force of water. Help was not at hand and three of her crew were lost from her liferafts.

Two more died aboard the Farr 40 *Business Post Naiad* (built in 1984) which capsized twice. On the first occasion the yacht was doing 4 knots under bare pole when a massive breaking wave rolled her over, breaking the mast and causing major structural damage. Harnesses held the crewmen on deck, and after the mast had been secured the yacht set off under power for shelter at Gabo Island. Some hours later another large breaking wave turned the boat over and she remained upside down for a period of four or five minutes. While the boat was inverted the owner-skipper suffered a fatal heart attack, and a crewman on deck was drowned through being unable to detach his safety harness in the same circumstances, probably, as when *Taka* capsized in the Japan–Guam race of 1991.

Finally a crewman was lost overboard from the Reichel/Pugh 43 *Sword of Orion* (built in 1993) when she was rolled through 360° as she headed back to Sydney after retiring from the race. As the yacht rolled, force of water broke the stanchion to which the boom had been lashed. The freed boom smashed the wheel and swept the helmsman over the side, parting his safety harness. With the mast gone and the engine off its mountings, rescue was impossible. Moreover all her ring frames had been broken and the deck to hull joint had split between the cockpit and the stern. After 12 hours the remaining crew were taken off.

Other yachts rolled and dismasted were the Young 12m VC Offshore *Stand Aside* (built in 1990), the Bashford Howison 41 *B52* (built in 1995), which remained inverted for three or four minutes, and the Jarkan 40, *Midnight Special* (built in 1995) which was rolled twice and just stayed afloat long enough for the crew to be rescued by helicopter. The Swan 44 *Loki* was rolled and had her cabin windows broken by an enormous wave, and the sturdy Cole 43, *Solo Globe Challenger* (ex *Rangatira* and built in 1984), a renowned seaboat, was rolled to 135° which caused loss of her mast, and a skylight hatch to break, allowing flood water to render inoperable all the essential electrics. Most of the crew were injured and were taken off, one with a broken leg, leaving just three to bring the boat in.

The 65ft (19.8m) *Team Jaguar*, after losing her mast, was struck by a breaking wave that submerged the boat to the companionway and brought her to a near vertical angle. All her deck beams were sprung and there was a real mess down below. It was what Peter Blake calls 'going down the mine' (see Foreword).

There is always something to be learnt from those who did complete the race successfully and accounts follow from the skippers of the winners of the three major classes. Firstly that of Ed Psaltis, skipper of the overall IMS winner *AFR Midnight Rambler*. She was tenth to finish, beating numerous larger yachts. He comments:

The 35ft (10.5m) *AFR Midnight Rambler* is of exotic GRP construction. There was no sign of hull/rig, keel joint damage although we put her through a horrible pounding. As long as no extremes are taken, modern construction does work. The fin keel is of lead, with no bulb, and she has no internal ballast. The angle of positive stability is 123°, and while still a modern, light competitive IMS design, her stability is higher than some of the very recent IMS designs. In addition to worldwide experience, the crew of seven had 50 Sydney–Hobarts between them.

During the eight hours when the breeze was 70 to 80 knots with very big waves, we just had the storm jib up. We were overpowered at times but mostly the helm felt good with just enough weather helm. Attempts were made to set a trysail but it created too much weather helm.

We had two important defensive weapons: speed and acceleration. Our usual speed was 7 knots and after a bad knockdown or confrontation with a big wave the speed would quickly accelerate up to this speed again due to the modern lightweight (while not extreme) design. Having speed and manoeuvrability was essential to steer through the big and confused seas. We were able to position ourselves best for each wave as it came, or steer around it. Otherwise the boat would have been a sitting duck.

Importantly during the storm we changed to a 'survival' watch system and had only two on deck at one time. One sat on the rail facing the storm, sheltering the helmsman from the bullet-like spray and called 'wave' when a big one came. The helmsman altered course to bring the bow into the wave, then pulled away sharply on the top of the wave and back onto the normal course. No helmsman should stay on watch for more than an hour in extreme conditions for, if concentration lapses, the outcome will be devastating.

AFR Midnight Rambler, designed and built by Robert Hick in 1995, has enough stability to keep going with the crew down below. I am told that some of the latest IMS yachts could not make ground to the south during the storm without all the crew on the rail.

I would never recommend a yacht to turn and run with the weather. Much better keep going into the wind and seas at about 60° apparent. Most boats that had severe trouble had retired and were running with the storm. In addition I would suggest that crew hook their safety lines to strong points situated at the main companionway before they come on deck and that they carry a personal strobe light or at least a waterproof torch in their wet weather gear.

A second account comes from Alex Whitworth, owner and skipper of the *Berrimilla*, a Brolga 33, designed by Professor Peter Joubert in 1969. She finished first overall in the Performance Handicap System division out of over 45 yachts, and had the big disadvantage of having to weather the storm in the night. The Brolga 33 is somewhat similar to an S&S 34, with deep V-shaped underwater sections, pronounced tumblehome and long overhangs. She is described by her owner as very strong and very stable with a range of stability of 136°. She came through the storm undamaged, though, he says, the hull took a real beating.

During the storm the same watchkeeping regime was adopted as *AFR Midnight Rambler* (ie two on deck, and changing every hour). The crew had 15 Sydney–Hobarts between them. Steering was made difficult by darkness and was mostly done by feel.

We sailed through the storm with just the trysail because I felt that we would have been seriously overpowered with the storm jib as well and she was handling all but the biggest breakers with no dramas. The trysail was sheeted to the spinnaker turning blocks on each quarter. We were sailing at around 60–70° apparent, averaging about 4 knots. It was generally possible to set the boat up for each wave, or avoid it, but the occasional breaker was either going too fast or coming from further abeam. On about ten occasions the boat was caught by one of these bigger breakers. She would be carried down the wave front at about an 80° angle of heel (ie on her beam-ends) on a wild surf, with the wave breaking right across the boat and filling the cockpit. A technique that evolved during this situation was to put the helm over to push the bow down the wave as the boat was being carried bodily sideways. In this way the sideways motion was converted into some forward motion and lessened the tripping effect of the keel. I am convinced that this technique helped us to avoid the worst effects of the breakers that did get us.

The boat is so stable that, once in the trough, she immediately stood upright, gathered speed and went on sailing, though on one occasion the boat was turned through 180°. With just the trysail up we could not tack so had to gybe which we felt was particularly hazardous. A wave breaking over the boat would fill the cockpit entirely and the storm boards were very necessary to keep water out of the cabin. The four cockpit drains are just about on the waterline when the cockpit is full and it takes an age to empty. Having a small swimming pool at the back of the boat tends to slow us down too.

Modestly, Alex Whitworth says that he suspects that *Berrimilla* was behind the worst of the storm and was quite lucky not to get rolled. The morning after the storm they saw a helicopter that was looking for *B52* which had been rolled in their area. Incidentally Professor Peter Joubert, who designed *Berrimilla*, was in the race in a larger but similar very stable design. His 43ft (13m) *Kingurra*, with 6 tons in her keel, got almost totally inverted by an enormous breaking wave but she righted herself 'in about five seconds' .

The winner, by some 12 hours, of the CHS division, comprising 12 yachts, was *Aera*, a Swan 46, a class of yachts renowned for their strong righting moment. The skipper said:

At midday on 27 December the storm hit with the wind building rapidly up to 60 knots from the west. Long experience of sailing a Swan 46 in heavy airs shows that the boat goes as fast under headsail only as she does with a mainsail set on almost all points of sailing. Thus, with an assured storm forecast, by this time *Aera* was under only her storm jib.

As the waves built up to a maximum of 10m (33ft) it became clear that it would not be safe to maintain the rhumb line so we bore off some 30–50°, bringing the true wind angle to 110–130°. The wind continued to build and was too much even for the storm jib, so we peeled to the storm staysail maintaining our course and 10–11 knots.

The wind strengthened to 70 knots for a period of two hours with gusts to 75 or 80 knots. Fifteen per cent of the surface was breaking and the wind was blowing the top off every wave. As a result there were long streaks of wind-blown water joining one crest to the next. The sea looked as if it was covered in a layer of smoke. Wavelength was about 100m (330ft) and the waves were not long-crested as one might expect, but diamond-shaped. During this period we suffered three or four small knockdowns, none more than 45°, and the cockpit filled seven or eight times. We kept a full watch of six on deck throughout, the most vulnerable person being the helmsman who was washed up against the pulpit a couple of times when a wave filled the cockpit.

In the next couple of hours the wind abated to 50 knots and we were able to set the storm trysail in addition to the storm staysail, and alter our course by 20–30° towards the rhumb line. However at about 1700 cloud cover became complete, we had sheeting rain and the wind built up to 65 knots. We were forced to drop the trysail and bear away to the old course. By now wavelength had increased to 150–200m (500–650ft).

Though we had been heading south-east at about the same speed as the low-pressure system we considered this safer than trying to turn back. However, the system was soon to move quickly towards the south allowing us to resume the rhumb line course and set more sail. By morning the storm was over. Our biggest problem had been our auto-inflating lifejackets that inflated when solid water came on board (see Chapter 8).

The great stiffness of the Swan prevented us from ever being knocked beyond 45° and it seems that the boats that got into difficulty were generally of lighter construction than *Aera*. Even so, we were unable to maintain the rhumb line course safely at the peak times of the storm. Many yachts were knocked down by seas on their beam. For example, *Loki*, a Swan 44 of similar design to *Aera*, tried to sail the rhumb line course but was nearly inverted by an extreme wave, suffering a broken coachroof window causing her to retire.

However, I believe there were other factors that allowed us to finish the race. Firstly, many yachts' storm jibs were too large for the conditions. Secondly, a very large number of yachts suffered gear failure. *Aera* was extremely carefully prepared by her regular crew and suffered no gear failure at all. It is worth mentioning that a small failure often leads to other problems, so the greatest attention to detail before the start of the race is vital. Finally, *Aera*'s crew was very experienced with over a hundred races of similar length between us and many of these races had been on the same boat. Familiarity with each other and the boat was another important factor.

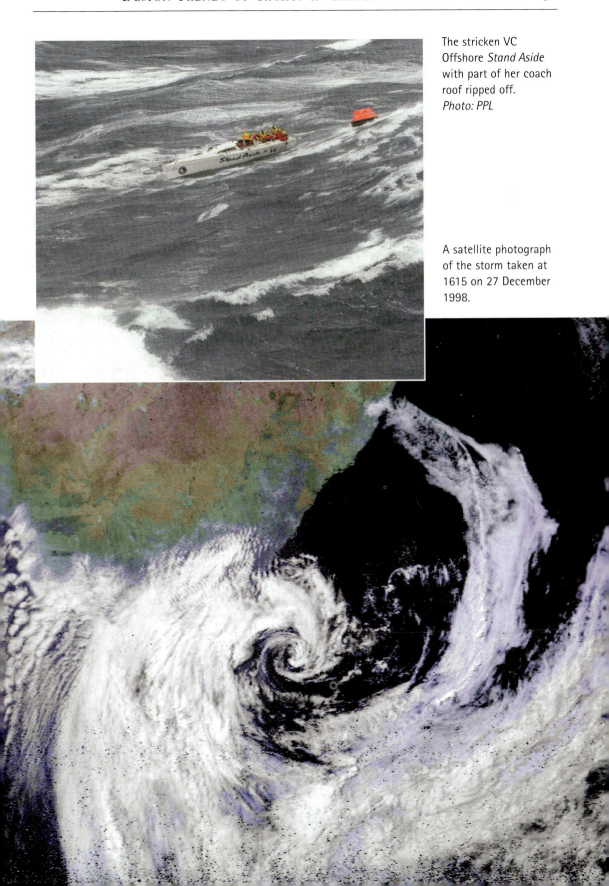

The stricken VC Offshore *Stand Aside* with part of her coach roof ripped off.
Photo: PPL

A satellite photograph of the storm taken at 1615 on 27 December 1998.

Some interesting comparisons can be made from these three accounts. We have three distinct types of yacht: a fairly moderate modern IMS type, a 30-year-old design, and a modern but conservatively designed Swan. All three of these yachts are amongst the stiffest in their respective classes.

The IMS yacht, *AFR Midnight Rambler*, managed to avoid getting into trouble by displaying great skill. She also had the advantage of daylight; nevertheless, at the same time several roughly similar but larger designs were rolled and suffered severe structural damage. The 30-year-old design, *Berrimilla*, resolutely and intelligently crewed, found quite big trouble in the dark but somehow every time flipped upright and undamaged. The large, stiff, strong, well-prepared Swan, *Aera*, again experiencing the worst part of the storm in daylight, with her experienced crew never becoming seriously worried at all. It was noteworthy that she carried a storm staysail as well as a storm jib. If the wind speed increases from storm to hurricane levels, sloops will need a spitfire jib, ie a storm jib of yet smaller size, if any sail is to be carried.

In the preceding chapter we learn that if a big enough wave breaks at a critical moment catching a yacht beam-on, she will capsize whatever her stability, but it is what happens afterwards that may be critical. Will she come back up again in about five seconds (as Peter Joubert's *Kingurra* did) or will she remain inverted from four to five minutes? Had *Business Post Naiad* recovered from her inversion as quickly as *Kingurra*, at least one life would not have been lost (see also Chapter 3).

Comparing *Berrimilla* with *Midnight Rambler* one finds a boat with more factors of safety built into her, but one capable of only half the speed. Incidentally it was extremely interesting to discover from Alex Whitworth that it may be possible to reduce the chances of being rolled by use of the helm to bring the bow down the wave.

Comparing *Aera* with *Midnight Rambler* we find a boat again with big factors of safety, not quite so elating to sail and, perhaps, twice the cost. *Midnight Rambler* probably represents a very good example of an IMS design. Nevertheless it remains questionable whether racing yachts in more extreme form are 'capable of withstanding heavy storms and are prepared to meet serious emergencies without the expectation of outside assistance', the supposed criteria for a Category 1 offshore race. The answer may never exactly be known, as human factors in storms tend to weigh so heavily.

Other possible lessons that emerged from the race were:

1 Need for improved means of finding those lost overboard.
2 The need for smaller storm sails in hurricane strength winds (see Chapter 17).
3 Too much paraphernalia attached to lifebuoys.
4 Insufficient knowledge of safety gear throughout crew.
5 Lack of effective radio communications from dismasted yachts.

The results of the Cruising Yacht Club of Australia's review of the race were not available at the time of going to print.

The trend from the stormier Sydney–Hobart races suggests that something has changed over 40 years:

1956 – 30 started, 28 finished (93%)	1984 – 150 started, 46 finished (31%)
1963 – 44 started, 34 finished (77%)	1993 – 105 started, 37 finished (35%)
1970 – 61 started, 47 finished (77%)	1998 – 115 started, 44 finished (38%)
1977 – 131 started, 72 finished (55%)	

Unless Australians are becoming soft, or storms are steadily becoming worse, neither of which seems likely, one might well feel that the trend is further evidence that commonly used racing handicap rules may be encouraging performance-orientated yachts to become less fit for ocean passages. The failure of some yachts to finish was solely due to mast/rig deficiency or structural problems, but in other cases failure to finish can be linked to low stability.

STABILITY OF RACING YACHTS

I am again grateful to Barry Deakin of the Wolfson Unit for his thoughts:

Traditionally, small cruising yachts had a range of stability of at least 150° and would therefore always return to upright if capsized. Such a stability range requirement is generally considered by modern designers to be unnecessarily conservative, and is certainly not readily
achievable with a modern hull form. In general, traditional forms with narrow beam and a
deep hull were more resistant to capsize, but breaking wave height in relation to boat size
is the overriding factor. Larger yachts are therefore safer in a given sea state, since they are
less likely to encounter a breaking wave of sufficient size to result in capsize. This fact has
led to proposals for stability requirements that vary with size (see Fig 3.1).

There is no doubt that there are many yachts which are vulnerable to being inverted by
breaking waves, and some of them are also unlikely to return to the upright, despite being
in storm conditions where further large waves will be encountered.

Casualty data appear to validate the standards developed, and suggest that the lessons of
the 1979 Fastnet Race may not have been taken to heart by the industry or the authorities,
despite further high profile casualties around the world. Unfortunately, as we all know, those
characteristics that have an adverse effect on safety in survival situations make the yacht fast,
spacious and comfortable in favourable conditions. They are valuable assets in the modern
yachting market, and authorities will be reluctant to try to enforce unpopular restrictions.

Buyers of sailing yachts should be provided with information to indicate realistically the
type of operation for which they are suitable. It would be irresponsible to market yachts as
ocean cruising yachts if they are vulnerable in terms of stability, or indeed any other aspect
of safety. Every individual is entitled to take measured risks, but one should not be misled
by marketing strategies into underestimating those risks.

Most yacht design offices now have facilities for computing the stability characteristics of

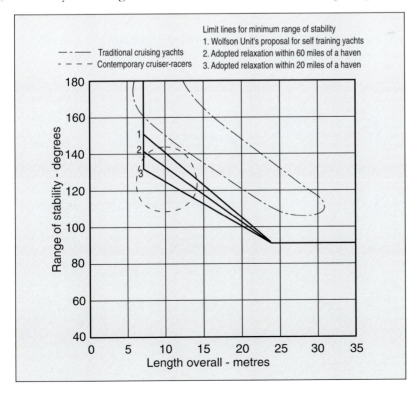

Figure 3.1 The two
sets of pecked lines
show that modern
racing yachts lie in an
area of a substantially
lower range of stability
than traditional
cruising yachts.

new designs and many incorporate a calculation of the range of stability into the design process. Not all of these computer programs are able to include the effects of coachroof and cockpit however, and these are of course fundamental to the stability at very large angles. There are many individuals and small companies involved in yacht design who do not have such facilities, and it is unlikely that they will commission a consultant to produce stability data, since there is no legal requirement nor public demand for such information.

Yacht designers tend to rely on their calculations for displacement and centre of gravity location. Inclining experiments, which are used to measure these values accurately, are virtually unheard of for cruising yachts, unless of course the yacht is also to be raced and undergoes an inclining experiment as part of its rating measurement. Since there have been no stability regulations for yachts, some designers have adopted their own targets and generally they appear to regard a range of stability of about 120° to be the basic requirement. This value may have been selected as a result of considerable publicity given to the USYRU recommendations in the mid-1980s, rather than being arrived at independently by the individuals.

There has been a reluctance on the part of rating authorities to demand detailed stability calculations from the designers of racing yachts. Until perhaps 20 years ago the technology was not readily available but more recently, with numerous computer programs available, specific stability requirements could have been incorporated into their rules. Fears of additional cost to the designers and problems associated with approval of results have perhaps deterred them. This attitude has led to an increased tendency to rely on approximate methods of assessment, based on a small number of principal dimensions.

An alarming illustration of the dangers of approximate assessments is given by a comparison of the stability curves for two examples of the same class of 28.5ft (8.7m) production cruising yacht (see Fig 3.2). The yacht with a range of 127° has a conventional rig as designed. The other with a range of only 96° has a mast furling mainsail and roller furling headsail fitted. The additional weight aloft on this yacht has reduced its range by 31°. The only way to identify such effects accurately is with an inclining experiment and a conventional stability calculation.

Thus, there are two aspects to stability assessment: the range needs to be determined properly: and there needs to be a sufficiently conservative minimum requirement. If an approximate method must be used an increased factor of safety should be introduced, for example by increasing the minimum requirement.

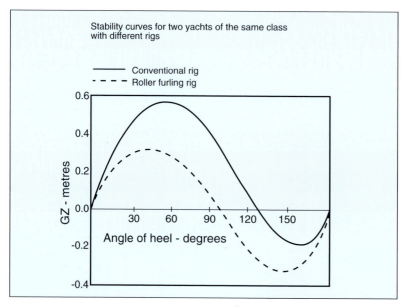

Stability curves for two yachts of the same class with different rigs

——— Conventional rig
- - - - Roller furling rig

Figure 3.2 A dramatic illustration of how a small yacht's range of positive stability can drop with modifications to the rig.

Yacht racing will never be 100% safe, but if the authorities wish to minimize the likelihood of fatalities through yachts having insufficient stability, the knowledge and techniques are there to be used, and they are now available at an acceptable cost. It appears that the result of existing racing rules has been to keep existing fleets competitive rather than to encourage increased safety in new designs. Improvements have now been made in the Whitbread Rule and if this example were followed by other race authorities, with a sufficiently stringent requirement, the general standard of safety would be raised. The researchers are making progress but the authorities seem to be hesitant about incorporating their findings.

Above Thierry Dubois clinging onto his capsized yacht which, by virtue of her extreme beam, is stable when inverted. Only by venting air from inside will she right herself. *Photo: AFP/PPL*

Left *Wild Thing* in the 1995 Sydney–Hobart Race demonstrates the full potential of modern racing yachts given an alert and competent crew. *Photo: Richard Bennett/PPL*

Clearly *Taka*'s stability range of 114° was not enough for an ocean storm if a yacht is to right herself quickly in the event of a total capsize. Compromise is allowable as vessels get bigger and Barry Deakin's figures in Fig 3.1 are worthy of note. He adds that the approximate methods of establishing the range of stability are acceptable for more stable craft but the more elaborate and accurate methods are necessary for craft in the lower range. This will include most racing boats.

Not only will a yacht's stability be significantly reduced by furling sails (Fig 3.2), but equally for radar, radar reflectors, spinnaker poles which fold up the mast, and mast steps. Even just loading up a yacht with food, and equipment which is stowed above the waterline, will have the same effect to a lesser degree, for example outboard motors, liferafts, food and equipment. The problem is not confined to smaller yachts. There are a number of super-yachts that only set their sails in gentle conditions due to heavy top hamper combined with shallow draft.

It was interesting that *Taka* self-righted after 45 minutes. A yacht should eventually self-right if she floods, and the effect of free surface water is to accelerate the process. Once righted there will usually be enough fore-and-aft structure to break up the free surface and discourage the yacht from inverting immediately, but there will be several tons of water to get rid of. Pumping out, by the way, is almost always preferable to taking to the liferaft.

The less lucky participants in the Vendée Globe Challenge singlehanded race of 1996–97 showed that there is still a rash of keel and stability weakness around the racing circuits. Far from bringing good ideas in for the cruising sailor, this race seems, up until now, to be breeding unforgiving yachts. At least the Vendée Globe type of yachts are now designed, like multihulls, with capsize in mind, eg with escape hatches fitted in the stern, etc, but it would be preferable that they have sufficient stability to right themselves quickly. One well-known case was Thierry Dubois's Open 60 *Amnesty International* which, in the 1996–97 Vendée Globe Race, remained firmly capsized in spite of large waves and the flooding of one of her stabilizing water tanks. The designer said that the boat had flooded as much as she was going to, and for the boat to right herself it would have been necessary to vent off air through a seacock to bring more water inside. In this event it might be prudent for competitors to establish at some point before the race the water level inside the boat which will cause her to sink! That Isabelle Autissier capsized in the South Pacific in February 1999, whilst taking part in the Around Alone race, and abandoned her yacht after being unable to right her, suggests no progress is being made in the realm of singlehanded competition yacht design.

The stability characteristics and, in particular, the angle of vanishing stability is information that can and should be obtained before a yacht is purchased for ocean voyaging. This information should include the effect of modifications such as furling sails, radar and other mast hamper, and also increasing displacement by the addition of fuel drums and motor bicycles on the upper deck and large quantities of stores and equipment down below. With this information one will have a good guide as to how stable a boat really is. In certain cases racing boats have acquired adequate or even abundant stability through using a bulb on the end of a high aspect keel, but such yachts have an unsuitably large draft should they ever be considered for cruising.

Other yachts have not righted themselves, as might be expected, when the keel has broken off. High aspect ratio keels, by virtue of their extra depth and smaller cross-sectional area, need considerable extra support. It is not so easy to tell at a glance how likely it is that such a keel will break off, though a surveyor is likely to give good advice. There is little to be lost in performance, or any other characteristic, by increasing the factor of safety in this region that is most easily done at the design stage. Of course keels of old-fashioned yachts are most unlikely to break off, but there is no need to go back to this style of design to achieve adequate strength.

QUESTIONABLE DESIGN FEATURES

Other modern features which buyers should be wary of are: large Perspex (acrylic) windows, weak coachroof structures, open centreboard casings, weak cockpit locker lids, weak steering arrangements, 'high tech' but unproven composite hull construction, off-centre hatchways, weak and unsecurable washboards, objects that rely on gravity to stay put, such as engines, batteries, anchors, fuel and fresh water tanks, and exhaust pipes which are not sufficiently well designed to stop water getting back to the engine. Many racing yachts, these days, have large shallow open cockpits with little protection from the elements, insufficient lockers, uncomfortable accommodation and fragile rigs.

Twin rudders are used more often in modern yachts, the rudders being offset from the centreline and angled outwards. Rudder damage can occur with this configuration owing to the keel no longer giving protection, and if one rudder is damaged the alternative one is usually only effective on one tack. The very high aspect ratio rudders of racing boats require two enormous bearings beneath their cockpit floors to function, and the bending moments are huge in return for small gains in efficiency. Structurally, a rudder supported by a skeg should be stronger than a blade, thus there is a good argument for using a skeg in the case of boats intended primarily for cruising. Not only is the rudder better supported but also it is much less likely to stall. The skeg must, of course, be very strongly built as failure may not only lead to the loss of steering capability but also create a hole below the waterline.

Straight or plumb bows are another characteristic of modern yachts encouraged by a rating rule. The elegant overhanging bow causes a rapid increase of buoyancy when the bow dips and discourages 'submarining', the straight bow does not.

CONCLUSION

One must appreciate that designers and builders are bound to try to give cruising yachts the sparkling performance characteristics of a racing boat if this is what people want. Thus every would-be buyer of an ocean cruising yacht clearly needs to be careful that he has a boat truly designed and built for the job – allowing for the extras he has in mind. Would-be buyers of performance yachts have to be more careful still. The quest for performance and excitement has, in some cases, been at the expense of passable stability, seakeeping qualities and strength. Moreover, in a fresh wind, possibly beyond the ability of an enthusiastic 'amateur' crew to control.

The implications for the prudent ocean cruising yachtsman might simply be to purchase a strong, stable proven design of vessel, unrelated to the current racing breeds and influenced by the sensible design characteristics given in Chapter 1 by Olin Stephens, the master designer of seaworthy yachts. Such thinking should produce a sensible craft. There is another argument worthy of consideration. If offshore or ocean racing crews are in need of help from the rescue services every time it blows more than force 8, there will come a time when governments will decide that yachtsmen are not able to manage their own affairs properly. They could take control of leisure craft safety regulations by creating all kinds of expensive and unsympathetic new legislation, to the detriment of all.

It is to be hoped that improvement of yacht design will continue but not at the expense of good stability and similar less obvious but important design features. Onus should always be on racing rule-makers to give precedence to seaworthy characteristics over maximization and equality of boat speed.

4 Spars and rigging considerations for heavy weather

MATTHEW SHEAHAN

Coastal-hopping in heavy weather conditions is one thing, long-distance bluewater cruising quite another. When the going gets tough many miles from land, self-sufficiency and confidence in the boat and her equipment are essential requirements.

As the primary driving force aboard the boat, the rig is fundamental to the crew's well-being in more ways than one. Lose the rig and there is a risk of having to cope with more than just the initial loss of motive power. Communications can be made inoperable and a longer passage time will put the food, water and fuel supplies in question. Depending on the type of craft, the motion of the boat may change completely as well, especially in bigger seas, and can make life very uncomfortable.

Prevention is always better than cure, and although it is never possible to guarantee the security of a yacht's rig, there are several ways of minimizing the risk. It is this approach that will be looked at first in this chapter, and then what to do if the worst does happen. But first a brief explanation of some of the most common types of rigs and what sets them apart from each other.

RIG CONFIGURATIONS

Although there are many historical reasons for the development of the wide variety of rigs in evidence today, the main reason for the differences is the practicality of handling a given sail area. Modern-day furling devices and reefing systems have done much to nudge up the size of sail plans that can be handled easily by, say, a crew of two. As boats get bigger, the configuration of the rig starts to play an important part in the manageability of the sail plan.

For boats of up to around 40ft (12m) LOA, Bermudan sloop rigs are by far the most popular as they are simple and easy to manage. However, above 40ft (12m) the cutter rig is popular. With this configuration, a staysail is flown from an inner forestay either instead of, or in conjunction with, the primary headsail. Breaking down the foretriangle area into two sails does make life easier for trimming, tacking and changing headsails. The configuration is particularly popular for coping with heavy weather when just the staysail and a deep-reefed mainsail can be set.

Since the advent of modern sail-handling systems, ketch and yawl rigs have become less popular. Yet they still have their place in reducing the total sail area into manageable sizes, especially on boats of 52ft (16m) LOA and above. Furthermore, having two masts means that there is at least the possibility of a spare mast, albeit smaller, in the event of losing the main mast. However, this will not always be the case, especially if a triatic stay – running from the top of the main mast to the top of the mizzen – is fitted. Having a mizzen mast can also provide a well-balanced heavy weather rig configuration too, where a staysail can be set on the main mast and a mizzen sail set aft.

Schooner rigs, where the forward-most mast is the shorter, offer similar advantages to ketches and yawls, where the total sail area is divided up into smaller individual areas. Again, this allows more options when it comes to balancing up the sail plan for heavy weather sailing on a given point of sail. And once more, in the event of losing one mast, there is at least a chance that there will be another still standing.

Although less popular, the unstayed mast configurations should be mentioned too. These are cat rigs with single large mainsails, swing rigs with a rotating mast and boom fixed unit, and junk rigs.

While providing several solutions to some of the potential problems and shortcomings of conventionally rigged spars, such configurations do have weaknesses of their own, particularly for the long-distance sailor. Having no rigging does mean that the spar is more likely to flex and, depending on the spar's material, is therefore more susceptible to fatigue in certain areas. Most builders of these types of spars are well aware of the problems, and it is true to say that this is less of an issue with carbon masts than those built in alloy. Nevertheless, while compression is the biggest problem for stayed spars, fatigue through flexing is the unstayed rig's biggest enemy. Lack of rigging also makes it more difficult to go aloft, especially while under way. A blessed excuse perhaps, but take time to consider how you would cope in such an event, before it happens for real.

In the 1981–2 Whitbread Round the World Race, *Ceramco New Zealand*, skippered by Peter Blake, lost her mast 150 miles north of Ascension Island when the port lower intermediate rod shroud broke where it had been bent around the lower spreader. The 50ft (15m) top section was recovered and lashed to the 11ft (3m) stump using a breadboard as a baseplate. The destination of Cape Town was 2455 miles away, but it was necessary to sail over 1000 miles more to stay in favourable winds. During the passage, *Ceramco*'s crew achieved one day's run of 238 miles. *Photo: PPL*

Perhaps the most important factor to bear in mind though, is that of setting storm sails. Few unstayed masts have attachments for inner forestays onto which storm jibs can be hanked, and some mast/mainsail arrangements have problems in fitting a trysail track. Such considerations must be borne in mind before heading off over the horizon.

A SEAWORTHY SPAR?

The biggest dilemma for many designers and prospective owners is whether to opt for a deck-stepped or keel-stepped mast. There is a continuing debate as to which is the most suitable for long-distance cruising, and there are advantages and disadvantages on either side. From a structural and spar design point of view, a keel-stepped mast should always be lighter, yet no less secure, than the same rig stepped on deck. Keel-stepped masts derive a large part of their security from the fact that they are 'built in' – as engineers would say – being supported at the mast heel and at the deck.

To use the same engineering terminology, deck-stepped masts on the other hand are 'pin-jointed' structures. In other words, without the rigging, a deck-stepped mast would fall over straight away. A keel-stepped mast would not – at least, not so easily!

When it comes to designing the mast section, a deck-stepped mast should always be constructed from a stiffer mast section – one having higher moments of inertia – compared to the keel-stepped alternative. Heavier masts can have a considerable effect on the stability and motion of the boat, as well as her performance, and although this may not be a key issue in some cases, it is nonetheless an important consideration.

Keel-stepped masts do have their disadvantages though. While it can be avoided (Fig 4.1), the most common is water leakage down the inside of the mast into the boat. A boat with a deck-stepped mast does not suffer this problem. In the worst case scenario of being

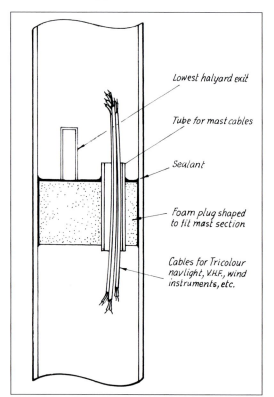

Figure 4.1 An example of a means by which a keel-stepped mast can be made to drain on deck rather than in the accommodation area.

Lowest halyard exit

Tube for mast cables

Sealant

Foam plug shaped to fit mast section

Cables for Tricolour navlight, V.H.F., wind instruments, etc.

dismasted, the bury section (the section below decks) of keel-stepped masts can sometimes cause damage below decks too, especially if the heel comes away from the mast step. This can happen if the boat is rolled or knocked down.

Although this type of damage is rare, a recent case in the Southern Ocean contributed to the loss of the boat as a watertight bulkhead was damaged. So preventative measures are important. They are simple too. Fastening the mast heel down to the mast step either by through-bolting, or by attaching a rigging screw strop to a hull attachment, is usually sufficient.

But what about the rest of the rig: what should be looked for or specified in a set of spars that will be fit for bad weather? Spreader roots, gooseneck attachments, shroud tangs and masthead units are the main areas to focus on. Although they all perform separate tasks, they do tend to fall into three categories: cast aluminium units, fabricated aluminium fittings and fabricated stainless steel fittings.

Cast alloy fittings are popular among production spar manufacturers as they are cheaper to produce in numbers and simple to fit to the spars, requiring only a few rivets or machine screws to fasten them (Fig 4.2). Although fine for normal coastal and occasional offshore sailing, castings like these can present more of a problem for longer-distance sailors for a number of reasons.

Aluminium castings are brittle when compared with alloy or steel fabrications, and consequently do not fare well if they receive sharp blows. In the case of a gooseneck, a crash gybe, transferring high shock loads along the boom, could be enough to damage a casting irreparably, whereas it might simply bend or distort a fabricated unit. Cast fittings do not like being distorted either. A spreader set at an incorrect angle can, when loaded, distort a casting to the extent that it fails completely. Again, a fabrication may be more tolerant of such misalignments.

But it has to be said that there are different views on this subject. One justification in favour of simple screw or rivet-on castings is that they are usually a stock item for the spar builder. As a result, they can easily be sent almost anywhere in the world and can often be fitted without specialist tools. The balance that needs to be struck when considering which system to go for is between the likelihood of failure, against the difficulty of repair.

In this respect there is one type of fitting that is not suitable for those travelling far afield. Spreader root castings welded to the mast wall itself should be avoided where possible, as not only are they more prone to failure, for the above reasons, and often reduce the strength of the mast wall locally, but should they be damaged, it is often difficult to repair the mast as the fitting cannot be removed easily. Indeed any arrangement where the spreader transmits its thrust to the mast wall rather than a through bar is to be avoided.

On the other hand, welding masthead units and sheave cages into a tube is not only acceptable for a robust spar, but also desirable, so long as the work is carried out properly. To achieve full strength, most types of aluminium alloy need to be heat treated from a 'soft state' to a 'hard state'. Subsequent welding heats up local areas of the mast section, usually at critical points, and lowers the mechanical properties of the alloy back towards the soft state.

The optimum procedure is to perform all welding tasks such as tapering, attaching masthead units, forestay attachments and sheave cages while the tube is in its soft state. Once complete, the tube is then heat treated to achieve its full strength. As far as finish is concerned, anodizing is technically the best means of protecting a mast against corrosion and is normally the most cost effective too for boats of up to around 43ft (13m) LOA.

Painted spars are the next best thing for larger boats, as there are few anodizing tanks that can cope with the size and length of large yacht masts. Furthermore, many people consider a paint finish to be prettier.

Paint finishes have improved significantly, and can offer good protection for an alloy spar so long as the surface is not damaged, but maintaining a perfect, scratch-free mast is a near impossibility. Although scratches and flaking paint are unlikely to cause structural problems themselves, one must keep an eye on any unusual signs that may indicate more serious corrosion beneath.

STAYING THE RIG

There are few statistics to prove it, but most spar manufacturers would agree that aside from poor maintenance and set-up, fatigue and rigging failure are among the most common reasons for dismastings aboard cruising boats. Fatigue cycles, where the fitting is effectively work hardened through repeated flexing, usually start as a result of poor articulation. This is particularly true of the shroud attachments to the mast where the less articulation that is present, the greater the risk of fatigue and subsequent failure. As is so often the case, all it takes is one inexpensive fitting to break to cause far more serious and costly damage to the mast.

So how is it possible to be sure that attachments are suitable? As a rule of thumb, pin and eye attachments are structurally the best as there is a greater chance of the eye rocking on the pin to accommodate different alignments (Fig 4.4). Fittings designed as ball and sockets – often referred to as stemball systems – have greater friction between their surfaces and are less likely to articulate (Figs 4.5 and 4.6). The result is fatigue cycles somewhere else in the fitting, usually some way down the stem of a swaged fitting or at the point where the wire exits the end fitting.

T-terminals and similar devices may well be suitable for many applications, but it has to be borne in mind that they will articulate less and need to be replaced on a more regular basis. The big problem is that, apart from the considerable expense of X-raying the terminals, there are no visual indications of how far the fatigue problem has progressed.

Another factor to consider is that few masts remain rigid in one place. Indeed, if they did, high shock loads would be transferred throughout the boat. Instead, masts do move in the boat and the rigging should be able to accommodate the full range of movement. But what is an acceptable amount and how should a mast best be stayed?

The wide range of basic configurations, plus the added combinations of the variety of multiple spreader arrangements, makes this area a difficult one to define precisely. If it was not for considerations of sheeting the headsail, the wider the chain plate base the better. But as a small sheeting angle is essential for good windward performance, a narrow chain plate base has to be offset by an increase in the number of spreaders up the mast. Larger craft often require discontinuous rigging once three or more sets of spreaders are used.

Generally, most boats are adequately stayed in the athwartships plane. It is achieving sufficient fore-and-aft support that causes most problems. Beating into a heavy seaway with a deep-reefed mainsail can be one of the most punishing situations for a mast. High shock loads transferred through the rigging, as the boat pitches and slams through each wave, can cause the mast to pump fore-and-aft. A deep-reefed mainsail can make the situation worse as the sail tries to pull the middle of the mast aft. Unless checked, this can cause a full inversion of the mast, ie when the middle of the spar bows aft. Under these conditions, masts can and do fail due to the high compression loads, especially when the boat drops off a wave. To prevent this it is important to stop the mast from moving too much in the fore-and-aft plane. Checkstays and running backstays prevent the mast from moving too far forward. Forward lowers or a babystay can help to prevent the mast moving aft, but the small angles where the stays meet the mast mean that an inner forestay should also be included for a belt and braces approach.

The inner forestay, as with the running backstays and checkstays, need not be permanent features and can be stowed by the mast in normal conditions. But for anyone considering trips where they may encounter heavy conditions, such stays are a must, especially on masthead rigged boats.

Figure 4.2 (above) Cast alloy spreader mounting.

Figure 4.3 (right) Note the lack of articulation of the forestay.

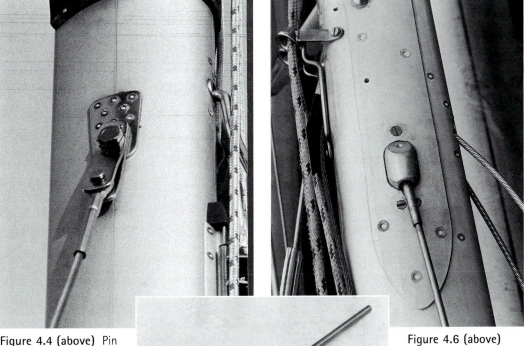

Figure 4.4 (above) Pin and eye attachment.

Figure 4.5 (right) Components of the stemball system.

Figure 4.6 (above) Exterior view of the stemball system.

With the wide popularity of furling headsail systems, it is advisable to make provision for an emergency forestay. Although generally reliable furling units can fail, and to be left with no headsails at all is unwelcome. Furthermore, even if the furling system works perfectly, when reefed heavily the shape of the remaining scrap of sail is too full and positioned too high up the forestay to act as a sensible storm jib. Setting a flat storm sail, low down, will drive the boat better and reduce heel – providing a much more comfortable ride. In most cases, an emergency forestay can easily be fitted to existing masts as well as new ones. A tang fitting positioned on the forward face of the mast, just below the main forestay fitting, and a tack fitting on deck are usually all that is required.

One popular concern of long-distance sailors is whether rod rigging should be chosen rather than the more conventional 1×19 wire. Although rod-rigged systems are generally more expensive than their equivalent in wire, the decision will usually depend upon ease of maintenance.

Conventional stainless steel wire is commonly available around the world and is easy to work with. Swaging tools are found in most popular ports and sailing areas, but for those travelling much farther afield, bolted cone and socket type (or swageless) fittings, such as the Norseman or Sta Lok-type terminals, require just a hacksaw and spanners to fit them. A further advantage is that these terminations can easily be re-made if any local damage to the wire is found or suspected.

Rod rigging, on the other hand, requires specialist tools to make the terminations and can be more prone to fatigue with few outward signs. Rod rigging does have advantages though. For a given diameter, rod stretches less than wire. This means that a mast can be secured more efficiently in the boat with less deflection of the mast itself, and that weight aloft can also be reduced, improving the performance and motion of the boat. It should also be said that on large cruisers, the scaling effect means that weight aloft becomes a serious issue for which rod rigging is frequently the only sensible option.

SHORTENING SAIL

While highly practical, affordable and, best of all, simple, roller reefing systems for main or genoa do have a few drawbacks that should be considered. Headsail furling gears are generally easier to get at than those used for in-mast mainsail furling and present less of a problem in the event of a failure. Furling mainsail systems can snag with the sail jammed in the section and refuse to come in or out which, in the teeth of a gale, could be very awkward. Even if the system is to be trusted completely, provision should be made for some other means of storm mainsail that doesn't rely on the furling device, such as a trysail track.

Unlike slab reefing systems or boom furling systems, where the weight is lowered each time a reef is taken in, vertical furling systems mean that the sail weight remains at the same height above the waterline. Keeping weight high up means that there is no stability improvement as the sail plan is reduced. This can lead to a slow heavy motion due to the inertia of a heavier spar with a furled sail inside it. Furthermore, with furling headsails, the increased windage of a rolled-up headsail over a bare forestay is much greater. Another significant drawback is that if the sail cannot be fully furled, the only way to get it down is to open it out fully before lowering it. This may not be feasible in severe conditions.

In-boom furling systems offer some advantages over their in-mast equivalents, especially when it comes to reducing weight aloft, but the problems of an even furl and the distance of the luff back from the aft face of the mast can cause problems.

Slab reefing is a practical and reliable method of reefing. The comforting thought is that in the worst case, there is a better chance that the sail can be lowered, although this is still by no means guaranteed, especially if a headboard car or batten sliders are fitted. Fully battened and semi-fully battened mainsail systems make the reefing process simpler to manage, especially if lazyjacks are fitted, by reducing the flogging of the mainsail as it is lowered. The sail also stows more easily on top of the boom.

Single line reefing systems, where the tack and the clew of the reefed mainsail are controlled by a single line, are also very popular and allow a mainsail to be reefed quickly and without having to leave the cockpit. However, one of the potential drawbacks with any control line led back to the cockpit is friction. In order to make the system work as smoothly as possible it is very important to ensure that the reef lines or halyards are kept as free from abrupt turns around lead blocks wherever possible.

CHECKING AND MAINTAINING THE RIG

How often the rig should be checked will depend entirely on the type of sailing undertaken. While every sailor should keep an eye on the rig all the time, there are practical limits. At the very minimum, weekend, home-based sailors should check their masts at the beginning and end of every season, with the mast being taken out of the boat for a thorough check at least every three years. At the other end of the scale, checking the mast and rigging while on passage should be a daily event. Whatever type of sailing is undertaken, the potential causes of damage or failure are more likely to be as a result of chafe, fatigue or corrosion than from the effects of overloading. In most cases, tell-tale signs of problems can be identified visually, while the mast is in situ, which is just as well as X-raying the mast and fittings would in most cases be impractical, extremely expensive, and sometimes inconclusive.

Aluminium alloy used for most spars has a high natural resistance to corrosion, resulting from the formation of the tough impervious oxide film on the surface of the aluminium when exposed to air. This oxide film, which is grey in colour, is self-repairing. So if removed by chafing or scratching, it will protect the aluminium from further corrosion, provided no dissimilar metals are in contact with the aluminium to cause electrolytic corrosion. However, any substantial corrosion at the base of the mast and at deck level should be treated seriously as these are high load areas for the mast. In these areas, dents in the mast wall can be a problem too and could cause the mast to buckle. This type of damage is not easy to repair without specialist tools and help.

Cracks are a particularly common starting point for mast or rigging failures and can be remedied so long as they are caught before they have had a chance to propagate too far. The areas to look at are wherever there is an exit or hole in the mast wall – especially if it is rectangular – for example, around halyard exits and where mast fittings penetrate the mast wall. Drilling a small hole at the end of the crack can, in most cases, stop the crack from travelling further, but it will only be a temporary measure and will need more elaborate attention as soon as possible.

Ensuring that all fastenings are secure is perhaps an obvious check, but one that is often overlooked, as is the free running of sheaves which, if jammed, can cause premature chafe and failure of halyards and control lines. If the mast is keel-stepped another area that is frequently ignored is the deck-level chock arrangement. The chocks should be so secured in place that the mast is prevented from moving at all.

While there are ways in which rigging terminations can be checked using electrical methods, a few simple checks can often reveal potential problems. Looking for broken strands or corrosion within the wire is the most obvious. Elongated eyes or bent pins are an indication of overloading and should be replaced. Alignment of rigging is another important check, as a stay or shroud that is distorted may fail from fatigue. As has already been mentioned, poor articulation is also very important and a common cause of fatigue-related

In the 1992–3 British Steel Global Challenge a number of bottlescrews cracked, and aboard *British Steel II* the mast was lost after the forestay bottlescrew failed on the leg between Rio and Auckland. A jury-rig was made using the boom and spinnaker pole, staysail sheets and reefing lines but, having been refuelled by a P&O tanker, she was able to complete much of the leg under power. *Photo: PPL*

rigging failures. All standing rigging attachments should have some degree of articulation in as many planes as possible. Another simple but essential check is to make sure that the standing rigging is secured to the spreader ends.

HEAVY WEATHER PROCEDURES UNDER WAY

Preparation in all areas of the boat is the key to riding out heavy weather conditions, and nowhere is it more important than with the rig. As with many other dramas at sea, all too often a catastrophic event is the culmination of several otherwise controllable or avoidable incidents. Be prepared. Ensure that the trysail will fit in its track by hoisting it, preferably without having to climb above deck level. Have enough sail ties ready to strap down the mainsail if it has to be lowered altogether, and ensure that there is a secure means of lashing the boom to the deck to prevent it being hurled about the cockpit. Life will be difficult enough with the boom in the cockpit instead of overhead, without the further complication of the spar sliding from one side of the boat to the other as the boat rolls in big seas.

Just as important is to ensure that all the heavy weather sails have been tried out, not just when tied up to the pontoon or swinging at a mooring, but under way and preferably when it is blowing. Anticipation is important too as it is far easier and safer to throw out a reef in calm waters, than it is to put one in when the weather has deteriorated. Anticipating the weather is particularly important if furling sails are used. A furled headsail can present considerable windage in gale conditions, to say nothing of the weight aloft. If the forecast is for heavy conditions, it may be prudent to take the sail down altogether and this means unfurling it completely – the last thing to be doing in 40 knots of wind! This also goes for furling mainsails. Although there is no additional windage when the main is furled, in extreme weather it may be sensible to lower the mainsail to reduce the centre of gravity.

WHEN THE WORST HAPPENS

Mast failures are frequently a result of rigging failures, and in many cases quick thinking can save the day – just. A shroud failure, be it a wire or terminal problem, often results in losing the mast. But if the helmsman is quick enough, and it is safe to do so, a smart tack with the jib left cleated will cause the boat to heave-to and allow the mast to be jury-rigged. In some situations it may not be possible to spend much time in this position, but at least it provides time to think about how the mast can best be supported. If a halyard is used to replace a shroud, bear in mind that the angle at the masthead will be very small as the halyard won't run over the spreaders. Using a jockey pole or spinnaker pole just above deck level as an outrigger may help to increase the angle at the masthead and improve the support of the spar.

A forestay or backstay failure is less likely to result in an instant dismasting, but it is still a serious problem and should be dealt with quickly. In this case the most important thing to do is to turn either downwind or upwind to take the load onto the intact stay, depending on which one is broken, and then rig temporary support using a spare spinnaker or genoa halyard. If the backstay fails upwind, don't panic. Leave the mainsheet cleated as the leech of the mainsail will help to support the mast. In many cases, be it shroud or stay that

A rain squall struck contenders for the British Admiral's Cup Team seconds after the start of a selection trial race, dismasting *Yeoman 25*. Her mast failed in compression as a result of the mainsail luff rope pulling out of the track, which allowed the mast to bend forward out of control until it broke. *Photo: Peter Bruce*

fails, it is important not to be too quick to lower the sails, especially if there is a big sea running, as the sails can often help to stabilize the motion of the boat and prevent the mast from panting. However, if the rigging failure happens in flat water and is simply a result of overstressing, dropping the sails may be the best option.

If the worst does happen and the mast falls over the side of the boat, there are two golden rules – get the spar away from the hull and don't start the engine until you are absolutely sure that the rigging cannot foul the propeller. Hull damage is a major consideration in the case of a dismasting, as is the issue of remaining safe on deck and not getting dragged overboard by tangled rigging. Extreme care is required, but also swift action. Cut the rig free to protect the boat, but do remember that the more that can be salvaged the better the chances are of setting up a jury-rig. Sometimes it is not possible to save any of the rig, so it is a good idea to have thought about how such a rig might be arranged with just the boom and the spinnaker poles.

SPARES AND TOOLS

The ideal tool kit is one that provides tools to deal with every component aboard. In reality, this is impractical and a compromise has to be reached. Basic tools should include drills, knives, hacksaws, screwdrivers, spanners, grips and wrenches, which are anyway usually considered essential for all kinds of shipboard tasks. Tools that are needed specifically for the rig might include the following:

> Rigging cutters (eg Felco) if 1×19 wire rigging is used. (Note that only an HT grade hacksaw blade, an angle grinder or a hydraulic cutter will cut rod rigging.)
> Club hammer
> Pipe wrench
> Extra large adjustable wrench and a length of hollow pipe to fit over it
> Sharp cold chisel
> Marlin spike
> Long tape measure
> Rivet gun

Spares

> Clevis pins
> Split pins
> Shackles
> Nuts and bolts
> Screws: machine and self-tapping
> Blocks
> Toggles
> Rigging terminals: swage and swageless
> A length of wire, longer than the longest stay aboard and no less than the biggest diameter, plus swageless fittings to match
> Bulldog clamps
> Mast and boom sleeving kit
> Rivets
> Zince chromate paste (or other insulating material)
> Seizing wire
> Tape
> Rope and cordage

5 Preparations for heavy weather

PETER BRUCE

After ships of his US Pacific fleet were seriously damaged or sunk in Typhoon Cobra on 18 December 1944 with the loss of 790 officers and men, Fleet Admiral Nimitz wrote a letter to the fleet which ended with the following comment: 'The time for taking all measures for a ship's safety is while able to do so. Nothing is more dangerous than for a seaman to be grudging in taking precautions lest they turn out to have been unnecessary. Safety at sea, for a thousand years, has depended upon exactly on the opposite philosophy.'

While some heavy weather is almost the inevitable lot of the ocean voyager, the majority of coastal sailors will be in a position to avoid it most of the time, very sensibly, by the exercise of discretion and by good planning. But meteorology is not an exact science, so there is always a chance of being caught out in a blow at sea however carefully one has studied the weather and listened to the weather forecasts. One can find oneself caught out in a storm anytime and anywhere. If this does happen, the aim should be to come through the experience safely, without damage, independently of outside assistance, and in as much comfort and good humour as the circumstances permit.

To achieve this aim, the wise skipper will make contingency plans and will practise for heavy weather either in harbour or in calm weather, knowing that he should expect no more than simple tasks to be undertaken by his crew when it comes on to blow. Storms can creep up insidiously on the crew of a vessel at sea; in a sailing boat, this often happens via a period of exhilaration as wind and wave exceed normal expectations. There follows a period when crews show a gradually decreasing tendency to make any additional effort, save that of attending to necessary reductions of sail, adjusting to discomfort or reconciling themselves to seasickness.

Clearly, a crew's energy and resources are best reserved for matters that cannot have been anticipated. A skipper with no inner doubts about the fitness of his vessel and equipment will find it easier to inspire his crew to make the special effort that may be needed in a storm. This chapter is written without a particular level of severity of weather in mind, but rather in acknowledgement of the fact that an unexpected encounter with heavy weather may occur at any time.

HARBOUR PREPARATIONS

One cannot buy safety nor guarantee survival, but one can buy equipment that in practised hands can improve safety. Predominately it is a crew's skill that will mostly affect the issue in an emergency.

Safety equipment comes in many forms and will vary according to the extent of the voyage. As mentioned by Olin Stephens in Chapter 1, a useful list of seamanlike measures to cope with eventualities in bad weather is provided by the Offshore Racing Council's Special Regulations. These regulations are compulsory for yachts in most offshore races worldwide, but cruising boat owners might also do well to study them, as they have been distilled from many years of experience. As already said, if he is to face bad weather with confidence, a skipper needs to do more than buy and mount the safety equipment that his conscience dictates or that complies with regulations. He and his crew must know how to use it through testing it in a non-threatening situation.

In addition to safety equipment, even the owner of a new vessel may need to make an occasional effort to keep on top of defects in a vessel's general equipment; in the case of an older boat, a constant effort may be necessary. In calm weather, the adaptable human quickly reconciles himself to such things as small leaks, quirky navigation lights, a seized hull valve, a defective pump, a shortage of mainsail ties and so on. Such shortcomings can assume enormous proportions in rough weather, creating an emergency out of something previously regarded as a trivial problem. Recording such faults in a 'defect book' is a helpful means of maintaining a boat in first-class condition.

Storm sails tend not to be used very often, and after use are returned to their bags with little thought for the future. It is wise, therefore, to check the storm sails for weak or broken stitching and sticky hanks at the start of every season.

In addition to commonplace failures, another potentially weak area lies with standby equipment. For example, when the jib furling gear breaks, will the alternative system be operable? When the GPS or Loran fails in fog, will there be batteries for the old radio direction finder set, and will it work? Likewise, the reserve bilge pump, the emergency navigation lights, and so on.

It has to be said that not all new boats are fit for heavy weather on delivery. Apart from the need for inherent structural strength, serious offshore owners will often have to carry out numerous modifications. For example, a separate trysail mast track can be added which runs down to near-deck level, allowing the sail to remain bagged at the foot of the mast ready for instant use. Lee cloths may have to be changed for ones of adequate size and strength; bolts may have to replace screws; penny washers changed for proper backing pieces for deck fittings; anchor well lids may need fastenings; mainsails may need sufficient reefing points; arrangements may be necessary to set a storm jib; adaptations may be necessary to deploy a parachute sea anchor, and so on. A surveyor's advice can be helpful in this situation.

When planning a vessel's chart portfolio, either before a voyage or during the lay-up period, consideration should be given to ensuring that there is adequate information in the event of being blown well off course, or having to find an unfamiliar port of refuge under the stress of bad weather. It is easy to imagine the anguish of being forced into an area of shoal waters without a chart. Adlard Coles himself, in Chapter 14, describes how he had to rely on a few discouraging notes in the *Cruising Association Handbook* to enter the shallow harbour of Walberswick in Suffolk, having been diverted there under duress of a North Sea gale from a point only 37 miles short of his destination of Dover.

PLANNING FOR DIRE SITUATIONS

A good heavy weather principle is to prepare for the worst and hope for the best. For example, Chay Blyth used to prepare himself on a flat calm day by staging the onset of a fictitious gale. Another method is to plan and practise for dire circumstances. Such action can have a negative effect on less experienced crew, so give them notice, ie 'Tomorrow morning at 10 am, safety drills!' Among the worst of all the perilous situations that should be considered are: one or more members of the crew falling overboard; the necessity to make to windward under sail in heavy weather to clear a lee shore; fire; capsize; or the need to abandon ship.

Man overboard

Looking at these events in turn, the man overboard situation comes to mind first. Indeed, in incidents involving a fatality where the lifeboat has been called out, it is the most common cause. There are three phases involved when someone is lost overboard: location; attachment; recovery on board and treatment.

In very high winds, such as those caused by tropical revolving storms, 'double-decker' waves often form where the lower level is steep and looks bad enough, but where the top level is truly awesome. This photograph is an example of a wave where the top level is breaking, taken by Captain de Lange in the north Atlantic in force 10–11.

At the risk of stating the obvious, location is much assisted by someone keeping the casualty in sight. One cannot assume that this will always be possible, so it is of equally heavy priority to practise recording the vessel's position, both with appropriate buoyant safety gear, and by using such navigational aids as may be available. In a real situation, in addition to the measures taken on board, outside help should be summoned without delay.

Two different methods for the retrieval of man overboard are in favour – the 'quick stop' and the 'reach-tack-reach' method. I instinctively adopted the 'quick stop' method with an entirely satisfactory result in my small yacht *Scarlet Runner* in 1973, when surfing downwind under spinnaker in an English Channel race. Immediately after the man was lost, the yacht, which had no engine, was turned into wind as the spinnaker was dropped. The sail backed across the foretriangle and was successfully gathered in as the boat beat back under mainsail to the man in the water. He was hauled in from the lee side at a point just aft of the shrouds.

The other method, taught by the Royal Yachting Association for many years, involves going onto a reach, followed by a tack and a reach back to the victim. It is preferable to spend time trying either one of them, rather than spending the time discussing which one to employ.

At first an effort may be necessary to get a crew to exercise a man overboard drill, but thereafter it will almost certainly be perceived as an important evolution, worthy of practice and discussion. The quick and seamanlike retrieval of some suitable object from the sea, without the use of the engine – as propellers so often catch a rope in a crisis – also provides a source of deserved satisfaction within a crew. Equally important is to prove by practical trial that the equipment intended for quick deployment, such as a horseshoe lifebuoy with a flashing light attached to it by a lanyard, can be used effectively in stressful circumstances. Experience, supported by trials in the USA, shows that a tangle is likely at the first attempt.

Every boat should have at least one means of lifting a casualty back on board. A stern bathing ladder is not the answer in a seaway. In particular, couples who sail on their own together should consider how to cope with the situation where the stronger and heavier partner has fallen over the side. The Seattle Sailing Foundation was inspired to study this aspect of the man overboard problem by some understandable but heartbreaking local tragedies. In one case a man, an experienced sailor, went overboard on a blustery day from the foredeck of his yacht. His wife, his sole crew, who was not experienced, had no idea what to do. Frozen with horror she steered straight until she hit the beach some time later. Her husband was never found. In another case, a skipper was lost and drowned even after being brought alongside, due to difficulties in hoisting him on board.

There is now on the market some very good equipment to aid the recovery of a man overboard, such as the Seattle (or life) sling, which deserves careful consideration. At the same time one should be aware that there may be a tendency these days to place too much reliance on technology, so it is best only to buy items that have withstood the stringency of thorough testing. Mike Golding carried 'personal EPIRBs' in the 1997 BT Round the World Race (Chapter 9). Rather than have the crew wear them, one or two were placed within easy reach of the helmsman who was instructed to throw them over the side if someone was lost.

A small waterproof torch carried in a foul weather jacket pocket as a back-up device is not only useful for finding things down below at night without disturbing the off-watch crew through using the cabin lights, but the torch might also act as a position indicator should one ever involuntarily part company with one's vessel.

Obviously prevention is better than cure, and in addition to non-slip surfaces and footgear, the value of a well-designed safety harness, built to the standard Offshore Racing

Council specification and adjusted so that one will not slip out, cannot be overestimated. Foredeck crews are most exposed, but they tend to be nimble and aware of the hazard, whereas those not used to being on the foredeck can be more at risk. Less obvious moments of exposure, but ones that have claimed lives, are those when crews unclip their safety harnesses to go below or have not yet clipped on when coming on deck. It is good practice to pass the clip up for the on-watch crew to clip on before progressing to the cockpit and vice versa. With practice, education, well-positioned strong points and jackstays, it should be possible to avoid ever being unclipped when on deck. It is worth mentioning that the harness should be clipped on in a way that prevents a person falling over the side rather than merely preventing him from being separated from his craft having done so.

In spite of more general use of safety harnesses, the possibility of losing someone overboard still remains. Two more common examples are when gentlemen are relieving themselves over the side, and when crew members are struck on the head by the boom in an unexpected gybe. Chances of survival, once in the water, are obviously much increased when a lifejacket is being worn. In the latter case, when the victim is unconscious, the facility of automatic inflation is desirable, but automatic inflation leads to much extra expense and effort as it often goes off when not required. Mike Golding disarmed the auto inflation capability during the BT Global Challenge Race of 1997.

There is something to be said for foul weather jackets with built-in safety harness and lifejacket, as the decision to put them on is then directly linked with windy or bad weather, and little effort is required. However, it is difficult to design built-in lifejackets with features to make them effective in rough water. For example, the experience of man overboard from the yacht *Hayley's Dream* in the 1989 Fastnet showed that it is necessary to incorporate a restraining arrangement, such as a crutch strap, to prevent the lifejacket riding up over the casualty's head. Another case, which occurred in the 1989–90 Whitbread Round the World Race, draws attention to the value of a spray guard to prevent the casualty drowning from inhaled spray. All such features can be achieved when the lifejacket is combined with a safety harness alone, an arrangement that would appear to optimize both safety and convenience.

In concluding this subject, it should be remembered that drowning, rather than hypothermia, is the predominant cause of loss of life in man overboard incidents.

A LEE SHORE

The next eventuality to be considered is a lee shore, which was once such a terrifying prospect to the crews of square-rigged vessels. Such is the weatherliness of modern craft that a lee shore is not now such a common cause for concern. Nevertheless, circumstances can come about when a yacht will only be saved from shipwreck by having the ability to make to windward under storm sails. Those who have a roller headsail system should be aware that, as the headsail is rolled in, it becomes baggy and increasingly inefficient as a windward sail. Some standard production yachts are neither supplied with storm sails at all, nor with provision to use them. To reduce the cost of the sail inventory, others are supplied with sails described as storm jibs that are too big for use in really severe weather.

Even when in possession of a sensibly sized storm jib, it should be remembered that, to be effective to windward, sheet leads and the point at which the jib is attached to the foredeck need careful thought and assessment. Ideally, the tack of the storm jib should be taken to a point somewhat aft of the stem fitting to obtain optimum balance and interaction between it and the mainsail/trysail. But to achieve this, a properly designed independent forestay, supported by running backstays, will be necessary. A tack pennant is usually advisable to raise the storm jib to match the height of the trysail or reefed main, and to give

greater clearance to waves breaking over the foredeck. In addition, sheet leads will need to be positioned further outboard than for the larger headsails to give a greater angle from the centreline. Finally, for yachts that use a headfoil system rather than hanks, consideration needs to be given to coping with an unusable foil. These devices are tough, but can be crushed by a spinnaker pole. Moreover, plastic versions have been known to simply fragment through cold temperatures or prolonged exposure to natural ultra-violet light.

Mainsails are often supplied without a sufficiently deep reef capability, ie the ability to reef to 25 per cent of the full area. This is, presumably, on the risky assumption that the engine will be used if it becomes too windy to sail or that most owners are not out in severe weather. Even if a good deep reef provision in the mainsail has been made, it is still important to ensure that the reefing line is located to create a really flat sail. A well-reefed but over-full mainsail is worse than an unreefed but well-flattened sail.

Assuming conditions warrant its use, a trysail is a most efficient sail, but it is usually difficult to set, due to the necessary height above the deck of the luff fastening arrangement – usually a slider gate – coupled with the proximity of the mainsail. Ideally, a separate mast track should be provided for the trysail. This allows the trysail to be bent on before the mainsail is lowered. Whatever system is used, a new trysail must be given at least one airing in calm conditions. Clearly, it is better to find that the sliders are the wrong size for the track in harbour, than when drifting onto a rocky lee shore in a force 10 storm. Sheeting positions should be tried with and without a serviceable boom. A good opportunity to put up storm sails might be when forced by lack of wind to make a passage under engine, or when racing has been cancelled due to bad weather.

Left Caught on a lee shore: *Gypsy Moth V* beached on the rocks during the BOC Challenge Race 1982. *Photo: Ace Marine/PPL*

Right The crew of *Oystercatcher* taking the opportunity to try their storm sails in the sheltered waters of Newport, Rhode Island, after racing had been cancelled due to the proximity of a hurricane. Torrential rain was falling while the photograph was taken. *Photo: Daniel Foster*

FIRE

Fortunately fires at sea are rare, but if they do occur in stormy conditions, as well they can, they become yet more difficult to deal with. The confined space of a yacht will rapidly fill with smoke and will soon have to be abandoned, with the possibility that there is no access to the radio, the liferaft or the flares. Quick thinking and action is imperative in this short period.

Electrical fires are the most likely in rough weather, caused by an ingress of salt water or by the yacht's movement creating a short circuit. Good design and construction will obviate most problems but the owner must ensure that his boat can stand extreme angles of heel and heavy shock without the possibility of a short circuit being created. If an electrical fire does occur, switching off power will help the situation if the problem is down-supply from the switch. However, most fires occur at the main power leads near the battery and these cannot be isolated by breakers or fuses. It is essential that the batteries cannot shift nor that anything can shift onto them. For example, there is a case where a fuel tank broke loose, shifting the battery, which then caused the main supply to short, hence causing a fire (see also Chapter 12).

CAPSIZE

The importance of a stable, strong and watertight hull has been referred to in earlier chapters of this book. The need for these features is particularly important in the dire situation of a capsize. To be prepared for a capsize, one should try to imagine one's vessel being held upside down in the sea, with ventilator plugs in place. Thus orientated, a well-designed and soundly built craft should have minimal leaks, even through the companionway or the cockpit lockers. Clearly, heavy items such as the engine, the galley stove, the deep freeze, all anchors – especially that extra-heavy emergency anchor deep in the bilge – batteries, gas cylinders, tanks and internal ballast should be installed with total inversion in mind. It might not be a bad thing if yachts were subject to an inversion test with full tanks when new. Not all would come through unscathed.

It might be thought that floorboards do not come into the category of items that should be secured so that they remain in place during an inversion, on the grounds that access to the bilges can often be useful, and perhaps even essential, in the event of being holed. A compromise is the best solution. One should leave the floorboard that gives access to the strum box unsecured, while other floorboards are screwed down with a minimum number of fastenings that can rapidly be removed in an emergency, or for cleaning.

Securing heavy items properly is half the battle; the other half entails educating the crew to conform to the time-honoured mariner's practice of 'securing for sea'. Adequate locker space and stowages are necessary to give this prescription a chance, but even so it will be found that stowing and securing all loose gear before leaving harbour, and keeping a vessel tidy thereafter, does not come naturally to most mortals. Nevertheless, unexpected events at sea can be so confounding that it does not always need a capsize to prove the wisdom of an orderly ship.

If a yacht is turned through 360° the mast is usually broken due to rig failure. It may be unrealistic to strengthen the rig so much as to make such failure impossible, but as most yachts are designed for 'ordinary' sailing, a degree of beefing up may be wise.

While on the subject of capsize it should be mentioned that a safety harness line should have a clip at both ends so that, in the event of a prolonged inversion or a vessel foundering (see *Waikikamukau*, Chapter 15), crew have a means of releasing themselves within immediate reach.

A Sinking Vessel

Our final worst situation is that moment when a liferaft will shortly be the only craft left afloat, and the moment has come to pull the inflation cord, or painter. An example of such a situation took place in a force 9 gale 1 mile off Salcombe on 11 August 1985. The 30ft (9.1m) sloop *Fidget*, built of mahogany on oak by Camper & Nicholson in 1939, fell about 20ft (6m) off the back of a wave in a very large cross-sea. She opened up and sank in about 30 seconds. The skipper, Simon Wilkinson, who habitually keeps a knife in the pocket of his foul weather jacket, only just had time to cut the liferaft and uninflated tender free from their lashings before *Fidget* foundered, and the crew were left swimming. It was fortunate that they were already wearing lifejackets, because there was an interval before the inflation cord, which was still attached to the yacht, came taut, and the liferaft inflated. Simon Wilkinson thinks that he and his crew might well have drowned if they had not been wearing lifejackets.

Should a vessel sink far from help, the best chance of being found these days lies with an emergency indicator beacon (EPIRB). This is a radio device, which in early versions transmitted on the aviation distress frequency 121.5MHz. The signal could be picked up by an aircraft or a satellite passing within line of sight, but would not be passed on by the satellite unless there was a ground receiving station within its horizon at that moment. The 121.5MHz beacon has been superseded by a beacon that operates on 406MHz in conjunction with a satellite system alone. This one has worldwide coverage, gives the identity of the casualty, a more accurate position, and is not so prone to spurious activation.

Raphael Dinelli standing on his stricken yacht shortly before she sank during the 1996 Vendee Globe Race. *Photo: RAAF/PPL*

The kind of event that *Fidget's* crew experienced is not one likely to have been prac-tised, though courses of instruction in survival exist and are rated as good value, in addi-tion to books on the subject. Apart from those who carry a Tinker Tramp combined dinghy and liferaft, the operation of a conventional liferaft is usually taken on trust. However, an opportunity to learn about one's liferaft occurs at the time of its annual inspection, when it will have to be inflated anyway. To witness an inflation, it is best to make an appointment with the servicing agent, who should be one authorized by the manufacturer, for an 'open-ing day'. A garden or marina inflation in the company of the crew is entertaining, but will certainly lead to extra cost. For example, the gas bottle is not used for a test inflation but is merely weighed and inspected, and replacement bottles are expensive to recharge and retest. Besides, it is quite easy to damage the fabric of a partially deflated liferaft when in transit back to the servicing agent. Nonetheless, it is possible for an owner to inflate the life-raft without using the gas bottle, and those who can trust their own judgement and know the technique for repacking do speak highly of carrying out their own annual inspection.

The merit of having additional items to supplement the liferaft's safety equipment pack will depend very much upon the circumstances; however, the concept of a grab-bag, or calamity-bag, filled with suitable sundry items deserves recognition. For example, a water-proofed VHF radio, dry clothing, space blankets, extra flares, food, water, writing materials, passports, money and crew medicines may one day reward the foresight involved. *Fidget's* crew, for example, were not to know they had been spotted, and would have been glad to have had some drinking water during the interval of 40 minutes while they were waiting to be picked up. Also, they were short of flares, one being faulty, and the others having been used immediately.

SEA PREPARATIONS FOR IMMINENT BAD WEATHER

A skipper should delegate various tasks within his crew to spread the load, and to take care of the situation if he himself were to be incapacitated or lost overboard. This means an organizational structure has to be formed, and though some people may go sailing to escape such duress, there is a clear need for it in times of crisis.

Likewise, it is always desirable to establish and maintain a watch routine so that crew can rest properly when off watch. With an experienced crew the watchkeeping routine will need no adjustment with the onset of bad weather. On the other hand, a less experienced and less well-prepared crew may find some members opting out while others are involved in one drama followed by another, leading to whole-crew exhaustion. This can be a recipe for disaster, as people do not tend to make good decisions when they are cold, wet, anxious and tired.

Quite often the situation, bad though it may be, does not require the whole watch on deck. Two people or even one person on deck may be enough to ensure the safety of the boat while conditions are stable. Others may best stay where it is warmer and drier.

It is suggested that all craft likely to be in the open sea could benefit from an owner's checklist covering actions to be taken in the face of an impending storm. Such measures will depend very much on the circumstances, such as the experience of the crew, the type of craft and her distance from base. The following list may be helpful to some, while others may consider the suggestions given here as being standard procedure before going to sea:

1 Issue seasickness pills.
2 Charge batteries.
3 Remove mainsail and stow in bag below decks. Set up inner forestay for storm jib, if appropriate. Rig trysail. Remove cockpit dodgers. Fold or remove cockpit sprayhood.
4 Check that windows and hatches are tightly closed. Fit or have ready ventilator cover plates. Attach hatchway and window storm screens. Put stopper, such as cork or plasticine, in hawse pipe.
5 Move storm sails, buckets, warps or other drag devices to a handy position, bearing in mind that it may be difficult and dangerous to open cockpit lockers during a storm.
6 Shut WC seacocks after a good pump through. Experience may show that other cocks need to be closed during bad weather. If shutting such seacocks could cause catastrophic results, an appropriate notice should be displayed. For example, a sign saying 'Engine cooling water cock closed' taped over the engine starter.
7 Plot position and, if a survival situation is anticipated, report this and intended movements to coastguards or shore authority. Put a dry towel, or absorbent material, within reach of the chart table. Start recording frequent barometer readings, or better still refer regularly to a barograph.
8 Check security of batteries and other heavy weights stowed below, such as anchors, toolboxes and tanks.
9 Put on appropriate clothing, such as thermal underwear, seaboots, gloves, etc. Musto HPX drysuits are remarkably good in gale conditions.
10 Pack a 'grab-bag'. In addition, seal spare clothing, bedding, matches, lavatory paper, food, water, hand held VHF radio, etc within clear heavy-duty polythene bags.
11 Pump bilges. Check pump handles are attached to the boat with lanyards and check the whereabouts of spares.
12 Put washboards into position, and secure their fastening arrangements.
13 Firmly secure latches of cockpit locker lids.
14 Check cockpit and anchor well drains are free. It may be helpful to blow through with an inflatable dinghy air pump or sink drain clearer.

15 Check deck items, such as the spinnaker pole, anchor, anchor well lid and liferaft are properly secured. Winch handles should not be left loose, and a spare should be kept below decks.

16 Check halyards are not twisted and the free ends of the lines on deck are stowed, so that they are not likely to go overboard and foul the propeller. Lead spare halyards etc clear of mast (to reduce noise).

17 Check navigation lights are working; hoist radar reflector.

18 Bring dinghy inboard and stow securely. Deflate an inflatable and stow below decks.

19 Consider renewing torch batteries and changing cooking gas cylinder.

20 Make up thermos flasks of soup and coffee. Make sandwiches and place in a watertight container.

21 Give the crew a good hot meal.

22 Secure and stow loose items below, especially in the galley area. If containers made of glass have to be brought onboard, such as, possibly, coffee or jam jars, they must either be packed away with great care or ditched. Put bagged sails at strategic points to break the falls of the crew.

23 Instruct crew members to put on their safety harnesses and lifejackets. Ensure that they are adjusted to fit snugly over storm clothing so that the wearer cannot slip out. Also, that the crew are familiar with the operating features and strap design so that they may be donned rapidly without assistance, if need be, in violent motion and darkness. Safety harnesses and lifejackets should usually be worn during the period of the storm.

24 Be ready to change down to storm canvas in good time.

25 If running, rig a heavy-duty main boom preventer to avoid accidental gybes. Ideally this should be rigged round a leading block forward and led back to the cockpit.

26 Rig a rope lattice within the cockpit to give greater security to its occupants.

27 Brief the crew on what to expect. Remind them of the importance of being hooked onto something really strong when on deck, of maintaining a good lookout, and of being aware of the position of flares, grab-bag, liferaft, sharp knife, etc.

28 Check rigging cutters. Ensure there is a lanyard on them.

29 Tape up all lockers without positive locking arrangements.

The well-prepared vessel, applying Admiral Nimitz's doctrine, is much more likely to come through a gruelling storm with only minor problems. Yet storms can be a tremendous test of endurance and, despite very careful preparation, much may depend upon the cool judgement, courage, physical fitness and tenacity of the skipper and crew.

6 *The use of drag devices in heavy weather*

PETER BRUCE

When it really comes on to blow it is safer to lie with the bow or stern into wind and wave, rather than beam-on. Choice of heavy weather tactics has been increased by the availability on the market of a large number of drag devices, the generic term for objects used over the bow or stern to hold a vessel end-on, and slow her down. The requirement to reduce speed is seldom necessary for strongly manned racing yachts such as those taking part in round the world races; on the other hand, for lightly crewed cruising yachts, slowing down can be a matter of dire urgency due to stormy weather and a crew's need to rest. Use of a drag device is an adjunct to heaving-to.

Drag devices fall into two categories: sea anchors in the form of *parachutes* that are streamed over the bow on a long line and are intended to hold the boat head-to-wind with a low rate of drift, and *drogues* that are trailed over the stern, and are designed to slow a boat down to a comfortable speed, keep the boat's stern into the sea, or act as an emergency steering device. At one time the term 'sea anchor' could mean 'a drogue' and vice versa, but in the USA they are coming to be thought of as different devices used in entirely different ways.

Once a parachute sea anchor has been successfully deployed in severe weather, the boat should need little further attention and the crew can relax. It is usually necessary to continue to steer when using a drogue, but in some combinations of hull and drogue the boat can be left to look after herself. Use of drag devices is gaining in popularity as they repeatedly prove their effectiveness. Simplicity and ease of use are important factors for the successful use of drag devices in unfavourable conditions. Also, a degree of skill and some specialized seamanship is necessary, as heavy loads are involved, especially for larger parachutes.

Sources of information

Information on drag devices can be obtained in a number of books from the USA. First is the *Drag Device Data Base*, published by Para-Anchors International – not to be confused with Para-Tech International or Para-Anchors (Australia). Another is *The Sea Anchor and Drogue Handbook* by Daniel Shewmon, published by Shewmon, Inc. There is also a significant report by the Wolfson Unit, Southampton, UK, published in 1988, which gives the results of tank tests of parachutes and drogues. Finally there is the *Storm Tactics Handbook* by the exceptional sailing couple Lin and Larry Pardey.

Victor Shane, author of the *Drag Device Data Book*, records the use of drag devices from all the different manufacturers. He has tremendous enthusiasm for drag devices and has collected over a hundred accounts of their (mostly) successful use. The style might leave some readers feeling a bit pressurized; nevertheless, the content is of very great interest and covers the use of drag devices of all sorts, many in really heavy weather. A number of skippers finish their report by stating that they would never go to sea again without a parachute.

The Shewmon book is a fund of independently derived detailed data, much of it constructional. He also highlights the characteristics of parachutes of his own design and compares them with the Para-Tech design.

The Wolfson Unit's report is blunt scientific fact. It is particularly interesting as in the ocean no one wave is exactly similar to another, so comparisons are not always valid. In the tests an exactly repeatable breaking wave equivalent to 5.85m (19ft 2in) in height was created in a tank in a wind of 40 knots. A number of 'typical hull shape' yacht models, equivalent to 10m (33ft) overall in length, were used in conjunction with two sizes of parachute and two types of drogue. Drogues were trialled both individually and in series.

The results demonstrated that, without assistance from a drogue, the models drifted broadside on to the breaking wave and were invariably capsized, sometimes by the breaking wave of 3.3m (11ft) which preceded the main one. What was surprising was that parachutes did not prevent yachts in the tank from being capsized. The sudden huge force of the breaking wave caused the parachute line to stretch and then, after the wave had passed, the model yacht would be carried forward by the elasticity in the line. Her momentum would take the boat past her original position, allow the line to go slack and cause even the large parachute to collapse, especially if the parachute had been pulled near the surface. Though this does not seem to happen at sea, the yacht would then turn beam-on to the direction of the waves and, before the parachute had redeployed itself and the slack in the line had been taken up, she would be capsized by the 3.3m (11ft) wave that followed the main one.

Drogues were much more successful. Provided there was tension in the drogue line when the breaking wave struck, and the yacht model was roughly stern-on to the breaking wave, she would invariably *not* capsize. Additionally, use of a drogue made it much easier for the rudder to hold the stern into the sea.

In summary, the Wolfson Unit trial results favoured drogues rather than parachute sea anchors, and series drogues rather than individual drogues. Of course no tank test can exactly reproduce conditions at sea, and the Wolfson Unit findings regarding parachutes is seldom, if ever, borne out in practice, possibly due to the difficulty of matching the parachute line to the line in the tank, but there are records at sea of the parachute line becoming slack, as happened in the tank, followed by a near capsize of the vessel. The possibility gives food for thought.

The *Storm Tactics Handbook*, among other valuable advice, gives detailed instructions on using a parachute sea anchor with a bridle or pendant line to angle a yacht some 50° from the waves, an ingenious refinement upon the basic system.

The need for further evaluation

There was a need to reconcile theoretical and practical assumptions from an impartial standpoint and learn the techniques for the deployment of drag devices. Thus trials were undertaken between 1996 and 1998 to evaluate, particularly from the practical point of view, purpose-built full-size parachutes, a much cheaper and smaller 'Bu-ord' parachute, and commonly used drogues. The trials were based on drag devices that were available in the UK and were offered for evaluation.

The trials were initially undertaken in calm weather with a view to working up to heavier weather using well-known types of cruising boat. These were a Rustler 36, a Hallberg Rassy 36, a Najad 391, a Warrior 35 and a Contessa 33.

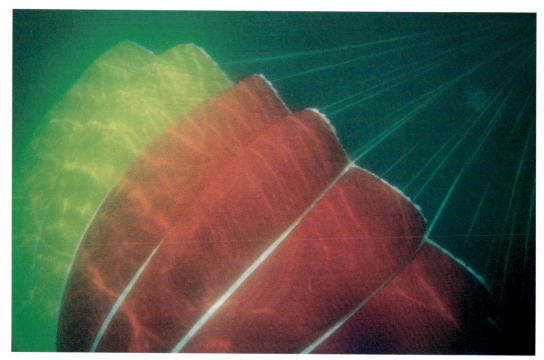

Once a parachute sea anchor is deployed it is in virtual hydraulic lock. *Photo: Richard Clifford*

For understandable reasons, force 6 to 7 was about as much wind as most owners wanted to go out into deliberately. Thus the trials were confined to conditions below which drag devices would normally be used. In spite of this anomaly, it was felt that much was learnt from the trials. It was observed when using the parachute anchor that the behaviours of the yachts were surprisingly consistent through the wind range experienced, giving some reason to believe that their behaviours would be similar in higher wind speeds. This view is supported at the Wolfson Unit.

PARACHUTE SEA ANCHORS

Early sea anchors used over the bow
John Voss, a retired Canadian sea captain of great experience who sailed around the world in a 38ft (11.6m) Indian war canoe at the turn of the nineteenth century, was one of the earliest successful proponents of the sea anchor. His canoe had a low rig with a small mizzen well aft, only 5ft 6in (1.7m) beam and only 2ft (0.6m) draft, all features that should suit the use of a small cone-shaped sea anchor. Subsequent attempts to emulate Captain Voss with similar sea anchors probably failed owing to the sea anchor having insufficient cross-sectional area and thus allowing excessive stern way.

In 1963 there is a brief record of Arthur Piver using a parachute as a sea anchor to ride out a great storm near Rarotonga aboard his trimaran. In 1965, on an expedition to Heard Island, the great explorer Bill Tilman hove-to by using a 32ft (9.8m) diameter parachute led from the bow of a 63ft (19.2m) steel schooner. He was surprised how well the parachute held a vessel of such size and weight into the wind until the bronze ring broke, to which the rigging (or shroud) lines were attached, and the parachute was lost, a point worthy of note.

Use of parachutes has probably come about from the availability of ex-military parachutes at San Pedro, California. The tuna fishing boats came to use them there, as did both

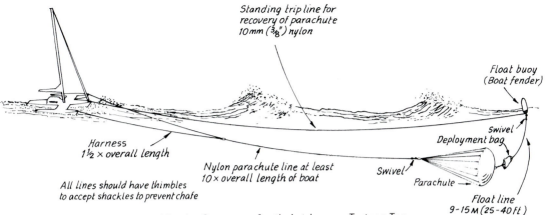

Figure 6.1 Sea anchor as used by the Casanovas for their trimaran *Tortuga Too*.

the multihull owners John and Joan Casanova, and the Pardeys in the late 1960s. The Casanovas used a parachute both to weather a succession of extreme storms experienced over many years of sailing in their trimaran *Tortuga Too*, and also simply to rest. At about the same time the Pardeys were experimenting in their monohull as well.

Why use a sea anchor?

When at sea in a small boat far from land the concept of a sea anchor, which could be compared with a mooring, is most attractive. Parachutes of appropriate size have little 'give', as if they were in hydraulic lock. There is a lot to be said, too, for presenting the bow into the wind and waves during a storm, as a boat is designed to take water flow from ahead.

Preparing a parachute sea anchor for deployment.
Photo: Peter Bruce

The parachute sea anchor has been pulled from the deployment bag. Note the float buoy in the form of a white fender. The red recovery buoy lies beyond.
Photo: Peter Bruce

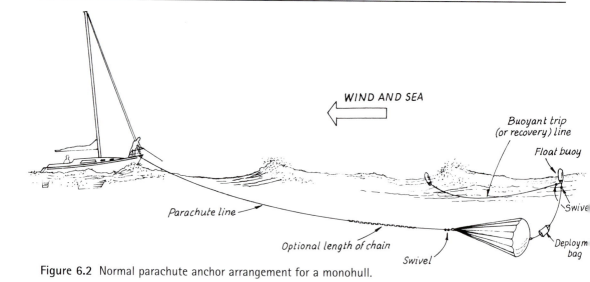

Figure 6.2 Normal parachute anchor arrangement for a monohull.

Besides, placing the bow into the sea by heaving-to or motoring into it are tactics with a good record of success.

For some yachts heaving-to is not straightforward. Many modern light-displacement yachts with fin keels do not heave-to comfortably. They are too lively and have insufficient underwater lateral area, so they yaw about and make tremendous leeway. It cannot be guaranteed that the bows will always face close enough into the waves to prevent capsize by an unusual wave, and the boat may be thrown backwards by a breaking wave causing damage to her rudder. It may be that some of the features that make a yacht unsuitable for heaving-to, such as low wetted surface area, are features that make her suitable for lying to a sea anchor. On the other hand, certain yachts, usually of heavy displacement, low freeboard and long keel, heave-to so well that their owners may feel that no other tactic is ever likely to be necessary.

Motoring into the sea can be another good storm tactic. The bow can be kept pointing into the waves and one can, to a certain extent, pick one's way around them. The disadvantages are that the tactic requires someone always at the helm with some skill, a powerful reliable engine, and adequate fuel.

Properly conceived parachute sea anchor systems have none of the above disadvantages, and might appear to some to be the ultimate solution and main line of defence (see Fig 6.2).

The parachute

At one time the only parachutes obtainable were those designed for aerial purposes. A good example is the Bu-ord parachute – the name originates from *Bureau of Ordnance*, which are American military surplus stores and can be found via the Internet. They were designed to haul a load out of the back of an airborne aircraft and are thus designed to take shock loads. These can work comparatively well for small craft and can be obtained cheaply. Sizes are said to go up to 18ft (5.5m) diameter, but smaller sizes are more generally obtainable. For years fishermen in the USA have used Bu-ord parachutes for lying-to at night or in bad weather rather than returning to harbour. They have been known to overcome the difficulty of obtaining larger sizes by putting a number of Bu-ord parachutes in series. One should remember that such ex-military stores are made available presumably because they are no longer suitable for their original purpose. They may be cheap, but they may not automatically be fit for sea use. Purpose-built parachutes, designed for use as a sea anchor, are manufactured in the USA, Australia and New Zealand in several sizes.

US SAILING's *Recommendations for Offshore Sailing* gives a parachute diameter of 35 per cent of overall length, but the UK trials suggested that it was sometimes preferable to go up one size. On the other hand, too large a parachute is not advisable as the larger the parachute the larger the loads and the greater the handling problems. The UK trials showed that long-keeled yachts tend to need larger parachutes than fin-keeled yachts because long-keeled yachts can take up a very stable broadside on attitude.

Para-Tech Engineering Co, Colorado, has a range of seven sizes of parachute from 6ft to 32ft (1.8 to 9.8m) diameter, the latter said to be suitable for boats up to 125ft (38m) in length. Shewmon parachutes are smaller for the same length of craft. The Para-Tech parachutes are supplied with a deployment bag, which is a fabric container that enables the parachute to open after it has been launched, rather than on deck.

There are other manufacturers and other less conventional forms of parachute such as the cruciform. In his Hallberg Rassy 29, my brother successfully lay bows-to an Atlantic storm in 1998 using a square-shaped builder's hoisting bag of low cost, said to be strong enough to lift a ton of sand.

Foredeck work

Sea anchors will require foredeck work at some stage and, if this work is left too late as a storm builds, it can become difficult and dangerous. For example, when Robin and Maggi Ansell set off in *Orca* (55ft (16.8m)) through the Great Barrier Reef bound for Alaska (Chapter 26), they decided to deploy their new sea anchor in the early stages of Cyclone Justin. Even though use of the sea anchor had been rehearsed, the task was not easy and after two hours of struggle the difficulties with the chafe guard had still not been resolved. Maggi Ansell said later that only with superhuman effort had Robin Ansell detached 10ft (3m) of $\frac{1}{2}$in (12mm) chain from the stern anchor, crawled forward again and attached it to the end of the parachute line. The yacht's motion was very severe, and when the load came on the chain, his ankle was caught between it and the toe rail and he was lucky to get away with severe bruising. She thought that to go on deck hourly to 'freshen the nip' would have been suicide.

Rather than struggle to lead the parachute line through the stem fitting as a storm builds, it is better to put the parachute line in position on leaving harbour. It should be led aft to the deployment bags in the cockpit locker along the outside of the guard rail, secured by breakable line.

Load

In addition to possible handling difficulties, the loads exerted by parachute sea anchors on their attachment points in heavy weather can be tremendous. Cleats, their fastenings, backing pieces and adjacent structure need to be up to the job. The Wolfson trials suggested that these should be enough to carry 80 per cent of the weight of the boat. An illustration of the sort of loads created is given by an account of a 40ft (12.2m) yacht, lying to an 18ft (5.5m) parachute in a North Sea gale of some 45 knots, with the parachute line attached to the windlass. When the first heavy load came on the line the windlass was torn out of the deck, taking with it the bow roller and most of the stem fitting. One should be aware that the larger the diameter of the parachute, the greater the loads it will impose. When cleats are judged to be not strong enough, a bridle can be used to spread the load over the boat. For example, the arms of the bridle can be led from the end of the chain to the port and starboard toe rail (see photo on next page) or to the primary winches. Stem fittings, being designed with ground anchors in mind, are usually the appropriate lead for the parachute line to pass through, but the drop nose pin intended to prevent the anchor chain from jumping out may need beefing up. Closed fairleads are also acceptable.

The yoke is attached at the toe rail on each side. Note the bolts along the toe rail which go through the hull-to-deck joint giving immense strength. *Photo: Peter Bruce*

The parachute line

Because the parachute is effectively a fixed object, the long rope line used for holding the sea anchor – which is often called a 'rode' in the USA – must have considerable elasticity. Only nylon will do. Nylon braid rope (equivalent to multiplait) is best, as this is the most elastic type and is torsionally stable. Hawser-laid nylon rope unlays with increasing load and will put twists in the rigging lines which will reduce the parachute's efficiency. Ropes other than nylon are designed not to stretch, for example those made from polyester, Spectra or Kevlar, and are not suitable.

The parachute line should have the same breaking strain as is appropriate for the main anchor because the line needs to stretch nicely but not break, even if subject to minor chafe. It should have stainless thimbles at both ends, since knots, particularly bowlines, will weaken it. Para-Tech stipulates the length of parachute line as 10 times boat length with a minimum of 300ft (91m). Daniel Shewmon recommends a minimum of 20 times the expected wave height, or even more because of the unpredictability of the severity of a storm. This requirement could lead to huge lengths of line to cope with, for example, the 40ft (12.2m) wave heights in the Auckland–Tonga storm of June 1994. Whichever method is used to decide length of parachute line, vessels have never suffered by having too long a line. John Kettlewell, for example, carries 800ft (244m) of line aboard his 32ft (9.8m) catamaran.

There is a case for putting a length of chain at one or other end of the parachute line, or half-way along it. This helps to reduce peak loading, help the parachute to stay well immersed, clear of flotsam and wave effects, and may allow the use of less line. In the trials, use of chain seemed to make little difference and when under load the parachute still appeared on the surface. Larry Pardey says that he likes to see his Bu-ord on the surface, and although if the parachute inverted this could flip the rigging line to the wrong side of the canopy, he has never known this to happen. Chain at the outer end or mid-point of the parachute line does make the task of recovery more onerous.

A length of parachute line can be heavy to handle. For example, a 448ft (136.5m) parachute line of ⅝in (16mm) eight-strand weighs 62lb (28kg) when dry, and 86lb (39kg) when wet. In addition to the parachute deployment bag, a purpose-built 'parachute line deployment bag' is recommended to avoid tangles and to save time, which might otherwise be spent in flaking out the line.

Above The parachute line led through the stem fitting will rapidly chafe through.
Photo: Peter Bruce

Left A yoke arrangement for a yacht with a toe rail. A length of $\frac{3}{8}$in (10mm) chain enclosed by a length of polythene hose takes the chafe at the stem fitting and cuts down on noise.
Photo: Peter Bruce

Nylon absorbs over four times as much water as polyester and, if the line is allowed to dry out after use without being thoroughly washed in fresh water, salt crystals will damage the fibres. Ice crystals will have a similar effect.

Chafe

Once deployed, the whole expensive and elaborate parachute anchor system can soon be lost if no proper provision is made for chafe. A bare rope, led through a normal stemhead fitting, is almost bound to chafe through in an hour or two. Anchors over the bow, boomkin stays or foul leads around the forestay will have the same effect. On the basis that one may spend a number of days lying to the parachute, a length of chain leading through the stem fitting is a sure way to give adequate long-term protection, but one should make provision for emergency release as chain cannot be cut. In the USA, double-lined firehose is also often used for protection against chafe, but chain is undoubtedly superior. If plastic hose is to be used, it should be inserted over the line before the eyes are spliced at each end. Small holes to take a lashing line should be drilled near the ends. Do not cut the tube lengthwise as split tube tends to work away from the point of contact.

The float

Parachutes above 12ft (3.7m) diameter need a float line and float secured to the apex of the parachute to ensure that the parachute takes up a suitable depth and not, under no load, a position on the end of the parachute line directly underneath the vessel. If this happens, the effort needed for recovery is tremendous and likely to defeat many crews. In one recorded instance (see Chapter 22) the line was cut by the crew and the parachute lost rather than hauling it all in. Fenders, conveniently, can be used as floats, and the bigger the better as it is nice to be able to spot where the parachute is whenever possible. Of course, white fenders do not show up particularly well when the sea is white with foam.

The float line should be of a length to keep the parachute at a depth of 33–49ft (10–15m), clear of wave effects. Parachutes do tend to come to the surface when the load is especially heavy. Larry Pardey says that he takes comfort from seeing the parachute at work and has never experienced any difficulties due to the parachute being at the surface. A swivel should be placed at the float end of the float line. If a length of chain is used at the parachute end of the parachute line, a single fender may not provide enough buoyancy.

The parachute sea anchor deployed. The float buoy is necessary if the load comes off the parachute.
Photo: Peter Bruce

Trip or recovery line

In addition to the float line, another 100–150ft (30–45m) of $\frac{3}{16}$in (5mm) soft buoyant line with a swivel should be used between the float and the recovery buoy, for all but small parachutes. By motoring up to the recovery buoy and bringing it aboard with a boathook, a large parachute can be collapsed and more easily recovered (see Fig 6.3). The trip line buoy should be easily distinguishable from the float buoy for obvious reasons. Trip lines permanently led back to the boat have been tried, but can often become tangled up in the parachute. They are seldom employed more than once, but if one perseveres one may acquire the knack and thus have the advantage of easier recovery. The technique for a 'standing' trip line, apparently, is to keep just the right amount of weight on the trip line rather than allow it to become too slack. The standing trip line is recommended in a current, such as the Aghulas or the Gulf Stream, when unusual effects, such as down-going eddies, may require that the parachute be tripped as a matter of urgency. It should be said that for a quiet life it is much better to deploy the parachute clear of currents.

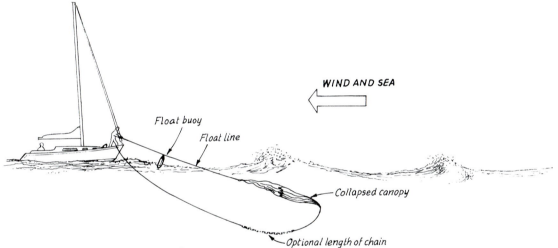

Figure 6.3 Recovering the parachute.

Swivels and shackles

Parachutes can rotate in use and therefore a swivel, which may turn at times when the parachute becomes less heavily loaded, is recommended by Para-Tech. There is some doubt as to whether a swivel does rotate under load but, if a swivel is used, it must be recognized as a frequent point of failure and needs to be of high quality with a greater breaking load than that of the parachute line. The same applies to shackles used to attach the parts of the system. When it comes to buying shackles and swivels, one can safely verge to the oversize. All shackle pins should, of course, be seized or double seized with Monel wire, seizing wire or a 'cable tie'.

Riding sail

In the trials the long-keeled yacht tended to lie nearly head-to-wind on a parachute sea anchor, but the fin-keeled yachts tended to yaw about, adding to discomfort and possibly hazard. If a yacht yaws about in strong winds at a mooring, possibly because the mast and/or hull generate lift, then she will probably yaw on a parachute sea anchor. The amount of yawing will also depend on whether a yacht has a lot of windage forward or aft. For example, a furled headsail will increase the amount of windage forward.

A purpose-made riding sail rigged on the backstay is advisable for yachts with no mizzen when lying-to a sea anchor. *Photo: Peter Bruce*

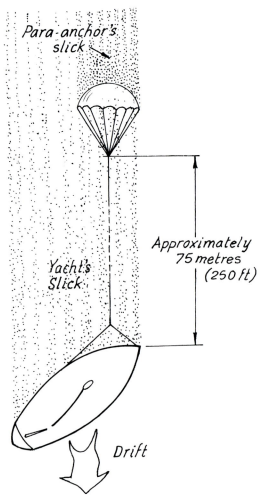

Para-anchor's slick

Yacht's Slick

Approximately 75 metres (250 ft)

Drift

Figure 6.4 Hove-to with triple-reefed main and 9ft (3m) diameter parachute anchor made of coarse-weave nylon stretchable fabric, which allows the water to sieve through under strain. Both boat and parachute anchor should be on the wave crest at the same time.

Yawls should be able to set a suitably small amount of mizzen to prevent yaw. Sloops may need some kind of riding sail rigged on the backstay. A storm jib set on the backstay tends to be too large. Best is a 'spitfire jib' of less than half the area of the storm jib and specially made for the backstay. Motoring slowly astern can also achieve the desired effect as well.

The Pardey method of deployment

Normal practice is to deploy the parachute straight over the bow, but there is an option to rig a Bu-ord parachute, with a deep-reefed mainsail or trysail set, so that the boat lies at an angle to wind and wave as described in Lin and Larry Pardey's *Storm Tactics Handbook*. The advantage of the arrangement is that the boat does not swing continuously through the wind, but stays at a more comfortable fixed angle, like being hove-to. In addition, the slick formed by the drift of the boat and the parachute may reduce the likelihood of waves break-

A parachute sea anchor rigged 'Pardey-style'. *Photo: Peter Bruce*

ing to weather (see Fig 6.4). It is sometimes said that the Bu-ord parachute is most suitable for the Pardey method of deployment, as it is more porous and therefore capable of taking a shock load.

A snatch block is used at the bow to accommodate the angled parachute line. Then a bridle, or pendant line, is taken from another block snatched onto the parachute line and led aft to a cockpit winch, directly or via a leading block – whichever gives the best lead. When the bridle is tensioned (and it may be necessary to veer some parachute line simultaneously to give enough slack to position the bridle block) the boat can be made to slew round to an angle that gives neither ahead nor astern movement.

Some yachts may need their stem fittings adapted to take the bow snatch block so it will lead the parachute line clear of obstructions. Larry Pardey likes to adjust the length of the parachute line so that the yacht and the parachute crest the waves at the same time.

Storm accounts in this book where the technique has been used, and the trials, showed that there is a huge weight on the bridle line when using the Pardey method and some deck fittings may not be up to it. The loads for yachts above 40ft (12.2m) are massive and may preclude the use of the Pardey method altogether. In some cases larger yachts naturally take up a good angle to the seas on a parachute, in which case the main objective is achieved without the need for a bridle line.

It was also found in the trials that the fin-keeled yachts, as opposed to the long-keeled yachts, were prone to tack over the lines in less than force 7. It seems that the longer and deeper the keel the better.

Riding to a sea anchor

The parachute sea anchor provides a remarkably secure mooring. Contrary to what one might think there is usually no undue load on rudders, probably no more than would be experienced at a ground anchor in deep and open water. It is recommended that the

An experimental cruxiform sea anchor on trial. This type of sea anchor is in the shape of a cross which forms a box shape when the leaves are brought together. It is cheaper to manufacture than a conventional parachute. *Photo: Peter Bruce*

rudder be lashed amidships. Though there are few records of rudder trouble while lying-to a sea anchor, the account of *Prisana II* (Chapter 25) is a notable exception.

Once set up correctly, the parachute needs no tending and therefore allows the crew to rest. This, for an exhausted crew, is a tremendous advantage, though in extreme conditions rest is a relative word as the hull will take a tremendous battering. As would be expected if it was possible to anchor in the open sea, a good deal of movement, such as severe pitching and heavy, quick rolling, is likely (see Chapters 26 and 27). Maximum drift rate is likely to be 1.5 knots, but is usually rather less.

It should be remembered that the boat, line and parachute are vulnerable to other craft when a parachute is deployed. One should use the VHF radio to put out a Sécurité message periodically, giving one's position and circumstances.

Recovery of the parachute

Small parachutes do not need float and trip lines and can be recovered by winching in the parachute line until a shroud line can be grabbed. Large parachutes (see Fig 6.3) are recovered by motoring gently into the wind, gathering in the line until most of it is on deck, then heading for the recovery buoy, picking this up and using the tripping line to haul in the deflated parachute. It can be heavy work requiring precise steering. A system of hand signals is advisable to assist the helmsman, who will not be able to see the direction and tension of the line. During the recovery process in rough conditions there is an evident risk of losing a man overboard, or catching the line round the propeller. Even in moderate conditions the task is tricky, and when the wet parachute is finally back on board it will inflate in the wind and be difficult to manage. Some not-so-young cruising couples, sailing on their own in yachts of over 40ft (12m), would probably find the recovery procedure difficult in any conditions. Nevertheless, practised and experienced shorthanded sailors do manage parachutes in severe weather.

CONCLUSIONS FOLLOWING SEA TRIALS OF PARACHUTE SEA ANCHORS

Accounts of successful deployments of parachutes in extreme weather continue to appear, and they amount to compelling evidence in their favour. After the trials it was clear that parachute sea anchors might be one of the safer means of coping with heavy weather. On the other hand, they are not a comfortable answer and large parachutes are not easy to recover by small crews.

Nevertheless, a parachute, for all the provisos, does meet the claims made. A parachute brings a fresh and welcome option to the seafarer, giving – once deployed – security without any effort on the part of the crew. Clearly a parachute will be worth its weight in gold in the event of a steering gear failure in prolonged rough weather, but as a method of coping with extreme severe heavy weather it may be no less valuable. For example, Deborah Schutz's account of the successful use of a parachute in a severe storm (Chapter 25) and the Ansells' account of the use of a parachute in Cyclone Justin (Chapter 26), to name but two, are convincing evidence that yachts using a parachute can weather ultimate conditions, and without active participation from their crew which, for cruising couples of retirement age or with young children, is just what is needed. A further welcome benefit of a parachute sea anchor, compared to running with a storm, is that the storm blows through more quickly.

When the direction of wind and sea are markedly different a yacht will lie-to the wind rather than to a sea anchor, and therefore be vulnerable to beam seas. Sea anchors may, and quite often do, become lost or tangled. They can impose heftier loads than their deck fastenings or their structures are able to take. Moreover, though carried, in the event they have not always been used because their deployment could possibly put their users at greater risk than they would otherwise be, especially as many people do not manage a successful deployment at their first attempt. One needs to allow for circumstances when it will not be possible to use the sea anchor by treating it as one of several options. Overall success is more certain with fully committed investment, preparation, good seamanship, timely deployment and practice.

If a decision is made to buy a parachute, purchasers are well advised to ensure that the parachute line and joining shackles are large and strong enough for the job, that their vessel has strong enough fittings to take the load, to make proper provision for chafe, and to try the parachute out for the first time in easy conditions.

DROGUES

Trailing objects astern to control speed and improve steering is an old and well-known tactic in heavy weather. Drogues are the purpose-made alternative to improvisation and have several other uses. For example, they have been successfully used as emergency steering devices and as devices for promoting directional stability, especially when entering narrow harbours or crossing bars.

When running before a growing ocean storm the speed generated by a vessel down the backs of the waves can often be elating. A wise skipper will recognize this to be a time for precautionary action. As wind and wave build up, so maybe does the load on the helm.

Above left Recovering a parachute single-handed can be a frustrating process. *Photo: Peter Bruce*

Above right Two strong men make the business of parachute recovery easier. *Photo: Peter Bruce*

Left *Warrior Shamaal* lying to a parachute sea anchor with storm jib set as a riding sail. Most storm jibs will be too large when it is blowing great guns. *Photo: Peter Bruce*

Left A parachute anchor deployment in the garden is advisable at the end of the season or after use.
Photo: Peter Bruce

Below A selection of drag devices used in the trials. The 448ft (136m) x $\frac{5}{8}$in (18mm) drogue parachute line is in the deployment bag (left). The Bu-ord parachute is in the centre, and the 18ft (5.5m) diameter Para-Tech parachute is centre right.
Photo: Peter Bruce

However, on top of a breaking wave, water flow past the rudder may be reversed, leading to loss of control and the possibility of broaching. The first step will be to reduce sail but, after that, use of a drogue of some sort may be invaluable to bring the boat down to a sensible and comfortable speed. Modern yachts seldom have 'balanced ends' and are thus not very directionally stable, so the beneficial effect of a drogue in maintaining a boat's course can be another large advantage.

Slowing the boat down and pointing the stern directly into the sea may result in more waves breaking over the stern than would otherwise occur. In fact, in stormy conditions it may lead to regular pooping. Accordingly, the aft-facing structure needs to be strongly built and, especially for a stern cockpit, the crew on deck well secured to their craft.

Using the vessel's anchor and chain over the stern is said to be effective. The weight of the anchor and chain takes the arrangement below surface effects, and the downward angle creates good drag. There are two disadvantages. There could be a disastrous outcome in shallow water, and recovery could prove to be tricky. A compromise might be to use the anchor chain alone. With a suitable arrangement of turning blocks it should be possible to use the windlass for recovery. These methods were not tried during our trials.

The established method is to use a drogue line of at least 330ft (100m), plus a weight and drag-producing device on the end. As with the parachute sea anchor, too much line is better than too little, though there are rare occasions with an unweighted drogue when, surprisingly, short lengths work best. Yet more line will be necessary to span longer ocean wavelengths, possibly built up from warps and spare rope. For optimum effectiveness the line should be secured to a bridle so that the load is split between attachment points on each quarter of the boat. This can be done by tying a rolling hitch to a point at least a boat length outboard, and securing the bridle line to the opposite stern cleat to the main line. After fastening it the bridle line is eased out, to middle the two lengths of the 'V' at an angle of 30°.

An essential feature of a drogue system is that the line should remain taut and as evenly loaded as possible. If the line becomes slack, a vessel immediately becomes vulnerable to being rolled, and shock loads on the vessel are likely. To prevent this, experimentation with the line length to bring the drogue into the ideal position relative to the waves is often recommended. It is said that the ideal position is when the drogue is in a trough when the vessel is half-way up the leading side of an overtaking wave. The trouble is that it may not be possible to see where the drogue is and, anyhow, waves are never quite uniform and sometimes not uniform at all. The best way of ensuring a consistent load is to have a very long line, and place sufficient weight on the end of the drogue line to keep it away from the worst of surface effects. When it is deep enough it will neither jump out of the water nor be much affected by the orbital motion within a wave. An alternative, probably better method is to deploy two drogues in series, so that if one drogue is carried forward by a breaking wave, another will still provide a braking force.

The Wolfson report recommends a sinker weight between 20–30kg (44–66lb), so that the drogue should operate at 10–15m (33–49ft) below the surface. Solid sinkers are awkward and heavy to move and stow, and have the potential to do serious damage when unsecured, though they do have a dual purpose as an 'angel' or 'chumb'. A suitable length of anchor chain or an anchor are often used as sinkers, and if diving equipment is kept on board, diving weights are suitable too. Should the drag slow the boat down too much, a little headsail or engine power may improve the situation.

The load can be very heavy, but rather less than that of the parachute. The Wolfson trials showed a peak load of 3.8 tonnes for the 10m (33ft) yacht when struck by a breaking wave. These heavy loads can be very dangerous, and great care should be taken that the line has a fairlead and that legs or feet of crew are not in the bight when the drogue is deployed.

Towing trials

With the aim of finding a suitable drogue to slow a vessel to a comfortable speed when running before a storm, it was desirable to establish by empirical means the drogue's effectiveness solely at creating drag. It was also desirable to compare commercially available products with arrangements improvised from what happens to be available – for example, to compare the performance of a relatively expensive purpose-made device with sails or an old motor car tyre. It was also useful to find out whether there were benefits in deploying drogues in series.

A towing trial was undertaken using a Najad 391 under power, as one can roughly equate the situation when motoring to running under bare pole. A fixed engine speed short of maximum was chosen, and the hull speed remeasured by the boat's log with the various drogues on tow. The line was 448ft (136.5m) of ⅝in (16mm) eight-strand.

When the drogue was fully weighted, as it should be, hand recovery was heavy work and a single person might need to allow an hour or more for the task. In one recovery in the open sea the line had to be let go when an especially heavy load came on it, a reminder that it is advisable to keep the bitter end secured. It is generally much easier to recover the drogue over the bow, and of course there is no reason why a power-driven sheet winch or capstan should not be used if available.

TRIAL RESULTS

Najad 391	Drag device	Boat speed (kt)	% of set speed
Engine rpm 2820	Nil	6.6	100
	Line alone	6.3	95
	HSD 300 Seabrake	(6.0)	(91)*
	Single car tyre	5.9	89
	No 3 genoa	5.8	88*
	Delta (48in)	5.5	83
	Series drogue	(5.3)	(80)*
	Galerider S (36in)	5.1	77
	Large single cone	4.6	70
	Home-made cone	4.3	65
	Delta (72in)	4.2	64
	Two cones in series	4.0	61
	No 3 genoa	3.8	58*
	Bu-ord para (10ft (3m))	(1.2)	(18)*

*Results are qualified in the text.

Further trials were undertaken to try to establish the amount of drag obtained by the various methods at low speed. The ideal drogue will cause the vessel to maintain a comfortable speed: neither too fast which might involve a broach, nor too slow, which could bring about the loss of steerage way. Clearly it is highly undesirable to be so tethered by a drogue that there is insufficient steerage way to bring the stern round to a breaking wave, thus one is looking for the minimum reduction in drag at low speed. For the purposes of the trial, 'low speed' was chosen to be 2 knots. If a drogue is over-effective, headsail can be set to ensure that steerage way is not lost.

TRIAL RESULTS

Najad 391	Drag device	Boat speed (kt)	% of set speed
Engine rpm 800	Nil	2	100
	Line alone	2	100
	No 3 genoa	2	100*
	HSD 300 Seabrake	2	100
	Single car tyre	1.7	85
	Galerider S (36in)	1.3	65
	Large single cone	1.3	65
	Drag device	1.2	60
	Delta (48in)	1.2	60
	Delta (72in)	1.0	50
	Series drogue	0.9	45
	Home-made cone	0.8	40
	No 3 genoa	0.7	35*
	Bu-ord para (10ft (3m))	0	0

* Results are qualified in the text.

The line alone

At one time, trailing warps alone was considered a primary storm tactic. They provided a degree of drag and gave a soothing effect to the waves. My father, Erroll Bruce, ran before hurricane strength winds in *Samuel Pepys* off Bermuda in May 1950, trailing warps. When Sir Robin Knox-Johnston sailed alone round the world in 1969 (the first to do so non-stop and singlehanded) he used a long warp in the form of a bight in severe weather. In addition, he used to set his storm jib sheeted amidships for directional stability, and *Suhaili* was so well balanced that, with the tiller lashed, he could retire to his bunk.

The performance of the line is much affected by depth of immersion, ie the deeper the line is immersed, the more even and effective the drag will be. Miles Smeeton, the veteran world-girdler of the 1960s, once remarked that the 360ft (110m) hawser he was streaming astern did not seem to be making much difference, and that he could occasionally see a big bight of the rope being carried forward on the crest of a wave in storms. Incidentally, he later advocates for his own boat, *Tzu Hang*, that some form of drogue should be attached to the line, but he never got round to doing it.

In the trials, the 448ft (136.5m) of ⅝in (16mm) eight-strand trailed over the stern on its own made a small but significant difference in drag. Of course, an even longer length of line comes to the same thing as a drogue. The difficulty is that so much rope may be needed to match the performance of a drogue (see Chapter 15) that it may be an all-day job to recover after the storm is through. It made no noticeable difference to the drag whether the line was towed in a bight or straight, and there are arguments for both methods. By allowing the line to stream straight behind it has a better chance of bridging the whole wavelength and therefore may produce a steadier pull. By using it in a bight there is a chance that it may discourage waves breaking astern, it is easier to recover, and less likely to be lost. The choice should probably depend upon the length of the line and the wavelength of the seas. A sea anchor line can, of course, double as a drogue line.

Long, heavy wet ropes are awkward to handle. For larger vessels it may be desirable to install a reel on deck from which the rope can be deployed either for a drogue or a sea anchor. A power-driven reel would be ideal. Smaller vessels can best use another 'deployment bag'. This bag contains the entire length of line and has a hole in the centre at the bottom. It can be put in the water enabling the line to run out without fouling anything. The deployment bag should be prevented from being carried down the line as it will seriously upset the operation of the drogue.

The handling difficulties and the expense of very long lines make a good case for using a good drogue, or drogues in series, in conjunction with a suitable length of line.

The series drogue

The beauty of the series drogue (see Fig 6.5) is that the pull is nearly uniform regardless of wave effects – a unique and very desirable feature given stories of drogues being picked up from astern by a breaking wave and carried forward. Another feature is that series drogues give good directional stability and many craft will maintain a course reasonably stern-on to the waves with the helm lashed amidships. On the other hand, making them is hard work and they are bulky to stow. With its delicate droguelets, the series drogue should not be used for any other purpose.

Figure 6.5 An effective drogue is the Jordan series drogue which uses hundreds of cones attached to a line streamed astern. An anchor at the end weighs the drogue down until the boat accelerates. This causes the drogue to rise and the drag to increase.

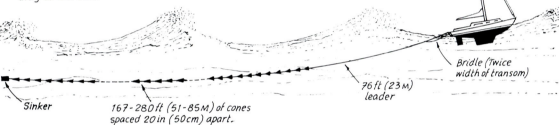

Bridle (Twice width of transom)

76 ft (23 M) leader

Sinker

167-280 ft (51-85 M) of cones spaced 20 in (50 cm) apart.

Part of a series drogue showing the droguelets.
Photo: Peter Bruce

Deploying a series drogue.
Photo: Peter Bruce

The series drogue used in the trials was designed for a 8.5m (28ft) yacht and had 110 cones attached to 18mm (¾in) multiplat and a 21kg (46.2lb) sinker. A series drogue for the Najad 391 should have 130 cones with a similar weight of sinker.

The series drogue provided a good pull in spite of being undersize. Recovery without a windlass was hard work and, when using a windlass, it was found that it was necessary to fold each individual cone to prevent part of the cone being trapped by the adjoining turn of line which caused the cone to be torn as it came away from the barrel. Putting a line and float, or a floated standing trip line, at the weighted end of the series drogue would aid recovery.

The cones will stand up to normal use but could be damaged in shallow water. Like the parachute anchor line, the 18mm (¾in) drogue line was very heavy to handle when wet.

The series drogue used for the trials was owned and constructed by Professor Nöel Dilly. As related in the *Drag Device Data Base*, he used it off the Azores, deployed from his Twister in force 10, and was deeply impressed by the beneficial effects of its steady pull. He is not alone. For example, Tony and Coryn Gooch have used a series drogue most successfully on their worldwide cruises to high latitudes in *Taonui*, both in bad weather and to rest. *Taonui* is long-keeled and holds her course admirably at 1.5 knots with the series drogue deployed. They use a bridle over the stern that can be adjusted to give the yacht a small angle away from dead downwind, which makes for a more comfortable ride.

Though not the most convenient of drogues to recover, the series drogue is one of the most effective.

The Galerider

The 36in (0.9m) Galerider (see photo on page 86) has good pulling power. It seemed to 'dig in' nicely in calm conditions. The hoop is highly sprung, so take care as it is withdrawn from its bag to avoid being hit in the face. Attractive features are low drag at low speed, ease of recovery, and the fact that it does not absorb much water. The hoop has to be doubled to fit the Galerider back into its bag and that makes it a little more difficult to handle on board than others. It is advisable to lash the doubled hoop with sail ties before putting it away.

In July 1994 Mary Harper, a solo sailor aged 79, used a Galerider from her LM30 under bare pole in a 'hard gale' in mid-Atlantic. She said she did not think she used the drogue correctly – the line was rather short – as she could not find the instructions; nevertheless, she found that it slowed her boat down to 5 knots and she was 'so happy with the results'. As related in Chapter 22, Michael and Doreen Ferguson also used a Galerider in the Queen's Birthday storm with good results once the line had been shortened in to 80–90ft (24–27m).

There are a number of favourable reports regarding the Galerider but – without a weight – it may operate too near the surface in extreme conditions to give a steady pull.

Seabrake

In his Foreword, Sir Peter Blake alludes to his most worrying time ever at sea in a wing-masted multihull. This was *Steinlager 1* in the Round Australia Yacht Race. He used a Seabrake to good effect, but at one point the drogue emerged from out of the face of a wave and became airborne. It was also damaged. The remedy was to replace the Seabrake, with 30ft (9m) of ½in (12mm) chain added to the drogue end. There were no further problems.

The Seabrake used for the trials was the HSD 300 hard version designed for vessels up to 33ft (10m) in length. (The larger fabric version, which takes up less space and is a more appropriate size for the yachts used in the trials (see Fig 6.6), seems to have a problem of availability.) The instructions for the solid Seabrake state that a chain of 11lb (5kg) minimum weight should be used in conjunction with a warp of three times the length of the vessel. Accordingly, 10ft (3m) of ⅜in (10mm) chain was used with 133ft (40m) of ⅝in (16mm)

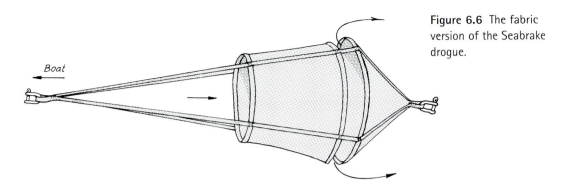

Figure 6.6 The fabric version of the Seabrake drogue.

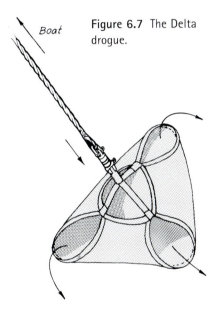

Figure 6.7 The Delta drogue.

nylon rope. Unless one happened to have just the right sized shackle it was found that two shackles were necessary to secure the Seabrake to the chain. The instructions also bade one to launch the drogue at very low speed. (It would be nice to be told what very low speed is, as it might not be convenient, or possible, to stop in a rising storm.) Three and a half knots was judged to be slow enough, and on going to the set revolutions the Seabrake gave more drag than its slender body would suggest.

It was tested with the small and short line recommended as well as with the line used for all the other tests, but there was little difference in the results. The HSD 300 version was significantly undersize for the boat, and the results might be thought reasonable for a drogue of only 12in (30cm) diameter and 22in (56cm) length. The Seabrake scores well by having low drag at low speed. However, space is at a premium in small craft and a solid drogue will not be popular aboard most craft.

The Delta

The 72in (1.8m) Delta (Fig 6.7) is intended for boats up to 45ft (13.7m) and the 48in (1.2m) Delta is intended for boats up to 35ft (10.7m). The Deltas are small drogues and therefore stow easily. They are also made of non-absorbent material, a heavy vinyl-coated fabric, and so can be simply dried with a wipe. The 72in (1.8m) Delta impressed with its pulling power. It seemed stable under load and did not break surface in calm conditions but, in Para-Tech's own publicity video, the (presumably) unweighted Delta could be seen breaking surface when towed behind a 29ft (8.8m) yacht in a seaway, and writhing about and breaking surface when towed behind a tug.

The Delta seems to have a possible disadvantage in that it provides a hefty drag at *low speeds*, making steering difficult at low speeds and recovery laborious. On the other hand, sail can be set to overcome the steering problem and the Delta gives a remarkable amount of drag for its size.

No 3 genoa

The use of a small genoa, 38 × 36 × 13ft (11.6 × 11 × 4m), was intended to establish whether satisfactory drag could be achieved without a purpose-made drogue. If a sail joined

The Galerider has good pulling power, but may need weighting to give a steady pull in extreme conditions. *Photo: Peter Bruce*

Launching the Delta drogue. *Photo: Peter Bruce*

by pieces of rope from its three corners was to open out like a parachute, one might expect some hefty pulling power. Using rigging lines of about 4ft (1.2m), the drag figure suggests that the sail did not open out and therefore only provided a very modest degree of usefulness. When longer rigging lines were used – a 15ft (4.6m) line from the head and two 25ft (7.6m) lines from the tack and the clew (to balance the sail approximately round the centre of effort) – it made a marked difference, as the results show. The sail gave colossal drag, probably more than would ever be required, especially at low speed, and performed more like a parachute sea anchor than a drogue.

Used either way, a disadvantage is that it is not easy to manage a sail on the upper deck in stormy conditions. Though the sail appeared to be stable, its asymmetrical shape could easily give rise to instability. A major advantage, however, is that sails are always on board and one does not have to buy additional equipment, and a minor advantage is that the sail can be dried off by hoisting it after use, not that this is always very convenient.

Many will prefer to use a proper drogue from a deployment bag rather than use their expensive sails for a purpose for which they were not designed. However, given long enough and balanced rigging lines, a small sail will work as a drogue and a large sail will work as a parachute sea anchor. For the latter, a full-size genoa would be more appropriate than the No 3.

The Bu-ord

Using the 10ft (3m) Bu-ord parachute as a drogue produced the most dramatic of the results. The yacht's propeller was unable to cope with the parachute at the rpm set for the trial and cavitated severely. It was necessary to reduce rpm from 2820 to 2000 to avoid cavitation when a speed of only 1.2 knots was achieved, indicating very high resistance. Without a float and recovery line attached to the apex, the parachute does tend to sink and then becomes extremely heavy and therefore hard work to recover. The Bu-ord absorbs quite a lot of water, but is small enough to be hung up, allowing it to dry out quite easily. It is soft and takes up very little space. The Bu-ord provides so much drag at all speeds that it is unlikely that steerage way can be maintained at all times.

Cone drogues

Cone or sleeve drogues (see photo below) are available in chandlers and are easy to make. These are the shapes that gave sea anchors a bad name, but in the small sizes available, if weighted, they seem to be no less effective than other drogues. Two were tested, one proprietary type with a 24in (61cm) diameter mouth and 4in (10cm) exit hole, and another of 30in (76cm) diameter and 3in (7.6m) exit which was home-made in two layers of parachute nylon. They were tried both singly and in series with 50ft (15.2m) between them and were

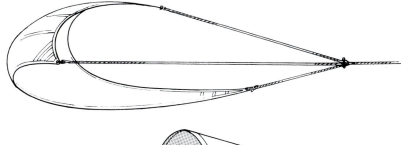

Figure 6.8 A strong headsail will make an effective drogue or sea anchor if the rigging lines are long enough.

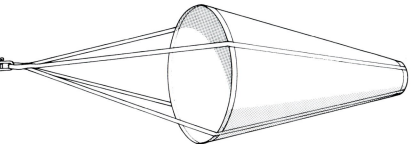

Figure 6.9 The cone drogue is very efficient.

A proprietory cone drogue.
Photo: Peter Bruce

Recovering drogues by hand is extremely hard work, especially when weighted. *Photo: Peter Bruce*

weighted with chain. The results of drag trials were impressive, both as a single drogue and when two were set up in series. The latter arrangement can be expected to give especially good results in a seaway as a single drogue is bound to be disadvantageously affected to some degree by wave effects.

A heavy-duty sewing machine was used to make the homemade drogue. An ordinary one could not manage.

The car tyre

The tyre seemed to produce a modest but useful amount of drag. For example, it doubled the amount of drag given by the line on its own. It had been expected that the tyre might porpoise or just skid along the surface, but there was no sign of this in calm conditions, though instances have been reliably reported in a seaway. A car tyre is an awkward, large object to stow and can mark paintwork. One should drill drain holes in the side of the tyre or remember to sponge out the inside after use. Some will find a dual purpose for a car tyre; for example, a tyre makes a good fender for the slimy walls, as it does not rotate.

CONCLUSIONS FOLLOWING SEA TRIALS OF DROGUES

The purpose-made drogues tested were strong, compact, easily handled, and gave an effective amount of drag, though it is thought that few owners of small craft will wish to find space for solid-built drogues such as the solid Seabrake or the Attenborough. It is tempting to choose a drogue that will perform well without being heavily weighted, but experience suggests, as does the Wolfson Unit report, that all drogues benefit from being held below the waves.

The amount of drag that will be needed will vary with the severity of the weather. Ideally one should have a drogue that will hold the stern of the boat firmly into the seas, slow the boat down to a comfortable speed, yet retain steerage way in the troughs of large waves from force 8 upwards. A most important requirement is that the line should never go slack. To bridge an ocean wavelength, the drogue line should be not less than 100m.

Directionally stable yachts using a drogue may be able to maintain a good downwind course using vane steering, an auto helm or with the helm lashed amidships, but many yachts will need to be hand-steered.

Small parachutes, such as Bu-ords, have been used over the stern of multihulls as drogues as well as over the bow as parachute sea anchors. Generally, monohulls will find the drag of a parachute too much to retain steerage way. At the other end of the scale a single weighted line, similar to the line used in the trials, will provide insufficient drag for most purposes. Ad hoc devices are not likely to be very effective either. The motor car tyre, for example, does not give much drag and can be the least trusted to stay submerged of all drogues.

Given the choice it is best to go for a weighted drogue that one feels one can handle and that gives a reasonable chance that the boat will still be steerable at low speed. If one can cope with the added complication, there is a good case for putting two purpose-made drogues in series to obviate further the effects of cyclical wave motion.

Though easier to manage, a drogue is not necessarily an alternative to a parachute. In the unlikely event of conditions becoming so extreme as to cause discontinuous load, for the yacht to be repeatedly pooped, to become unsteerable or to pitch-pole, then she is probably better off with her bow facing into the seas, hove-to, under power, or lying to a parachute sea anchor – the decision best made early rather than late.

However, it is generally accepted that all craft are safer 'end-on' to the waves rather than 'broadside-on' when it really comes on to blow. Thus owners of craft that do not heave-to comfortably will be better off having any well-tried drag device, whether deployed over the bow or the stern, rather than nothing at all.

CHAPTER

7 *The meteorology of heavy weather*

RICHARD EBLING

(This is written for the benefit of sailors, not meteorologists, and therefore many of the finer points have been simplified or glossed over.)

These days, with the vast amount of weather information that is available to the sailor, in theory there is no need to be caught out, but no meteorologist can truthfully put his hand on his heart and always guarantee 100 per cent satisfaction for 24-hour forecast products, let alone those that look ahead for the best part of a week.

OBTAINING OFFSHORE DATA

Sailing from a UK port should mean access to services such at MetFAX, which is a source of not only a text forecast with outlooks for the north Atlantic or Biscay, but charts covering an area between 70°N–40°N and 40°W–15°E for up to four days ahead, all for the cost of a couple of pints of beer. In France, SEAFAX provides a similar service (equal to five bottles of the cheapest vin rouge). Australia too certainly offers a dial-up service, but having spoken to Admiral's Cup competitors from the USA it would seem that as yet US fax forecasts would not be detailed enough for cruising or passage planning, but that the NOAA VHF forecasts are good for shorter periods.

At sea it is no longer necessary to receive actual and 24-hour forecast coded charts by Morse, which then require plotting and drawing by hand (as it was 30 years ago). For many years radiofax has provided charts for up to six days ahead in some parts of the world, either using a dedicated receiver/printer or, more recently, the ubiquitous laptop plugged into an AF output socket on the ship's radio.

Technology has brought about both the Internet and the use of worldwide mobile phones – phones that use the terrestrial GSM network where there is one, automatically switching to the Iridium satcomm network when out of range of a land-based transmitter. On the Internet, six-day charts are again freely available: free, that is, apart from the cost of the phone call – though on board this will mean 'mobile prices'.

STRONG WINDS

Outside the tropics, the two most common causes of heavy weather associated with depressions are either the development of a secondary low, thereby causing the isobars to be squeezed closer together, or the straightforward unexpected deepening of an existing low centre. It was this squeezing of the isobars on the south-east and eastern flank of the main depression as a secondary low swept through which led to at least a doubling of the expected gradient that caught out Adlard Coles as he crossed the North Sea (see Chapter 14). It is probably as well that he hove-to when and where he did as the south-westerly wind would have been even stronger through the Straits of Dover, accelerating as it funnelled between the converging English and French coastlines.

With reports in this book coming from many sources, it may be appropriate to comment on wind profiles. Friction reduces wind blowing over the sea to about 80% of the wind speed above the boundary or friction layer, and friction overland reduces the wind to about 40%. In the scale of winds reported by masthead anemometers, however, there are further factors that are worth looking at, especially when you bear in mind that weather forecasts are all based on the height of a standard (land-based) anemometer – 33ft (10m) above ground level – a height probably chosen as being just above touch-down for aircraft.

Height in feet above the surface																		
10	20	30	33	40	50	60	70	80	90	100	120	140	160	180	200	250	300	
Factor over the sea																		
0.89	0.95	0.99	1.00	1.02	1.04	1.06	1.08	1.09	1.11	1.12	1.14	1.16	1.17	1.18	1.20	1.22	1.25	
Factor over the land																		
0.74	0.88	0.98	1.00	1.05	1.11	1.16	1.21	1.25	1.29	1.32	1.38	1.44	1.48	1.53	1.57	1.66	1.74	

For example, if the forecast is for 30 knots (force 7), with an anemometer 50ft (15m) above the waterline, the expected mean speed should be around 30 × 1.04 = 31.2 knots, and on a 160ft (49m) lighthouse such as the Fastnet, 30 × 1.48 = 44.4 knots could be recorded: a good force 9! I said 'recorded', as reported wind speed observations on meteorological broadcasts *should* always be corrected for both altitude and exposure. They are in the UK, but may not always be elsewhere, especially in some of the more remote corners of the globe.

It is also perhaps worth remembering the 'weight of the air'. In 24 knots the wind exerts a pressure of 2.3lb/sq ft, but a little under half as fast again, a wind of 34 knots, will exert 4.6lb/sq ft, while at 48 knots it exerts 9.2lb/sq ft (doubling the wind speed means 4 times the pressure). So even for sails of equal area the 'heeling factor' in a given wind relates very much to the height of the sail's centre of pressure. Increased height of the centre of pressure means increased wind speed, and therefore increased pressure multiplied by an increased heeling moment.

To avoid confusion, unless otherwise stated, all diagrams and meteorological theories refer to the northern hemisphere, ie cyclonic flow is anticlockwise, and anticyclonic flow is clockwise. If you find the look of weather charts confusing as you cross the equator, a tip is to pick up the chart by the bottom edge and hold it against a strong light, a sunlit window for example. This has the effect of reversing references to north/south, but keeps east/west the same, once more giving a familiar look to the shape of the frontal systems.

SECONDARY LOWS

Without access to weather charts, trying to identify conditions leading to the development of a secondary low is next to impossible, as both surface and 'upper air charts' are needed. This of course presupposes an onboard weatherfax, which is becoming more commonplace. These give access to a reliable source of charts that are big enough and detailed enough to work on. Scouring the weather facsimile schedules (I personally prefer the 'Klingenfuss Facsimile Guide' rather than 'ALRS 3', as worldwide examples are included) will show references to combined 'surface/1000–500hPa' and to '500hPa/1000–500hPa thickness charts'. (Strictly speaking, the correct SI unit for barometric pressure is the hecto Pascal, and documents such as weather charts and radiofax schedules will use hPa, but mercifully 1hPa = 1mb and I will use the more familiar unit.)

The charts that should be of most use will be:

1 Surface analyses, probably labelled ASXX or FSXX (**A**ctual **S**urface or **F**orecast **S**urface)
2 Thickness charts, probably labelled AUXX or FUXX (**A**ctual **U**pper-air or **F**orecast **U**pper-air)

Use of the word 'thickness' should bring home to us that the atmosphere is three-dimensional, and that it is not enough to consider what happens just at the surface. Average atmospheric pressure is 1013mb, and since pressure decreases with height, the vertical distance between the level at which the pressure is 1000mb and the level at which the pressure is 500mb is known as the 'thickness' of the lower half of the atmosphere, the lowest 28 000ft (5.5km) or so which, after all, is where most of the weather is.

Cold air is denser than warm air, therefore if the thickness value is low the air is cold, and if the thickness value is high then the air is warm (see Fig 7.1). Warm sectors with their relatively homogeneous contents will be shown as areas with very little change in value.

Many weatherfax charts or chartlets will have lines omitted for clarity. If we take a surface chart with isobars, which is probably the most familiar, filling in many of the missing isobars will be reasonably obvious, but in some cases it won't be possible. Fig 7.2 illustrates possible flow across a col. (Because low and high pressure systems can be thought of as valleys and mountain peaks some geographic terms are used, such as ridge or trough. A col or saddle point is a high valley between two mountains, which at the same time is a ridge between the lower ground on either side of the mountains.)

The size of your weatherfax chart will of course depend on the receiver/printer used, but the 500mb/1000–500mb chart is normally broadcast in the largest format possible and will probably be complete in as much as all the necessary lines will be there, but since it is not a surface chart, it will of course have no isobars or fronts shown; on the other hand, the surface forecast charts may have some thickness lines included so that it may well be

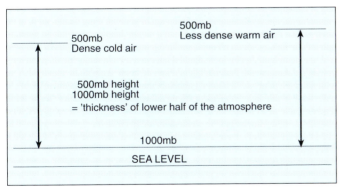

Figure 7.1 Variation of pressure with height due to variation in temperature.

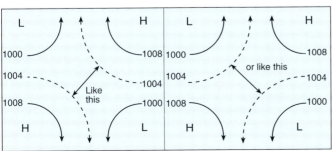

Figure 7.2 Where should the missing isobars be drawn?

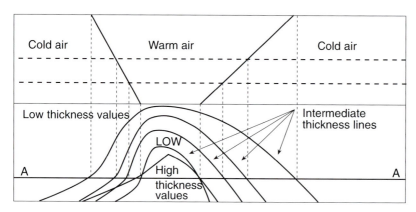

Figure 7.3 Plan view of met chart with thickness lines. How 3-D information is displayed on 2-D meteorological charts. Vertical section at A–A.

necessary to use one chart in order to complete the other. (On combined charts the thickness lines are normally the ones that are dashed or dotted.)

Once it is understood what is being looked for, the practice is very straightforward (Fig 7.3). Just as tightly drawn depth contours on a marine chart (a steep gradient) will denote rapid shoaling, fronts or, more correctly, frontal zones are areas of change where either cold air is being replaced by warmer or vice versa. Whereas warm sectors with their relatively uniform contents contain few thickness lines, in frontal zones the greater the contrast in temperature, the closer the thickness lines will be, and the steeper will be the 'thermal gradient'. At a warm front cold air is replaced by warmer less dense air, and so the thickness values will rise, falling again at the cold front as the warm air is replaced by cold air once more.

Forecasting development of secondary lows

In an ideal world the surface and upper air features should be closely related, as in Fig 7.4, but unfortunately this is not always the case. Sometimes the thickness lines are bunched along the warm front, or along the cold, and sometimes even cross into the warm sector. Secondary lows tend to form where the thickness lines are bunched together.

In Fig 7.5a the thickness lines are bunching where they run nearly parallel to the cold front for a considerable distance. In conditions such as these the distance from the point of development of a secondary low – as a cold front wave – from the point of occlusion is likely to be in the region of 1200–1500nm, with the new low moving generally in a direction parallel to the thickness lines or the isobars within the warm sector. This is probably the most common way in which secondary depressions form.

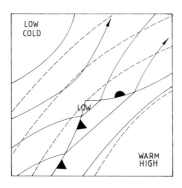
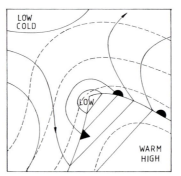
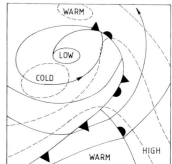

Figure 7.4 Three stages in the development from a frontal wave to an occluded frontal system showing the relationship between isobars, fronts and thickness lines.

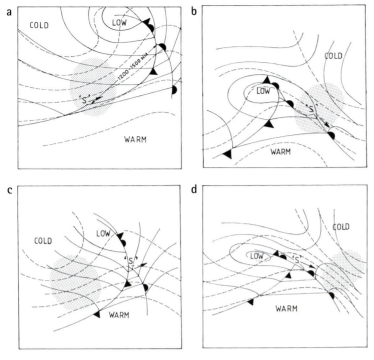

Figure 7.5 Thickness patterns associated with the development of secondary lows and their direction of movement.
a) Secondary low development as a wave on the cold front.
b) Secondary lows on a warm front.
c) Secondary low developing at the triple point.
d) Least common case of a secondary low developing at the triple point.

In Fig 7.5b the secondary low develops as a warm front wave. The bunching of the thickness lines in this case is seen to be just ahead of the warm front with a distinct ridging over the warm sector, and the resulting depression moving along the thickness lines. (Compare this with Fig 7.5d where the bunching is nearer to the triple point.)

The development of a secondary low – as a triple point low – (Fig 7.5c) is again quite common. In this case the thickness lines will no longer be parallel to the cold front. Some will cross the warm sector, while the rest will turn pole-wards (north) just before they reach the occlusion. Again in this case the movement of the secondary low will be in the general direction of the thickness lines or isobars within the warm sector.

In Fig 7.5d, as in 7.5c, some thickness lines cross the warm sector, and bunching is seen to be closer to the triple point than in 7.5b. This case is the least likely development.

In all cases, the driving force behind any development of a secondary low is the strongest thermal contrast, which is shown on a chart by the bunching of the thickness lines.

The following questions should be asked:

1 Is the strongest thermal contrast along and parallel to the cold front? If so, watch out for cold front waves.
2 Is the strongest thermal contrast along and parallel to the warm front? If so, watch out for warm front waves.
3 Is the strongest thermal contrast across rather than along the front? If so, expect a triple point low to develop.

EXPLOSIVE DEEPENING

Development of weather systems is normally fairly well forecast, so if depressions do suddenly deepen unexpectedly, more often than not it is a case of explosive deepening (which is defined as deepening at over 24mb in a day). This usually happens during the winter months, and nearly always occurs over the oceans, with the western north Atlantic being one of the world's preferred areas. However, explosive deepening of depressions can occur at any time, even in mid-summer, especially if the tail end of any ex-tropical revolving storm is involved.

If the signs leading up to one of these events have slipped through the professional forecasters' net, it is very unlikely that the yachtsman will have any additional information to guide him except that of a steadily falling barometer. With no other information to go on, a good rule is that falls of 10mb in 3 hours will be followed by a gale (force 8). While the falls may not be particularly rapid, to the rear of the depression the pressure rise may be. (In the October 1987 storm, the barometer at Hurn Airport fell some 33mb in 18 hours at an average of 5.5mb/3hr or 1.8mb/hr, but later the barometer rose 50mb in 15 hours! It peaked at 12.2mb in the hour 0400–0500 UTC. Rises of over 10mb in 1 hour covered an area from Lyme Bay and the Isle of Wight to Reading.)

Initially, the strongest winds may very well be contained within the warm sector, but once the explosive deepening gets under way, storm or even hurricane force winds (force 10–12) can occur over a comma-shaped arc (seen shaded in Fig 7.6) in the cold air behind the cold front, as cold dry air from high in the atmosphere is dragged down and swept into the circulation. The dryness of this entrained air is responsible for areas with clear skies, as reported during the 1979 Fastnet Race.

However, just because the wind speed is increasing it does not necessarily mean that the associated fronts will also speed up. Pressure falling along a trough line (Fig 7.7a), such as a cold front, will sharpen the trough, tightening the pressure gradient each side of the front without affecting the gradient measured along the front.

The distance apart of the isobars measured along the trough – in this case, a measurement of 'x' units, remains constant even though the distance apart of the isobars 'y' has now decreased. Very rapid post-frontal pressure rises will of course also have the same net result.

LEE LOWS

Depressions can also be caused by high ground. Examination of the chart will show a 'hole in the isobars' or wide space in an apparently regular circulation about the main depression, and it is within this empty space that a lee low may form.

As air is forced to rise over a range of mountains, in general the curve of the isobars becomes more anticyclonic. Likewise, on the leeward side of the high ground with descend-

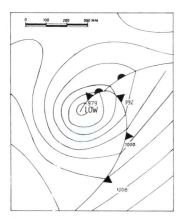

Figure 7.6 Comma–shaped arc of enhanced wind due to the intrusion of subsided air.

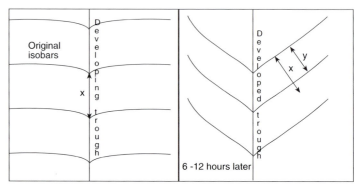

Figure 7.7 Isobar spacing along a developing trough may remain constant in spite of closer isobars and strengthening winds.
Y = tighter gradient, therefore increased wind speed compared with X.

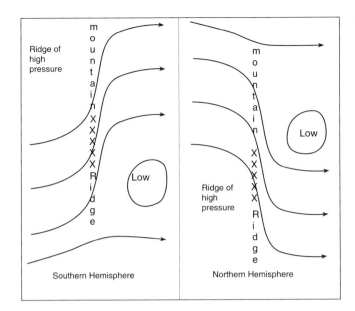

Figure 7.8 Development of a lee low as an eddy due to the distortion of isobars crossing high ground.

ing flow the isobars become more cyclonic. As well as marked troughing to the lee of mountains, lee depressions can also develop. In the same way, water flowing past an obstruction will form eddies that break away to be carried in the stream.

Often the only evidence for drawing a discrete circulation around these centres is gleaned from satellite analysis. In the mid-1950s, with an anticyclone over Greenland and northerly winds over the UK, charts would be drawn with perhaps very little in the way of isobars due to lack of observations to suggest a lee low to the south-east of Iceland. It was perhaps only with the arrival of unexpected prolonged snow in Scotland that we would be aware that one of these eddies had broken away from its source and been carried along embedded within the flow, arriving as a polar low.

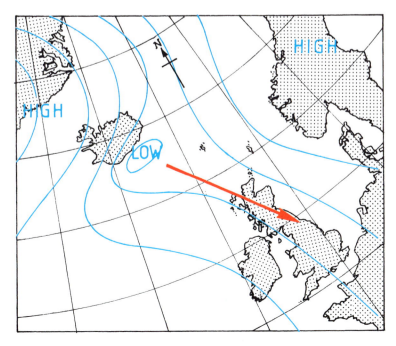

Figure 7.9 Polar low developing as a lee low before breaking away to be carried southwards across Scotland and possibly eastern England.

HIGH PRESSURE GENERATED WINDS

Unexpected strong winds may also be caused by anticyclones that fail to move away as expected, with little, if any, indication from an onboard barometer. An example of this involved John Wilson, who in a UFO34 (see Chapter 16) ran into extreme weather south of Iceland that was the result of a complex area of low pressure in mid-Atlantic. On Friday 11 May 1979, a small depression crossed Scotland followed by an area of light winds as a col followed, crossing Rockall early in the day, and then Scotland in the late evening. Meanwhile, the main Atlantic low at around 45°N 40°W appeared to consist of three centres with the lowest pressure around 980mb. On the Saturday, the lows moved north-east at about 20 knots, with troughing towards Iceland. But the blocking high pressure over the Greenland icecap was, if anything, still building – increasing the pressure gradient (50 knots) over and to the south of Iceland, leading to the very high wind speeds he experienced. On the Sunday, pressure over Greenland was still high, maintaining easterlies of a similar strength over Iceland and over the sea areas to the south and east, as the depression, now a single centre of 987mb, began to track east-north-east around 60°N. It was not until this stage late on Sunday and into Monday that the Greenland pressures began to fall as the low moved away from Iceland.

The reluctance of an area of high pressure to move was also evident in the 1994 Queen's Birthday storm (Chapter 22) when some 80 yachts were caught out in a storm as they sailed together from New Zealand to winter in the tropical Pacific islands. Again the closest isobars (and strongest) were in the quadrant squashed against the anticyclone centred over or close to New Zealand.

ANTICYCLONE WINDS

The wind circulating around a centre is acted upon by centrifugal forces acting away from the centre. In an anticyclone the pressure gradient force acts outwards as well, so that around high pressure both forces act in the same direction. Around a low the pressure gradient acts towards the centre, in other words, the centrifugal force is acting against the pressure gradient, reducing its strength (Fig 7.10). *Thus around an anticyclone winds are stronger for a given isobar spacing than around a depression.*

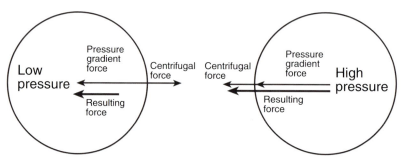

Figure 7.10 Forces acting on air under cyclonic and anticyclonic motion.

CONVERGENCE/DIVERGENCE

When winds meet, either spiralling into a depression or perhaps when a sea breeze blowing inland meets the land breeze, the air has to go somewhere. If the convergence is at the surface the air obviously cannot sink, so it must rise. Convergence also occurs when moving air is slowed down. Obviously air that is rising will expand and cool, and if the air is cooled sufficiently any moisture will condense into clouds. In the same way divergence at

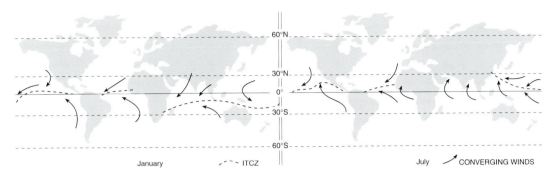

Figure 7.11 Trade winds converging towards the equator in January and July.

Figure 7.12 Satellite view of the ITCZ on 24 October 1998.

the surface can only be satisfied if the air aloft is subsiding – in which case the air will be compressed, warmed, and any moisture particles will evaporate.

With north-east trades in the northern hemisphere blowing towards the south-east trades of the south, there must be a front and a line of convergence separating these two flows. It was once thought that there was convergence along the entire length of this intertropical convergence zone (ITCZ), but it is now accepted that the actual convergence occurs only here and there. Nevertheless, the ITCZ is a breeding area for tropical storms – although they may not develop precisely on the ITCZ. Fig 7.12 shows a photo montage of several infra red satellite pictures. In these the coldest (highest) clouds are brightest.

The bright clouds associated with the ITCZ can be seen over the Atlantic from Nicaragua to the Cameroon, across Africa close to the equator, with a rather large area of bright clouds to the south of India and over Indonesia. Over the Pacific the main activity seems to be just south of the Hawaiian islands, thus showing a series of convergence areas rather than the continuous belt that had been thought to exist.

TROPICAL REVOLVING STORMS

1   Charts displaying tracks of tropical revolving storms (TRS) (Fig 7.13) show that formation does not occur within 5° north or south of the equator.

2   High water vapour content is required. In order to supply both the water vapour and a

sufficient source of heat for convection, sea temperature in excess of 79°F (26°C) is essential, allowing the air to contain typically 0.7–0.9oz (20–25g) of water per 2.2lb (1kg) of air (2% of the air will in fact be water vapour!). As the moist air within the circulation rises, expands and cools, condensation takes place, releasing large amounts of energy in the form of latent heat.

Tropical revolving storms

Area and local name	Jan	Feb	Mar	Apr	May	Jun	Jul	Aug	Sep	Oct	Nov	Dec	Average No per year	Average of over F11 per year
N Atlantic, W Indies (hurricane)					?	——	——	====	====	====	——	?	10	5
NE Pacific (hurricane)					?	——	====	====	====	——	?		15	7
NW Pacific (typhoon)				?	——	——	====	====	====	——	——	?	25–30	15–20
N Indian Ocean, Bay of Bengal (cyclone)		?	——	====	====	——	——	——		====	====	?	2–5	1–2
N Indian Ocean Arabian Sea (cyclone)		?	——	====	——			?		——	====	?	1–2	1
S Indian Ocean W of 80°E (cyclone)	====	====	==—	——	?						?	——	5–7	2
Australia W, NW, N and Queensland coast (cyclone)	====	====	==—	——							?	——	2–3	1
Fiji, Samoa, New Zealand (N Island) (cyclone)	====	====	====	——	?						?	——	7	2

—— main season   ==== period of greatest activity   ? period affected if season is early/late

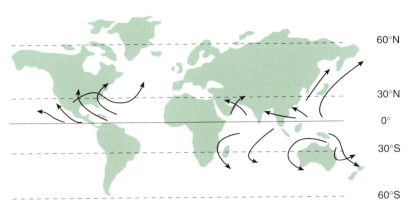

Figure 7.13 Typical tracks of tropical revolving storms.

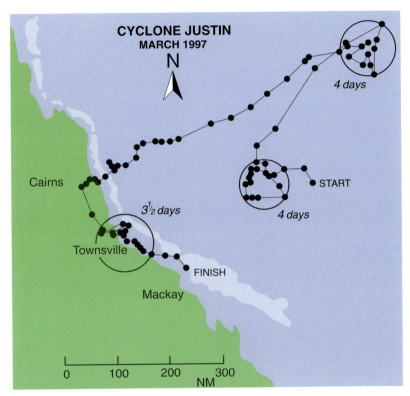

Figure 7.14 Justin's erratic track for some 20 days.

A thunderstorm over East Falkland viewed from Pebble Island. Although the main storm was 30–40 miles to the east, on flying some 50 miles south-east to Goose Green, the last 15 miles were through hail. Note the effect of the stronger southerly wind towards the top of the cloud, producing the typical anvil head.
Photo: Richard Ebling.

3 The released latent heat needs to be contained within the vertical column of the circulation and therefore TRS need to be well away from the influence of any jet streams.
4 Eventually a small amount of the rising air at the top of the system turns inwards and sinks. This dry air is then responsible for the clear eye of the storm.

The initial track of a TRS is mainly westwards, typically at 10–15 knots, with a slight pole-wards component (Fig 7.13), steered by the tropospheric flow. Somewhere between 20° and 30° away from the equator, depending on the position of the high pressure belt, the track usually curves increasingly pole-wards at 20–30 knots. As the system leaves the tropical circulation, steering will be governed by the westerly winds of the mid-latitude troposphere.

Not that all TRS do as expected. Looking at the charts for *Orca's* last cruise (see Chapter 26) I was surprised at the lack of movement of Cyclone Justin – just 180nm in nine days (3–12 March). With dew points and sea temperatures in the mid to high twenties, Justin's slow movement can only have been due to lack of any steering flow throughout the height of the cyclone until around 12 March, when Justin headed north-east towards New Guinea for three or four days before returning to hit the coast near Cairns and then to travel south down the coast towards Mackay.

The moral of this is that although tropical storms should curve away from the equator, in reality they are very unpredictable and a close eye on the barometer is required. Within the tropics the diurnal variation of pressure (the atmospheric tide) of perhaps up to 3mb may mask early warning of approaching systems. It is normal for tendencies of ±0.5mb/hour to occur around 1 and 7 o'clock am and pm local time.

THUNDERSTORMS

On a smaller scale to tropical revolving storms, thunderstorms are also fuelled by convective processes. What is needed is 'conditionally unstable air', allowing a parcel of saturated air to be buoyant and to rise, when an adjacent parcel of dry air does not. (Indeed, were the parcel of dry air to be lifted it would sink again to its starting point.) In the lowest 10 000ft (3048m) of the atmosphere dry air cools with height at around 37°F (3°C)/1000ft (300m), and at about half that rate if the air is saturated, due to the release of latent heat as moisture is condensed out. The trigger to start this movement could be heating from below,

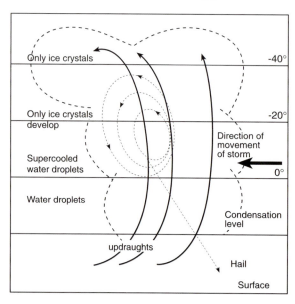

Figure 7.15 Development of hail stones within a cumulonimbus cloud.

or cooling from above, or ascent as air is forced to rise over high ground in the case of air mass storms, or is forced to rise as a front approaches. Convergence near a front can give rise to some of the severest storms, but another requirement for severe storms is a marked change of wind velocity with height which tilts the updraft.

The updraft is almost self-perpetuating as it is fuelled by the latent heat released by condensation. The small 'cloud' droplets that originally form have a slow drop speed, and will easily be carried up in the strong updrafts – giving them the chance of growing larger.

Since within a cloud 'the higher the colder', at around –4°F (–20°C) ice crystals develop. Higher in the cloud as temperatures get even lower, more and more of the updraft consists of ice rather than water, until temperatures reach –40°F (–40°C) by which time the cloud consists only of ice crystals.

A classic hurricane viewed from a satellite. Note that the date is during the height of the hurricane season and its latitude lies betweeen 20°N and 30°N when it could well recurve. *Photo: Internet*

As the droplets/ice particles grow they become heavier, and because the updraft is no longer vertical, falling ice/water will leave the saturated updraft and fall into drier air – where evaporation takes place. The latent heat required for this cools the adjacent air – generating negative buoyancy and hence the downdraft. Not only is the downdraft due to the coldness (density) of the air, but the falling precipitation also drags air down with it (due to friction).

When this downdraft hits the surface it rapidly spreads out as a cold pool giving rise not only to a rapid or even violent increase in wind speed, but also changes in direction. As the cold pool and its 'gust front' undercut the surrounding air so conditions become ripe for development of a new up-current of air. In storms with many updrafts, the falling ice/water may enter another updraft and so be carried upwards once more, providing the opportunity for further growth (this process can be repeated many times). For example, examination of large hail stones will show many 'shells', as layers have progressively built up.

A thunderstorm can also be considered as a very efficient electrical generator even though the exact electrical mechanism is unknown. Fields of 100kV/m to 400kV/m develop within the storm, a positive charge at the top, a negative charge towards the bottom of the cloud, and an induced positive area on the ground immediately below the cloud. It may well have been this 'build-up' under cloud that affected Bill Cooper aboard his steel ketch just before she was struck by lightning (see Chapter 15).

Once a critical field strength has been generated (1 000 000kV/m), a lightning discharge takes place, temporarily neutralizing the field, but build-up is immediately recommenced as long as the cell is still active. The lightning stroke can be cloud to cloud, either within the same cloud or to an adjacent cloud; or cloud to ground, ground in this case being either land or sea.

A ground stroke (land or sea) is initiated by a 'stepped leader'. This is a surge of electrons that move downwards at about 164ft (50m) per single microsecond, and after a pause of about 50 microseconds, a second step takes place, this sequence being repeated until the leader reaches the ground. A charge will then move rapidly upwards along the path taken by the leader. After about 0.01 seconds another stroke occurs. (Up to 30 or 40 strokes have been observed in the same channel.) Cloud to cloud strokes also consist of a stepped leader and a return stroke.

While the strength and direction of local winds generated by air being drawn into a thunderstorm will be a combination of both the in-flowing air and the pre-existing wind, the cold downdraft wind will be blowing out from the storm, arriving as a chilly squall with a sudden increase in speed and change of direction, undercutting the surrounding air in the same manner as a cold front.

TORNADOES

Strong updrafts are also needed for tornadoes; this time the updraft is also rotating, initially at an altitude somewhere between 10 000ft and 20 000ft (3000m–6000m). As the rotation increases, the local pressure gradient across the rotating core, and the local centrifugal force about the core, come into balance, and the system is now called a meso-cyclone. By this time most if not all of the flow is drawn in at its lower end, and this in turn extends the rotating core lower and lower until it reaches the surface.

Near the surface, however, friction prevents the balance between the local centrifugal force and the local pressure gradient, and so air streams in towards the centre. The funnel cloud that extends from the cloud base is mainly condensation caused by the decreasing pressure, but if it extends to near the surface, spray will be swept up over the sea and dust and debris will be swept up over land.

Strong or violent tornadoes are, thankfully, only found over land, when theoretically a maximum speed of 313 knots is possible. Weak tornadoes may also form beneath the rapidly growing cloud that develops over a gust front – perhaps around the fringe of a thunderstorm where funnel clouds and waterspouts may occasionally be seen.

In conclusion, if professional forecasters are not 100 per cent accurate, then amateurs with fewer facilities are unlikely to do better. Nevertheless, if information is available, it is good to have the knowledge to be able to interpret such information correctly, and it is very satisfying too.

8 Waves

SHELDON BACON

WAVE GROWTH

A yacht is far from land, becalmed on a glassy sea; and then the wind appears. What now happens to the surface of the sea? If the wind were a perfectly steady and uniform airflow and the sea surface were perfectly flat and smooth there would be no waves generated. The friction between air and sea would drive a current in the sea, but some irregularity in the wind is needed to disturb an initially smooth sea surface to begin to generate waves.

The real wind is gusty, blustery and turbulent. There is an atmospheric boundary layer about 330ft (100m) high above the sea surface within which the airflow is directly affected by the presence of the sea surface. This induces turbulence on scales from millimetres to tens of metres (also the air/sea temperature difference can induce circulation in the wind to over 3280ft (1km) above the surface). The turbulence is carried along by the overall flow of the wind, and it is this turbulence that starts up the wave motion on the sea. This is the initial phase of wave growth, and it is relatively slow.

Once there are some waves present, a very rapid (in fact exponential) phase of wave growth takes place. The more waves there are, the rougher the sea surface is, so the more turbulence is generated in the wind, which produces still more waves, and so on. However, this process cannot continue for ever. For any given wind speed, low or high, a state of saturation is reached when energy input to the waves by the wind is balanced by dissipation of energy from the wavefield, either by waves travelling out of the generation region, or by breaking. The exponential growth phase does not tail off to the steady state however; it gets carried away and, for a short time, energy is pumped into the waves that the waves cannot hold. This is called overshoot, and it can be dangerous for yachts because the wavefield will have to lose energy by waves breaking at a greater rate than during the saturation phase.

Ultimately, the sea state reaches a steady state which will not change until the wind changes its speed and/or direction. If the wind should increase further, the waves will continue to grow; if it decreases, dissipation will remove more energy than the new lower wind speed is injecting, and the waves will become lower. If there is a change in direction, potentially the most dangerous possibility in extreme conditions, a new sea will develop on top of the declining old one, resulting in a cross-sea, and it will develop rapidly since the sea is already rough and the wind turbulent.

With the passing of a wave. water particles travel in nearly circular paths. At the surface, the diameter of the circles is the crest-to-trough height of the wave. At the top of the crest, the water is travelling straight forwards; at the bottom of the trough, straight back. At some point on the front and rear faces of the wave, the water travels straight up and straight down. The water is also in motion below the surface, to a depth that depends on the length of the wave. Consider, for example, a 66ft (20m) long wave: at 16ft (5m) depth (25% of the wavelength), the particle speeds are 20% of their surface values, and at 66ft (20m) depth (one wavelength), only 0.1%. This becomes very important in regions of shoal water: if there is seabed in the way at a depth where the wave is trying to influence water motion, the wave can feel the bottom.

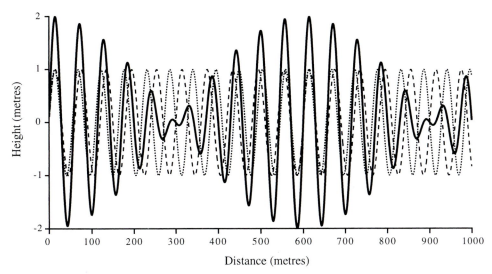

Figure 8.1 This is a demonstration of the formation of wave groups by the addition of similar waves. In this example there are two basic waves, one of length 177ft (54m) crest-to-crest (dotted) and the other 197ft (60m) crest-to-crest (dashed); they are both 7ft (2m) high crest-to-trough. The height of the resulting wave (solid line) varies between 13ft (4m) crest-to-trough and zero. It is made of waves at the average length of the two basic waves 187ft (57m) wrapped in an envelope whose length depends on the difference between the basic waves: the smaller the difference, the longer the groups made by the envelope.

There is a unique connection between the length, period and speed of a wave, which can take any height, but for any one length of wave, there is only one possible speed and one possible period. Long waves travel faster than short waves (in deep water), so if many waves all of different lengths are produced in one place, which occurs during a storm, the longer waves that are generated will travel out of the area of the storm faster than the shorter ones. This is the origin of swell: fast-moving, long waves that may arrive in advance of an approaching storm. Wave shape changes as the wave becomes steeper: long, low swell waves are rounded and vertically symmetrical (sinusoidal), but as steepness increases they become asymmetrical: more peaked at the crest and flat in the trough (trochoidal).

If two waves of similar lengths are added, another important phenomenon arises, that of wave grouping. If the crest of one coincides with the crest of the other (or a trough with a trough), the resulting height is the sum of the two, but if a crest coincides with a trough, the two waves cancel. The single wave resulting from the addition of two looks different: there is now an envelope around the short-wave basic wave train that groups the individual waves into 'packets'. This is illustrated in Fig 8.1, which shows two waves of the same height but slightly (10%) different lengths added. Now the two waves travel at different speeds according to their lengths: the longer one faster than the shorter. This will cause the envelope to travel forwards as the crests and troughs move in and out of phase, so that the envelope has a forward velocity of its own called the group velocity. This is related to the difference in speed between the two waves, so the envelope can move quite slowly forwards while within each resultant group, the individual waves rise at the back, move forwards through the group, and finally disappear at the front of the group. This can be seen happening within ships' wakes, for example.

After presenting some of the basics of wave growth, propagation and decay, the following sections consider wave height prediction, global wave climate and extreme waves.

WAVE PREDICTION

Here is a recipe for reasonably accurate prediction of wave height. If a quick estimate is required, skip parts (1) to (5) below and go straight to (6), which will at worst result in an over-estimate.

Wave height depends (among other things) on wind speed, fetch (distance upwind to 'where the wind starts' – either the coast or the far side of an approaching weather system) and duration (length of time the wind has been blowing). If the wind blows at the same speed in the same direction for long enough, the waves will stop growing and will have become fully developed; so we proceed to treat three cases: the growing fetch-limited sea, the growing duration-limited sea, and the fully developed sea.

Accordingly, there are three decision graphs for deciding which case applies, and three prediction graphs for providing the estimate of wave height for the relevant case. This is how they work.

1 First establish your 'case': decide on the wind speed (in knots), fetch (in nautical miles) and duration (in hours). Call these values W, F and D. Fig 8.2 shows limiting duration as a function of wind speed and fetch, and it provides the answer to the first question: is the case duration-limited or fetch-limited? Find what duration in Fig 8.2 corresponds to W and F. If D is greater than this value, the case is fetch-limited, so go to (2) below. If D is less than this value, the case is duration-limited, so go to (3) below.

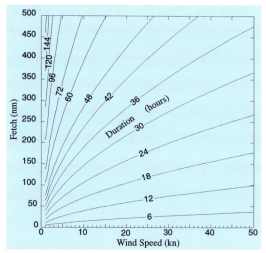

Figure 8.2 First decision graph. Given a known situation described by wind speed, fetch and duration, use this graph to decide whether the case is fetch–limited or duration–limited.

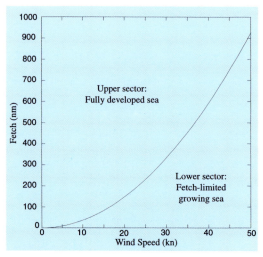

Figure 8.3 Second decision graph. If the first decision graph has shown that fetch-limiting is relevant, use this graph to decide whether the sea is really fetch–limited or actually fully developed.

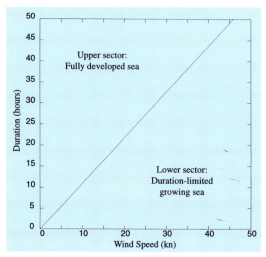

Figure 8.4 Third decision graph. If the first decision graph has shown that duration–limiting is relevant, use this graph to decide whether the sea is really duration-limited or actually fully developed.

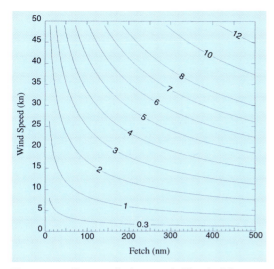

Figure 8.5 First prediction graph. The decision graphs have led to the conclusion that the sea is fetch-limited and growing. Use this graph to predict wave height (Hs, metres) given fetch and wind speed.

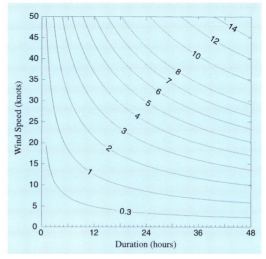

Figure 8.6 Second prediction graph. The decision graphs have led to the conclusion that the sea is duration-limited and growing. Use this graph to predict wave height (Hs, metres) given duration and wind speed.

2 Is the case really fetch-limited, or is the sea fully developed? Turn to Fig 8.3. Find what sector of the plot wind speed W and fetch F fall into. If the sea is fetch-limited and growing, go to (4) below. If the sea is fully developed, go to (6).

3 Is the case really duration-limited, or is the sea fully developed? Turn to Fig 8.4. Find what sector of the plot wind speed W and duration D fall into. If the sea is duration-limited and growing, go to (5) below. If the sea is fully developed, go to (6).

4 Fetch-limited growing sea: use Fig 8.5 to predict wave height for fetch F and wind speed W.

5 Duration-limited growing sea: use Fig 8.6 to predict wave height for duration D and wind speed W.

6 Fully developed sea: use Fig 8.7 to predict wave height for wind speed W.

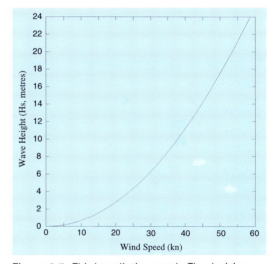

Figure 8.7 Third prediction graph. The decision graphs have led to the conclusion that the sea is fully developed. Use this graph to predict wave height (Hs, metres) given wind speed.

Here is a worked example. Say you are in the north Atlantic, 300 miles from the east coast of America, and you anticipate 25 knots of wind from the west to last for 24 hours. The limiting duration from Fig 8.2 is 36 hours. Our case (24 hours) is less than this, so proceed to Fig 8.4, from which we see that 25 knots for 24 hours is in the duration-limited growing sea sector. Finally, looking at Fig 8.6, we get a wave height of about 13ft (4m) for our case.

Of course, this is not the full story. Rates of decay are less easy to compute, if the weather is easing. Shallow water effects come into play when the water depth is less than half the wavelength. For waves of 5–10 second period (typical open-ocean values), meaning

165–482ft (50–150m) wavelength, water depths of 82–246ft (25–75m) and less will begin to affect the behaviour of the waves. They will become steeper until eventually they break, usually in the very shallow water near a beach called the surf zone, but in very severe weather (very high/long waves), they can break over offshore banks. Waves can also be made steeper or less steep by running into or away from a current. This is commonly seen in coastal waters over tidal cycles, but is also relevant for strong offshore currents like the Gulf Stream or the Kuroshio, which are notorious for their steep confused seas whenever the waves run against the current. Swell, which will increase the average wave height just by being around, also slightly increases the growth rate of waves in the presence of wind.

A GLOBAL TOUR

Observation of the waves of the world's oceans by satellite has been underway for a sufficiently long time that a meaningful picture of the global wave climate can be presented. This section will describe the global mean wave climate as measured between 1985 and 1996 by a sequence of satellites. The instrument used is the Satellite Radar Altimeter, which, from a height of 435 miles (700km) is able to measure the sea surface wave height to an accuracy of 1in (2.5cm), comparable to the best surface-based (ships and buoys) instruments.

The data are shown in Figs 8.8 to 8.11, being the global mean wave height distributions for January, April, July and October. The wave heights are in metres, and the measure actually used is significant wave height, which is a scientific measure close to what an observer would estimate visually. January and July are shown because they are the peaks of summer and winter winds (for both northern and southern hemispheres); the intermediate seasons are seen in the other two figures.

View of a small freshwater loch in Uig, Isle of Lewis, on 8 October 1995. The fetch was 600ft (183m) and the wind was south to south-west, gusting 61–78 knots.
Photo: Murray Macleod

The idealized picture of global atmospheric pressure is: low pressure at the equator (the Doldrums), high pressure about 30° north and south latitude (the Horse Latitudes), low pressure about 60° north and south latitude, and finally the polar highs. Light or variable winds are ascribed to these locations. The strong winds that blow between these alternating belts of high and low pressure are well known: the trades between the equator and 30° (north-east trades in the northern hemisphere, south-east in the southern). Between 30° and 60°, the northern hemisphere experiences south-westerlies and the southern hemisphere north-westerlies (the Roaring Forties); and between 60° and the pole, south-easterlies blow off the Antarctic, and north-easterlies off the Arctic. How do the waves conform in reality to this scheme?

There are some obvious features in these figures. The northern winter appears as rough seas in the north Atlantic and north Pacific from about 35°N in both oceans and continues up past Iceland in the Atlantic. Average wave heights in the northern deep ocean winter are in excess of 16ft (5m), with hardly a trace left in the summer. The southern winter appears as a great belt of rough seas extending from about 35°S to close to the Antarctic continent in about 65–70°S. In great contrast to the northern hemisphere however, in the southern summer the seas don't reduce nearly so much: from over 16ft (5m) to 10–13ft (3–4m). In further contrast, the equatorial Atlantic and Pacific are relatively placid much of the time. The calms under the Horse Latitudes show up clearly in the north Atlantic, less clearly in the north Pacific, and not at all obviously in the southern hemisphere, where the seasonal advance and retreat of the Roaring Forties sends waves northwards beyond 20°S.

Plainly there is much more to the story beyond the simple 'banded' model, and the most significant missing ingredient is *land*. Land soaks up and gives out heat much faster than the sea, both on time scales of a day and of a year. Where there is no (or little) land, the sea has a moderating effect on the wind regime, so that the degree of variation between summer and winter is smoothed out. This applies in the Southern Ocean wind belt (the Roaring Forties). The great land masses of the northern hemisphere cause the reverse to happen. Changes between seasons are amplified, particularly in that the northern summer is a lot calmer than the southern summer.

Land has other effects on the sea. The figures show the effect of sheltering. Enclosed seas are much calmer on average than the open ocean: look at the Caribbean, the Mediterranean, the Baltic, the seas of the East Indies, and others. As well as the generally short fetch in enclosed seas, they get little or no swell, and the presence of swell promotes wave growth (as well as contributing to the total wave height). There are shadow zones 'behind' Iceland, the Hawaiian islands, New Zealand and, very noticeably, east of southern Argentina over a thick slice of the south Atlantic.

Probably the most significant large-scale effect of land on conditions at sea is the monsoon (the word 'monsoon' derives from the Arabic for season). In the northern summer, the Asian landmass heats up, creating an enormous low-pressure area centred near the Himalayas. Winds blow around it anticlockwise, and it affects most of Asia, from the equatorial Indian Ocean, past the China Sea to the seas around Japan. In the northern winter, everything reverses: the cold generates a continental high (this centred over Mongolia), the winds blow clockwise, etc. On the figures, the waves caused by monsoon winds appear particularly in July in the Arabian Sea, where the south-west monsoon is strong, and in the China Sea east of the Philippines in January, where the north-east monsoon is strong.

EXTREME WAVES

There are two sorts of extreme (meaning very high) waves: those that crop up in the normal course of events and those caused by rather unusual circumstances. Properly speaking,

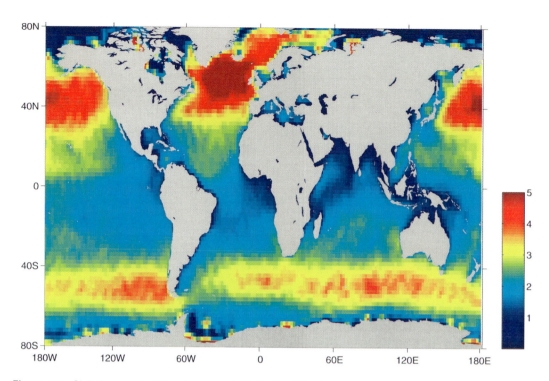

Figure 8.8 Global mean significant wave height (metres) for January.

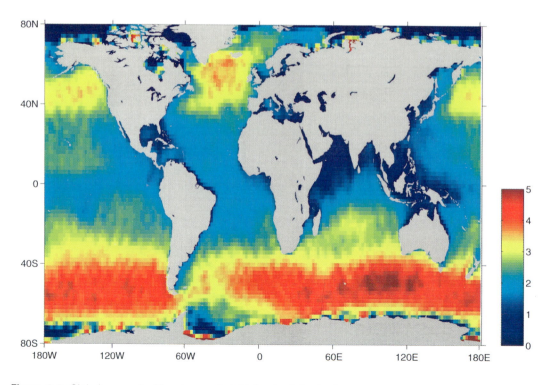

Figure 8.9 Global mean significant wave height (metres) for April.

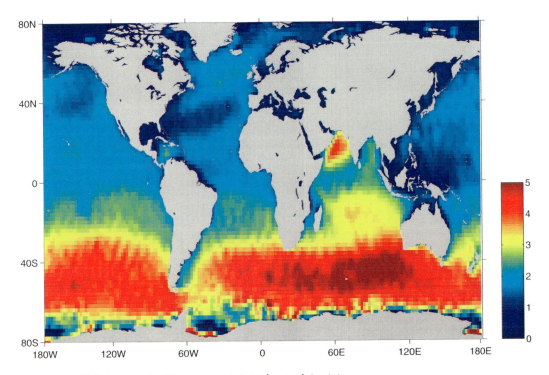

Figure 8.10 Global mean significant wave height (metres) for July.

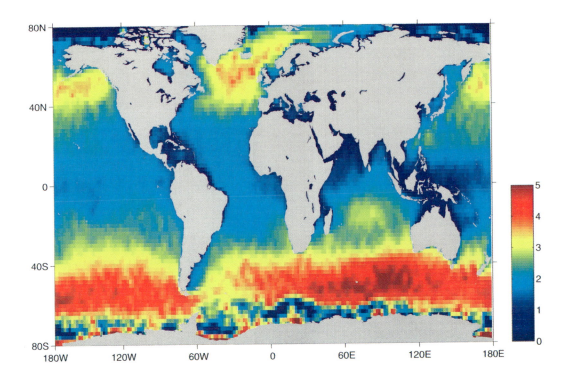

Figure 8.11 Global mean significant wave height (metres) for October.

the latter class are those that are usually referred to as 'freak waves', which we deal with first. The Japanese word *tsunami* was borrowed to replace 'tidal wave' (they have no connection with tides), and it refers to very long, very fast waves produced by marine geological activity: volcanic eruptions, undersea earthquakes, and the like. Some particularly notable examples are the waves produced by the Lisbon earthquake of 1704 and the explosion of Krakatoa in 1883. In the latter case we know that the waves crossed the Pacific Ocean in 12 hours, travelling at 300 knots. Tsunami wavelengths are around 100nm, with 10 to 20 minutes between crests. These waves are hardly noticeable in the open ocean, being not at all steep. They acquire their destructive power by steepening and increasing height as they run into shallow water.

One might legitimately refer to freak waves in the Agulhas Current region off South Africa, which seems to be uniquely blessed both in its reputation for high, steep waves and deep troughs ('holes') in damaging and sinking ships. This is due to the combination of oceanographic, meteorological and even orographic features that combine to produce those conditions. There are the long east-going waves propagating out of the Roaring Forties. They run into the strong Agulhas Current itself (similar in strength and character to the Gulf Stream and Kuroshio, reaching up to 4 or 5 knots) running south-west and west on the east and south coasts of South Africa. Coastal lows (see Chapter 7) influenced by the presence of the Karoo plateau (over 0.6 miles (1km) high) and the Drakensberg (over 1.8 miles (3km) high) can add more strong winds; and the physical effects of wave trapping and focusing caused by meanders and rings in the Agulhas, on scales of many tens or hundreds of miles, add further to the confusion.

Tropical revolving storms (typhoons and hurricanes) cause localized wave conditions rather different from the background average. They originate up to about 30° away from the equator, and if they move more than about 40° from the equator, they turn into

The series of photos on these two pages show the Channel lightvessel while on tow to her station in December 1978. At the time the towing vessel was hove-to off the Lizard in an easterly force 9–10. *Photo: Ambrose Greenway*

'ordinary' extra-tropical depressions. For example, the West Indies and north Atlantic have about nine per year; the western north Pacific, including the South China Sea, get about 30 per year. The worst of the strong winds (above force 8) and resulting high seas tend to be confined to a radius of about 100nm of the centre of the storm.

Time is an important factor when thinking about extremes proper. Referring back to Figs 8.8 and 8.11, remember that they show monthly averages. In any ordinary month, there is likely to be a day that is double the average. Now, thinking about individual waves rather than averages: for a given significant wave height Hs, in any three-hour period the most likely highest individual wave will be about twice Hs. The longer you look, the higher the likely highest wave. Engineers like to use the 50-year return height as an offshore design parameter. This means the highest Hs seen on average once in 50 years, based on three-hourly estimates of Hs. In an enclosed or semi-enclosed sea like the North Sea, this might be 20–26ft (6–8m). In the open ocean the 50-year return value of Hs is over 66ft (20m) for the north Atlantic, when the highest individual wave would be over 131ft (40m). Extremes, and waves intermediate in height between average and extreme, and waves lower than average, can all occur for a given Hs because of the shifting relationship between all the different component waves of different lengths in any sea state.

Sixty foot waves experienced in the Southern Ocean. Les Powles found that his self-steering gear worked even in extreme wind speeds. *Photo: Les Powles*

9 *Managing a large amateur racing crew*

MIKE GOLDING

This chapter is largely based on experiences aboard the steel 67ft (20.4m) cutter *Group 4*, with a crew of 14 during two BT Global Challenge events, and a singlehanded record-breaking voyage. These, of course, were races around the world, and hardly a cruise. However, out on the ocean in stormy weather there are many similarities between cruising and racing. The right things have to be done in an equally competent way at the right moment. One can't afford to be sloppy just because one is not racing.

The BT Global Challenge is often described as going 'the wrong way' around the world, but in the case of the most recent race, offwind sailing time was much the same as the time spent sailing to windward. Thus many of the principles learnt during both the British Steel and the BT Global Challenge will apply to more normal racing and cruising. For example, the axioms: 'Eat before you are hungry – Wrap up before you are cold – Sleep before you are tired' are just as appropriate to cruising in a 20ft (6m) sloop with a crew of two as racing in a 120ft (36m) schooner with a crew of 28.

By all means drive the crew hard but, essentially, both crew and boat must be fully prepared before an ocean voyage. In the case of the crew this means that they will work together when the chips are down – as they often are in high latitudes – and there is such confidence among the whole crew that not only do they all feel that what is being done is right, but also that no one need be scared. Build confidence so that the crew is mentally prepared and practised for bad weather. Undercurrents caused by mistrust form easily enough when circumstances are really bad, so this confidence level has to be very high. Such was the spirit developed among the crew of *Group 4* during the course of the most recent BT Global Challenge race that we felt like a steamroller going down a hill. Once it had got going, nothing could stop it.

SAFETY

The principal risk in offshore sailing is losing someone overboard. Safety harnesses combined with lifejackets are much easier to put on and less cumbersome than they used to be. However, the commonly fitted auto-inflate facility can be irritating or even dangerous, and on *Group 4* this was disarmed. The skipper or watchleader can decide that safety harnesses are to be worn, but on *Group 4* there was an unspoken rule that if anyone on watch decided that it was time for a harness and put theirs on, everyone else should do so too. It just seemed to happen.

There should be a rule that it is the individual's responsibility for clipping themselves on, and no one should be criticized for being slow through careful use of clips. People who are really slow with their clips are best employed in the aft end of the boat if possible. Clips should be attached up-wave of the crew member and in a manner to minimize the amount of slack in the safety line. No one should ever use shrouds as attachment points as, in the event of a severe knockdown, the person can find themselves up at the spreaders when the boat rights herself.

When undertaking foredeck work, such as sail changes, it is tempting for those concerned to decide who is to do what when they get there. There are several good reasons why time on the foredeck should be minimized, safety being one, so crews should be taught to have the conflab in the cockpit beforehand.

MAN OVERBOARD

The quick stop system is the best, and man overboard drill should be practised until everyone in the crew is familiar with the procedure – in particular, practise how to release the danbuoy and ensure all know where the man overboard button is. Personal EPIRBs are valuable to have on board, but can be a nuisance to carry around. As they are buoyant they make good markers. On *Group 4* one was attached to the danbuoy, another to the horseshoe lifebuoy, and a third stowed within easy reach of the helm, so it could be chucked over the side if necessary.

Two recovery systems were used. One was a scramble net and the other a 'Tribuckle', which allowed the man overboard to be parbuckled back on deck.

MOTIVATING THE CREW

Some of the principles that one might apply are as follows. Aim to keep everyone 'on board', meaning by that that all hearts and minds are working together for the vessel. Employ a structured plan. Ascertain what each crew member's personal aspirations are. For example, if someone wants to be a watchleader and yet is never allowed near the wheel, then one has to tell them why. Get involved with everything that takes place on board. Never ask someone to do something that one would not be prepared to do oneself. Be prepared to help out in any job if circumstances warrant it. Single out extraordinary good actions and make sure credit goes to those who deserve it. Make sure that the skipper does not take the credit for what others in the crew have done. Be absolutely fair. Make sure that praise reflects the effort involved in achieving something. For example, one should not confine praise just to those whose experience or natural skill makes their task easy. Respond to 'inputs' (formal crew suggestions), even if one later changes the system back to what it was beforehand.

Try to turn around the crew members who are not pulling their weight rather than belittle them. Educate those who are repeatedly not getting something quite right by gentle, light-hearted public ribbing. Discourage in-fighting. Discourage the formation of cliques or elite groups, as otherwise someone will be left at the bottom of the barrel. Even 'couples' can constitute a clique, so do not allow affectionate relationships to become too obvious. Give incentives. For example, at one point I offered to make breakfast if *Group 4* managed to get 15 miles ahead of the rest of the fleet. It worked.

The aim should be to complete the voyage successfully with no serious injuries, and for everyone to leave the boat feeling happy to have been there.

CREW ORGANIZATION

Obviously the skipper must not plan on staying awake for the duration of the voyage; thus there must be a degree of delegation. In a large crew this could mean there are two 'mates' or watchleaders. In a smaller crew there will be just one 'mate'. In any event the mates must know when to call the skipper. Criteria for this will depend entirely upon the circumstances. For example, if the skipper is also the strategist when racing, he will want, if he is like me, to be called if a change in the situation is such that a tactical decision may need to be considered. The criteria will be extended depending upon the experience of the watch-leader. It will tend to include unexpected events and matters that give rise to concern, such as potential collisions. Less experienced sailors will need a full briefing, and one must be careful not to heap greater responsibility upon the watchleader than he or she can shoulder. For example, when taking the family on their first sail one will have to work up from short day passages to Channel crossings. Most experienced skippers will favour a structured crew organization and will delegate tasks to their crew at which they are already good.

Exceptions to this general rule are some professional crews where there seems to be no structure at all. The skipper knows that each of his crew can do any job on the boat competently, and he allows his crew to develop their own pecking order based upon ardour and ability. Those who come out bottom will end up doing the chores, and usually everybody accepts this. Such a method can work well, but if the noisiest and most aggressive get to the top of the heap rather than the best sailors, teamwork suffers and the crew is vulnerable to overheating. The occasional meltdown does, of course, occur.

WATCHKEEPING

It is important to employ one watchkeeping system and to stick to it. *Group 4* used two six-hour watches during the day and three four-hour watches at night. Individuals take turns to be out of the watchkeeping system for a day to be 'mother watch' (ie to act as cook, etc). This makes a nice break in the routine. However, key people such as bowman, helmsman and watchleader remain in place, regardless. Everyone else is in the 'mother watch' pool.

In severe conditions the organization has to be stiffened by a 'storm mother', this being someone selected from the watch system who has the strength, the skill and the stamina to keep the watch on deck going in bad weather.

In normal weather the whole watch on duty should be on deck trimming sails, etc, but in severe weather it is preferable to have some of the watch under cover. On *Group 4* there was a deckhouse 'red light area' where part of the duty watch could rest with their eyes shut, dressed for the prevailing conditions. They were not allowed in the saloon in wet gear. Meanwhile on deck there would be a helmsman, someone on deck beside him and one in the hatchway to act as a communication link.

A rule employed on *Group 4* was that no one could go below from the outgoing watch before everyone was up on deck from the relief watch. This system discouraged late arrivals and gave more time for a proper and detailed turnover.

The watch on deck was encouraged to keep noise down, so that the watch below could sleep without unnecessary interruption.

CLOTHING

For high-latitude work good clothing is essential. The *Group 4* crew mainly used Musto clothing, and it was felt that they were a lot better off with breathable fabric. There were some longevity problems, and the occasional feeling that there were small water molecules knocking about that had achieved the impossible and penetrated the Goretex membrane. The Musto one-piece suits were awesomely good in the Southern Ocean, though one could need help to get into them. As one has little ability to control one's temperature, in warmer latitudes they could become uncomfortably hot.

It was found that the use of cotton clothing spoilt the three-layer system, so the only cotton material on board were the crew shirts worn when entering and leaving harbour. Tactel fibre for underwear not only felt good, but dried quickly after getting wet, or after washing. Silk underwear was comfortable and warm in less extreme conditions and was pleasantly cool in the tropics. An ordinary towel around the neck was considered unnecessary and became just something else that required drying. On the other hand, Polartech scarves did work.

Regarding gloves, three levels of protection were used. Pittard, or ordinary sailing gloves, gave the first degree of protection. Splashdown neoprene gloves gave a second degree of protection and then, in extreme weather conditions, Goretex mountaineers' gloves with huge gauntlets and liners provided the final level. Only four pairs of gauntlets were carried, but everyone had their own liners. It was noticed, incidentally, that the cuticles of one's fingernails go white in cold weather; thus one could see how many legs someone had done in the Southern Ocean without having to ask!

For eye protection from heavy spray, industrial plastic safety goggles provided the best protection. Ski goggles were not so good as they have foam linings that carry water, and consequently they become uncomfortable after a while.

Musto M2 sea boots with liners served well, and were satisfactory for those who do not habitually suffer from cold feet. Leather lined boots were warmer, but were usually too low cut for the Southern Ocean.

Overall, one should emphasize that one can't get away with anything other than high-quality clothing, and the major brand names are the best. Even so, one has to accept that there are times when one is just going to get wet.

Group 4 was equipped with interior heating, and while this was still working it kept the level of condensation down nicely. When it failed, crew comfort was markedly affected and there were failures of electronic equipment. Even when weight considerations are paramount I would always have a heating system fitted. Now that such equipment is readily available there is no point in making life harder than it already is.

Group 4 seen at the start of the 1997 BT Global Challenge. *Photo: Norsk Data*
Inset: Goggles provide good protection against stinging spray and allow a better lookout to be kept. *Photo: Peter Bruce*

FOOD AND DRINK

Mainly dehydrated food was used aboard *Group 4*, and much thought was given to achieving a good vitamin balance. For the Southern Ocean legs, food was chosen for high calorific value; otherwise, good quality hot meals were served, regardless of the weather and climate. It was felt important to create a culture that does not allow anything to deviate from the norm. An enhanced orange juice liquid called Refresh was used to encourage the crew to drink a lot. It could be heated up in cold weather, was high in calorific value, was vitamin C enhanced – *and* tasted good.

SEASICKNESS

Taking a pill in good time can reduce seasickness. The higher the morale, the less inclined people are to be seasick.

WEATHER

Modern weather information is of high quality, so one should tap into all the weather data available. One person from each watch should be designated as the weather watcher and trained to make use of all the facilities. In addition to a navigational log, a wind log was kept since data-logging equipment was banned in the Challenge Race. Entries were instigated by the GPS alarm every 10 minutes. On several occasions, the records made led to tactical gains.

HEAVY WEATHER TACTICS

As weather deteriorates I am big on changing down early, rather than hanging on to the limit with existing sail area. In bad weather one should keep going in the required direction as long as is feasible. If this becomes impossible it is safest to remain under way as long as one can. However, if the weather deteriorates further, one should be aware that it might be necessary to make the decision that the boat must be managed solely with survival in mind, rather than making the destination or doing well in a race. One should also think beyond the storm, to when it is moderating and past.

Be ready to make sail changes at the point when wind and sea conditions require them. When going to windward, little progress will be made until the sail combination is right. Again when racing to windward, head for the centre of the depression where the isobars are closest to obtain the quickest shift in the wind at the earliest moment. In one such instance *Group 4* found herself in the comparatively windless eye of a depression and changed up to her full sail plan to maintain maximum speed. However, on arriving at the edge of the eye of the storm she was knocked flat in the gusts. Rather than try to reduce sail area in such conditions, she was sailed back to within the eye where it was much easier to change back to appropriate storm sails for the conditions outside the eye.

HARBOUR TIME

A good time to have a massive clean up is 24 hours after arrival in harbour. After that, each member of the crew should be given an area of responsibility and will have been nominated to deal with one or other of the defects that will have been recorded on the just-completed leg. On *Group 4* these could be done at any time while the yacht was in harbour. One of the watchleaders was nominated to be 'chaser' to ensure that jobs were being progressed and completed on time. The aim was to achieve a general feeling that the next leg had been won before it had even been started thanks to thorough preparation. For example, sails were inspected inch by inch, sharp points that could tear a sail were ruthlessly eliminated and, rather than taking a large number of spares, equipment was checked over and over and over again. Preparation, above everything, is the key to success.

10 Crew fitness for heavy weather

NOËL DILLY & CATHY FOSTER

Hopefully, one's preparations for heavy weather will have been so appropriate and carried out in such good time that no tremendous exertion will be necessary when it comes on to blow. However, one cannot be sure that this will be so, and it is important that both skipper and crew are at the peak of their physical ability when this is most needed. Seasickness is an obvious cause of unfitness, but lack of sleep and an unsuitable diet can also be relevant.

Before tackling these subjects it should be said that suitable clothing for heavy weather is obviously important. A good oilskin (or foul weather gear if you prefer) is effective up to force 7 or so. If time is spent on deck when the rigging really starts to howl, water soon seems to work its way into the innermost layers, especially if activity is necessary. Cold can become as much of an enemy as the wind.

Mike Golding's remarks on clothing are helpful in Chapter 9. In particular, 'one-piece breathable suits' such as those made by Musto can be a godsend in extreme weather.

SEASICKNESS BY NOËL DILLY

When we stop being self-propelled animals, and step aboard some device that moves, we incur the risk of motion sickness. Some cynics have suggested that this was an evolutionary expedient to inhibit travel and so preserve the purity of the local gene pool. Seasickness or naupathia (from the Greek word ship-suffering) is probably the oldest form of motion sickness recognized by man. From the Argonauts to the astronauts, a surprisingly high number of people have been motion sick. Anyone who has a normal ear is susceptible. This was first discovered when a deaf mute institute took 70 inmates on a cruise and, despite a storm, none of them was seasick.

Although most people adapt rapidly, there are a few who suffer from seasickness all the time that they spend afloat. Children less than two years old are immune, but we are most susceptible between the ages of two and twelve years. It is surprising, to learn that excessively fit exercise freaks are very susceptible to seasickness, but not space sickness.

Although individual subjects differ in their degree of susceptibility, there are also sexual and racial differences. Women, especially during menstruation and pregnancy, are 70 per cent more vulnerable than age-matched men. Asian races, especially the Chinese, get sick more quickly. Seasickness is not unique to humans, as many pet owners have found to their discomfort when taking their animals to sea.

While seasickness is generally not life threatening, it markedly reduces the quality of life. It usually culminates in cyclical nausea and vomiting. Although there is a large psychogenic element in seasickness (ie originating in the mind), one does not have to be conscious to be seasick.

There is no obvious evolutionary explanation for seasickness, so why should the mechanism still exist after millions of years of evolution if it serves no obvious purpose? Motion sickness is the result of activation by an artificial stimulus (unnatural motion) of mechanisms that do have a function (removal of poisons from the stomach). Why should unnatural motion provoke this response? Well, because very tiny doses of poisonous neurotoxins provide just the same disturbance of the signals to the brain from the eyes, the ears and the limbs as does the motion of a boat. The brain interprets these signals as indicating the first signs of an ingested poison, and one vomits to get rid of the poison! The accompanying nausea might also serve as a reminder to the individual to avoid such poisons in the future.

Much research has been done on the causes of seasickness. The most accepted theory is the sensory mismatch hypothesis, which holds that the brain is confused by conflicting information from the eyes, ears and the body's other position indications. The sensory inputs to the brain do not conform to the expected pattern. For example, the eyes looking at the chart are telling the brain that the chart is still, but the ears are telling the brain that the boat is moving about. Ultimately the interactions between the brain, the gut and increasing nausea activates what is loosely described as a vomiting centre in the brain, and afterwards one feels temporarily better until the cycle is repeated.

Fear also plays a role. Many studies have shown that there is increased activity in the 'fight and flight' part of the nervous system associated with vomiting.

Feeling nauseated is often associated with a specific activity like cooking, navigating or getting dressed into foul weather gear. When watching out for the condition in others there are several signs, apart from the victim becoming pale. Sometimes they sweat profusely, yawn and cough. They withdraw from the general activity and become listless and apathetic.

What about treatment?
Strategy – prevention is the aim of the game
The simplest and the most effective approach for the vast majority of sailors is to frequently, but slowly, increase exposure to the motion that produces sickness. While pushing the limits of each exposure there is good evidence to suggest that the best technique is to lie in the supine position (face upwards with only a thin pillow). The head should be lodged still, with other pillows, and the eyes closed. This will increase the time before the onset of nausea. Before one takes these extreme measures, some people manage to survive by looking at a fixed point on the distant horizon. Keeping the axis of vision at an angle of 45° above the horizon will reduce the receptor stimulation. Reading should be avoided.

A well-ventilated cabin is important, and going out on deck for a breath of fresh air is helpful. It is advisable to avoid alcoholic or dietary excesses before or during sailing. Small amounts of fluids and simple foods should be taken frequently during extended periods of exposure.

Despite the conventional wisdom of not eating before exposure, there is good scientific evidence that food may suppress seasickness; a light meal comprised mainly of carbohydrates is beneficial to many.

Non-drug treatment
Ginger
Ginger has been cultivated for so long that the plant is unknown in the wild state. The spice ginger has a very good reputation as a seasickness remedy, and two major scientific studies have found it to be superior to a placebo (pretend pill). It has also been used with success in treating both post-operative nausea and sickness following radiotherapy. But a study of its effectiveness in controlling space sickness in astronauts found no benefits.

Taking in reefs as it begins to blow up requires good foul weather gear and a sound stomach. *Photo: Peter Bruce*

The Chinese recommend a dose of about 1g taken at least half an hour before travelling. Some Chinese crews chew little pieces of ginger root continuously until they acclimatize. Western experiments suggest a smaller dose, somewhere between one-third to one-fifth of a teaspoon of dried ginger (up to $\frac{1}{2}$g), is appropriate. At this dosage, six gingersnap biscuits or a pint of ginger ale (not fizzy ginger beer) might just provide an adequate dose. Since ginger has few if any side effects, the dose can be repeated whenever necessary.

Alternative remedies

Alternative treatments such as acupressure bands applied at the wrist over the P6 or Nei Knan acupuncture point seem to work for some people. Although there is a lack of scientific evidence regarding their effectiveness, it has been shown that any treatment is better than nothing.

Other simple remedies, such as sugary sports drinks (Gatorade, Lucozade) and warm tea can be remarkably effective.

Drug treatment

Motion sickness is more easily prevented than cured. Whatever drug is chosen, the timing of the doses is a key factor in the efficacy of the treatment. Starting the treatment 8 to 12 hours before sailing produces a more successful outcome than starting once the symptoms begin.

There are a bewildering array of remedies on the market, suggesting that no single drug works for everybody, and that once one has found one that works one should not bother to change. The table below lists some common ones. The drugs can basically be divided into two groups: first, the short-acting ones such as hyoscine, therefore the drug of choice for a Channel dash; and second, the longer-acting ones such as meclozine and promethazine, which are suitable for cruises requiring several consecutive days at sea. Before starting a cruise, longer-acting drugs have to be taken earlier than the short-acting alternatives.

Non-proprietary name	Proprietary name (amount of drug in each tablet)	Oral dose (No of doses per day)	Remarks
Meclozine	Ancolan (Australia) Bonamine (Canada and Germany) Sea-Legs (UK) (25mg)	50mg (1)	Low incidence of side effects. May cause sleepiness, good for prolonged treatment. You can even start taking it the night before you set off.
Promethazine hydrochloride	Phenergan (universal name) (25mg)	25mg (1–3)	Best taken in evening. Sleepiness fairly common. The 'knockout drop' also comes as a sugar-free syrup, very useful for children. It is also available for injection for treatment of the long-term hopelessly seasick.
Promethazine theoclate	Avomine (UK and Australia) (25mg)	25mg (1–3)	Probably the same as promethazine hydrochloride.
Diphenhydramine	Benadryl (UK) (25mg)	50–100mg (3)	May cause sleepiness and more effective as an antihistamine than when used for motion sickness.
Cyclizine	Marzine (France, Italy and Germany, Marezine in USA) (50mg)	50mg (3)	Low incidence of side effects. Good for prolonged treatment. No longer obtainable in UK due to hallucinatory properties.
Hyoscine (hyoscine hydrobromide)	Hyoscine is universal name but also Kwells (UK and Australia) Sereen tabs (UK) Travacalm (with antihistamine mixed in; Boots, UK) (0.3mg)	0.6mg (3)	Useful in single doses for short journeys. Side effects too troublesome for prolonged use. Its great advantage is that it starts working within half an hour and will be absorbed if sucked. Skin patches are also available (Scopoderm).
Dimenhydrinate	Dramamine (universal name) (50mg)	50–100mg (3)	Medium term of action, about six to eight hours. Does cause sleepiness.
Cinnarizine	Stugeron (universal name) (15 mg)	30mg (3)	Medium action. Pleasant tasting and may be sucked or chewed. Many people find it very effective.

The *Card* power reaching under No 3 genoa and reefed mainsail in 55 knots (true) in the south Atlantic. At this stage, most sufferers have overcome sea-sickness.
Photo: Rick Tomlinson

If your particular favourite is not on this list, do not worry. If it works, stick with it. We know that the actual act of *treating* seasickness will cure 30 per cent of sufferers even if the treatment itself is apparently useless. Whatever drug is used it is important not to exceed the stated doses and to tell someone what you are taking. If you have worked through most of this list without success, then it is probably worthwhile trying one of the sedating anti-histamines like Phenergan.

The most effective (in controlled trials) over-the-counter medication is the antihistamine Dramamine (dimenhydrinate).

Experiments suggest that the most effective treatment is a combined therapy using scopo-lamine (hyoscine) plus dexamphetamine, or the antihistamine promethazine plus ephedrine. However, since some of these drugs have been abused, prescriptions for these combinations are almost impossible to obtain.

Of the easily available drugs, scopolamine, which has been used for treating motion sick-ness since the 1940s and as a hallucinogen for centuries, is likely to be the best choice. The active ingredient is hyoscine. The major disadvantage of this drug is its side effects. In lower doses they include drowsiness and dry mouth, and higher doses produce profound side effects, such as hallucinations. It also has some unpleasant interactions with alcohol.

For the really determined sufferer it is often effective to use a sedative such as diazepam as an adjunct to the seasickness remedy. In the USA, some people advocate Prozac!

After nausea has begun

The 'skin patch' preparation of hyoscine 'Scopoderm' forms the mainstay of treatment after the symptoms have started. They are the ideal means of delivering a quick-acting remedy to vomiting sufferers. The drug acts rapidly. It is absorbed through the skin and is an easy alternative to taking the drugs by mouth. However, the manufacturers are having problems with crystallization of the drug, and it was withdrawn temporarily in the UK.

The other potential treatments are with suppositories or, more elaborately, by injection, neither of which are attractive, but do work in emergency situations. After two or three days, an attempt should be made to stop any medication by slowly reducing the frequency and amount of the drug taken. Most drugs of prevention have side effects, which include the hazards of sleepiness, blurred vision and a dry mouth.

Managing a seasick crew

A seasick person on deck must be wearing a harness and be clipped on. The greatest danger of seasickness is falling overboard while vomiting.

Management really has two phases. Managing someone who feels nauseous, and then managing someone who has vomited.

If the victims are just feeling queasy, they can often still be valuable members of the crew, and the age-old, but extremely effective, treatment of getting them to take the helm works. When these people go off watch, try to place them in an amidships berth. Although many sufferers will object and be macho, it is a good idea to help them take off their foulies and assist them into the berth, doing things like fixing the lee cloths for them.

Those who have vomited usually fall into two groups: the remarkable-recovery lot, and the moribund. The rapid recoverers can be treated like the first group. However, the low self-esteem, loss of morale and near-suicidal feelings of the major sufferer have to be experienced to be believed. They cannot just be left in the cockpit. The risks of falling overboard, hypothermia, dehydration and other serious problems make it essential that they are taken below.

You will have to undress them, zip them into a warm sleeping bag, give them a bucket, a handful of tissues, and a bottle of water. Better than plain water during seasickness or dehydration recovery is an isotonic solution. This fluid mimics the salinity of the human body and is therefore more rapidly absorbed. For example, the World Health Organization produces a sachet which, when mixed with water, is called a 'WHO solution'. Many other brands are available such as Dioralyte in the UK, Gastrolyte in Australia.

It is suggested that sufferers lie flat with their eyes closed. A child's spill-proof mug is an effective way of serving drinks. However, one has to look at the overall picture when treating these people. They need to be cosseted and protected, but they are useless. Remember that someone must sail the yacht, and useless seasick crew should not monopolize the best berths. The hard workers need these berths to maintain optimum rest off watch.

If during a long passage you do become acclimatized, do not gloat just yet. There is a form of seasickness associated with returning to the land after a long voyage – mal de débarquement. Treatment is identical, and a quick cure is to go back to sea.

One should remember that recovery takes place rapidly on arrival in harbour. Several children owe their existence to seasickness having brought about the removal of several doses of the contraceptive pill!

Even if someone has overcome seasickness, a storm at sea can make enormous demands upon one's vitality. Cathy Foster now gives advice drawn from the racing world on how to optimize one's physical and mental energy.

SLEEP AND DIET MANAGEMENT BY CATHY FOSTER

Sleep

As all offshore sailors know, the symptoms of lack of sleep are: a slowdown in reaction times, lack of alertness, a lessening in the ability to see well, moodiness, and a reduction in intellectual performance. Moreover, when extremely tired, very convincing hallucinations are common.

Knowledge gained from the racing sphere can be readily adapted for use in extended bad weather. The French have done the most research into sleep deprivation, using either solo, shorthanded or multi-crewed offshore races of varying lengths over the last six years such as the Figaro, the BT Challenge Round the World Race and the Jules Verne Trophy. Their research, which has led to sailors competing with electrodes on their heads to read their brain activity and monitor their sleep patterns both while racing and during their recovery onshore, has come up with some interesting facts. Dr Jean-Yves Chauve, the doctor most involved in the French offshore scene, used this electronic gadgetry when he found that individuals are unable to reliably self-monitor either the amount of sleep gained or the quality of it.

Jean-Yves Chauve reports that solo sailors in the Figaro (made up of 4 to 5 races, each one lasting 3 to 5 days) can adapt to get all the necessary recuperative sleep required in short periods, often around 20 minutes, followed by spontaneous waking without an alarm. In this situation the need to be on the lookout for change or disaster is the primary motivation. By using relaxation techniques they can train to get to sleep quickly, so that only 1 to 1½ minutes of the 20-minute period is lost in trying to get to sleep. Sufficient body warmth and food is also critical in getting to sleep quickly.

If the conditions are not imminently dangerous, Jean-Yves Chauve has found that many sailors work best with sleep periods totalling around 6 hours a day. Various sailors have found that 2 sleep periods of around 3 hours each seem to be natural in a day, starting around 2 pm and 2 am. Each person is different and, if aware enough, they can identify their preferred activity times, which can be added into any rest pattern calculation – the simplest example of this being those who prefer to be 'early birds' as opposed to 'night owls'. Some people can work for extended periods of time at a high performance level on cat-naps (10 to 20-minute rests) before collapsing; others need regular sleep periods. In the end the best system depends on each sailor's ability to relax and the clever choice of the length of sleep deprivation relating to the psychological and/or performance needs of the moment, as well as the awareness of potential danger when switching off to sleep.

Synchronizing the biological clock to circadian (day and night) rhythms has proved very important. This is especially so during the second half of the night when not only does the sailor become less alert as a result of various biological functions that only operate at this time, but also because the temperature of the body reduces. An interesting fact is that 65 per cent of major catastrophes happen between midnight and 6 am.

In order to reduce breakage and injuries, sailors in the Figaro, the British Steel Challenge and the Vendée Globe learnt to plan ahead, making critical manoeuvres and decisions in the 'day' time whenever possible.

Because offshore sailing is a 24-hour activity, it is important to be as alert as possible during the night. Aboard *Commodore Explorer*, the 80ft (24m) catamaran that was first to sail around the world in under 80 days, the crew operated a watch system matched as much as possible to circadian and personal rhythms. The watches were calculated on a 23-hour day to take account of the boat sailing fast and gaining on the sun. Since being 'off watch' also includes eating, socializing and dressing and undressing time, care had to be taken to build in enough time to sleep. They tried to stick to a system whereby the first half of the sleep period was not disturbed except in dire emergencies – only the second half could be upset for performance sail changes, etc. As a result, the crew had few physical accidents or social problems.

In fully crewed 3 to 5-day races, such a structured approach is not possible because the body cannot adapt quickly enough to any watch system or because the crew are sleeping on the rail for performance reasons. To reduce the risk of damage or disaster, many prudent skippers insist on the crew taking their regular inshore racing positions for manoeuvres at night, especially during gybes, since a sleepy body is more likely to react correctly instinctively in a familiar role. However, the research highlights the importance of making sure that the decision-makers get enough quality sleep to stay alert under duress, especially in the middle of the night when core body temperatures are at their lowest.

Under normal circumstances the human body is very responsive to changes in the environment. For instance, 'night' will always tend to relate to when the sky is dark. The timing of 'day' and 'night' can be moved, but the body needs time and a regular pattern to adapt to new timing. For example, it seems to take about 3 days to settle into a watch system.

Working hard whilst taking seas 'green' over the bow needs carbohydrates. *Photo: Rick Tomlinson*

However, once the pattern is set it should remain. Attempts to alternate the 2 to 6 am watch by adopting a system moving progressively forward will leave everyone suffering from permanent 'jet lag'. The symptoms are headaches, loss of appetite, irregularities in bowel movement, poor concentration, fatigue during the new day time, and yet an inability to sleep properly at night. They are caused by the mismatch between the body clock running on the 'old' time and the new environment with new time cues, such as differences of sunrise and sunset, light intensity, and day and night temperature changes within each watch period. It has been found that attempting to adopt a new sleep pattern before a race has not worked since the body when sailing will respond to environmental cues that do not exist onshore; moreover, the adrenaline accompanying the start is enough to upset all sleep patterns.

Fitness
The fitter the crew is, the more they will be able to endure sleep deprivation. The blood circulation also gets sluggish with the long hours of holding one position. Latest research indicates that the ability to endure depends on keeping up carbohydrate stores in the body. Unfit people will rely strongly on working anaerobically at an earlier stage in a race, which eats up energy sources derived from carbohydrates, whereas fit people will consume their fat energy stores first, since they will be working aerobically until fatigue sets in. Additionally, being fitter will bring quicker recovery when the boat finally gets to the dock.

The body also needs to be in balance with itself before the start – well rested and not coping with alcohol poisoning. There is nothing worse than starting a long race with a hangover. In addition, frenetic running around getting the boat ready on the morning of the big race, or working all hours in the office until the last minute, will mean that the body is not fully rested. The top crews will go to the pre-race parties, but not to all of them, and they'll be back and in bed before the early hours of the morning.

Alcohol, caffeine and smoking all inhibit the ability to get good sleep. Alcohol and caffeine together are especially likely to reduce the amount of sleep each night, although personal addictions may override any attempt to stick to the theory. The solo sailors tend to stay off caffeine and alcohol for 6–9 months prior to a major race in order to get the maximum effect from one dose in emergencies.

Mood changes

Mood changes are another effect of sleep deprivation. There is a marked tendency to focus only on personal needs. This seems to transfer into feelings of martyrdom, boredom if not feeling involved, and insecurity in crew members who are either new or uncertain as to their continued future with the boat. 'Showing off' can be the result. In addition, most people become intolerant of their fellow crew members, which shows up in edginess, sarcasm, resentment, temper loss and a more defined sense of 'territory' on board.

Getting to sleep

When conditions are tough it will be important to grab whatever sleep is possible. Yet some people find it very difficult to sleep offshore. It can be the boat's motion, the noise, or thoughts that go round and round. What's happening on deck? Will I roll off the bunk if I sleep? When will I ever be warm again? I'm on my own – what if a ship doesn't see me and I'm asleep?

It is important to stop taking responsibility when off duty and to trust the crew sailing the boat to do the job. Obviously yacht skippers find this very difficult. It must be made clear to those on watch that those off watch should not be disturbed by small issues that should be sorted out by the crew on watch. Trust is an important issue.

Sleepers must ensure that they are physically constrained from falling about by using the lee cloths, and it is worth mentioning that it is best not to sleep on deck because the deck is uncomfortable, one can roll off, or be in the way if the wind changes.

But getting to sleep as soon as possible needs more than immobility, comfort and trust; it is necessary also to turn off the mind. This can best be achieved by taking control of one's breathing in the manner used for relaxation exercises. The benefits of such techniques come with practice.

Incidentally, one of the technical achievements of recent years has been the development of thermal sleeping bags (obtainable from mountaineering shops) which, when combined with body heat, allow damp bodies and clothes to dry out.

Diet

There is plenty of sport science research to prove that personal output in terms of performance (mental as well as physical) is only as good as dietary input, and there are numerous stories told about offshore food disasters.

The prime requirement is a balanced menu with bland seasonings, since most people cannot tolerate strong flavours offshore. A balanced diet should contain carbohydrates, protein, roughage (essential for healthy bowel movement), fats, minerals and vitamins, especially vitamin C. Clearly, the nationality of a crew will influence the choice of menu since the 'comfort giving' element of food is a consideration as well as its nutritional value, and crews like to eat what is familiar to them. However, thought does need to be given to another factor – the performance-enhancing side to nutrition.

Carbohydrates, ie sugars, cereals, wheat products, beans, bananas, rice and pasta, are essential to increase and sustain energy resources. Recent research indicates that carbohydrate depletion leads to mood changes, making people irritable and lethargic. The brain's analytical capability also lessens, which affects, for example, one's decision-making ability. To counteract these effects carbohydrates must form a major part of a ship's diet. Another less obvious aid to performance is that of taking electrolytes suspended in liquid to replace essential salts lost through sweat in hot weather.

In the colder climates, one hot meal every 24 hours and facilities for frequent hot drinks will add to the morale of the crew while maintaining a warm core body temperature.

Liquid is very important to prevent under-performance through dehydration, both physically and mentally, so plenty of water should be consumed. For optimum performance, urine should remain the colour of pale straw; dark yellow indicates an insufficient liquid intake.

11 Handling motor yachts in heavy weather

DAG PIKE

In very rough conditions, planing boats need to come down to displacement speeds, so initially methods of handling boats at speeds of below 10 knots will be covered. While the displacement hull is primarily built to operate at these speeds, the planing boat is very definitely not, so in a later section the particular problems of handling planing vessels at slow speeds in stormy seas will be discussed.

Rough seas are considered to be those in which the throttles cannot be left set and the boat left to take its course. Instead, speed has to be reduced or throttles operated continuously to negotiate the boat through the waves. Much depends on the size and construction of the vessel as to what will constitute rough seas, but in general these will be seas generated by winds of force 6 and upwards.

DISPLACEMENT CRAFT

Head seas

A displacement boat works in a comparatively small speed range. When operating in a head sea the main thing to do is find a speed at which the boat runs comfortably. Provided the boat is strongly built it is possible to find a speed even in quite rough seas where the boat will lift over the wave and drop down the other side without too much discomfort to the craft or the crew. Matching the speed to the conditions is the secret of operating in head seas, provided the waves have a normal gradient and a wavelength that allows the boat to operate without any undue change in attitude. When a displacement boat is driven hard into a head sea, the bow will lift to the wave and then become unsupported as the wave crest passes aft. In this situation, the bow will drop to restore equilibrium before lifting once more to the next wave. The problems start in a short, steep sea when the bow may not have time to lift to the next wave, particularly as the stern will still be raised under the influence of the wave that has just passed. A slower speed will give the boat more time to adjust to the changing wave profile and will thus help to make the motion easier. In a boat with a fine bow there is a greater risk of the bow burying into a head sea because it has less buoyancy.

If the vessel is driven too hard in a head sea, then there is a real danger of a wave breaking on board as the bow is forced through, rather than over, a wave. Water has surprising weight, and with solid water breaking on board in this way there is a risk of structural damage. In this situation, the most vulnerable parts of the boat are the wheelhouse windows. Although I have never experienced them breaking, despite seeing tons of water crashing down on many occasions, others report this experience.

When trying to find a comfortable speed for operating in particular conditions, it is important to ensure that sufficient speed is maintained to give steerage way. At a slow speed the response of the helm will be slower and the bow could fall quite a way off course before the corrective action on the rudder starts to take effect. If, at this time, a wave should rise and strike against the weather bow, then the slow rudder response could mean that the boat will be knocked round, beam-on to the sea, before the corrective action is effective. In this situation, opening the throttles is one way to get a fairly immediate improvement in control, and this can bring the boat back on course quickly without any rapid increase in velocity. The safe minimum speed to maintain steerage way will vary from boat to boat, but it is unlikely to be less than 3 knots and will be more with craft that have small rudders. The risk of being knocked off course is greatest with a breaking wave where the water is actually travelling towards the boat as this exerts a considerable force on the bow.

If the sea conditions reach the point where the boat has to be forced hard in order to maintain steerage way in deteriorating conditions, then the time has come to start nursing the boat over the waves. This is when the throttle can be used to good effect. By opening the throttle as the wave approaches, the bow of the boat will lift and a burst of engine power will also improve the steering effect. As the bow lifts to the wave, the throttle should be eased off before the bow punches through the crest. Easing the throttle will cause the bow to drop slightly, thus reducing the tendency for it to fall heavily into the trough. As the next wave approaches one has to be ready to open the throttle again.

By using this throttling technique, reasonably comfortable progress can be made to windward. More control will be felt and one will be well prepared if a larger than normal wave comes along. However, this type of operation does require considerable concentration because there is always the risk of being caught out of step by the irregularity of the waves and, of course, for that larger-than-normal wave.

Beam seas

Running with the wind and sea on the beam in moderate seas has the disadvantage of discomfort, due to the heavy rolling that is likely to occur. In these conditions, full speed can generally be used on a displacement boat without any real problems arising because the boat is lifting bodily on the waves, and the bow and stern have little movement in relation to each other. However, occasionally the boat drops off the edge of a fairly steep wave front and that can be both uncomfortable and a little frightening so, as the beam seas start to get rougher, more care has to be taken.

Running with the sea on the beam exposes a large area of boat to the approaching waves and in stormy seas this can make the craft vulnerable. The transition from what is an uncomfortable beam sea to a dangerous one will depend a great deal on the type and characteristics of the craft, but once the waves have started to break then, again, more care has to be taken.

There are two main problems with beam seas. First, as the waves become steeper, the boat will try to adjust to the tilted surface of the sea and, consequently, will heel to quite a large angle. This in itself is not too serious, provided the range of stability of the boat is adequate, but it has to be remembered that the wind will also be pressing on the windward side of the boat, tending to increase the angle of the heel. The second problem is more serious and occurs when breaking waves are encountered. When the surface of the water is moving bodily to leeward it can exert very great pressures on the windward side of the vessel. The pressures are resisted by the still water on the lee side which produces a turning moment that could develop to the point where the boat will capsize. In these conditions there is the risk of seas breaking on board, because many displacement boats have reduced freeboard amidships. These breaking seas could fill a cockpit or other deck openings which makes the predicament worse, so that there will come a time when operating in a beam sea is not the optimum way to go.

The distressed fishing boat *Lynnmore* 'dodging' in seas described as 40–50ft (12–15m) high, accompanied by a mean wind speed of 60–65 knots. The term 'dodging' entails keeping a vessel's bows into the seas, using only the minimum of power to maintain steerage way, and is the fisherman's preferred storm tactic.
Photo: Kieran Murray

Fortunately, a wave rarely breaks along a long front, but tends to do so in patches so that, with anticipation, it is possible to avoid breaking waves in beam seas. This means watching the sea ahead carefully and anticipating which part of the wave crest is going to break, and then either reducing speed to let the wave break in front of the boat, or turning into or away from the wind to pass behind or in front of the breaking crest. Even in moderate breaking seas, life can be made a lot more comfortable on board by this method of avoiding the largest of the waves and steering round the unfriendlier-looking crests. In moderate seas there is not too much to worry about if things go wrong, but once the seas start to break then the stakes become higher and one has to be much more cautious.

If, in a beam sea, a situation occurs where a wave that is about to break is bearing down on the boat and it is too late to reduce speed, then there are three options. The course can be maintained, hoping that the boat will cope, one can head into the wave, or bear away from it. A lot will depend on the type and capabilities of the boat, but the best action would normally be to turn away from the wave, because this has the advantage of buying time and it will also reduce the impact of the wave on the boat which is then moving away from it. The breaking crest often rolls only a limited way to leeward and one can escape the breaking water altogether by this action. If it is decided to turn away from a breaking wave in this fashion, then the throttles should be opened wide, both to get the maximum steering effect and to keep the distance from the breaking crest as large as possible. If the opposite course of action is chosen and one heads into the wave, then reducing speed will probably be necessary to reduce the impact of the wave.

A point to notice when running in a beam sea is that one often sees the waves approaching on the quarter starting to break. You may think yourself very lucky that you keep missing these breaking waves, but they are, in fact, caused by the wash of the boat combining with the approaching wave to create an unstable wave which consequently breaks when otherwise it would not have done so. Such seas seem to have little force in them.

Following seas

Running before a heavy following sea has the reputation of being the seaman's nightmare, conjuring up visions of broaching, capsizing or being swamped. Much of this fear stems from sailing boats, where running before a sea may be the only option left under extreme conditions. There is no doubt that running before a following sea has its dangers, but provided they are recognized, they can be compensated for and the dangers can be minimized.

At first glance, it would appear that running before a sea and travelling in the same direction as the wind and sea would be a far safer course to take than battling against the waves. However, a boat is controlled by the rudder and it needs a good flow of water to be effective. If the water flow is reduced or even reversed because of an overtaking breaking wave, then there will be much less control of the craft, or control could be lost altogether, and it is this factor that presents the major hazard in a following sea. An average open sea wave will be travelling at somewhere between two and three times the speed of the average displacement boat, so it will take some time to pass on to the boat.

When the crest of the wave is approaching the stern, this face of the wave is the steepest part and the bow will be pointing downwards towards the trough. In this position, gravity will exert a downward pull on the boat, combining with the thrust from the propeller into an increased forward motion down the slope. Similarly, when the boat is on the back of the wave with the bow pointing upwards, it is, to all intents and purposes, going uphill and the speed will be correspondingly reduced. These involuntary increases and decreases in speed can be controlled to a degree by opening and closing the throttle as the circumstances dictate, and unless the waves are breaking it should be possible to retain adequate control over the boat.

The Weymouth lifeboat almost submerged by a breaking sea while undergoing trials off Portland Bill.
Photo: HMS *Osprey*

In a breaking wave, the surface water is moving forwards in the direction of travel of the wave at a speed slightly in excess of the speed of the wave. This forward movement of the breaking crest is transient, starting as the wave crest becomes unstable and ending when the wave has reached stability again. The behaviour of a boat in a breaking following sea will depend, to a certain extent, on the position of the boat in relation to the crest as it breaks and on the design of the vessel itself. If the wave rises up and starts to break immediately astern of the boat, then there is a real danger that the breaking crest will fall onto the craft. This is more likely to be a problem with the type of heavy breaking wave found when waves approach shallow water, rather than the open sea breaking wave which tends to have a more rolling type of crest.

One thing in favour of the boat at this stage is that the downward angle of the boat on the forward surface of the wave will help to increase the speed of the craft, and might even enable it to accelerate away sufficiently to escape the breaking crest. If not, the crest, in falling, will accelerate and take the boat with it, which will also help to increase the momentum, particularly if the boat has a large transom stern which faces the oncoming rush of water. With a double-ended boat, also known as canoe stern, the theory is that the pointed stern divides the oncoming water and allows it to pass safely along each side of the boat.

A craft that is accelerating under the combined influences of the rush of breaking water at the stern and the downward slope of the face of the wave would probably be all right if the boat could just keep accelerating in this way. However, as the stern is lifted by the rush of water the time comes when the bow of the boat starts to bury into the next wave ahead. This means that the bow starts to act as a pivot and also starts to put up considerable resistance to the forward rush. It is at this point that the risk of broaching occurs, with the bow trying to stop and the stern trying to swing to one side or the other under the influence of the rush of water. This strong turning effect can turn the boat broadside-on in the classical broaching situation. Once broadside-on the sea the turning moment reduces, but is then replaced by a capsizing moment similar to that which can be found in a beam sea. Even if the boat escapes this particular situation, it could well find itself vulnerable to the next wave that comes along, because it is unlikely that it will have recovered in time and achieved the steerage way necessary to cope with the situation.

A deep-draft vessel with its rudder well immersed should still retain steerage control in this following breaking sea situation, whereas the shallow-draft boat could be much more vulnerable. The hull design of the boat also has a bearing on its behaviour, and a boat with a sharply angled forefoot is likely to create a pivot point more readily than one with a cut-away forefoot. A transom stern also makes the boat more vulnerable.

Found in this situation with a breaking wave approaching at the stern, there is not a great deal that can be done, other than try to keep the boat absolutely square on to the sea for as long as possible. This will demand concentration and hard work with the steering wheel, although the rudder could become virtually ineffective in these conditions. As a general rule, the throttle should be opened as wide as possible to try to run from the breaking wave or at least reduce its impact, and to retain steerage control for as long as possible. This will also have the effect of lifting the bow to a certain extent and it will also help to reduce the impact of the wave at the stern.

When running before a following sea that may be large, but is not breaking, full throttle should be used to maintain steering control. One should try to keep pace with the waves as far as possible. In these conditions it may be noticed that the waves astern are starting to break, but this is again usually the influence of the wash of the boat combining with the crest which causes it to break. This can be a significant problem when crossing a harbour bar in a following sea, and I have seen quite harmless-looking waves suddenly rear up astern in this situation. It seems that the extra disturbance caused by the progress of the boat is enough to turn the waves into an unstable form, although in theory these breaking waves that are assisted by the wash should not cause any problems, even though they present a frightening picture when looking astern.

When running in front of a moderate following sea that is not breaking, there can still be a considerable change in the trim of the craft as a wave passes underneath. In this case the change in angle is more noticeable than in a head sea because the wave takes longer to pass under the vessel, giving it longer to adapt to the angles of the different faces of the waves. When the crest of the wave is passing underneath, the boat suddenly feels rather unstable. This is due to the fact that because the boat is only supported amidships, rather than over its whole length, her stability is considerably reduced at this point. This is a fairly transient situation and stability is rapidly restored as the wave passes, but if running at a speed close to that of the wave, this period of instability could last for longer, and it might be sensible to consider reducing speed to allow the wave crest to pass more quickly and thus reduce the periods of instability.

One problem found on many boats when operating in a following sea is that the visibility astern is not as good as it might be. It helps a great deal to have a good view astern and on each quarter as well, but many boats lack this facility.

With a well-found vessel, running before a heavy following sea can be a very exciting experience. I have travelled down the Irish Sea in a 48ft (14.5m) lifeboat on a wild night when the wind was blowing up to force 10. The first hour or two were quite frightening while we became used to the conditions, but once we had gained confidence that the boat was adequate for the job, we could revel in the excitement of rushing like an express train down the face of a wave, or so it seemed, and then watching out through the windows in the top of the wheelhouse, for the next wave approaching from astern. I think an unnecessary dread of following seas has been built up among the small-boat fraternity, but one needs a sound boat before taking chances in a following sea, or indeed in any rough sea.

In conditions where the sea is starting to become rough when running before it, a quite dangerous situation can build up because one is unaware of just how bad things are getting and because, to a certain extent, the boat is running in harmony with the sea. The lack of impact of the waves in a following sea can lull one into a false sense of security. Thus it is a sensible precaution to stop every now and again, turn round, and head into the sea, just to see what conditions are really like. It might be frightening to realize just how the waves are building up, but it is better to be frightened in this way than to be caught out unawares.

PLANING BOATS

If operating a planing boat at displacement speed, then one is more vulnerable than one would be in a displacement boat in the same conditions. There are two reasons for this. First, if one is at the point where one has to slow down to displacement speeds in a planing vessel, then conditions are probably becoming quite bad anyway and, second, a planing boat is not running at its optimum at displacement speeds, either in terms of hull shape or in terms of control.

From the point of view of hull shape, planing boats tend to have fine bows and full sterns, which is not usually a happy combination in rough seas. At the bow there can be a lack of freeboard if the boat has a reverse sheer. This, combined with a fine bow, gives a lack of buoyancy in this area which can mean that the bow buries readily into both a head sea and a following sea. The craft is also much lighter and probably more affected by wind, so that it may be more difficult to maintain steerage way at low speeds in a planing boat because the bow will tend to fly off to one side or the other. This situation will be exaggerated because the rudders are always smaller and are therefore less effective at slow speeds, although on vessels fitted with outboards or stern drives, where the propeller thrust is used for steering, good steering can usually be maintained at low speeds.

A delicate hand will be needed on the throttles at displacement speeds because a small movement of the throttle can produce quite a large variation in the speed. However, one can use this to good effect when needed to nurse the boat through the waves, and one will probably use the throttle a lot more on this type of boat, short bursts on the throttle being used to help maintain heading and to help lift the bow to approaching waves.

The tactics of operating a planing boat in rough conditions can often mean that rather than reducing speed when operating in a head sea, one should look for an alternative heading for the boat on which it can still be operated at higher speeds. For instance, whereas a planing vessel may well have to slow right down in a head sea, it can still maintain good speed in beam seas or in following seas particularly, and this could well be a safer course to take, rather than running the boat at displacement speeds on the original course. Much will depend on the destination and what the options are. High speed in a following sea will often be safer than for a displacement boat operating in the same conditions because the high speed allows the helmsman to dictate his position with respect to the waves.

Most long-distance cruisers are of the displacement type because this is where fuel economy for long distances is achieved. However, an increasing number of semi-displacement long-distance cruisers are appearing, most of them trawler yachts of one type or another, but some planing, deep-V boats are able to achieve respectable ranges for cruising. The big difference between these types and displacement hulls is the influence of the dynamic stability on the performance. The dynamics created by the forward motion help to stabilize the hull at speed, but one will also notice a much greater response to the throttle, not only in the speed of the hull, but in its trim angle. This change in trim angle can be used to good effect to help progress in rough seas and it can even be effective at quite low speeds, down to those found on displacement hulls.

Indeed, it would be fair to say that the primary means of control in semi-displacement and planing hulls is the throttle. By varying the propeller thrust with the throttle one has the ability to raise or lower the bow, but the throttle also has a vital role to play in the speed at which one impacts with approaching waves. This speed of approach, to a certain extent, determines whether the boat will fly off the top of a wave or not. Although it looks photographically spectacular when a boat does this, it is not an efficient means of progress, because every time the boat flies or even partially flies off a wave the propeller is losing effect but, more importantly, it puts an enormous stress on the boat, the machinery and the crew. When we were setting a record round Britain a few years ago in a 50ft (15m) deep-V, we made it a rule that the hull should never leave the water. In this way we felt we might be able to cope with standing up in a fast boat for 44 hours.

Few cruising yachts are likely to attempt such heroics, but the same rule applies. If one does hit bad weather, particularly head seas, then careful throttle control is vital to give the boat as gentle a ride as possible, but this doesn't necessarily mean that one has to come down to displacement speeds. In many cases the bow should be kept up to reduce the chance of water coming over the foredeck, and accordingly, one can use the change of trim that usually occurs at around 12–15 knots, when the hull tries to climb over its own bow wave, to keep the bow up.

Unless the sea gets too rough, it is possible with a deep-V hull to get it up and running so that it stays virtually at a level trim despite the impact of the waves which try to upset the trim. Much will depend on the wave size, but if the boat is trimmed properly she can run virtually across the top of the waves with the control of the attitude of the boat being exercised solely by the use of the throttle. The biggest problem with this is actually getting the vessel up into this situation, and it does mean that one may have to negotiate several waves rather uncomfortably as the boat builds up speed, and then levels out as she starts to move at high speed.

Getting a craft trimmed in this way is a real joy and the boat really sings as she flies along. It requires careful setting up, using the power trim, the flaps and then, finally, the throttle to keep the balance, as passing waves have varying influences on the hull. When one has a boat up and running in this way, it is possible to make very rapid progress to windward even though the waves can be quite large. However, it does require some degree of courage to take the bull by the horns and get the boat up into this situation.

It is not just a technique for use on sports cruisers. When I was delivering the world's first large deep-V hull from Britain to Greece we managed to get it up and running in this way when the Mistral started to kick up a nasty sea in the Mediterranean. The boat was an 85ft (26m) patrol boat for the Greek Navy, and the choices were to wallow at displacement speeds for a long night at sea, or try the high speed technique to make harbour in a couple of hours in the rapidly freshening wind. This is probably a technique to use when running for shelter rather than when general cruising. It needs a strong boat and it is not likely to be effective on semi-displacement craft.

When running like this, concentration is needed because there is always the risk that a bigger wave than normal will come along and upset the delicate balance of the boat. A good throttleman will read the waves and concentrate very closely on each one as it approaches, adjusting the throttle almost by instinct as the craft meets the wave, so that the bow slices through the top without the wave imparting too much lift, allowing the boat to continue on an almost even keel. With the Greek boat it took a fair amount of courage to wind the boat up and open the throttles, and we suffered a few nasty bangs as we hit the first two or three waves, but soon after the boat really got up on top and, with the flaps down, away we went, travelling at close to 30 knots in conditions where I would never have thought it possible for a boat of this size.

One of the major ingredients when running a planing boat in rough seas is to use the throttle very delicately. The tendency, when a larger wave is seen approaching, is to bring the throttle right back to reduce the impact between wave and boat, but this will bring the boat off the plane, the bow will drop, and there is every chance that the larger wave will come curling down the deck as the bow buries in it, rather than passing under the hull. In most cases only a slight reduction of the throttle setting will be needed to adjust to the approaching wave. This will not change the trim of the boat too dramatically, and one will find oneself making much better progress. This is one of the reasons why I favour throttle controls separate from the gear lever, because then one has a much wider range of movement which allows for the more sensitive control necessary for this type of driving.

Head seas

We have already covered most of the aspects of head sea handling when using the throttle. Getting the boat up and running on the tops of the waves may have limited application, and one is much less likely to take these sorts of chances with a cruising boat, which is less well designed to cope with the heavy impact that can result if things get out of hand. It is also unlikely on a cruising craft that one can maintain the necessary level of concentration for any length of time, and very often the visibility from the steering position is not good enough to enable one to read the waves easily. Reflections in the windscreen, and even the windscreen itself (if it has been sprayed with water), can greatly reduce the ability to read the waves ahead.

In these conditions, one will be more likely to find a throttle setting at which the boat runs comfortably and let the boat do the work. In moderate seas one can often make good progress in this way, and certainly if one is on a long passage, this takes a lot of the tension out of driving and makes for a more comfortable life. In moderate conditions one can also set the autopilot and have a nice gentle cruise, but always in a planing boat one must remember the wide variety of shapes and sizes of waves that can be met at sea. If one does decide to set the throttle in this way, then the speed at which one is running must leave an adequate margin for the boat to ride comfortably over larger than normal waves, without danger or too much discomfort.

If conditions start to deteriorate one will find oneself easing back on the throttle, because the motion of the boat will soon indicate whether one is pushing things too hard. Fortunately, with most modern, fast cruising craft the weak point in the boat (and the one that generally starts to complain first) is the crew itself, and this is a good safety factor. If the motion starts to get uncomfortable for the crew, then one is probably pushing the vessel too hard, and easing back the throttle should find a more comfortable speed.

When conditions get to the point where it is difficult to find a comfortable speed and still keep the boat on the plane, then one is faced with two options. The first is to ease back and come off the plane and operate the boat in the displacement mode, but the low freeboard at the bow of most planing boats does not always make this a comfortable option. If one has any doubts about one's own capabilities, then this is probably the wise course of action to adopt. The main secret of fast boat driving into a head sea is to match the speed of the craft to the conditions, and the throttle is the main control to work with. Obviously, one may benefit from adjusting the flaps to help keep the bow down when one is on the plane, and normally if one finds oneself reducing speed one will almost certainly want to bring in the power trim if it is fitted, which will also help to balance the boat to the conditions.

The other option open is to alter course. Even a 20° alteration can make a significant difference to the way the boat behaves. Altering course off the wind may not get one moving on the direct course to the destination, but it will have the effect of extending the wavelength, which in turn reduces the wave gradient, which in turn will give a more comfortable ride. One will need to experiment to find the best amount to alter course, and there may be times when one needs to turn up into a big wave and reduce speed, or turn away and open the throttles to escape from the section of a wave that is breaking.

Beam seas

A planing craft in beam seas can be quite an exhilarating ride. If one wants to make rapid progress in waves, then one has to concentrate hard, and even in beam seas it is necessary to read the waves ahead all the time, otherwise one can find oneself caught out and experience several unpleasant moments. If the waves come in a regular pattern, then it would simply be a question of the boat lifting over the wave as it passed underneath and dropping down into the trough in a nice rhythmical way. However, waves are far from regular, and one becomes very aware of this when running in a beam sea. It is easy to find oneself with a wave suddenly presenting what appears to be a near-vertical face as the boat approaches, and then equally quickly that wave seems to disappear and one drops into a trough. The boat can suffer some quite heavy impacts dropping off waves in this way, but one can avoid much of this if the steering and throttle controls are used to good effect.

If one watches the waves, particularly in a beam sea, one will notice that some are considerably higher than others, some having gentle gradients, others having steep gradients and with peaks and troughs. Very rarely does one get a long wave front. It is quite easy to see where the flatter areas of sea are and, by using the throttle and steering, one can often steer around the worst of the waves, which tend to form in localized peaks. It is surprising how comfortable a ride one has if one drives the boat in this way. However, there is no doubt it needs quite a lot of concentration and a sensitive hand on the throttle and steering. It is often difficult to get good steering control in these conditions because one has only one hand on the steering wheel, and it can pay to concentrate on just one of these controls, normally the steering wheel, so that one can really use this to good effect, leaving the throttle setting at a speed that is comfortable for the conditions.

With the wind on the beam one will find that the boat will steer off the wind much more easily than trying to steer into it, so heading downwind will be the normal course in taking evasive action from threatening wave crests. Having said that, when one steers off the wind, the waves are still coming from ahead, so one may have to steer further off to actually miss a particular wave. By steering into the wind, on the other hand, one will get a better chance to let the wave pass across the bow and run into the smoother water behind. Every wave is different, and one will have to make an assessment of each one at the time. A point to remember here, as far as navigation is concerned, is that if one keeps turning off in the same direction one will, in effect, be steering a course quite different from that intended.

Even when the wind is not exactly on the beam and one is steering a course 30–40° from the wind, one can still adopt this same technique of driving the boat through or round the lower parts of the wave to make good progress. These are tactics that one can adopt even in quite rough seas, but as the seas get rougher the consequences of making a mistake become greater and one will need to concentrate that bit harder. It can be a very exhilarating ride, but one must always be aware of the risks one is taking and the consequences of getting out of step with the waves.

Mention needs to be made of the way in which fast boats, particularly those of the deep-V type, lean into the wind under the influence of the rudders. This is obviously most pronounced when the wind is on the beam. Obviously, if there are flaps fitted to the vessel, then one can level the boat up so that it runs true, but even then, if one is using the steering to avoid the worst of the seas, whichever way you turn will cause the boat to lean. This is one of the primary causes of an uncomfortable ride in a beam sea. It will particularly be the case if one takes the option of pointing the bow up into the wind to avoid a nasty sea ahead, and there is always the risk here that there can be a heavy wave impact on the flat of the V of the hull. One will get this effect whichever way one turns, and the only way to avoid it is to use the steering gently so that one does not upset the transverse trim of the boat too much.

Following seas

Running before a following sea in a powerboat can be exciting. Not only can one often employ full throttle in this situation, but one feels that one can do so with comparative safety, because the speed of encounter with the waves is much slower than with a head sea. The speed at which the waves travel is determined by their wavelength, so that smaller waves will be travelling at 12–15 knots and the larger waves, perhaps those generated by a force 5–6 wind, may be travelling at between 15 and 20 knots. Certainly, in coastal waters one is unlikely to find waves travelling at more than 20 knots unless, of course, there are swells where the wavelength can be considerably longer and the wave travels faster accordingly, but these waves tend to have a very gentle gradient which is unlikely to impinge on one's progress. With a moderate-speed planing boat, one will be overtaking following sea waves, even travelling at twice the speed of the waves, so that the period of encounter allows the boat to recover from each wave in turn without any dramatic change of attitude of trim.

With boats capable of speeds up to around 30 knots, it is often possible to simply set the throttle and let the boat take its course while still making rapid speed downwind. Much will depend on the size of the waves and their speed of travel. One of the problems is that, as the craft climbs up the back of the wave it tends to lose speed because it is, in effect, climbing uphill, and then when it gets to the crest it tends to sit there for a moment until enough of the bow projects over the steeper leeward face of the wave to cause it to drop with a quite sudden change of trim. This all tends to happen in slow motion. Relatively speaking, with the boat on the crest of the wave travelling little faster than the wave itself, there is a marked change in attitude as the boat drops down the leeward face of the wave, and at the same time suddenly accelerates. This acceleration is under the impetus of the throttle and of gravity. In rough conditions, and depending a great deal on the speed and type of the boat and the speed of the waves, one can find the bow of the vessel burying quite heavily into the next wave in front as it rushes on the downhill slope. Certainly, with a boat with a full bow, one will find the impact of the boat into the wave quite harsh, giving a very uncomfortable motion.

Concentration can be needed when crossing a harbour bar. *Photo: Dag Pike*

There are two remedies in this situation if it becomes uncomfortable, which is likely if the wind and waves start to increase. First, if one has the potential to increase speed, this will have the effect of reducing the time that the boat spends on the crest of the wave, thus reducing the dramatic change of trim at the crest. Second, if one does not have the potential to increase speed one can reduce it so that one tends to ride with the bow on the upward slope of the wave, virtually keeping pace with the wave. If the wave should disappear in front or break, then one can open the throttles and accelerate over it. This will give one a slower and more comfortable ride, and is the tactic to adopt if one finds the sea conditions starting to rise to the point where one feels one ought to nurse the boat. Sitting on the back of the wave in this fashion also requires a fair degree of concentration, and a bigger wave may come up behind you – which could well be travelling faster than the boat and one could have a potential broaching situation on one's hands, unless one recognizes it and accelerates away.

In rough conditions, say force 7 or upwards, running in a following sea in a planing boat can be one of the safest means of progress, provided of course that one has a sound and reliable vessel. One can still make rapid progress in this direction, at least travelling roughly at the speed of the waves, simply by sitting on the back of a wave and waiting for that wave to collapse or break before driving onwards. It is not really a wise tactic to adopt if one has a long way to travel, because one will soon get tired and lose concentration. As already stated, concentration is the name of the game because mistakes can soon get one into trouble.

The same technique can be used if one is entering harbour where there is breaking surf on the bar and one has to drive the boat in through this with the wind and sea behind. In many situations, such as a harbour entrance, it would be untenable for a displacement boat because of the risk of broaching and losing control as the waves overtake. In a planing boat one is much more able to dictate one's position in relation to the waves, and here one can keep the craft riding on the back of a wave as one goes in. If the wave breaks, then one drives over it to place the boat on the back of the next wave in front, and so on until one is through the broken water. It requires nerve and concentration, and this is not the time when one can afford to have anything go wrong with the boat, but it is a feasible way of tackling breaking waves.

In following seas one problem that can be encountered is a certain loss of stability, particularly when travelling at lower planing speeds, say around 18 or 20 knots. Here the dynamic stability of the hull, generated by the boat moving through the water, will be much less and it will be further reduced if one is in breaking water where the water is moving ahead. One will find this aspect most noticeable when one passes through the crest of a wave where the inherent stability of the hull is also reduced. This can cause the boat to lean over, so that if one does fly the boat at this stage she could land very heavily on the flat of one side of the hull. While such a loss of stability is not likely to be dangerous to the point of capsize, it can make handling the boat more difficult. Once again, it is a question of using the throttles at the right time to increase the dynamic response and to get the bow up as one comes through the crest of the wave if this sort of instability is felt to be developing. This will be apparent by the rolling of the boat and by sloppiness in the steering. As so often with a high-speed craft when one gets to this situation, the solution is to put on more power rather than to close the throttles.

At slower speeds in following seas one will generally want to keep the flaps up in order to give the bow as much lift as possible so that the bow doesn't drop off as one overtakes a wave. At these slower speeds one will bring the power trim in, if fitted, for the same reason. Both of these controls have less effect at slower speeds anyway.

In planing and semi-displacement boats one cannot relax in rough seas in the way that one might with a displacement boat. The boats tend to be more lightly built so that they are less resistant to wave impact, so even by slowing down to displacement speed one will not always find the best solution, particularly if the bow drops at the same time as will certainly happen with a fully planing hull. Semi-displacement hulls tend to be better because they have a fuller bow.

The need for concentration in faster boats has been mentioned constantly, but this can become a problem at night when it can be difficult to see what the waves are doing. This is the time to set the boat on the most comfortable and least demanding course, irrespective of destination. Again a lot will depend on the conditions, but somewhere with the sea about 30–45° on the bow will give the best ride, where one runs at reduced speed and leaves a reserve to cope with those larger than average waves when they come along.

COPING WITH EXTREMES

When conditions turn bad, the best place to be is in harbour. However, it can sometimes be more dangerous to try to enter harbour than to stay out at sea. Some of the worst sea conditions can be found in harbour entrances, so the first decision one has to make when bad weather arrives is whether to stay out at sea or whether to make for harbour. It is never an easy decision because the thought of harbour always seems so attractive, but before heading for harbour consider the conditions in the entrance, particularly if the harbour lies downwind and it is wide open to the seas. One could find particularly bad conditions in the harbour entrance just when one thinks one has reached safety and can start to relax.

When out at sea, the first thing to consider is speed. Speed, comfort and stress are directly related, and a slower speed can solve many problems when bad weather is encountered. However, don't reduce speed to the point that steerage way is lost, otherwise one can be vulnerable to breaking waves. Unless one has steering control one will not be able to maintain a desired heading, and that could bring as much trouble as going too fast. If the sea builds up to the point where one feels unhappy, then one must look at what resources one has in order to cope. When things get really bad, then it is time to go into a survival mode with the object of weathering the storm until things improve.

There are no magic solutions in these situations and the decisions will be based to a large degree on the type of vessel, the nature of the conditions, and one's experience and ability to cope. In these extreme conditions, lifeboats are expected to cope and to have something left to help others in trouble. We can take a lesson from lifeboats and the way they operate, but it is to be remembered that much of the safety of lifeboats in rough seas is determined long before they actually put to sea. The boats are strongly built, their equipment is sound, and the crews are well trained and fit. These are all prerequisites for survival in bad conditions, but there is always the risk of being caught out, and the prudent sailor will make some mental as well as practical preparations for this by ensuring that both he and his craft are in good condition before putting to sea.

When caught out in worsening conditions, the first thing to do is to make an assessment of the situation. What are the weak points in the boat and its equipment? Is the crew fit for the task ahead? Where is the nearest shelter and safety? The first concern should be with the boat and where she might let one down. If she has large areas of glass windows one might be reluctant to push the boat into a head sea. If she has a rear cockpit, one might want to avoid the risk of a sea breaking over the stern in a following sea.

As far as machinery goes, one will be concerned about the amount of fuel remaining and the reliability of the engines and propulsion, and auxiliary systems such as the electrics. In rough seas it only needs a small failure which, in itself, may not be too serious, but which can start off a chain reaction of events that can lead to disaster. I remember coming across a boat at sea that was on fire in rough conditions, a pretty serious situation that had started because of a steering failure! The steering was a wire and pulley system; the wire frayed and then finally broke. Given time, such a condition would not have been too difficult to fix, but without steering, the boat turned broadside-on and was rolling very heavily. This made it difficult to effect the repair but, much more seriously, the rolling set the poorly secured battery sliding about, which eventually broke the main battery cable. The short-circuit that resulted started a fire, and the single occupant was lucky to get out alive. This may be an exceptional case, but any failure in the boat or its systems can add to one's worries. Preparation is an important weapon in heavy weather, so make sure everything is well battened down and secured. When assessing the situation one should take all factors into account, and if one remains unhappy with any of them one should go into the survival mode earlier, which may then allow one to reach safety before the conditions deteriorate too far.

Methods of heaving-to in a powerboat tend to require the boat to be driven, which means that one may have to spend long hours at the controls. There are alternatives, and one of them is simply to close the boat down and leave her to her own devices. I don't think this would be my choice, but I know of several cases where powerboats left to drift have come through unscathed. The problem is that we tend to hear about the ones that made it rather than those that simply disappeared without trace. Even when very tired, keeping some semblance of control is better than just letting the boat drift. If one has nothing to do, one tends to give up mentally – and that is not a good state of mind for survival. In a strong displacement vessel one would probably get away with it, but in a light planing boat the chances would not be so good.

One can drive the boat on a course that seems sympathetic to the boat and the sea, but the good skipper tries to keep something up his sleeve. There are the traditional methods of coping with rough seas, such as using drogues, sea anchors and oil. The use of this equipment may often be talked about, but few modern skippers have the experience of using this equipment and fewer still have used them for survival. They are certainly not the solution to all your problems, as they are often portrayed, but they are worthy of consideration if only to know when to reject them.

The universally proclaimed panacea for all desperate situations at sea is that of spreading oil on the water. There is no doubt that the correct type of oil used under certain circumstances can have a beneficial effect, but this is limited and miracles must not be expected. The recommended oil is unrefined fish oil, normally supplied as 'storm oil'.

It is rare to find a boat carrying oil for the specific purpose of spreading it on the water, so that when the need for it arises, the only oil likely to be available is either lubricating oil or diesel oil. Diesel oil is almost useless, but lubricating oil will have some effect. It is less viscous than the optimum and it will spread readily on the water, but its effect in reducing the breaking of waves will be less than fish oil. On balance, though, I do not think much of the idea of using oil.

Drogues, sea anchors and oil can be some of the weapons available to help cope with extreme conditions, but the best weapon of all is a fit crew who think about what they are doing and how they are doing it. In a slow displacement boat the best approach is to drive the boat at slow speed, probably head to the sea or just off the bow. In a planing boat one may be best running before the waves, provided that one has enough speed to travel faster than the waves. Failing this, turn and point the strongest part of the boat, the bow, into or close into the waves and maintain steerage way, but little more, to reduce the stresses as much as possible.

12 Multihull tactics in heavy weather

GAVIN LESUEUR

HEAVY WEATHER OPTIONS

Multihull sailing uses many of the seamanship skills necessary to take any vessel to sea. The way one manages heavy weather aboard a multihull should depend on knowledge of the multihull's characteristics in heavy weather, the proximity of safe shelter, the direction in which one intends to sail, and dangers such as a lee shore, reefs, shipping routes and sea conditions.

This chapter concentrates on the areas in which multihulls differ from monohulls in handling heavy weather. It considers design characteristics, preparations for heavy weather, and the tactics, techniques and equipment that may be employed.

MULTIHULL DESIGN CHARACTERISTICS IN HEAVY WEATHER CONDITIONS

The design variability of multihulls is vast. Fast racing trimarans differ dramatically from Polynesian-style catamarans or the traditional cruising catamaran or trimaran; nevertheless, all have features in common. They utilize beam rather than ballast for stability. They are shallow-drafted, even if fitted with keels. Many will dramatically increase their leeway with raised daggerboards or centreboard. Rigs have to withstand higher loads owing to the high initial stability. The deck area is generally larger. Motion varies considerably between designs, but in general is more stable on a lateral plane and more pronounced in fore-and-aft moment than for equivalent-sized monohulls. All these common features determine the techniques that enable the crews of multihulls to survive and handle heavy weather conditions safely.

In choosing a multihull for bluewater sailing the considerations include size (length and beam), payload, construction and design. For example, some designs are limited by their ability to take the weight of substantial cruising stores, despite in all other respects being 'heavy weather seaworthy'.

Payload is a significant design feature. As a general rule, about one-third of the weight of the vessel can be carried safely. Depending on where a multihull is sailing and how long the passages are, features such as water and fuel capacity can have significant effects on performance. Multihulls carrying half their weight in payload are usually overloaded and put the structural integrity at risk.

The choice of catamaran versus trimaran is fairly subjective. Both can have equal performance, although as a general rule the trimaran will sail to windward slightly better, has more of a monohull feel, and needs more helm attention off the wind in big seas. Bluewater catamarans have lots of design choices – bridgedeck or not, trampoline or solid foredeck, keels or centreboards. These variables affect weight and windward ability and thus performance. The traditional cruising catamaran will usually sail well off the wind, has a unique feel in comparison to trimarans and monohulls and, if designed so to perform, will sail well to windward.

Both keels and centreboards have advantages and disadvantages. A keel makes grounding or drying out easier and protects the propeller, but keels do not usually allow as good performance to windward as centreboards, and they cannot be retracted to increase leeway when this is needed.

Many of the features that can make a multihull suitable for heavy weather sailing are inherent in the basic design. To reduce the possibility of capsize the vessel should be able to deploy drogues or parachute sea anchors. This necessitates very strong tether points for bridling and controlling the rode length. Deck fixtures, hatches and windows need to be strong enough to handle wave impact, and the sail wardrobe should include an efficient storm jib and storm mainsail (usually a fourth reef). On deck, adequate lifeline attachment points are needed to allow safe access to all areas of the vessel. Design features to enhance survival after a capsize should include escape hatches, non-skid under wing decks, liferaft access, survival tools and supplies.

Specific hull design features for heavy weather sailing vary widely. At a minimum, the structural integrity should be well engineered, the vessel balanced to reduce pitching and with adequate beam for the rig size to reduce capsize risk. Modern cruising catamarans and trimarans are designed to have collision bulkheads and enough spare flotation to remain afloat despite hull penetration. Most have reserve buoyancy in the bows to reduce nose-diving or pitch-poling risks.

The choice of outboard or inboard engine is significant. For catamarans the option also includes a single pod mount or twin engines mounted in the hulls. Diesel engines are the most fuel-efficient, have adequate power for propulsion as well as auxiliary (generator or freezer) use, and the fuel is least flammable. The drawback is that they are also the heaviest and have a higher initial cost. Petrol engines are popular with their lighter weight, especially the modern four-stroke engines with high-thrust propellers and reversing exhaust systems. Outboards are generally mounted on the stern rather than in the hulls or in front of the rudders. This means that the propellers often aerate when motoring in heavy seas, resulting in poor performance to windward in these conditions. On catamarans twin engines give excellent manoeuvrability and provide a back-up should one fail or need maintenance.

Avoiding Heavy Weather

The worst of most weather patterns can usually be avoided through good forecasting and using a multihull's speed to avoid the area, sail to a safe harbour, or at least sail into the area of least effect. To do this one needs to be realistic about the average speed the multihull can maintain. This takes good log records and the ability to look at the figures and extrapolate from them to more extreme conditions. Often one may be trying to slow down so that one can reduce fatigue and handle worsening conditions.

In most circumnavigation races around England and Australia the comparative speeds averaged over the entire routes ranged from 9 knots for the 60ft (18m) racing trimarans to about 5 knots for the cruising catamarans. These figures include calms and storms, drifting and running with drogues. The average speed for around the world non-stop by the largest racing trimarans and catamarans is still only about 15 knots. To avoid weather patterns, sometimes one may have to sail only 50nm or less to reach a safe port or anchorage. To plan upon high average speeds to find safety is flirting with danger. Be realistic. There are a few rules that determine where to sail in cyclonic conditions. Multihull sailors should know these rules whenever they sail in waters affected by cyclones.

The ability to sail at speed away from an area can also be used to gain sea room so that the multihull can either stream a drogue or, in the most extreme circumstances, lie-to a parachute sea anchor. Alternatively, the aim may be simply to avoid shipping lanes so that in poor visibility and extreme conditions there is less risk of being run down while stopped.

The key to using a multihull's speed to avoid heavy weather is to know realistically what speed the vessel will do in the prevailing and expected conditions.

DECK PREPARATION FOR HEAVY WEATHER

When a storm is approaching and it has to be confronted at sea, the deck should be set up to make life safer and easier. The multihull will be confronting high winds and waves that will break both over the boat and up through the trampoline decks. One may need to tow drogues or set a parachute sea anchor, set storm headsails, storm-reefed mainsails or reduce to bare poles. Emergency tools and equipment should be accessible, and preparations should be made for possible capsize. The time to think through the plan is at the first hint of bad weather in prospect, not when the storm is nigh.

The following can be done on deck to prepare a multihull for the worst. Stow all deck objects below if possible. Double-lash everything that has to remain on deck (eg dinghy, sailboard, spare fuel tanks). Try not to leave anything on the trampoline netting. Wave action from under the boat can be as destructive as a wave smashing onto the boat from above. The worst position for a dinghy is on the trampoline net. Remove all unnecessary lines, stowing them below for quick and easy access. Lines dragging overboard will inevitably tangle with the rudder system. A multihull's shallow draft and lower displacement causes its sterns to rise out of the water regularly and any trailed line invites disaster.

If the multihull has a dinghy mounted on a targa or davit bar, then remove the motor and cover the dinghy so that it cannot be pooped. This may mean inverting it or bringing it on deck. Inflatables should be deflated.

Prepare the parachute sea anchor and drogue lines and have both ready for deployment. Anticipate worsening weather rather than wait until it may no longer be safe to go on deck to launch the equipment.

Give the helmsman ready access to such essential equipment as suitable clothing and wet weather gear, a white signalling flare should other shipping venture near, access to plenty of snacks and drink, binoculars and a torch.

HEAVY WEATHER MULTIHULL SAILS

No multihull should leave its mooring without a storm jib. These can be lifesavers, as on a lee shore one has to be able to make ground to windward. The storm jib can also be essential when running downwind under warps or a drogue, as it gives the directional control to enable the bows to be kept downwind. The windward performance of a multihull in a storm is dependent on a balanced rig, and in extreme conditions this may take the form of a storm jib and rotating aerofoil mast section.

Roller furling headsails do not work as storm sails. This is because the foot of the sail climbs upward as most headsails are furled. Sail area up high is not where it is needed in a gale. Moreover, a half-rolled headsail usually has no shape and is distorted to the point that it often provides more drag than drive to windward. Multihulls with roller furling headsails should have a cutter rig arrangement, or staysail, to enable the storm jib to be hanked on inside the fully furled headsail. In extreme conditions remove the headsail completely from the furler.

Catamarans often have lower forestay tension than other yachts, and as a result cause increased fatigue on roller furling extrusions. Watch the joints carefully for wear, and do not wait until the rivets or screws fail before repairing them. A familiar problem is that the extrusions separate and, when one comes to furl the headsail, the bottom extrusion turns but the ones above the break do not, so the sail then tears and remains stuck aloft.

A storm trysail is rarely seen on multihulls. Not only is a storm not the time to be bending on a new sail, but many fully battened mainsails are not readily removed. The more practical alternative is to have an equally strong fourth 'storm' reef section in the mainsail. This section of the sail needs to be heavily reinforced at both the tack, clew and along the reefed foot. To qualify under category 'O' (the highest offshore standard), the smallest area of reefed mainsail must be less than 15 per cent of the total mainsail area. To make this area work efficiently it is important that the reefed section of sail lying in the lazyjacks is firmly stowed. A line of reef eyelets is essential. The Cunningham eye section at the front of the sail needs to be secured firmly both to the mast track and to the boom or deck. It is sometimes necessary to lash the Cunningham eye to the mast with a stout line.

Storm Sailing to Windward

As a tactic in heavy weather, sailing to windward on a multihull has some advantages. One remains in control. The bows of the multihull have momentum to punch through waves, and the worst breakers can be avoided, or at least approached at the optimum angle. But it is usually wet, uncomfortable and stressful on both the vessel, its helmsman and crew.

There are many times that one may need to sail to windward. Examples include having to claw off a lee shore or sail away from a worsening weather pattern. To point effectively in heavy weather a multihull should have well-reefed sails with narrow sheeting angles and some shape. Flat blades sheeted widely do not allow a multihull to point. Sails should be adjusted as wind strength increases, adjusting the sheeting points to allow the sails to twist. This is achieved by moving the jib sheeting point further out and back, and by easing the main traveller down the track and easing the mainsheet slightly.

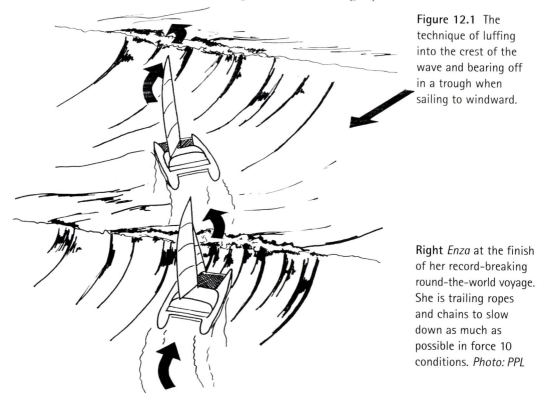

Figure 12.1 The technique of luffing into the crest of the wave and bearing off in a trough when sailing to windward.

Right *Enza* at the finish of her record-breaking round-the-world voyage. She is trailing ropes and chains to slow down as much as possible in force 10 conditions. *Photo: PPL*

As a general rule, if one thinks one may need to reef, then reef! Reef to the gust strength, not the average strength. Multihulls should always have sheeting systems that are simple and foolproof. Never leave a rope in a self-tailing winch, and always ensure the loose end of loaded sheets can run freely. Assume that they can get caught, and always have at hand a knife suitable for cutting them quickly. Risk of capsize is greatly reduced if one has instant control of the sails.

Centreboards and daggerboards

A catamaran's leeward daggerboard should be partially raised and also the windward board partially raised as conditions worsen. This increases leeway, but will lower the risk of capsize by reducing the boat's lateral resistance. This is especially important if the windward hull is raised or hit by a steep large wave. Try not to get beam-on to breaking waves. If this occurs, raise the centreboard or both daggerboards completely. A trimaran's centreboard should similarly be raised to achieve the same effect.

Use of engines

Motorsailing with diesel engines and a storm jib and/or deeply reefed mainsail is a very effective way of clawing to windward in heavy weather conditions. Enough sail is needed to keep the boat driving and balanced.

Tacking and stalling

Tacking in rough seas with minimal sail and the centreboards partially raised can be difficult and dangerous. The danger is stalling part way through the tack and falling backwards on a wave. If it seems likely that the boat will stall during a tack in heavy weather conditions, then a controlled gybe with no mainsail set should be considered. If the rudders are not firmly held they can turn rapidly to their limit and even break. Capsize is possible if the multihull slides sideways without forward motion. Having to back the jib and reverse around

is fraught with risk. If in doubt, run off and gybe to get onto the new tack. One will lose some windward ground, but one may lose much more by attempting, but failing, a tack. Never attempt to tack or gybe if there is a possibility that there may be too much sail up.

Crew fatigue

Exposure   The speed of a multihull creates a high apparent wind when sailing to windward. Exposure, leading to overwhelming crew fatigue, is a common problem. The best solution is to have an enclosed helm position. As a minimum the helmsman should have adequate wet weather gear including a fully enclosed helmet. The head is a major source of heat loss, and wind-driven salt spray rapidly reduces any sort of forward vision. Whether one uses a lightweight surfing helmet, a canopy, dodger or simple spray shield, ensure one's protection system is up to the job. Most wharves have a fire hose. Ask to borrow it for a few minutes and blast the helm area to see if everything holds up!

Motion   Sailing in a multihull to windward in short steep seas can be very uncomfortable. The motion can be quick, jerky and the hulls may leap off the back of waves and plummet into the following troughs. The solution to reducing this motion is simple. Slow down. It sounds easy and it is. To slow down one can either reduce sail further or tow a drogue, which will even out the vessel's speed. The aim is to keep driving forward and to roll over waves rather than leap over them.

Hull fatigue

The fatigue factor on beams and rig increases enormously when pounding to windward. Dropping off the back of a wave often gives false readings on masthead wind instruments. This 'flicking effect' results in stories of 70 knot winds when, in reality, the strength might have been half that figure. Nevertheless, apparent wind experienced when driving to windward is stronger than the true wind, and both equipment and rig must be designed and prepared for it. Sailing to windward into big, steep waves requires skilful helm work. One often needs to bear away sharply at the top of these waves to prevent falling off the peaks.

STORM SAILING DOWNWIND

Downwind sailing can be an exhilarating ride. Racing multihulls can surf regularly at over 25 knots, although most cruising multihulls are at risk of broaching or losing rudder control at speeds over 20 knots. It is important to remember that wave fronts travel at varying speeds. A 10ft (3m) wave may travel at 20 knots; a large storm wave at up to 40 knots. The speed of a multihull combined with the acceleration provided by a large wave can suddenly change the feeling of stability to quite the opposite.

Tactics in downwind heavy weather sailing outweigh all design considerations. Even so, multihulls best suited for these conditions have large buoyant bows, centralized weight and strong drogue attachment points.

Running downwind as a storm survival tactic requires understanding of the weather. Most areas have a typical storm track. Being aware of this, and of the changes in wind direction, will enable an assessment to be made as to where one should head. It is essential that an accurate log is kept of wind direction to determine one's tactics. Plot the storm front on a chart and determine tactics, taking into account position and sailing ability.

Downwind storm sailing needs sea room and lots of it. Under drogue and warps a multihull may still average up to 10 knots – 240 miles a day. Without a drogue, a multihull will start surfing as the wind and waves build. By reducing sail the tendency to surf will be reduced, but eventually most multihulls will surf under bare poles in storm conditions.

When sailing downwind it is important to note the true wind speed every few minutes.

Because of the high boat speed of a multihull the true wind can be deceptively strong compared to the apparent wind. For example, a multihull may be able to carry two reefs and a working jib in 20 knots of apparent wind, while sailing downwind at 15 knots boat speed. The problem occurs when one has to round up to reef in 35 knots of true wind! Carry the amount of sail for the true wind, not the apparent wind. Reef to the gust strength. Just one experience of rounding up when overpowered in gale conditions is one experience too many.

When trailing warps or drogues, bridle them for directional stability. Capsize often occurs when broached or hit by a rogue wave coming from a different direction. A bridled drogue will slow any tendency to turn a multihull sideways to a wave face. Despite the best preparation, any vessel can be overwhelmed by a huge breaking wave. Try not to sail directly down waves or at right angles to their direction. It is best to sail down the face at a slight angle with control. If one has to sail straight down the face, always tow an efficient drogue.

STOPPING

There are three recognized techniques for stopping at sea: parachute sea anchoring, lying a'hull, and heaving-to.

Parachute sea anchors

It is possible to anchor at sea – not to the seabed, but to the ocean itself. The multihull will then be moving at only a little more than the rate of the water currents. Parachute sea anchoring is the ultimate survival technique when the crew is exhausted, the conditions appalling, and the multihull at risk of capsize. It can also be a way of 'parking at sea', a useful skill when awaiting tides or daylight to enter ports or to stop downwind drift if the boat is crippled by damage or cannot sail off a lee shore.

Parachute sea anchor manufacturers recommend parachute sizes according to the displacement of a multihull. The size is important because if the parachute is too small the bows will blow off and allow the vessel to become beam-on to the approaching waves. If the parachute sea anchor does not hold the bows into the wind, then do not set it off the

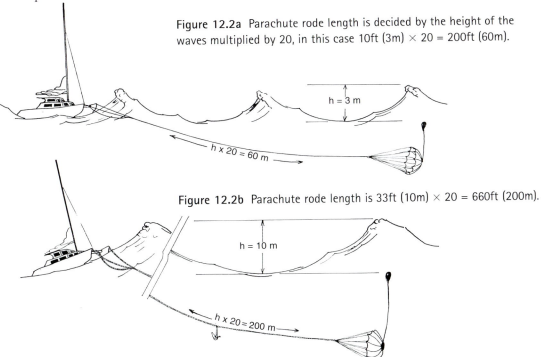

Figure 12.2a Parachute rode length is decided by the height of the waves multiplied by 20, in this case 10ft (3m) × 20 = 200ft (60m).

h = 3 m

h x 20 = 60 m

Figure 12.2b Parachute rode length is 33ft (10m) × 20 = 660ft (200m).

h = 10 m

h x 20 = 200 m

bow. It can be set off the stern as a drogue but should be replaced with a bigger unit. Parachute sea anchors should be set from the bow of the multihull on a nylon line usually called the 'rode' or 'tether'. A bridle should be attached to the rode and run through the blocks on the outboard bows. The free ends of the bridle lines must be secured to strongly attached cleats. Keep the arrangement simple.

The rode should be able to stretch, therefore nylon is preferred over polyester or Dacron. The rope diameter should be equal to the multihull's normal anchor line (which is ideal). The minimum recommended rode length is 20 times the expected height of the waves. The use of a weight or some chain, located mid-scope, provides catenary/mechanical shock absorption. This can be added after deployment if needed, by feeding it down on a snatch block.

A sea anchor parachute needs a small float attached to a line tied to the discharge outlet (the small opening in the top of the parachute). This stops the parachute from sinking too far below the surface and pulling the bows down. Trip lines are not used on most multihulls because they cause foul-ups. It is best to have the main tether line on a strong winch so that it can be winched home when the weather moderates.

When preparing for heavy weather, the bagged parachute can be stored in the cockpit with the lines attached and ready. Similarly, the bridle arrangement should be pre-set. The parachute is now able to be set without having to untangle and run lines in an emergency.

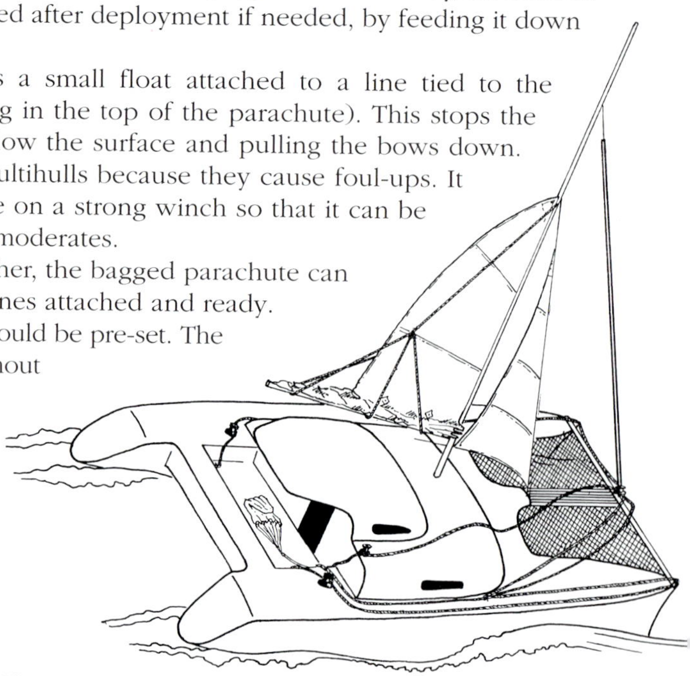

Figure 12.3 When preparing for heavy weather, the bagged parachute anchor can be stored in the cockpit with lines attached and ready.

Launching the parachute sea anchor

Before launching, wet the parachute to help it sink rather than inflate in the wind. The safest launching technique involves rounding up into the wind (either under sail or motoring). Then, dropping all sail immediately, secure the rudder amidships and, as the multihull drifts off to one side, deploy the parachute over the windward bow – never the leeward side. Control the rode run with a turn around a winch. As it runs give enough tension to fill the parachute and turn the bows into the wind. Secure the rode firmly and set the bridle lines. Check all chafe points. When finished, check all chafe points again!

Figure 12.4 Before launching, wet the parachute, round up into the wind, drop the sails, secure the helm amidships, and deploy the parachute over the windward bow.

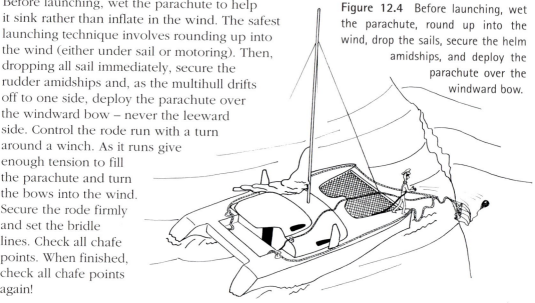

Centreboards should be lowered to reduce side-to-side swinging motion (yawing). To keep the centre of lateral resistance forward, raise the rudders if possible, or lock them in the amidships position.

Parachute sea anchor problems   If a multihull is being yanked off wave tops and driven through waves, pulling the deck hardware and possibly the parachute to bits, then the rode needs to be longer and deeper. Add an anchor to the line as a catenary and lengthen the rode to reduce peak loads in the line.

Strand rope may untwist under load. This rotation might twist up the shroud lines and reduce the effective diameter of the parachute. Braided nylon is better. Swivels rarely help as they do not readily swivel under load.

Retrieval of a parachute sea anchor   Trip lines back to the boat are a potential cause of tangles and are not recommended. A trip line on a float, or a float line plus recovery line, may be necessary in a seaway – though many seem to manage without. Before recovering the parachute sea anchor wait for calmer weather. Simply motor up to the float or the parachute while winching or hauling the rode. If not using a float, the parachute will not break its shape until one of the shroud lines is reached; but just haul on one of these and the chute will collapse.

Parachute sea anchor care   Salt-water crystals drying in the parachute material will weaken the material in due course. Keep the parachute wet until it can be rinsed thoroughly in fresh water, dried and re-bagged. Storing the parachute in sealed garbage bags is one suggestion.

Lying a'hull

Lying a'hull is dropping all sails and drifting under bare poles at the whim of the wind and waves. A multihull will usually adopt an angle somewhere around beam-on to the sea. Waves may break over the hulls with tremendous impact and will pound against the hulls from underneath. High loads are put on beam structures. Small multihulls can be tripped and flipped over. Lying a'hull in storm conditions is only a tactic to be considered for the larger multihull.

A multihull lying a'hull will drift downwind at speeds of up to 5 knots. Lightweight multihulls with the centreboards raised often turn slightly downwind as the centre of lateral resistance is moved aft and the hulls 'sail'. In moderate conditions this is fairly comfortable. In storm conditions it is not.

Heaving-to

Heaving-to means having the helm turned so that the multihull is trying to round up into the wind, but the headsail is aback (sheeted on the wrong side) and the mainsail set normally. Depending on the hull shape, lateral resistance of keels and multihull length, the resultant motion will vary from sailing slowly forward to drifting on a broad reach. In moderate conditions it is a good way to pull up and rest, or perform tasks such as a repair.

Multihulls should be trialled lying a'hull and hove-to. Only by testing will one know how the craft will respond and this should be undertaken prior to an emergency. A global positioning satellite (GPS) navigator is invaluable when hove-to. It will give details of drift and current position with far superior accuracy to dead-reckoning.

DROGUES AND WARPS IN A STORM

A line and chain warp towed astern will slow a multihull in moderate conditions, but when sailing downwind in more severe conditions it will be usually necessary to tow some more efficient drag-creating device behind (ie a drogue). A drogue and bridle should always be ready for deployment. It can be used to reduce overall speed, to stop, or for slow surfing down waves, to reduce broaching tendencies by stabilizing direction, and to ease the load on the rudders and helm. A bridle-mounted drogue can even be used as emergency steering. When sailing downwind under storm sails a drogue may be essential to stop pitch-poling or broaching. This is especially true in gusty conditions with steep seas. Centreboards should be raised when running downwind with a drogue to move the centre of lateral resistance toward the stern and thus reduce yawing. If the drogue is to be effective, it must remain submerged. To achieve this, it must have an adequate length of towline and it may also be necessary to keep the drogue underwater with some kind of weight such as chain.

DROGUE TYPES

In an emergency, ground anchors have been used for towing astern. These twist, spin and roll and may cause dramatic knots in the rode or chain. A CQR anchor works reasonably well if towed backwards from the crown. Anchor chain alone can also be towed, and the drag can be increased by tying it into a big knot. No matter which anchor is used the multihull will be slowed. A car tyre drogue is often advocated as a cheap drogue. These work until one really needs them: at high speeds they sit on the water surface and skid. A much better idea is to set up a drogue specifically designed for the purpose. There are a number of proprietary drogues available, ranging from moulded plastic or metal devices through to cloth cones and small parachute shapes.

Larger multihulls require a substantial device to handle the high loads needed to slow them down. The proprietary drogues come in different sizes designed for these loads. The metal conical drogues have specialized slots that open at a pre-adjusted setting. These slots increase the turbulence and thus slow the boat speed. The smaller, plastic conical drogues have fixed slots that work continuously. These are generally suitable for multihulls up to 39ft (12m) in length. The drawback of the metal or plastic conical drogues is that they take up valuable storage space.

Figure 12.5 A compact lightweight drag device can be made of material in the form of a miniature parachute or cone, and has the advantage that it can be stored easily.

A compact, lightweight drag device can be made of material or webbing. They can be like miniature parachutes or cone shaped. Water is caught in the wide end of the cone and leaves at the narrow end. Excess and discharging water creates turbulence to retard forward movement. The advantage of a material drogue is that it is stowed in a small bag and can be permanently stored in a cockpit locker or hung in a transom bag.

SETTING UP A DROGUE

The drogue tether or rode should be able to stretch. Braided nylon is best as stranded nylon has the tendency to unravel under heavy loads. Dacron or polyester lines have reduced elasticity and thus, to avoid snatch loads, a longer rode length is required if these are used. Rode diameter

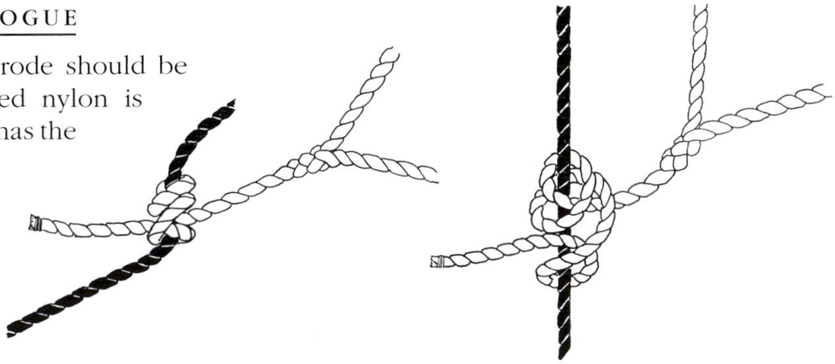

Figure 12.6 The rolling hitch is required for the second bridle line.

should be equivalent to the normal anchor rode specification.

All drogues are useless stored away and untested. The set-up of the lines is critical for them to work properly. A bridle should be used to achieve maximum directional stability. If a bridle is used, then it needs to be tested to ensure that the tether length can easily be adjusted. The bridle should be between 1.5 and 2.5 times the multihull beam. Bridle arms that are too short can impose severe hull loads and are not so effective at preventing yaw. If the lines are too long they will probably twist. This is not a major problem in itself as the twist should stop and leave enough length in the bridle arms for them to remain effective. The difficulty occurs in untangling the twist when adjustment is needed.

A good bridle arrangement is to rig it permanently and, when required for use, secure the rode to it using a rolling hitch, leaving enough spare slack length of rode so that it may be attached to a stern cleat as back-up. Steering is possible both by using the helm and by adjusting the bridle arm lengths. It may be necessary to have some centreboard down.

The tether length is critical to drogue operation. If the drogue is in the face of the following wave when a multihull starts to surf, then it may leap out of the wave and surf down in parallel with the multihull. Conical metal and plastic drogues often 'porpoise' and need a short length of chain attached to them to prevent this tendency. The drogue tether should be adjusted regularly to be a half wavelength out of synchronization with the boat, ie at least one and a half waves behind when on the peak of a wave. When the multihull starts to surf, the drogue has to be pulled through the following wave, thereby retarding the multihull's acceleration.

Wave and sea states change with tide, sea bottom and wind conditions. As waves build in height they increase in length. For effective use of a drag device the tether must be adjustable and the length reviewed regularly. Do not wait for the drogue to stop working before adjusting it.

More than one drogue can be used at once. In an emergency, where one has run downwind and one needs as much drag and directional stability as possible, many lines, preferably tied together to form a long single line, can be run astern. In an extreme emergency one may have to use lines such as halyards. To rethread mast halyards afterwards, have a 'mouse line' available. This is a $\frac{1}{8}-\frac{1}{4}$in (3–5mm) diameter line that is attached to the end of the halyard before the halyard is removed. It is left in the place of the halyard so that it can be used to pull the halyard back. However, since the loss of halyards could be catastrophic, it is better to have an abundance of spare stretchy line suitable for the purpose. Sheet and halyard lines have minimal stretch and elasticity, so do not use them exclusively as either drogue or sea anchor rodes. The aim is to achieve maximum elasticity to reduce strains on the line, the attachments and the hulls.

Swivels do not stop rode twists or stranded ropes from unravelling. Under load they simply do not work, except to add some weight to the line. Beware of stainless steel swivels that can have undetectable fatigue problems owing to salt crystal corrosion. Sudden failure of stainless steel components has led to the total loss of drogues and sea anchors.

WING MASTS IN A STORM

It is virtually impossible to feather a wing mast so that it will not create drive. Without sails the mast will control the yacht, often taking the multihull in different directions to the rudder and/or drogues. As a general rule, if one is sailing under a wing mast alone then the wing mast rules. To balance the boat a very tiny storm jib is often needed. It will not make the boat go much faster, but it will stop the wing mast from taking control.

Lying to a sea anchor with a wing mast is not much fun. It knocks the deck gear around and pushes waves over the boat as the multihull sails on the sea anchor. Only use a sea anchor on a multihull with a wing mast as a last resort, and then use it over the stern unless you can set a small sail well aft to make the multihull feather into the wind.

Pin or lock the wing mast fore-and-aft when 'stopping' in a storm. It then behaves like a normal mast and does not tend to drive the boat forward at excessive speed. Never let the wing mast rotation control become loose in high winds, as violent oscillations can develop and regaining control could easily cause injuries. Always lock the mast rotation control in both directions. This counters sea-induced inertia forces and will stop oscillations developing.

AFTER A CAPSIZE

When sailing in extreme conditions any multihull is at risk of capsize. This is a fact of life, and is not necessarily the death of crew or yacht. Be prepared. Always wear a safety harness that can be released under load so that one is not trapped outside an inverted hull. Have a capsize plan ready before setting out. This includes inverted cabin access, securing of cupboards, sails, tools and emergency survival rations. Successful heavy weather sailing means being organized for an emergency, having back-ups prepared, and knowing what to do ahead of the problem occurring. Only step *up* into a liferaft. A multihull is the best survival platform and should be left only when rescue is absolutely assured.

SUMMARY

Multihulls in heavy weather are no more a cause of concern than any other well-designed yacht with an experienced crew. The techniques needed to sail a multihull successfully in storm conditions differ from those of monohulls, although similar rules often apply. Sail with caution, learn the limitations, and prepare for the worst. Above all, it is important to have practised the techniques for ultimate survival before an emergency arises. The time to learn how to set a drogue or parachute is not in one's first storm. The time to discover how a catamaran or trimaran drifts under bare poles is not as a cyclone is bearing down. Nor should one have to guess the time needed to cover the distance to clear a severe weather pattern.

Surviving heavy weather sailing is an attitude, and forethought, experience and practice using the methods described will all help to develop it.

13 Monohull heavy weather tactics

PETER BRUCE

Military officers are fond of saying that few plans survive first contact with the enemy, and the same may be said for the plans of the crew of a small vessel encountering heavy weather for the first time. Such plans as have been made have to be flexible. Unexpected events are likely to occur, the weather forecast is often a simplified overview, and people's behaviour may be unpredictable under duress of prolonged exposure to blinding spray, fear, cold temperature, wearying noise and violent motion. One can be fairly sure, however, that crews, boats and equipment that have done well in previous storms will do so again.

Regardless of the expected wind strength, there are courses of action that can be taken before the weather takes control that can much reduce the chances of disaster. Vessels should be placed to avoid lee shores, shoal water, currents, tidal races, headlands and areas marked on charts as having overfalls. Once the storm has struck, while a vessel is still afloat, however cold and uncomfortable the conditions, her crew should neither seek nor accept offers of rescue, nor take to the liferaft without very good reason, for to do so may incur graver risks than enduring the storm. One should be very cautious about taking a tow in a seaway, too. Few modern craft have adequate strong points for such a situation even when the master of the towing vessel has the patience and skill to maintain a low enough speed.

Apart from these recommendations there is no universally applicable advice to be offered: there is no one simple remedy. If only there was. Every skipper should plan suitable tactics, carefully taking into account the characteristics of his boat, and be prepared to adopt them in good time. Some courses of action are, of course, heavily committing, and once decided upon are hard to change. In this concluding chapter of Part 1 an attempt will be made to summarize the various tactics available to the skipper of a monohulled sailing boat in heavy weather.

Drag devices, particularly parachutes, have established their worth and can be counted as important additional options for coping with heavy weather, but not the only option. The tactics that are described in this chapter have been employed in one or more of the accounts of heavy weather in this book and their effectiveness in actual circumstances can best be judged by referring to them. It is not possible to specify the exact wind strength when the various options can be recommended due to the number of variables involved. Obviously, the size of the craft is of considerable relevance, and in storms big is beautiful. But other factors count heavily too, such as the nature of the seas, the design and strength of boat, and the size and strength of the crew. In broad terms, this chapter covers courses of action to consider when the wind speed exceeds force 9, to force 10 and above.

It is evident from Adlard Coles's own modest accounts that he was skilful at choosing the moment to shorten sail. As he advocates, this should be undertaken in advance of immediate necessity, despite a natural reluctance to do so in the hope that the weather may show an improvement. He was of the opinion that, when cruising in bad weather, it will be prudent to adjust sail area for the squalls and gusts rather than for the mean force. He was also a believer in running with no more sail than can be carried if close-hauled, thereby avoiding the need for frenzied reefing action in the event of a man overboard, or a bad landfall. Obviously, the longer sail reduction is deferred, the harder it is to start, and the greater the risk of damage meantime. Incidentally this applies to all heavy weather tactics, in that bold and resolute decisions are best made before a situation becomes desperate. Likewise, serious problems are often best dealt with as soon as they occur.

When bad weather is approaching, most people, very sensibly, make for a safe harbour. But once caught out in a storm there is much to be said for enduring it rather than continuing to run for shelter, as breaking waves in shallow water can be infinitely more of a hazard than the open sea. Besides, if entry into harbour becomes unwise or impossible, the loss of sea room is irrevocable.

When beset by a storm, the human objective is to remain as safe and as comfortable as possible. As far as the boat is concerned, the aim is to avoid sinking, being rolled over, pitch-poled or otherwise suffering damage to hull, rig and sails. As Adlard Coles says, the wind dictates the amount of sail that can be carried and can also cause loss of sails, rigging or mast; but it is the breaking seas that do the more dangerous damage to hull and superstructure. There is great energy bound up within a wave, and major forces are at work when a breaking sea strikes a boat. A boat can also be picked up by a breaking sea and accelerated to an alarming speed. A moment later the boat may be flung into the still water in the trough of the wave where she will stop almost instantly. It is at this point that serious damage to crew and boat is likely to occur. Clearly, it is desirable to avoid breaking waves but, if this is not possible, then the waves should be taken within 20° of either the bow or the stern. Before the days of self-draining cockpits, being pooped, ie a wave breaking over the stern, was a major hazard to yachtsmen. It is now less of a problem, but remains a danger to motorboats open at the stern, to yachts with unusually large cockpits, or with low bridgedecks that require washboards or doors in place to prevent a sea sweeping down below.

PRESSING ON

As increasingly severe weather overtakes a craft, a seaman's instinct encourages him to continue to maintain his approximate course while reducing sail appropriately. When the destination is to windward and the crew has the determination to press on, perhaps under storm jib or trysail alone, despite the uncomfortable motion, this is commendable and, incidentally, is a policy that has won many races. The helmsman's technique is to close-reach across the troughs, then head up into the waves, and bear away hard on the top to avoid a slam. Likewise, when reaching, the helmsman will luff into the wave crests and bear away in the troughs.

The crew will be heartened by continuing in the desired direction, and hand steering – unlike heaving-to or lying a'hull – provides an opportunity to avoid breaking waves. As a storm tactic, this type of action has its merits only when the crew is strong enough to persevere and while it is still possible to make progress under storm sails. For example, it was a tactic adopted by Ed Psaltis, skipper of the overall winner of the stormy 1998 Sydney–Hobart Race (see Chapter 3), under storm jib alone, and is particularly appropriate in daylight for beamy IMS racing yachts with low underwater lateral area and low range of stability. To paraphrase Ed Psaltis, 'Having speed and acceleration gives manoeuvrability to steer through big and confused seas. It is possible to position the yacht best for each wave as it comes, or steer around it. Without speed, acceleration and manoeuvrability a boat is a sitting duck to large waves.'

As conditions deteriorate further, any size of sail set, however small, can become over-powering. At first the helmsman will luff to reduce the angle of heel, but the flogging sail will cause the whole boat to shake violently. On the other hand, when the helmsman reaches off to gather speed, the boat will be thrown on her beam-ends across the seas. At first some middle ground will be found between these extremes, but as wind and wave increase there comes a point when it may be necessary to consider other options, especially if the helmsman's difficulties are about to be increased by darkness.

HEAVING-TO

Sabre, a 34ft (10.4m) steel cutter with a crew of two, was one of the few centre-stage yachts that survived the June 1994 Pacific storm virtually undamaged. She sailed through the eye of the storm and undoubtedly experienced as bad conditions as any without any rolls or knockdowns. Her crew commented afterwards: 'Our boat is prepared with very rough con-ditions in mind and, lying hove-to, has proved herself on several occasions.'

When it comes on to blow it is better to heave-to early rather than late, and indications that the time is ripe usually come from the helm. If control is becoming difficult or the helm is feeling spongy as a result of water aeration, it is time to heave-to. If waves are breaking, plan to round up between the waves that are about to break. One can often find a good area of water just behind a wave that has recently broken. At night, breaking waves can be heard and sometimes the phosphorescence can be seen.

One can heave-to either by backing the headsail or by tacking and leaving the jib sheet made up, accompanied by a mainsail appropriately reefed for the conditions, or a trysail. The helm should be secured with heavy shock-cord or rope so as to hold the boat's bow towards the wind, and adjustments then made to the sheets and the helm until the boat is at her most comfortable. At this point she will probably be moving gently forward at a knot or two and as about as fast to leeward.

In the right design of boat the increase in comfort that can be derived from heaving-to in a seaway has to be experienced to be believed. Noise and motion are promptly much reduced and there is no longer a need for a helmsman, though it is important to check for chafe. Thus heaving-to is a good expedient to adopt, not only in heavy weather but also for having a meal in comfort or when an uncertain pilotage situation demands time for thought. On no account should one try to back an overlapping headsail in order to heave-to, as there is a high chance of bursting the sail on the spreaders.

Storm jibs, deep-reefed mainsails or trysails are sometimes employed on their own, as for example in the case described by Sir Peter Blake in the Foreword. On this occasion a trysail and storm jib were set to ride out Hurricane David, but the storm jib was soon taken down. In these instances it is more likely that a helmsman will be necessary. Given the choice, it is better to set a deep-reefed mainsail or trysail on its own rather than a storm jib set on its own. This is particularly so when the storm jib is set on the forestay rather than an inner stay position as the centre of effort may then be too far forward to keep the bow into the wind.

A deeply reefed mainsail works as well as a trysail but should not be considered an alter-native as mainsails can easily be torn, and are not designed to work efficiently if the boom breaks. A trysail can be used with or without the boom. If it is necessary to run before the wind or to work to windward, use of the boom will make life easier and more comfortable. On the other hand, if reaching or fetching, the sail will work well without the boom, and the boom will be less of a hazard to the crew.

Traditional remedies best suit traditional boats. When hove-to a yacht should lie about 50° to the wind, but unfortunately not all fin-keeled yachts will heave-to untended in a sea, probably because they lack underwater lateral area. In particular, light-displacement yachts with slim high-aspect ratio keels may not stay at a constant angle to the wind and can dance about while making great speed to leeward. The problem with such boats is that when it seems advisable to slow right down, rather like a supersonic aircraft they won't (see Chapter 3). Heaving-to is a time-honoured and seamanlike tactic to employ in moderate to severe conditions, and owners of many craft may need no other. However, owners of some modern yachts will find that heaving-to can become neither comfortable nor safe, and there is always the chance that any yacht lying hove-to can be caught by a large breaking wave.

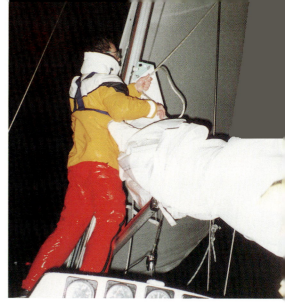

If caught out in a storm at sea it may be wise to lower the mainsail, take it off the boom, and stow it below to reduce windage. *Photo: Peter Bruce*

Lying a'Hull

If heaving-to seems no longer sensible it may be tempting to resort to lying a'hull, ie taking off all sail, lashing the helm – usually slightly to leeward – closing all hatches securely, and letting nature take her course. The ease with which types of yacht will lie a'hull is variable. Broadly speaking, old-fashioned narrow-beam heavy-displacement yachts often lie a'hull well, while light-displacement beamy yachts often do not. Nevertheless, lying a'hull was the most popular survival tactic in the generally lightish-displacement 1979 Fastnet fleet (Chapter 17). Harry Whale lay a'hull off Ushant aboard *Muddle Thru* in the great English Channel storm of 1987 (Chapter 19) and *Tir Nan Og* survived hurricane force winds lying a'hull off Brazil (Chapter 18). It is a tactic employed by many yachtsmen – and not always of dire necessity. In a sufficient force of wind the windage of the mast alone provides stability, like a steadying sail, and the turbulence caused by the yacht's drift may reduce the chances of waves breaking to windward. As an illustration of a vessel's ability to look after herself during a storm, one may recall that most of the vessels abandoned in the Fastnet race were later found bobbing about in the swell with hatches left wide open.

Lying a'hull may seem relatively comfortable, often more so than other tactics, but it gives a false sense of security. The problem, of course, is that the boat is vulnerable to breaking waves from broadside on and, to paraphrase Andrew Claughton in Chapter 2, 'breaking waves do not have to be very big to roll any sort of small craft right over, whatever her hull features'. The consequences of a roll-over can be most dramatic down below – more so than one might imagine – and the chances of the mast being lost are high. This occurrence, apart from the obvious effect on mobility, can lead to all kinds of immediate problems – not the least of these is that the lack of damping effect of the mast, without which a yacht's roll inertia is halved, results in quicker and more unpleasant motion with a much-increased chance of being rolled yet again.

While on the melancholy subject of capsize it may be significant that several yachts have been rolled over just as a storm seems to have abated. Examples are Bill King in *Galway Blazer* in 1968, *Sayula II* in the first Whitbread Round the World Race in 1973, Michael Richey in *Jester* in 1986, and the Swan 46 at sea in the October 1987 storm, described in Chapter 19. This is a phenomenon called 'overshoot', for which Sheldon Bacon provides the explanation in Chapter 8. Another contributory factor may be the shift of wind direction as a front goes through, when the effect of two wave trains crossing at an angle is known to produce regions of extreme wave height where the seas may break heavily.

Having pointed out the dangers of lying a'hull, to try to put matters into perspective it should be mentioned that world girdlers such as Alec Rose, Nicholas Davies and Alan and Kathy Webb, albeit with heavy-displacement boats, have found the practice of lying a'hull entirely satisfactory for weathering the gales of a normal world circumnavigation. For such solidly built vessels it is quite a rare event to encounter the sort of weather that does not allow lying a'hull without a high risk of capsize, but there are enough examples in this book of yachts being rolled over while lying a'hull to show that the tactic, sooner or later, may lead to being rolled through 360°. For this to happen a craft has to be caught broadside on just as a wave breaks, so luck plays a strong part.

USE OF ENGINE

Nowadays the diesel engine is a generally reliable item of equipment that can be used to good effect when managing under sail would be difficult, such as entering and leaving a berth. The old-fashioned view that 'to use an engine is unseamanlike' may have been based upon more than just prejudice, for early auxiliary engines were not always dependable while running, nor easy to start, and it was wise not to encourage over-reliance on them. Moreover, the high chance of catching a rope round the propeller in a stressful situation is well known.

Nevertheless, the competent use of an engine was demonstrated in the extraordinary account of *Pendragon* in Hurricane Carol (Chapter 15) and also Alain Catherineau's celebrated rescue feat in the 1979 Fastnet (Chapter 17). One is not likely to be able to make directly into the sea under auxiliary engine or tack through the wind in storm conditions but, bearing in mind that even a bare pole will provide some aerodynamic lift, it may be possible to make across the seas to windward. There may often be circumstances when it will be safer to 'heave-to under engine' rather than lie a'hull, especially when running before a storm is inappropriate due to a lee shore. In this case the use of an engine, either in combination with sails or without, may be highly desirable, though lubrication of some engines will not work at a large angle of heel. It should not be forgotten that skippers of power craft have no option but to 'heave-to under engine'.

When running before the sea it may be significant that the old-fashioned British lifeboat with a speed of 8 knots could not always be handled confidently without the use of a drogue in combination with the engines. Coxswains of modern lifeboats, with a speed of 18 knots, find they have no such trouble as they can power their way clear of breaking seas. Bearing in mind the opening sentence of this chapter, which suggests that flexibility may be necessary when facing severe weather, yachtsmen should regard the use of an engine as another string to their bow, and be ready to use it when the situation justifies, after carefully checking for ropes over the side. Having started the engine it should be regularly checked (Chapter 16).

Damien 1 is knocked down by a breaking wave which caught her beam-on.
Photo: Jérôme Poncet

The 36ft (10m) schooner *Halcyon* lying a'hull when caught out in an unforecast storm 300 miles east of Cape Hatteras in October 1981. Mean wind speed was 50 knots and seas were 25–30ft (8–9m) with large breakers. *Photo: Douglas Perkins*

RUNNING BEFORE THE SEAS

There is nothing new about the tactic of letting a vessel run freely before the sea, when sea room permits. Apparent wind is reduced, motion is more comfortable, and the risk of being rolled becomes less likely than when lying a'hull. When considering extreme conditions, running with full directional control is vitally important to avoid the breakers and keep the stern at the optimum angle to the waves to avoid broaching. This is not easy, especially at night, though experienced planing dinghy helmsmen and surfers may have an advantage. In a confused sea, waves can come unexpectedly from odd quarters, necessitating a quick response from the helmsman and boat. Clearly the speed of the boat has to lie within a range necessary to achieve good control. If speed is too slow, the boat does not respond quickly enough, and if too fast, especially in darkness, the helmsman may not be able to react in time to avoid pitch-poling or a broach, both of which can have very serious repercussions.

Some craft undoubtedly handle better than others when running before the seas, and it might be easy to assume that displacement is the controlling factor. The situation is not so clear cut, with a combination of design factors such as the degree of balance of the ends affecting the issue, as described by Olin Stephens in Chapter 1. In any case an overly low-geared wheel is a considerable disadvantage. The corollary is that in the case of a high-geared wheel, or a tiller, some degree of physical strength is likely to be needed on the helm. It is worth mentioning at this point that vane self-steering can work in up to 50 knots of wind speed or more, and can be invaluable for shorthanded crews in heavy weather.

The tough professional crews of the 60ft (18.3m) yachts in the Whitbread Round the World Race find exhilaration in the downwind 'sleigh-rides' through the southern oceans under as much sail as they can carry. Their technique is to luff across the trough to maintain speed, then to bear away almost square to the wave, just as the crest arrives, to encourage the boat to surf down the wave. It is similar to methods used by dinghy sailors and Malibu board surfers and requires some skill, strength and a great deal of concentration, especially when carrying maximum possible sail. Such crews will have perhaps six or eight expert racing helmsmen to share the steering task, whereas the average cruising boat may not have more than one, for whom the task of steering may become extremely wearisome after not many hours. Thus the average cruising yacht should only run before the seas while it is clearly safe and comfortable to do so. Many vessels have come to grief by pursuing this tactic too long.

Shortly after the US Coast Guard cutter arrived on the scene, the schooner was overturned by a particularly large breaking wave and quickly sank. Her sole crew – visible by the stern of the capsized craft – was rescued by an 180ft (55m) Avon rigid inflatable boat. *Photo: Douglas Perkins*

RUNNING WITH WARPS

As already mentioned, it is important to try to find an appropriate speed for good steering when running before a storm. Towing warps as a means of keeping the stern to the seas, while flattening the breakers behind and helping to reduce the yacht's speed to a more desirable level, may sound archaic to some, but it is a technique still used by experienced seamen, particularly in shorthanded situations. First, warps, having more than one use, are usually available, easy to stow, and uncomplicated. Furthermore, one can control the length of rope paid out to ensure a steady pull. Too short a warp and breaking crests can carry it forward so that there is no retarding force at all. A long warp, unlike a single drogue, can span a whole wavelength, so making the pull more constant. Warps intended for securing alongside will not be long enough for spanning an ocean wave. Thus for ocean passages one should be looking at a length of 400ft (122m) or more. Even experienced warp-users such as Sir Robin Knox-Johnston relate the ease with which warps can tangle when being paid out in the sort of conditions when they can help; thus preparation and skill are necessary in their deployment.

When Sir Robin Knox-Johnston encountered heavy weather in the southern oceans he put out 600ft (183m) of 2in (5cm) circumference warp in the form of a bight, lashed the helm tightly amidships, and went to sleep. He says:

The warp held the heavily built *Suhaili* firmly stern-to the waves. She lay very comfortably, regardless of the wave height, in forces of at least 12 on the Beaufort scale when the sea was white with spindrift. *Suhaili* drifted downwind at an average of about 2 knots in big stuff and strong blows with only a storm jib set right forward, sheeted tight amidships. If she tended to yaw, the force on the jib increased the more she came round, tending to push her back downwind. *Suhaili* has a canoe-type stern, or Norwegian type if you prefer, and this meant that there was no great resistance to the waves as they rolled past, they were just divided. The warp stretched quite a lot in surges, but that was to be expected. Had I been able to get the warps out in 1989. I am sure that we would have been all right, and I am intending to make a couple of rope reels, which I shall hang from the deckhead in the fo'c'sle, so in future I can lead the warps directly over the stern if I need them in a hurry.

Bernard Moitessier's experience with warps during a survival storm in the South Pacific in 1965–6 is often quoted. The 40ft (12.2m) yacht *Joshua* was towing 'five long hawsers varying in length from 100ft (30.5m) to 300ft (91.4m), with iron ballast attached and supplemented by a heavy net used for loading ships'. At the onset of the storm it seems possible that this arrangement was successful, but once the wave height and length reached a certain point, the yacht failed to respond to the wheel, and the warps did not prevent her from surfing down the crests. Not finding these circumstances satisfactory, eventually Moitessier cut the warps, whereupon he found himself in a much more comfortable situation.

Towing warps behind the Kelly 32 catamaran *Anna Louise*. In this case the warps pulled out of the water at times, failing to produce a steady load. *Photo: Richard Herbert*

Interestingly, Dr David Lewis, returning from the USA after the 1960 singlehanded Transatlantic Race, recounts a similar experience. He had been running under staysail alone, but after the sheet fairlead had pulled out of the deck with the increasing wind strength, he lowered the sail and streamed 120ft (36.6m) of warp in a bight. At once, he says, his boat became unmanageable, and even when he did succeed in steering down the seas, the breaking waves would carry the warp alongside. There are more examples of such difficulties described in the 1979 Fastnet Race account (Chapter 17).

Tony Marchaj explains the apparent anomaly regarding use of warps to some extent in his book entitled *Seaworthiness: The Forgotten Factor* (published by Adlard Coles Nautical). He believes that, in a fast-growing sea, wave height increases more quickly than wavelength, producing especially steep seas. As waves develop in size there will be a time when their wavelength is twice a given boat's length. At this point the bow will arrive in the trough just as the stern is at the top of the crest. With steep enough seas as a result of the fast-growing effect, one can see that there may be a tendency for the boat in this attitude to topple, ie pitch-pole or broach, especially as the water particles driven by the orbital action within a wave will be moving forward at the crest of the wave, reducing the effectiveness of the rudder. When a boat has been designed with the rudder placed well aft, the control situation may be further aggravated as a result of 'ventilation', a term used to describe the situation when the rudder may be lifted partly out of the water or its efficiency reduced by aeration. Moreover, if a yacht is overtaken by a breaking wave the water flow upon which the rudder relies can be reversed.

In very short steep seas, when a boat could topple and when the rudder may be less effective than usual, many yachtsmen have felt that they would benefit from the use of some drag device to prevent their vessel broaching or pitch-poling. Tony Marchaj suggests that when the wavelength has had time to develop further there will be a need for less drag and more speed to evade breaking crests and awkward cross-seas in the troughs, hence a need to discard the use of warps as the wave system matures. Nevertheless, this does not explain why those such as David Lewis and Bernard Moitessier had control difficulties with warps streamed after seas had had ample time to grow, and others, such as Sir Robin Knox-Johnston and Geoffrey Francis (Chapter 15), did not.

The explanation seems to lie in the length and height of waves compared with the length of warp used. If Bernard Moitessier used warps, as he says, of up to only 300ft (91.4m) in seas of wavelength 500–560ft (152–171m) one could expect, through the orbital movement within a wave, his warps to be ineffective at times. Likewise, allowing for the bight, David Lewis's warp only extended 60ft (18.3m) in waves that he estimated to be 150ft (46m) in length.

After disposing of his warps Moitessier found that it was an advantage to luff a little at the arrival of each wave crest to take the sea 15–20° on the quarter. He was now in the same situation as the Webbs in *Supertramp* (Chapter 15) and using the same tactics. These two are not alone in preferring to run free with the seas slightly on the quarter. Not only does it reduce the chances of pitch-poling, but also – like a surfer – by steering across the waves one may be able to avoid the worst of the breaking crests. When the face of the wave is exceptionally steep there will be a very fine balance between pitch-poling and broaching, and in this case the helmsman may have to weave his boat down the wave to optimize the situation.

The experience of Bernard Moitessier and others leads one to the view that to avoid being pitch-poled, rolled over or being pooped, boat speed must be kept at a level to give directional stability at all times. Of course, once huge seas have had the time to develop, it is usually in the troughs of the waves that problems occur. Here the boat's speed is no longer being helped by gravity, and the shelter of the adjacent wave crest may reduce wind strength. Nonetheless, in the trough of a wave, the need for directional stability remains as vital as elsewhere. Thus warp drag has to be adjusted, or enough sail has to be set, to take the craft safely through the troughs, accepting that at other times even with warps streamed, this may mean that a boat could be surfing at what may seem to be an unnatural rate. Some boats, like *Suhaili*, may be directionally stable when towing warps with helm lashed; others may demand competent helmsmanship, but probably to a lesser degree than when running completely free.

An auxiliary engine can possibly provide the additional drive needed to achieve good steering control in the troughs. It might be helpful to illustrate this point with an extract from an account by Richard Clifford when cruising off Ireland in his Warrior 35, *Warrior Shamaal*, in August 1979. As luck would have it, he found himself alone at sea in the midst of the infamous Fastnet storm of 1979. It may be of note that it was not his first storm.

A modern lifeboat almost buried by a breaking head sea. It is easy to imagine that a small vessel might be capsized if caught beam-on to such waves. *Photo: Ian Watson.*

I dropped off my crew in Glengariff on 13 August and sailed gently down Bantry Bay, then headed south-west out into the Atlantic. At 0400 the next morning the wind was too much for the storm jib, so I handed it and lay a'hull. Very soon afterwards *Warrior Shamaal* was knocked flat by a large breaking wave. I grabbed a bucket and bailed, found the bilge pump and pumped, and fought my way to the wheel to try to get the boat to run downwind, but she would not come round. The next extra large wave again filled the cockpit and the saloon to just above the cabin sole. When we came back on an even keel I noticed that the liferaft was floating in its container beside the boat, the bilge pump handle had gone and the anchor had come out of its well on the foredeck. The immediate problem was to stay afloat, so I rushed below, got the heads bilge pump handle, and put the washboards in position. Still *Warrior Shamaal* would not run downwind and yet another wave bowled the boat over, filling the cockpit and pouring water below. By this time the liferaft had inflated itself and broken adrift.

I was not prepared to set my 98sq ft (9.1sq m) storm jib as it would have been too big: my 50sq ft (15.2sq m) spitfire jib was in my garage! So I started my 15hp auxiliary engine and with this ticking over in gear I was able to keep the stern into the wind with an occasional burst of full throttle after my concentration had lapsed.

Suddenly we were at the top of an extra big wave. *Warrior Shamaal* hung at the top then plunged forward in a horrifying nose-down attitude. Her bows plunged into the trough and I fully expected to continue on down, or the stern to flip over, pitch-poling the yacht. With a shudder we pulled out of the dive and rushed on with the next mountainous wave.

Tactics had to be changed again, so between waves I passed a mooring line from one cockpit winch aft around the self-steering, and back into the cockpit. My 300ft (91m) warp is coiled and seized with sailmaker's twine every 60–70ft (18.3–21m) to avoid tangles. I attached the end of this onto the mooring line and paid out each coil until the whole bight of rope was more or less floating astern. Still running ahead on the engine and towing the bight, I experienced no further problems.

In this account we not only have an engine being used to good effect, but we again see that lying a'hull may not be a satisfactory tactic in extreme conditions. Furthermore, we see that warps were thought to be necessary to avoid broaching or pitch-poling during the period when the seas were developing rapidly in height and steepness.

On balance it appears that warps streamed astern on their own can work well in extreme storms so long as the warp arrangement is long enough to span a whole wavelength of the seas. The shorter the warps are in relation to the wavelength, the lower the proportion of time when the warps are providing effective drag. Consequently a collection of short warps may slow a boat down below the speed necessary to steer, or for the boat to steer herself, yet they may provide insufficient drag to prevent wild surfing when the orbital movement within the wave is moving in the same direction as the boat.

Having established that a long length of warp would seem one form of desirable equipment for heavy weather, it is worth quoting from Michael Richey's experiences in July 1981. He was returning to the UK from Bermuda in his famous 25ft (7.6m) Folkboat *Jester* when he was overtaken by a fierce storm from the south-south-west. He writes:

How to handle a boat in extreme conditions is a matter for judgement and much will depend upon one's knowledge of how the boat behaves. Perhaps there are no hard and fast rules. In *Jester* I have never felt the need to tow warps, although I have often run before gales. Now, under self-steering, we were surfing down the slopes of heavy seas and the tops were beginning to fall off. My fear was that she might bury her head and pitch-pole. It seemed essential to slow the boat down. I carried on board a 11lb (5kg) Bruce anchor as a kedge, and since the Bruce is reputed to be hydrodynamically stable I reckoned it should tow like a paravane. Accordingly I streamed the anchor over the starboard quarter, on some 75ft (23m) of line, taking the end – with some difficulty, as one must crawl out to it – to the cleat. This immediately slowed the boat down to about half her speed and kept the stern nicely into the seas, preventing her from slewing about. So we spent the night of 9–10 July, the storm rising in violence and with a general situation of discomfort, but *Jester* well under control.

This report encourages an alternative to the use of very long warps during a storm.

USING DROGUES

Warps have several disadvantages. The warp, or series of warps knotted together, may need to be very long to provide enough drag and also to bridge a whole wavelength. Not every yacht carries enough line and, even if it does, the crew may not have the will and patience to handle a long length of rope in bad weather, and when the storm is over there is the dreary task of bringing the line back on board.

Much the same effect as that of a warp can be achieved by using a line in conjunction with a weighted drogue. A good drogue will provide the same drag as hundreds of feet of rope but, better still, it will provide strong resistance when the boat is tending to go too fast and disproportionately less when the boat slows down and is in danger of losing steerage way. Additionally, a suitably weighted drogue will operate clear of surface effects. Given the choice, a good weighted drogue is much more efficient, easier to manage, and it is more likely to do what is needed. Fuller details are in Chapter 6.

The disadvantage of any form of effective drogue is that it will hold the stern aggressively into the seas, increasing the chances of the boat being pooped. Centre-cockpit vessels are to be preferred when using drogues. It may be necessary to steer when using a drogue, but some vessels will be steered by an autopilot and a few others, particularly long-keeled yachts, will steer themselves with the helm lashed. As in the case of warps, there may come a point as waves mature when a drogue will give more hindrance than help and the boat is better off without. Alternatively, waves may develop so much that there is a risk that the yacht may pitch-pole, as happened to *Silver Shadow* in the Queen's Birthday storm of 1994 (Chapter 22). If the boat is of a type that does not heave-to comfortably, and there is a danger of pitch-poling, the options are to motor into the sea or deploy a parachute sea anchor.

USING PARACHUTE SEA ANCHORS

If running before a storm, perhaps using a drogue or warps, a point may be anticipated when the vessel is in danger of being pitch-poled, a lee shore is becoming an issue, or the crew is too exhausted to continue to steer. A remedy in these circumstances is to deploy a parachute sea anchor, and for some yachtsmen this tactic is now their first line of defence. The advantage of a correctly deployed parachute is that it will hold a yacht bows-on to the seas, and when struck by a breaking wave she will not be rolled or pitch-poled, however large that wave may be.

Of course it is not necessary for the situation to become desperate before deploying a parachute sea anchor, and it will be much easier to set it up before the storm breaks. There are plenty of recorded instances to be found in yachting magazines and in the *Drag Device Data Base* when a parachute sea anchor has proved to be an advantage. The parachute sea anchor has come of age, but for success a number of conditions have to be met. The parachute has to be big and strong enough, and the parachute line has to be long enough and of the correct diameter. Moreover, all the components of the system including the securing points on the boat have to be solid enough to take the considerable load. Many people do not achieve a good deployment at their first attempt, and recovery can be difficult.

There are no half measures in the use of a parachute, but there are growing numbers

After two severe knockdowns while lying a'hull, Ernest and Val Haigh tied together 600ft (183m) of heavy line and trailed it astern. The improvement was immediate. *Photo: Ernest and Val Haigh*

of yachtsmen who, having successfully used a parachute, now would not be without one, in spite of the uncomfortable motion when the parachute is deployed. One variation, developed by the remarkable couple Lin and Larry Pardey on lying head-to-wind and -sea on a parachute sea anchor, is to set up the parachute line at an angle using a snatch block on a pendant line led from aft. With a trysail or deep-reefed mainsail set, a boat can be much more comfortable than when the parachute is directly over the bow, but many accounts suggest that this method may take time to perfect. The technique appears to be most suitable for long-keeled yachts under 40ft (12.2m) such as the Pardeys' own yacht *Taleisin*. More information is to be found in Chapters 6, 25, 26 and 27.

USING OIL

There has never been any doubt that oil on troubled waters provides a calming influence. Some scientists attribute the mechanism to something called the 'Marangoni Effect'. A rider of probably academic interest is that a film of vegetable oil, which has a high elasticity, is said to work better than a film of mineral oil. However, there are precious few recent records of small craft using oil of any sort to their benefit during severe weather. It may be significant that whereas British lifeboats were fitted with a small tank of 'wave subduing oil' – a vegetable oil called Garnet 46 – the oil was seldom used, and modern lifeboats no longer carry it. We have the instance of HMS *Birmingham* using oil in the 1987 English Channel storm to assist a vessel in distress (Chapter 19). The captain had good reason to use it and the opportunity to study its effectiveness; in this case the oil could be seen to be working, but the problem was to position it so as to be useful. Oil was certainly helpful to Group Captain Geoffrey Francis during the typhoon described later (Chapter 15), where he attributes his survival to an abundant supply of rope and tractor vaporizing oil. One must give credit to him for making the best use of his resources; however, not many craft would be likely to carry around 100 gallons of oil on deck in case a tropical revolving storm occurred. Nevertheless, there is no doubt that oil can be a lifesaver in the right place.

A feature of many storm experiences is that crews are often forced to work through a variety of tactics as conditions worsen beyond previous experience, and it becomes obvious that something different has to be done. Instinct and improvisation come to one's aid, but we can be sure that the people who deserve to come off best are those who have the resolve to keep on top of the situation, who have chosen and thoroughly prepared their vessels and crews for heavy weather and, when necessary, have alternative measures in mind.

This book illustrates that there is no one answer to survival in heavy weather, yet there is a great deal that can be done to optimize one's chances. At the same time one must not forget Adlard Coles' words from Chapter 15: 'No yacht, however sound, and no crew, however experienced, is immune from the dangers of the sea.'

PART *2*

STORM EXPERIENCES

14 North Sea gale

ADLARD COLES

The first occasions on which I got properly 'caught out' in gales occurred in 1925. That is not to say that I had no previous experience of gales, for in 1923 I had made a long cruise with two undergraduate friends in my 7-tonner *Annette* to the Baltic. It happened to be a year of particularly bad weather, and as a result we experienced a number of gales in which we broke the boom, parted a shroud, pulled out the bobstay, sprang the mast, and suffered much minor damage. But all this occurred near coastal waters and we were never caught in the open sea beyond reach of harbour.

In 1925 my wife and I bought a 12 ton gaff ketch at Riga, which we renamed *Annette II*. She was a heavy double-ender of Scandinavian design measuring 29ft 7in (9m) overall and no less than 11ft 4in (3.5m) in beam. The draft was 3ft 9in (1.1m) or 7ft 9in (2.4m), with the centreboard down, and the sail area was 430sq ft (40sq m). She was fitted with a hot-bulb semi-diesel engine, which I could rarely get to work. Everything about this yacht was heavy and solid. She seemed huge after the first *Annette*, which was of light displacement and only 19ft (5.8m) on the waterline.

My wife and I had a wonderful cruise in *Annette II*, sailing from the strange historic port of Riga to Gotland and Öland, and then to Sweden and Denmark, before passing through the Kiel Canal to the North Sea, and westwards past the Frisian islands to IJmuiden in Holland.

We had a fair amount of bad weather during the cruise and were hove-to west of Öland Rev lightvessel in a gale, but it only lasted about six hours. The real gale was reserved for the last lap of the voyage, when at dawn on 18 September 1925 *Annette II* sailed out of IJmuiden on the sandy coast of Holland bound for Dover. Her staysail, mainsail and mizzen were set close-hauled to a light southerly breeze and she could just lay a little south of west. The yacht sailed steadily seawards over the grey waves, the Dutch coast gradually fading to a pencilled line, until it was finally lost as the distance increased and the hands of the cabin clock marked the passing hours.

During the morning, the wind backed and freshened. Occasionally, spray whipped across the deck and tumbled along the lee scuppers before running back into the sea. The backing wind, an ominous sign, had the merit of enabling the course to be altered to the south towards the Maas lightvessel, and progress was good.

At sunset *Annette II* passed the lightvessel, some 15 miles west-south-west of the Hook of Holland, leaving her a few miles to the eastward. The evening meal was prepared and eaten, and by the time the crockery had been washed and stowed away, night was upon us. The wind moderated and headed and the tide was foul for six hours so, although the yacht sailed well throughout the night, she failed to bring the Schouwen lightship abeam by morning.

The ketch *Annette II* in the Stint See, Riga, at the start of her cruise to England. An Estonian family is bidding farewell.

Despite the light wind and sea it had been by no means an idle night, for we had to keep a vigilant watch as we sailed through a fleet of fishing boats, and from time to time ships crossed our course, so for much of the night both of us were on deck. The yacht's navigation lights were inefficient, but I had bought two hurricane lamps at IJmuiden, one with red glass and the other green, which were kept in the cockpit and shown as required.

At dawn (19 September) my wife was at the helm and it was my turn on watch. I have never shared a poet's love of the dawn at sea. It is then that the long sleepless hours make themselves felt. The dawn is grey, the sea is grey. It is cold and damp and one gets hungry. *Annette II* was just ploughing over a waste of empty sea, for the low Dutch islands were far below the horizon. The glass was falling steadily and the wind was freshening again. We had no wireless and, therefore, no weather forecasts, but the conditions were a warning in themselves. The only cheerful prospect was that the wind had backed so we could lay the course and were making fine progress with a fair tide.

Throughout the morning *Annette II* sailed in a welter of foam on her course for the North Hinder lightvessel. After lunch I began to feel anxious, as we had failed to sight the lightship, when happily a spidery red form was vaguely discerned in the distance ahead. I had made the common mistake of overestimating the distance made good. We passed close to the lightship just before 1500, and her crew turned out to greet us. I had no time to respond to their friendly hails, for a squall stuck us and I was busy reefing the mainsail and setting the storm jib.

By then it was blowing half a gale and the barometer had fallen no less than 20mb since early morning. From the yacht's position, the Sandettie lightship lay about 30 miles to the south. The distance from the Sandettie to Dover is only a matter of another 20, so we determined to carry on and get to Dover or another port on the English side of the North Sea.

On we sailed, with the wind continuing to harden all the time. The wind had backed to a little east of south, and with shoals off the coast of Belgium little over 20 miles to windward, the seas, although rough, were not high. The hours slipped by as *Annette II* held on her course, and the glass continued to fall. It dropped another 7mb, making a total fall of 27mb.

Towards sunset *Annette II* was more than half-way from the North Hinder to the Sandettie lightship. The sun was low and fiercely yellow, and gradually a great bank of purple cloud spread across the sky, covering the whole horizon to the southward. The sun became hidden behind the cloud as it advanced, but a wan light lit up the white-capped sea.

Then it arrived. The first squall was on us. The seas were obscured in the whiteness of pelting rain, and there was a sizzling noise. The yacht heeled far over, the wind whistled in the rigging with every sail, every stay and sheet hardened under the strain. The seas leapt short, steep and breaking. One came aboard heavily and broke over the cabin top and cascaded off to leeward. The yacht was hard pressed with her lee rail under in spite of that tremendous beam, and I let the mainsheet fly. That eased her, and I sheeted the storm jib to weather and belayed it. I sheeted in the reefed main and mizzen hard and, with the helm lashed slightly down, the yacht lay hove-to on the port tack.

For a while I sat in the steering well. The force of the wind was stunning. The rain was torrential, ironing out the breaking seas with its pelting drops, leaving only the deep furrows. The squall was accompanied by thunder and lightning.

Annette II lay hove-to very well. The heavy oak hatch to the companionway was closed, and the dinghy was well secured on the foredeck by four lashings. The yacht seemed safe enough, but she might have been better without the mainsail, though I did not lower it. With the onslaught of the gale the wind veered to the south-west, at once dispelling any hope of fetching to Dover. The yacht was slowly drifting towards the middle of the North Sea. There was no danger in that direction for many hours to come, but if the wind veered to west or north-west the Belgian shoals and coast would be under the lee.

There was nothing to be done. Seizing my chance between the seas, I opened the hatch and slipped into the warm interior of the cabin. In the meantime my wife had been busy with the lamps, filling and trimming them: white, red and green. She jammed them between the cabin table and a bunk, where they were ready for use. She had also prepared malted milk, and this, together with some dry biscuits, formed our evening meal.

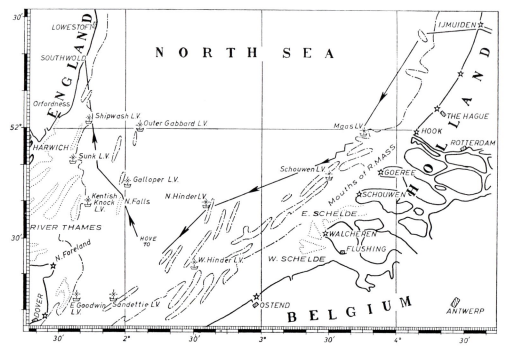

Figure 14.1 The course of *Annette II* in the North Sea gale, September 1925.

Night was soon upon us. There was nothing to do but lie as best we could in our bunks. We took watches in turn to open the hatch and look out for the lights of approaching ships and to see that all was well. Down below in the cabin it was wretched. The atmosphere was close and damp, for leaks had developed in the deck and round the coachroof and there was condensation everywhere. The ceaseless hammering and shaking as the seas struck the boat were wearying, and as the sea rose we had to use continual effort to prevent ourselves being thrown out of our bunks. We were both very wet, as the violent rain and spray had penetrated our oilskins, so that when we went below the wet clothes gave a feeling of clammy dampness. Neither of us slept, but we dozed a little from time to time.

When one or other of us went on deck we occasionally saw the lights of ships sufficiently close to warrant exhibiting one or other of the flickering hurricane lamps. On deck the scene was impressive in the extreme. The seas were black, but their formation was outlined by the gleam of the breaking crests. They came in sinister procession. The bows of the boat would rise to meet one, then down it would fall on the sloping mass of water into the trough, before rising again in time to climb the next. Sometimes the top of a sea would break aboard green and fall with a thud on the top of the cabin roof to stream aft in a cascade of water over the closed companion doors into the cockpit.

There was tremendous noise: the wind in the mast and rigging, the hiss of advancing breakers and the splash of running water. Above all raged a non-stop thrumming and vibration in the rigging. I believe the sea steadily increased, for the motion became worse and worse. Two of the lamps got smashed, but it did not matter much, as they flickered so much when exposed to the wind that there was little chance of them being seen. Moreover, we grew lethargic and our visits to the deck became less and less frequent; we were quite game to accept the chance of one in a thousand of being run down.

The position was wild in the extreme: we were hove-to in the night of a severe gale, surrounded at a distance of about 20 miles, except to the north, by a broken circle of shoals, on which the seas would break heavily. We were absolutely in the hands of chance. At the time we were profoundly miserable. We just lay in our bunks only half asleep. The position was not imminently dangerous so long as the wind did not shift to the west.

The night went by steadily, time passing neither slowly nor quickly. The hours went by until the moment arrived when in the dark cabin one could discern the outline of the porthole against the dim light of approaching day. We had only a vague idea of our position and my wife very appropriately suggested that I should go on deck again while it was still dark to see whether the lights of any lightships were in sight. On my reckoning there was little prospect of this, and I remained as I was for a few minutes before summoning energy to do my wife's bidding. Then I climbed out and stepped up into the cockpit. It was bitterly cold on deck and a big sea was running, but the wind was less vicious. It was still dark and, to my surprise, I saw at intervals the loom of several flashing lights reflected in the sky to the west. There must have been a clearance in the visibility. My wife's intuition was right. Then, suddenly, away on the starboard beam I saw distinctly the glow of a distant red light. It disappeared. It came again. A long interval and there it was again!

I had been anxious about our position, but in a few seconds the situation was utterly changed. Unfamiliar as I was with the Thames estuary, I could not be misled by two red flashes. On the face of the whole chart it could mean only one thing: the Galloper lightship (the character of the light has since been changed).

The wind, which had shifted from time to time during the night, was south-south-west. I unlashed the helm, sheeted the jib to leeward, and bore away to the north-west. As the yacht gathered way with the sheets eased she crashed over the seas, and the wind hurled the spray across the boat in massive sheets. With a roar a big sea flung itself aboard, struck the dinghy, and fell on the cabin top. A few minutes later another reared up and came crashing over the yacht, breaking in a solid mass over the companion cover, and struck me a heavy blow across the chest. My wife joined me on deck. All night we had lain in our bunks damp to the skin and, now in the bitter cold before dawn, the driving water constantly penetrated our oilskins and chilled us to the bone. We were both pretty tired after the sleepless night and the effort of keeping ourselves from rolling off our bunks. We were also hungry, for under these conditions cooking had been almost impossible.

We had a few sips of whisky and Riga balsam. The latter was a potent drink which we had bought in Riga. It was rather an unpleasant bitter taste like medicine, but I fancy it has a very high alcoholic content and is warming. The edge of hunger was relieved by eating macaroons which we had bought at IJmuiden; they were wet, for a sea arrived at the exact moment that we opened the tin. It was rather an odd kind of breakfast and an odd time to have it, but basically it was alcohol, sugar and protein – a good mixture when one is tired and cold.

In a wild welter of foam-capped seas *Annette II* sailed on. Time after time she was swept by seas. But the knowledge of the yacht's position gave us confidence. We could see the friendly red flashes of the Galloper lightship and before dawn it came abeam. The sea was then tremendous and very confused, as we were crossing shallower water in the vicinity of the North Falls.

My wife sat beside me, trying to identify the looms of the distant lights. The steering was too heavy for her, but she was cheerful and took a full share in any work to be done. An hour after we had passed the Galloper, the distant lights still remained below the horizon. Before long even the looms could no longer be distinguished against the lightening sky.

Navigation posed problems, as I was totally unfamiliar with the east coast of England and I was unable to leave the deck to go below to lay proper courses. I had charts of the Continental coast, but the only ones I had of the east coast of England were a small-scale chart of the North Sea and an old Blue Back on an equally small scale. Harwich was little over 20 miles away, but the approaches would be tricky without a proper chart and the wind was likely to veer and head us. On the other hand, Lowestoft appeared to have an easy approach. It was nearly 50 miles distant, but even if the wind veered to the west it would still be free and the passage would take less than 10 hours sailing. So we eased the sheets and altered to the estimated new course.

Running before the gale with the wind on the quarter, *Annette II* was very hard on the helm. I was very cold and it was exhausting work. The hours passed slowly. My wife tried to take a spell at steering, but the effort to hold a steady course before the big following seas was beyond her physical strength.

At length the time arrived when land should be in sight, but there was nothing to be seen except sea and more sea in every direction. Nevertheless, the gale had moderated and we passed a few ships.

At last my wife (who has exceptionally good sight) declared she could see something like land on the port bow. I could see nothing of it myself, but I knew she must be right and that the end of our difficulties was in sight. This cheered us immensely. My wife went below and got a primus going to heat the cabin. There was a shambles in the cabin from articles thrown adrift during the gale. The water in the bilges had risen to the cabin sole and everything was soaked. But the sea was moderating under the partial lee of the land and presently my wife appeared on deck with a tin of cold baked beans, which between us we devoured hungrily. She then took a watch, for the yacht was becoming easier on the helm, and I went below into the warmth of the cabin, peeled off my oilskins and slowly changed into dry clothes. When I returned on deck to resume steering, with dry clothes on and a shot of whisky inside me, I felt a different man, but my wife, who was also wet through, would not change.

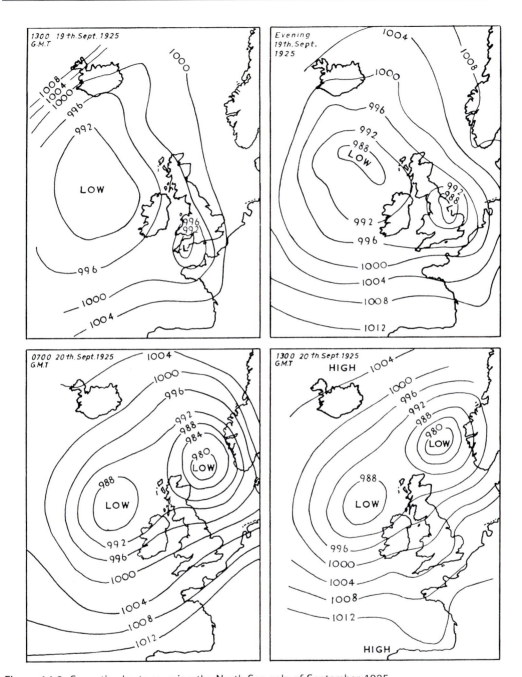

Figure 14.2 Synoptic charts covering the North Sea gale of September 1925.

A low coast was abeam, and short brown seas replaced the confused mass of grey. A black buoy was passed, the sun appeared, but the minutes still seemed like hours. At last we saw a town on the port bow and after some consideration came to the conclusion that it was Southwold. It came nearer and, through glasses, we distinguished two long low wooden piers. References to the *Cruising Association Handbook* gave a few notes on the shallow harbour at Walberswick that were far from encouraging, but on nearer approach we realized that we had a leading wind up the reach between the piers. The yacht was steered more inshore, the entrance came near, and we could see the seas breaking on either side. I calculated that it was two hours after high water. I took two soundings with the lead, before sailing on straight for the piers. *Annette II* foamed up the narrow entrance between the piers and her anchor was let go in the calm of harbour. The voyage was at an end.

It may be of interest to add that the name *Annette II* was adopted by me as a pseudonym in my early book *Close Hauled* for Arthur Ransome's *Racundra*. When I sold *Annette II* the new owner installed a new engine and reverted to the original name of *Racundra*. Since the war her whereabouts had been something of a mystery until a yachtsman identified her, by means of a photograph, sailing and apparently in good condition in the Mediterranean.

CONCLUSIONS

The weather was featured in the Sunday and Monday newspapers, which described the weekend as the worst of the year, with 'violent' gales and fierce rainstorms. The disturbance was reported as developing off the north coast of Spain early on Saturday morning and travelling north-east across England at a rate of 40–45 knots, but the accompanying synoptic charts show that the cause of the trouble was a deepening secondary. At Dungeness the wind was 35 knots (force 8) sustained from 0900 on Saturday evening till 1700 on Sunday. At Calshot, Hampshire, and Spurn Head, Yorkshire, it reached about 43 knots (force 9). Many vessels were in distress round the coasts.

From these reports, it seems reasonable to regard the gale as experienced by *Annette II* in the North Sea as mean of force 8 for a few hours, falling on Sunday morning to force 7, as recorded at Calais at 0700. The frontal squalls when *Annette II* lay hove-to could have been anything up to 50 or 60 knots, possibly bringing the mean up to force 9 on the Beaufort scale for an hour or so. The following lessons were learnt from our cruise in *Annette II* and the gale on the last lap.

1 **Sail area**   A yacht with a very small sail area, such as *Annette II*, is so slow in light and moderate winds that, without auxiliary power, she is a sitting duck for gales when on long passages.
2 **Time**   Our holiday was drawing to an end when we were caught out, otherwise we would probably have taken shelter long before the gale started. Shortage of time and the need to get a yacht to her home port in a hurry are the most common causes of cruising yachts getting caught out.
3 **Heaving-to**   The yacht hove-to well without coming up into the wind or forereaching too much. No doubt the long, straight keel and the sail plan distributed over three low sails helped her performance. Leeway, however, must have been considerable.
4 **Rain**   From later experience I can confirm that torrential rain, so violent that the surface of the sea smokes with it, has the temporary effect of taking some of the viciousness out of the seas.
5 **Tiredness**   On arrival in port we had been 53 hours at sea in narrow waters, out of which we had perhaps a total of 4 to 6 hours of sleep. We felt tired, but we quickly brightened up ashore in front of a blazing fire at the Bell Inn. It is probable that in heavy weather, when sleep is dificult because of the din, the lack of it is not exhausting provided that the crew can get a reasonable amount of rest in their bunks. People suffering from insomnia carry on with relatively little sleep.

The passing hardship made no apparent impression on my wife, who had taken it all calmly and uncomplainingly, but years later she told me that for weeks afterwards she suffered from nightmares of huge seas.

15 A variety of storms and weather phenomena, 1938–1997

ADLARD COLES & PETER BRUCE

When Adlard Coles started to write *Heavy Weather Sailing* in the 1960s he drew mainly from his own experiences because there were not many recorded accounts of small craft in very severe weather at that time. Of course the number of oceangoing yachts then was tiny compared with today. When small craft were overtaken by extremely rough weather there was often a scarcity of information from which comparisons could be made. For example, corroborative weather information was not so easily available and anemometers were not fitted, so good information was probably lost through sailors not having enough solid facts on which to hang their accounts. In addition to his personal accounts, Adlard Coles assembled a number of stories in a chapter originally entitled 'Survival Storms', where there was enough background information available to give authenticity. These are reproduced in this chapter either because some of them were long-held yardsticks of severity or there is something extraordinary about them – for example, William Mathers' decision to go to sea in a hurricane.

Adlard Coles' collection of storm stories gives the background to the thinking of 40 years ago or more, particularly regarding the use of sea anchors which, clearly, were not highly regarded. (Explanation may lie in the projected area, as modern parachute anchors have vastly more projected area than those used 80 years ago.)

Following Adlard Coles' section, some more recent reports of storms have been added to this chapter. In addition there are some accounts of heavy weather caused by thunderstorms, waterspouts and tornadoes. These events, which are often short-lived, can sometimes be as life threatening as any normal storm.

Adlard Coles writes:

The difference between a gale and what has become known as a 'survival' storm is that in the former, with winds of force 8 or perhaps 9 (say 30 to 45 knots mean velocity), the skipper and crew retain control and can take the measures that they think best, whereas in a survival storm of force 10 or over, perhaps gusting at hurricane strength, wind and sea become the masters. For skipper and crew it is then a battle to keep the yacht afloat. The course is dictated by the need to take the breaking crests of the seas at the best angle. Where yachts more commonly get caught out in storms and hurricanes is on the western side of the Atlantic. It is for this reason that I have turned to America and the American magazine *Yachting* for information about survival storms, as the principal danger area lies on the route between the New England yachting centres and Bermuda, Florida and the Caribbean. The principal hazards are the tropical storms, with closed isobars and mean wind force between 34 and 63 knots, and the hurricanes of 64 knots or more, with gusts possibly reaching 170 knots.

Hurricanes as a rule occur between June and November and principally in September, but there can be out-of-season ones at pretty well any time of the year. According to Captain Edwin T Harding, US Navy (the author of *Heavy Weather Guide* and a meteorological specialist in the subject), waves of 35–40ft (11–12m) are not uncommon in an average hurricane and, in giant storms, build up to 45–50 ft (14–15m). Waves even higher have been reported, but happily they are very rare.

Bermuda yachtsmen tell me that during the winter there are severe storms in the Atlantic which, while not termed hurricanes, are equally formidable. They may last for a duration of three days with winds reaching the vicinity of 85 knots, well above hurricane force. Yachts do not always survive such severe storms. For example, the 70ft (21m) schooner *Margot* or *HSH (Home Sweet Home)* left Bermuda at 1700 on a January evening bound south. The weather forecast was good for 50 miles south of Bermuda, but by 2000 the same night the wind reached 85 knots locally and for the next week the minimum winds recorded at Bermuda were 50 knots. The schooner has never been heard of since. It is thought that she went down on the first evening while running under bare poles, and that her extra large cockpit and unsafe companionway resulted in her being flooded by a following sea. It is not known whether she was towing warps or whether her loss could have been averted had she done so.

Another example of a winter storm was that experienced by the 68ft (21m) schooner *Curlew*, which left Mystic, Connecticut, in a fresh north-westerly on Sunday 11 November 1962, bound for the Caribbean for charter service. She was skippered by Captain David Skellon, an Englishman, and the mate was Ed Owe, a Connecticut sailor. The two of them were the only deep-water sailors aboard, and they took the helm in turns during the whole of the nights in the bad weather that followed. By Wednesday morning the wind was northerly, about force 10, and the yacht was running under bare poles. A number of troubles had already developed, the most serious being the failure of the braking screw that kept the propeller shaft from turning, and a bad leak in the propeller-shaft packing. The bilge pump operated by the main engine seemed only just capable of keeping ahead of the leak.

The storm steadily increased during Wednesday and throughout the night. *Curlew* had entered the Gulf Stream, where the seas became more dangerous. In the second watch the following morning she suffered her first real broach, and was knocked flat on her beam-ends for almost three minutes before she slowly righted. After straightening the yacht's course out before the storm, the crew streamed a 3in (7.6cm) warp astern in a long loop, with drags lashed to it.

On Thursday the seas were higher than ever and the wind was estimated as gusting 75–80 knots. At 0700 a mountainous sea broke over the full length of the ship and stove in the main cabin skylight. As a result of Mayday calls to Bermuda, *Curlew* was spotted by a search plane and at 1400 the USS *Compass Island* hove into sight.

The yacht then continued to run under bare poles on her course for Bermuda, with *Compass Island* standing by and giving course instructions by radio telephone. That night *Curlew*, under a lee created by *Compass Island*, succeeded in getting within a quarter of a mile of the flashing buoy off St George's Harbour. Shelter was at last at hand. But the wind must have shifted, and it was so violent that no further progress could be made against it, even with the help of her powerful engine. It was impossible to gain harbour and *Curlew* had to run off. By then the yacht's condition was critical and, as the weather forecast predicted a continuance of the storm for another 24 hours, it was decided to run off and abandon her.

The schooner *Curlew* in distress in the Atlantic storm, north of Bermuda, with winds gusting up to 85 knots. *Photo: USS Compass Island*

Curlew manoeuvred alongside under the lee of *Compass Island*, but in doing so broke her bowsprit and carried away her foremast and shrouds against the ship's side. Nevertheless, all the crew were rescued by *Compass Island* without injury by means of cargo nets – a creditable performance at night with wind little below hurricane force.

Three days later it was reported that *Curlew* had been sighted. She was located and towed back safely into St George's Harbour. By then there was some 5ft (1.5m) of water above the cabin sole and everything below had been smashed, but after survey it was found that the hull was undamaged. All her seams and fastenings were as good as new. She is Everdur fastened, mahogany planked over white oak, with teak decks.

Curlew's was a remarkable survival of a storm stated to be the largest low-pressure in the area for 40 years. The 56ft (17m) schooner *Windfall*, which left Mystic at the same time as *Curlew* on the same course for Bermuda, sank in the storm. Her crew, when last seen by a freighter, were hanging onto wreckage, but the weather was so bad that the freighter was not able to do anything to help them. Nine other ships were in distress at the same time as *Curlew* and, altogether, the sea on this occasion claimed over 144 lives.

What is confirmed by the experiences in this storm is that once wind and sea have risen to or near hurricane force there is no knowing what will happen. *Windfall* sank, but *Curlew* survived, despite being partly waterlogged. Her tactic of running off, streaming warps, may have saved her, but despite this she broached several times. It is probable that *Windfall* may also have streamed warps, because it was the recognized method of coping with following seas.

Adlard Coles' comments were:

1 **The value of mechanical aids** It was the engine-operated bilge pump in *Curlew* that enabled the leak to be kept under control.
2 **The weakness of many steering wheels** Five spokes of *Curlew*'s wheel were broken when a man was swept against it by breaking seas. Damage to wheels is by no means rare in gales.
3 **Broaching** In a storm, however violent, broaching is not necessarily disastrous.

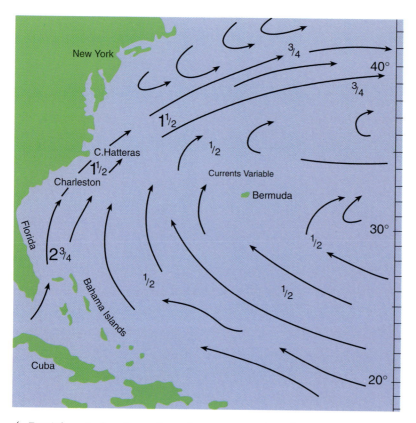

Figure 15.1 The Gulf Stream current (approx rate in knots). The diagram shows average summer conditions, but the stream varies in direction and rate in knots and is often much stronger than shown. It causes exceptional seas when the wind is contrary to the stream and its meanders provide a time-honoured speculation for navigators in the Bermuda Race.

4 **Partial waterlogging** A yacht may survive despite being partly waterlogged. This is evidenced both by *Tzu Hang* (which is referred to later in this chapter) and *Curlew* in circumstances where one would imagine survival to have been impossible. After she had been abandoned *Curlew* must have drifted out into the full force of the storm, and yet left to herself she remained afloat lying a'hull with water several feet above her cabin sole.

5 **Coming alongside** In hurricane conditions the rescuing vessel has great difficulty – sometimes finding it impossible – to lie alongside a yacht without damaging her in order to take off her crew. A rescuing vessel has to lie close alongside, and in heavy seas there is a grave risk of the yacht's mast breaking against the rescuing boat's side. The mast may then provide an additional hazard, as the broken part and rigging will flail around, and may prove a lethal weapon if it strikes the crew or rescuers as they are climbing the scrambling nets. The alternative procedure that might be used for rescue (such as the survivors of *Windfall* clinging to wreckage) would be to try to make a lee and drift inflatable liferafts to anyone overboard, as ships' lifeboats are useless under these conditions. The difficulty would be that the rescuing vessel would drift rapidly to leeward down on the yacht, so great skill in handling the former craft would be required.

Curlew may not have experienced the worst conditions of the Gulf Stream, as in her position the wind appears to have been blowing across rather than against the stream, though there is nothing certain about its course or velocity. Normally, the maximum strength of the Gulf Stream is found in the Straits of Florida and where it flows northwards towards Cape Hatteras. Here, in northerly gales against the stream, the seas in the axis of the stream are more dangerous to a yacht in an ordinary gale than those in a storm or possibly even a hurricane in the open Atlantic. This accounts possibly for the loss of *Revenoc*, one of the most deeply felt yachting disasters on the American side of the Atlantic.

Revenoc was a Sparkman & Stephens designed, outside-ballasted, centreboard yawl. Her dimensions were 42ft 7in (13m) LOA, 29ft 7in (9m) LWL, 11ft 10in beam (3.6m), 4ft 6in (1.4m) draft, with a sail area of 883sq ft (82sq m). She was built to the highest specification and was particularly well equipped for cruising and ocean racing.

On 1 January 1958 the yawl sailed from Key West bound for Miami. In her sailed her owner and skipper, Harvey Conover, his son Lawrence Conover, their two wives, and William Fluegelman. The crew were highly experienced. Harvey Conover was a veteran deep-water sailor who had sailed since boyhood and was a former commodore of the Cruising Club of America. His son, aged 26, had been brought up with boats and was a first-class seaman. William Fluegelman had sailed a great deal with the Conovers and was a former Coast Guardsman. Mrs Harvey Conover was an able and experienced hand and Mrs Lawrence Conover had also sailed extensively in the two *Revenocs*.

On 2 January a north-north-east gale gusting 65 knots struck the area without warning. The Weather Bureau summary as reported in *Yachting* read: 'A big high pressure area over south-eastern US was pushing back a broad, not especially severe, cold front south-easterly across Florida, the Florida Straits and the Bahamas. Meanwhile a small, intense low pressure centre (not reported until Thursday, when *Revenoc* was expected at Miami) suddenly developed on Wednesday over western Cuba, moving north-east across the path of the front. As they approached each other, the clockwise wind pattern of the front and the counter-clockwise wind around the low centre, both blowing from a generally north-north-east direction, combined to set up a sudden gale with terrific gusts in the Florida Straits before daylight Thursday.'

The seas under these conditions on the axis of the Gulf Stream would have been fantastic. It was in this storm that *Revenoc* was lost with all hands. No trace of her was ever found except for her swamped dinghy, which drifted ashore near Jupiter Inlet on 6 January, having been carried northward by the current.

The loss may have been caused by many things. Most probably it could have been by being run down by a ship at night, because shipping is heavy where she was caught out and a yacht's lights may be lost in the seas and spray of a gale. It could also have been accounted for by a mast over the side damaging the hull beyond repair before it could be cleared away, by the yacht being driven onto outlying coral reefs, or by a rogue sea stoving in the superstructure or decks or rolling her over.

The answer will never be known, but the tactics adopted in *Revenoc* can be guessed at. In an article by Carlton Mitchell in *Yachting* of June 1956 an extract was quoted from a letter by Harvey Conover, after he had been caught out before in a Gulf Stream storm in *Revenoc*. In this gale (gusting 56–65 knots) he had run at 2 or 3 knots under bare poles towing warps

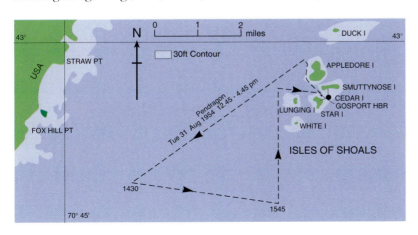

Figure 15.2 The course of *Pendragon* during Hurricane Carol.

so satisfactorily that he thought the yawl would take almost anything by this means. So, provided he had enough sea room, it is most probable that *Revenoc* was running before the storm trailing warps (and perhaps sails) on her last voyage. This is conjecture and the only lesson to be learnt from the tragedy is that no yacht, however sound, and no crew, however experienced, are immune from the dangers of the sea.

Returning now to the subject of hurricanes, let us consider Jean Gau's 29ft 6in (9m) ketch *Atom*, caught out in the path of Hurricane Carrie in September 1957, about 360 miles south of Montauk Point, Long Island. She survived lying a'hull streaming one warp and with oil bags secured to the weather rigging screws. There are four points which may have helped her in weathering the storm. After crossing the Atlantic, her bottom was so foul that she lay almost dormant in the water. Her draft was only 4ft (1.2m) and she had 2 tons of iron on her keel and 2 tons of inside ballast. She was thus of a type that would be difficult to capsize, and there would be less tendency to be tripped by a long shallow keel than a deep narrow one. It is probable that she had a low rig, though I have no particulars of this. *Atom* was in the track of Carrie, but about 160 miles to the northward of Bermuda, Carrie changed her mind, and sped off eastward across the Atlantic and finally made a precise landfall on the Fastnet Rock off south-western Ireland. As I have no particulars of *Atom's* course to compare with the track of the hurricane, I do not know whether she was anywhere near the centre, but even if she avoided the worst she would have been involved in gales so severe that they might come into survival storm category.

Atom's evidence is thus in favour of lying a'hull, but on 26 February 1966 the ketch was caught again between Durban and Cape Town. She lay a'hull with wind and sea on her port beam, but on this occasion she was completely rolled over through 360°. She lost all her spars and sails. Jean Gau was asleep below at the time and fortunately suffered no incapacitating injury. He spent the next 14 hours pumping the bilges (filled to the cabin sole), cutting away spars threatening to damage the hull, clearing rigging, and finally coping with the horrid job of drying out the engine. Then, under power, he managed to get to Mossel Bay, some 75 miles distant.

The *Atom* had a reliable anemometer, which recorded the wind velocity of 60 knots. Whether this was in gusts or at the mean speed on the Beaufort scale (which at 60 knots would be force 11) one does not know.

Jean Gau's experiences show that one can voyage time after time across the oceans without harm, but it takes only one freak wave of particular size and shape, catching the boat on the wrong foot, to do real and sometimes disastrous damage.

One of the most remarkable stories of yacht survival in a hurricane was that of *Pendragon*, which was involved in Hurricane Carol in 1954.

Pendragon was lying in the somewhat insecure Gosport harbour at the Isles of Shoals, situated in the Atlantic to the north-east of Boston. She is a cutter measuring 41ft (12.5m) LOA, 30ft (9.1m) LWL, 10ft beam (3m) and 6ft 3in (1.9m) draft, built by Nevins in 1935. Her crew consisted of William H Mathers and his wife Myra and two friends, Mr and Mrs Smoot.

Meanwhile, Hurricane Carol had stalled over North Carolina, but on the Tuesday morning, 31 August, came the startling news that she was well on her way again, moving up the New England coast. The warning arrived too late to make a better harbour. In *Pendragon* all preparations were carried out for Carol's arrival, but at the height of the storm a kedge began to drag and *Pendragon's* cable had to be cut to clear her. The wind was too strong to enable them to regain shelter under the lee of the breakwater upwind under engine, so in order to avoid going on the rocks *Pendragon* proceeded to sea in the dangerous quadrant of the hurricane.

Once in the open, the seas were found to be mountainous and the full weight of the hurricane winds was experienced. What we are concerned with here, however, is the method adopted so that the yacht could survive. The extraordinary thing is that she was handled under engine. This is the only occasion that I have heard of where an engine was used in an auxiliary yacht in open water during a gale, let alone in a hurricane. It seems to me that the average auxiliary engine would be useless even at force 7, though I have never tried the experiment at sea. So I wrote to Mr Mathers and from his answer it appears that it was done in this way.

The engine was a four-cylinder Gray with a rating of 25hp. It was fitted with a 2:1 reduction gear giving a propeller speed of about 800rpm in the hurricane. The propeller was 18in (45.7cm) diameter with a relatively flat pitch. In the hurricane, *Pendragon* was steered in the troughs beam-to the seas. The crests were about 300–400ft (91–122m) apart. In the troughs (where the yacht was under the partial lee of the waves), the engine gave enough power to give a speed of about 2.5 knots, which gave her skipper sufficient control to luff to the breaking crests of the seas, sufficiently to prevent her from being rolled over.

Pendragon's course is shown in Fig 15.2. First she ran before the storm and her rather fine bow seemed to bury and 'her stern would lift, which made the rudder almost useless. At the bottom of each wave she would turn one way or another at her own discretion and roll badly. In one of the troughs she rolled so far that she took in green water over the cockpit coaming.'

Owing to the dangers and the outlying rocks off Duck Island, *Pendragon* could not be run off to east or north-east away from the centre of the hurricane. For this reason, after clearing Appledore Island, William Mathers rounded onto the port tack heading south-west, although this would bring her nearer the centre of the storm. At about 1400 the sky cleared considerably in the west and the wind definitely let up. Half an hour later the wind veered from south-east to south and south-west, and *Pendragon* was able to lay to the east and south-east. A tiny patch of blue – a beautiful deep blue – appeared and disappeared before returning again and gave moments of warmth and better visibility. At 1545 the lighthouse on one of the islands in the Isles of Shoals was seen.

The yacht was run off to the northward and an hour later she was safely back in harbour. As Myra Mathers puts it, 'it did seem somewhat incongruous to crash around for four hours unable to see anything and end up exactly where we started'.

The only accident occurred when a sea hit *Pendragon* on the port quarter, just as the helmsmen were being changed and the yacht was momentarily off course. Myra Mathers had handed the tiller to her husband and was sliding past him when she was catapulted head first into the sea and drifted 25ft (7.6m) to leeward. Her head struck a stanchion as she went overboard.

By a stroke of good fortune, the sea had knocked the yacht to a standstill and the hurricane winds quickly drove her to leeward to Myra Mathers, who was then picked up. Much the same thing happened when *Tzu Hang* was pitch-poled in the Pacific, which is referred to later, and Beryl Smeeton was thrown 30yd (27m) to leeward. As the yacht had been dismasted, she was partially waterlogged and lay motionless. Beryl Smeeton, although injured, swam to the floating wreckage of the mizzen mast and pulled herself along to the side of *Tzu Hang*.

In both yachts the difficulty was to pull the survivor, weighed down by sodden clothes, out of the water into the safety of the cockpit. Myra Mathers was temporarily entangled round a stanchion, but once this was realized, she was quickly hauled on board *Pendragon*. The rescue of Beryl Smeeton in *Tzu Hang* was even harder, because she was unable to help, with the use of only one arm, owing to the injury to her shoulder. It took the combined strength of the two men to get her on board.

Hurricane Carol, in which *Pendragon* was involved, was intense, causing tremendous damage and insurance claims. During its unexpected dart up the New England coast, it blew down a 630ft (192m) television tower on the roof of the radio station at Lynn, Massachusetts, so no further weather forecasts were received from that source. It also toppled over a crane on the breakwater at the Isles of Shoals just before *Pendragon* started on her hurricane cruise. It is remarkable that, although *Pendragon* was rolled over until her spreaders were in the water and the cockpit filled, she survived with no more damage than might occur in an ordinary gale. She fared better at sea in the hurricane than most of the yachts that had taken shelter in harbour, where houses broke up and floated down on the anchored vessels, and boards, planks and other land objects took to the air, striking rigging and endangering crews. Great numbers of yachts broke their moorings or dragged their anchors and went ashore.

Points to note are:

1   It was only William Mathers' quick decision to put to sea that saved *Pendragon* from the fate that befell many yachts in harbour. Big ships sometimes leave port when hurricanes are anticipated, as they are safer in deep water far from land, but it is unusual for a yacht to do so.
2   Attention is drawn to the difficulty of recovering a man or woman overboard even when alongside the yacht. The added weight of sodden clothes and the violent motion of a yacht in a storm combine to make the task unexpectedly difficult. This is particularly significant when a yacht's crew consists of two only, such as the owner and his wife.
3   A yacht provided with enough power and with a big slow-revolving propeller of low pitch may be able to survive a hurricane, as *Pendragon* did. In her case, the seas seem to have been so immense and so long that enough speed could be obtained in the troughs to luff to the crests, but I doubt whether this would be possible in short and very confused seas. Furthermore, I do not think *Pendragon*'s tactics could be adopted by a yacht equipped with a normal high-revving propeller.

Most of the gales and storms that I have described occurred in waters frequented by yachts and thus they afford practical examples of what can happen when engaged in ordinary cruising on the American side of the Atlantic, but some of the worst storms and the highest seas are found in the high southern latitudes, where yachts rarely sail except for the occasional world voyagers or Cape Horners.

The classic example of a storm of supreme violence in the South Pacific Ocean was afforded by William Albert Robinson when he was caught out in one in 1952 about 40° 45' 50S. Robinson had circumnavigated the globe and is one of the best-known and most experienced deep-sea cruising men of his generation. He had had experiences of other storms and recorded hurricanes, but the storm that he describes as 'The Ultimate Storm' in his book *To the Great Southern Sea* was by far the greatest that he had experienced in a lifetime of deep-sea voyaging.

His yacht was named *Varua*. She was a brigantine of 70ft (21m) overall length, designed by the late Starling Burgess in consultation with her owner for deep-sea voyaging, to be capable of weathering exceptional gales and storms and able to run before them cleanly with little risk of broaching-to. As yachts go she was a big vessel, and she owes her survival to size, design and her owner's experience. I do not think any ordinary yacht, such as yours or mine, could have lived through the ordeal that she encountered.

During the storm *Varua* lay-to under forestaysail and lower staysail until the seas reached such a height and steepness that her sails were alternately blanketed in the troughs and blasted by gusts on the crests. They were then lowered and *Varua* lay a'hull. Instead of lashing the helm down, the wheel was lashed amidships and, finding her natural drift, the brigantine fell off several points and headed slowly downwind with the seas on her quarter. Oil was used and Robinson states that the slick was more effective than when the boat was hove-to, when most of it was blown to leeward.

The gale backed slowly from north-east to north, and towards midnight *Varua* began to get out of control. 'The seas were so huge and concave at this point that the whole upper third seemed to collapse and roar vertically down on us. Our oil had little or no effect now, as the surface water was all being blown to leeward.'

Robinson unlashed the wheel and ran her off downwind dead before the storm, gathering speed under bare poles to 6 or 7 knots. As he considered this dangerous, he let go five 75ft (23m) lengths of 2in (5cm) warps plus 656ft (200m) of smaller lines. This reduced her speed to 3 or 4 knots and she steered under perfect control, and the oil slick seemed more effective at this lower speed. Nevertheless, at times she ran down a sea and buried her bowsprit in the trough before rising again. Robinson says that if *Varua* had not been trailing drags she might have run right down. As he puts it, 'When a 50 ton, 70ft (21.3m) vessel surfboards shudderingly down the face of a great sea on its breaking crest, you have experienced something.'

Tzu Hang, in her attempts to round Cape Horn from the Pacific to the Atlantic, was involved in survival storms in much the same latitudes as *Varua*. On the first occasion she was manned by a crew of three, consisting of her owner, Brigadier Miles Smeeton, his wife Beryl, and John Guzwell of *Trekka* fame. In this attempt to round Cape Horn she was pitchpoled, stern over bow, when running streaming 361ft (110m) of 3in (7.6cm) hawser. During the second attempt, when she was sailed by Miles Smeeton and his wife alone, another storm was encountered. This time *Tzu Hang* lay a'hull, but she suffered a complete rollover. On both occasions the yacht was dismasted, severely damaged and partly waterlogged. The seas that did the damage must have been 'freak' waves, formed by a combination of wave trains with unlimited fetch in the wastes of the Pacific. 'Sometimes', wrote Miles Smeeton, in *Once is Enough*, 'a wave would seem to break down all its front, a rolling cascading mass of white foam, pouring down the whole surface of the wave like an avalanche down a mountainside'.

A view of the Southern Ocean by Les Powles. He estimates the wave height to have been 60ft (18.3m).

In weather conditions such as these, few yachts would live with-out sustaining damage, whatever their type and whatever the method of defence adopted. The astonishing thing was that she sur-vived at all. *Tzu Hang* had a tough crew, and temporary repairs were effected on each occasion, but had the seas that did the dam-age been quickly followed by others equally formidable, she surely must have gone to the bottom. Possibly the dismastings enabled her to ride the seas better and thus saved her from this catastrophe, but *Doubloon* (as described in earlier editions of *Heavy Weather Sailing*) was rolled over again after she had been dismasted, so one cannot be sure of this.

On the other hand, there are many examples of yachts that have sailed in the Roaring Forties and round Cape Horn without incident or near disaster. This was the 'impossible route' chosen by the Argentine Vito Dumas for the great singlehanded voyage he described in his book *Alone through the Roaring Forties*. Dumas' yacht *Lehg 11* was a 31ft 2in (9.4m) Norwegian type from the board of Manual M Campos, and was a modernized version of the old Rio de la Plata whaleboats, somewhat akin to a Colin Archer double-ender. She was designed for the purpose of ocean voyaging, with a long keel, and to be easy to steer in all weathers. The ballast keel was 3.5 tons of iron and the design provided a high degree of reserve buoyancy. No inside ballast was carried. The success of the design was proved by the apparent ease of steering singlehanded without the modern aid of self-steering. There must have been plen-ty of buoyancy in her pointed stern to have survived the seas that Dumas experienced. In his voyage it was not a matter of a gale here and there but of almost continuous dirty weather – with winds on occasions estimated to be gusting up to 70 knots. His tactics in heavy weather were origi-nal. 'As regards a sea anchor' he writes, 'I have one point of view which settled the ques-tion for me; I would never give such an object sea room. I am convinced that a boat can stand up to any sea, comfortably enough, under sail. She has freedom of movement and can lift to the sea. Should the wind force exceed 50 knots I would say, contrary to the opin-ion that following seas play havoc by breaking on deck, that one of my favourite pleasures was to run through squalls on a mattress of foam. My speed on these surf riding occasions exceeded 15 knots: I then presented the stern to another wave and began this exciting pas-time anew.'

Some readers may regard the speed of 15 knots as exaggerated, but the exact speed is immaterial and what is clear is that *Lehg 11* experienced the right length of ocean sea to enable her to surf for appreciable periods at far above her theoretical maximum speed. Dumas does not give any detailed description or advice on how this surfing was accom-plished, or of how he managed without self-steering. Surfing in ocean seas can be danger-ous on account of the risk of being thrown down into the trough and pitch-poled. However this may be, Dumas ran before gales at about 5 knots and succeeded in sailing round the world in the most dangerous waters that can be found, and arriving at the end of the voyage with his boat in perfect condition.

There are more recent examples of yachts that have voyaged in the dangerous waters of the South Pacific and rounded the Horn without resort to streaming warps or any of the conventional methods of weathering gales and storms. When Sir Francis Chichester round-ed the Horn in *Gypsy Moth IV* in March 1967, after making a remarkably accurate landfall

Close-up picture of a following sea. It is difficult to understand how any yacht, or even a small ship, can survive in such seas. *Photo: de Lange*

without a fix of sun or stars for three days and little sleep for a week, he was running under storm jib. It was evidently blowing very hard, with the violent gusts and high seas for which the Horn is notorious. *Gypsy Moth*'s cockpit was filled on five occasions and once it took 15 minutes for the water to drain away, which provides further evidence of the inadequacy of the drains in self-emptying cockpits.

Gypsy Moth IV ran under storm jib, and there is no mention of her streaming warps. Her speed seems to have been between 5 knots and later 7 knots, so this affords another example of a yacht maintaining considerable speed when running in heavy seas before a gale.

Much valuable evidence on the subject of running before storms comes from Bernard Moitessier, who, in 1967, was awarded the Blue Water medal of the Cruising Club of America and the Wren Medal for Seamanship of the Royal Cruising Club for his outstanding voyage from Moorea to Alicante via Cape Horn. His book entitled *Cap Horn à la Voile* recounts his experiences but, in the meantime, I am indebted to him and the *Royal Cruising Club Journal* and *Cruising Club News* (published by the CCA) for the following information.

Joshua, in which the voyage was made, is a 39.6ft (12m) double-ended Bermudan ketch of 12.1ft (3.7m) beam and 5.25ft (1.6m) draft, designed by Jean Knocker. She is of steel construction and has a fixed keel. The sail area of 960sq ft (89sq m) is considerable for a yacht undertaking such long-distance voyages. A feature of her design is the 'pilot's post', which is a metal cupola from which she is steered. *Joshua* left Moorea (the island west of Tahiti) on 23 November 1965 and rounded Cape Horn on 11 January 1966, 49 days later.

As it chanced, the wind was moderate from the north-west when Cape Horn was rounded. No difficulty was experienced, and as with *Tzu Hang*, it was in the South Pacific that *Joshua* encountered a 'survival' storm in which she nearly foundered. This storm lasted six days and was caused by two low pressure systems. Moitessier had no anemometer, but he estimates that the wind was at hurricane force in the gusts, which suggests that the mean strength would be about force 10 or perhaps force 11. In the South Pacific, given six days for the seas to build up, this would be a 'survival' storm. The seas were reported to have been absolutely gigantic and their length was estimated to have been about 500–560ft (152–171m), breaking without interruption from 650ft to nearly 1000ft (198–305m), leaving acres of white water behind them. They were described as being 'absolutely unbelievable'.

Joshua at first ran before this storm towing five long hawsers, varying in length from 100 to 300ft (30–91m), with iron ballast attached and supplemented by a heavy net used for loading ships. These afforded so much drag that the yacht failed to respond quickly enough to the wheel. They also failed to prevent her surfing on the crests of the gigantic waves. On one wave, which Moitessier says was not especially large, but just about the right size for surfing, *Joshua* took off like an arrow, with the warps behind her as if 'dragging a fishing line', and buried herself in the wave at an angle of 30°, so that the forward end of the boat was buried up to the ventilator abaft the mast. Another wave taken in the same way might have caused *Joshua* to pitch-pole just as *Tzu Hang* had done and been dismasted, but happily the next really dangerously breaking sea caught the yacht at an angle and Moitessier thinks it is this that saved her from surfing and pitch-poling. It was then that he remembered the Dumas technique of running in gales at about 5 knots and putting the helm down on the arrival of each wave sufficiently to luff a little so as to take the wave at about 15° to 20° on the quarter. By this means a yacht will not be thrown forward surfing and in danger of pitch-poling because she is at an angle to the sea, nor will she be rolled over as she is not abeam to the sea, but there must remain some risk of a broach-to.

Accordingly, Moitessier cut the warps and released *Joshua* from the drag. From that moment she was safe, following the Dumas technique of running fast and taking the seas 15° to 20° on the quarter. Moitessier says that *Joshua* could not possibly have survived except by this means. This ties up very closely with the experiences of Warren Brown, who ran in *Force Seven* before a hurricane at speed, taking the seas on the quarter. There is much to be learnt from Moitessier's theory of running which is referred to below:

1 In extreme storms in the South Pacific the ordinary methods of surviving storms are not enough. A sea anchor would be useless. Heaving-to would be out of the question. Streaming warps may not prevent surfing at perhaps 15 knots with the risk of pitch-poling.
2 *Joshua* was of steel construction and, in her owner's opinion, would not have survived without it. She was constantly struck by seas sweeping over the whole vessel up to the mast. These would have carried away any timber deckhouse, and disaster would have followed. *Joshua* was steered from a steel pilot cupola. It was not safe on deck, even with lifelines, as the yacht sometimes disappeared completely below the sea. Moitessier also recommends that any yacht planning world voyaging should have a flush deck if she is of wood construction.

3 It is recommended that storm sails should be small and not too heavy and cumbersome. I think this applies to any sails such as a storm trysail. The old-fashioned ones used to be very heavy for the sake of strength, but cumbersome heavy weather sails are difficult to handle and to set. There is no need for very heavy sails, especially now that synthetic fibre is used, because the area is so small that canvas of even moderate weight is very strong in relation to the area.

4 Moitessier states and then repeats that 'no one can claim he will not founder in these latitudes'. This confirms the opinion of other deep-sea cruising men that a time can come when no yacht can be certain of survival, whatever her size or rig may be.

5 Moitessier does not say a great deal about the form of the seas that he found most dangerous. He describes such seas as 'crazy', which is, of course, the equivalent of 'freak' or 'rogue'. Such seas usually have heavy cascading crests, but Moitessier states that this is not necessarily the case, as the most dangerous seas in the South Pacific are very steep, not necessarily breaking, which pick up and throw the boat into the trough and can cause pitch-poling. He also refers to waves much bigger than the others and coming from a different direction. For a yacht to be pitch-poled requires a sea of such immense size that it is not likely to be encountered except in very exceptional storms and with the unlimited fetch of the ocean.

Bernard Moitessier described the seas that *Joshua* encountered in the South Pacific as 'breaking without interruption from 650ft to nearly 1000ft'. He ran under bare pole, taking them 15° to 20° on the quarter to avoid being pitch-poled. The yacht was of steel construction, steered from within a steel cupola.
Photo: de Lange

Thus far Adlard Coles. I have added four Pacific Ocean accounts to Adlard Coles' collection of storms as further examples of experiences of extreme weather, besides accounts of extremely strong squalls that may have been associated with thunderstorms, tornadoes and waterspouts. These latter two events are comparatively rare, but the outcome can be quite dramatic.

The first is a story where survival involved the use of oil and warps. On 2 May 1938 Group Captain Geoffrey Francis was caught out in a typhoon while taking his new 57ft (17m) ketch *Ma-On-Shan* on passage south from Hong Kong. Happily he had an abundant supply of the two items, rope and oil, which he used to good effect. He had taken the oil in case he ran out of wind, and the rope because he felt it was sure to come in useful. During the typhoon he deployed between 900ft and 1200ft (366m) of a huge length of hairy natural fibre rope from the stern in one long line and used a marlin spike to puncture in turn the 25 4-gallon cans of tractor vaporizing oil that had been stowed aft of the main mast. Though typhoon-sized waves were breaking all round the vessel as she ran under bare poles at hull speed, significantly none broke immediately behind her.

The seas were kept as much on the quarter as Geoffrey Francis dared he believed he was in the dangerous quadrant of the typhoon and the steady pull of the warp was most effective in preventing *Ma-On-Shan* from broaching. He remained convinced that it was the combination of the large quantity of oil used, and the warp streamed in very long lengths, that saved the boat. It was not easy to say how much rope was streamed, but if the wavelengths were between 450ft and 600ft (122–183m), as seems possible, they would probably have been long enough to span a whole wavelength of a typhoon wave.

Incidentally, the *Ma-On-Shan* had been spotted by the P&O passenger liner *Rawalpindi* shortly before the arrival of the typhoon and, when *Ma-On-Shan* eventually made Saigon, Geoffrey Francis found he was unable to cash any cheques. His friends and associates back at his home base in Singapore had been told by the *Rawalpindi's* officers that the *Ma-On-Shan* must have been lost in the typhoon, and a stop had been put on his bank account.

The second story comes from Alby Burgin, an Australian who sailed the 37ft (11.3m) *Rival*, a Vashti design by Alan Buchanan, through Cyclone Emily on a race from Brisbane to Gladstone, in 1972:

The wind was recorded at Bustard Head lighthouse at 132 knots and, within a radius of 15 miles from our position, two large fishing trawlers, a steel yacht and a trimaran broke up and sank with the loss of 12 lives. The waves running in shallow water against the current were 30ft (9.1m) high, very steep, and coming to a point where the top 3 or 4ft (0.9 to 1.2m) were being blown off. Horizontal water was everywhere; visibility was about 50ft (15m) and the noise was deafening.

We were under storm jib and I was the only person on deck at the time, the crew being down below behind securely fixed storm boards. If I'd held my head up, the wind and water would have cut my eyes out; as it was, the force of them was hurting even through my wet weather gear and undergarments. Waves were crashing continuously over the bow and rolling along *Rival's* deck across the overflowing cockpit. The compass in front of the tiller was mainly under water.

The boat was managing the conditions fairly well until an exceptionally large wave, like an enormous green and white breaking verandah, crashed onto the deck, taking off hand rails, the liferaft, and breaking the plate glass windows of the coachroof. The tremendous weight of water buckled my knees and rolled *Rival* through 360°. My lifeline had been fastened to a large teak cleat, but when the yacht was upside down I found myself loose in the turbulent sea. The first thing that came into my mind was to stay underwater to allow the sea to wash me away from the yacht. If I surfaced too quickly, I had visions of bashing my head on the rolling yacht or hanging myself in the rigging. When I estimated I was clear, I found I could not make headway to the surface. I realized that I must be waterlogged, having been exposed on deck for many hours. My next thought was to get rid of my wet weather gear, which I managed to do while still underwater – I was glad that I never wear sea boots, which are almost impossible to get off underwater. Only then was I able to get to the surface, to find the dismasted *Rival* 20ft (6.1m) away. I swam to the yacht and my crew, being on deck by this time, helped me back on board. I had lacerations to both arms and face. When the cyclone had passed over, we jury-rigged and sailed into Gladstone. Then I had time to wonder at the serious injuries I would have received from the deck gear had my lifeline not broken.

Alby Burgin is well known in Australia for his epic voyages undertaken at an age when most yachtsmen have retired to their gardens. This brief and understated description of the survival of a fully fledged cyclone demonstrates that, provided the crew can remain with their craft, and provided that craft is very strongly built and can float like a bottle (see Chapter 1), there is no reason to give up hope. When *Rival* was rolled it is noteworthy that her storm boards (washboards) were securely in place.

The third Pacific account is of an Australian yacht race that will long be remembered for the loss of four yachtsmen who were drowned when their yachts sank. This was the JOG Tasman Cup on 15 April 1983, with a 44-mile overnight course from Sydney harbour, south along the exposed coastline to a buoy off Port Hacking, and back. The forecast was for 20–30 knot south to south-west winds as well as south-easterly swell, giving a beat down to Port Hacking. It seems that the wind that materialized was much as forecast, but it created a secondary swell across the one from the south-east. In addition, there was a south-going current running offshore – locally known as the 'set'– and the whole combination created some very steep breaking waves.

The first yacht to get into trouble was the *Montego Bay*, a Hood 23 production boat with an experienced crew. After falling heavily off several waves she was found to be making water. The crew decided to abandon the race but, in spite of some spirited work with a bucket, the boat sank rather quickly. Just before this happened they had succeeded in firing two flares, but had obtained no acknowledgement from their Mayday transmission and were too late to reach their lifejackets in the cockpit locker. There seems to have been some confusion in the two boats of the racing fleet that saw the flares as to whether there was a genuine emergency, and it was not until three hours later that a yacht returning to Sydney after abandoning the race happened to encounter two of *Montego Bay*'s crew in the water, and raised the alarm. Two more of the crew were picked up half an hour later, but a fifth man was never found.

Meanwhile another yacht, the Farr 727 *Waikikamukau* with a crew of four, had also sunk. She had been capsized by a particularly large breaking wave, and with no washboards in place she had filled rapidly through her main companionway. The crew was attached to the boat with their safety harnesses, but one of them was unable to detach his safety harness before the stern of the yacht submerged and he was drowned. Another crewman had great difficulty in kicking off his sea boots, which were hampering his ability to swim. None of the crew was wearing lifejackets, and the horseshoe lifebuoy stowed in the stern sheets of *Waikikamukau* had gone down with her. The three remaining crew quickly separated in the heavy seas and darkness.

In the end, there was only one survivor, who had to swim for 10 hours before being picked up by a passing fishing boat. He reported that both helicopters and rescue craft, who were still looking for the fifth man from the *Montego Bay*, had repeatedly passed close by him, but had failed to spot him or hear his cries. As it was, he was only seen by someone who was leaning over the side of the fishing boat being seasick.

But for the warmth of the water, no one would ever have known what had happened to the two yachts and their crews, and there were many hard lessons learnt from the tragedy of this race. The importance of lifejackets is clearly one of them. Another is the importance of having washboards (or storm boards) in place in the main hatchway in big, breaking seas.

A less distressing event took place in the South Pacific in February 1985 when an experienced Australian couple, Alan and Kathy Webb, with their 16-year-old daughter, Portia, were overtaken by a survival storm. The heavily built 45ft (13.7m) steel cutter *Supertramp*, in which her owners had great confidence, had been designed for world cruising with a moderate fin keel, a skeg-hung rudder and immense strength.

They arrived in the Roaring Forties with Easter Island 450 miles to the west and Chile some 1400 miles to the east (40° 20'S, 101° 37'W) to be confronted by a plummeting barometer and 80 knot winds that continued for 36 hours. The self-steering soon broke, and Alan Webb was left to steer for the duration as they ran under bare pole in winds they estimated at force 12. Huge breaking seas developed, aggravated and confused by squalls. The Webbs make a practice of lying a'hull with the wheel lashed to windward in gales, but in this instance Kathy Webb says it would have been impossible to heave-to as they would certainly have been capsized.

Alan comments: 'When running down waves of this extreme height, *Supertramp* developed too much speed, but by surfing down them at an angle, I found I could remain high on the crest and also take speed off the yacht. It was vital to keep her on top of the first tier, high upon the shoulder of the wave, by steering about 20° across its face rather than let slip into the trough. We still stood a chance of being rolled over, but a slow roll-over would do much less damage than being pitch-poled at speed.' The Webbs have since wondered whether they might have hoisted their storm jib in the lulls to give steerage way, but conclude that their speed under bare pole seldom dropped below 4 knots, and for the rest of the time any sail would have been too much.

Several other interesting points came from the experience. First, Alan Webb felt his beach surfing experience was helpful in negotiating the breaking seas. He was also helped by the fact that *Supertramp* was extremely controllable under bare pole, and could even be gybed when lying a'hull. Another good feature of the boat was her centre cockpit with 10in (25cm) coamings and large-diameter drain holes. Finally, they mention 'Polar Mitts', given to them by a Canadian icebreaker in the Magellan Straits, as the only effective gloves they have ever come across for wet, freezing conditions.

There are dramatic local changes in the weather from good to bad that are seldom forecast, and are over so quickly that their severity is often doubted by those who were not there. They could account for a number of losses of vessels without trace in what might appear to have been not very severe conditions. For example, the British barque *Marques* was racing from Bermuda to Nova Scotia in 1984. At about 0800 she was 80 miles north of Bermuda in moderate weather when a hurricane force wind hit the ship 'out of the blue'. She capsized and only those on deck survived, the remainder being trapped below. One of the explanations was that she was hit by a microburst, a localized downdraft associated with a thunderstorm. There was no doubt that thunderstorms were about that morning, though the *Marques* was apparently not particularly close.

Bill Cooper has a good account of an extraordinary experience in the Bermuda triangle aboard his 58ft (17.7m) steel ketch *Fare Well* in June 1982. He, his disabled wife Laurel and a lady friend, Nora, had sailed from Bermuda heading for New England when they heard on the radio that Hurricane Alberta was coming their way. The forecast gave conditions in which 'elderly gentlefolk should not be at sea', but they had nowhere else to go. Having made relatively light work of the hurricane, happily quite distant, something totally unexpected and quite sinister then took place:

Bill and Laurel Cooper's *Fare Well*, which was thought to have encountered a waterspout at night. *Photo: Bill Cooper*

Matawa is a traditional 34ft × 9ft × 6ft (10.5m × 2.7m × 1.8m) yacht designed by Morgan Giles and built of plywood by Cardnell Bros in 1947. *Photo: Peter Bruce*

By the evening of 19 June we were hove-to under storm jib and very close-reefed mainsail. Our wind was averaging 40 knots with the gusts going well off the clock. I think the seas were about 15ft (4.6m). These conditions persisted all night; the average wind was not rising much, but the seas built up a bit, and I estimated 20ft (6m) in the morning watch. Each broadside wave shot a little jet of cold water through the perished rubber sealing of the deckhouse window onto the protesting form of Laurel in the stand-by berth. Otherwise, all was dry and sound below. The yacht was behaving very well indeed. The decks were awash most of the time, but the high poop had only spray, and the cockpit, which is really a sheltered area at deck level, had had no green sea, but enough itinerant slosh to justify one storm board in the hatchway.

The storm centre was then reported to be in position 41°N, 66°W, some 170 miles away to the north-west, and probably the closest we came to it. Our position was based on DR, of course, for we had seen no sunshine for some time.

A feature of these violent and fast moving storms is that the advanced semi-circle has strong winds over a much greater radius. Behind the storm the radius was only 50 miles, and conditions soon started to improve. The sea was slow to give up, but the wind moderated quite quickly. We tacked when reasonably sure the storm had passed, and headed 290°T, leaving our reduced sail up for the night.

When I took over the watch at 0400 on 20 June the wind had eased to force 4, but the seas were still considerable, though not dangerous. We rolled badly, and the main was not filling properly. I furled it, and decided to set the genoa and mizzen to get some way and stability. It was very dark, and raining heavily. There had been a couple of thunderstorms during the night producing moderate squalls: there was thunder about at that time, but nothing exciting.

I had got the mizzen half-way up when I heard, rather than saw, what looked like a wall of very heavy rain approaching. In a second or two it arrived, rain of unbelievable intensity. I had been glad of our cockpit shelter, but it was of no help against this sort of rain, when even the splashes wet everything. Then the wind arrived before I had time even to move. It came across the few yards of water I could see, blowing the waves flat. It hit us an almost solid blow, and we were flung over to starboard; how far I cannot say for there was no point of reference, but certainly more than 90°, and I fell onto the starboard bench at the limit of my lifeline. While we were over, a sea broke and swept us, wresting the boom from the gallows, parting lashing and gaskets.

I scrambled up as the ship righted. The mizzen blew out. The main boom shook like a slipper in a puppy's mouth and, with a loud report, the 14oz (397g) main split and blew to shreds. The genoa, which had been rolled up, stretched in the wind and, without the core turning, allowed a few feet to unroll; the clew then blew out. My oilskin was ripped open; all buttons were gone and the zip pulled apart.

As I tried to gather myself to deal with matters I felt all the power to move leave me. I stood holding the leather-covered wheel feeling strangely euphoric as if being drawn steadily upward off my feet. The feeling went on and on as if time had stopped, and I could not breathe, though my lungs were full. I could not move at all.

Then the lightning struck. Instantly, tension disappeared. The whole space around the yacht seemed to be glowing, but I had absolutely no sense of time. I was aware of Nora appearing in the hatch followed by Laurel, looking very white. Both had been rudely propelled from their bunks when the gust had heeled us over, and all the above had taken place while they scrambled to the deck, say 20 or 30 seconds. Laurel describes me as standing motionless at the wheel, mouth wide open, with water streaming down me as if I were standing under a waterfall. I had to be roused to move. Presumably I was in a state of shock.

The ladies turned to, and gradually I joined in, largely doing as I was told. Together we tamed the main boom, which had broken its gooseneck. When it was safely in the gallows we bundled together the collection of streamers that had been a mainsail. The mizzen was grappled in. The genoa was more of a problem. The sheets had slackened as the clew pulled out, and had tied themselves into a spaghetti knot so tight we could neither furl the sail, nor get it down its extrusion core. I did not fancy my chances half-way up the forestay at that time, so we let it go.

There was big trouble in the engine room, and compass deviation went from zero to 90°W, then slowly to 25°W, which only came to light through logging the direction of the swell; but what was it, apart from the lightning, that struck the ketch at 0430 that morning? Bill Cooper now thinks that he encountered a tornado with waterspout. Presumably it was the lightning strike that caused the magnetic anomaly, or was it the tornado?

Harry Franks had a slightly similar experience in 1997 off Ushant in the 34ft (10.5m) Morgan Giles designed wooden sloop *Matawa*:

We were coming to the end of our summer cruise in *Matawa*; she celebrating her 50th birthday this year. After a quiet night a little way up the River Elorn attached to a convenient buoy, we had taken the ebb out of the Rade and were heading for Ushant.

The wind was light and on our beam from the north and we were intermittently sailing and motoring, wanting to make Ushant in good time for a run ashore that evening. A few showers were threatened and there was some thunder about, but it looked like an uneventful sail as we passed Pierres Noir South Cardinal and headed for Pierres Vertes buoy. I was on the helm and the rest of the crew were variously loitering below, navigating, sleeping, reading, etc. We had the engine on to hold us up to windward, as the land breeze that had helped us out of the Rade had given way to the forecast northerly. The rather jagged rocks of Les Pierres Noir were coming and going in the poor visibility to starboard, but we were well clear of them and to leeward.

I was idly wondering what the likelihood of a lightning strike on our metal mast was as the thunder rolled around us when suddenly 'BANG', over we went as a massive gust hit us. For a moment I had that frightening feeling, remembered from dinghy sailing in times past, that we were going to go right over as I hung on desperately to avoid being pitched over the lee rail. Thankfully, *Matawa* did the right thing and slowly came into the wind, giving me the chance to check sheets. Down below, Henry on the windward bunk had been thrown across onto Michael junior on the leeward one and Tim, in the forepeak, was sure we were going to capsize. With the wind came torrential rain and much reduced visibility, and we were now, it seemed to me, being driven towards the rocks.

Fortunately Mike senior had recovered from the initial shock quickly, thrown oilskins on and was soon on deck. 'Foresail down' was in order and this we soon managed, though as I checked away the foresheet, I had a glimpse of the comprehensive shredding of the sail – fortunately not a new one. Still we were out of control and the wind seemed to be turning us around like a top, the sea flat but stirred by driven wavelets. By this time Tim was also on deck and we had hands to lower the main; those rocks looming in the mind closer by the second as we were driven on. Down came the main and I finally began to feel that I had some control, thankful that the engine was still on. I steered due south as gradually the wind subsided and the rain eased off from its frantic pelting. Soon, and with much relief, the rocks appeared still to north of us – as I half expected us to have been driven past them! Fifteen minutes later we had the main up again, soon after that the No 2 genoa, and we were able to get back on our old course.

One hour later we were at anchor in Lampaul. We did, however, notice that one or two other boats had their oilskins out to dry which reassured us that we had not been hallucinating. The whole episode had only lasted half an hour at the most.

In retrospect, I suspect that we had experienced a mini tornado-cum-windspout. This is surely why I had the impression of being driven at will through all points of the compass while we reduced sail. What warning had we had of such an 'event'? The navigator says that he had noticed the sky going dark; but obviously not dramatically enough to mention it to me. I suspect that I had not noticed it because I was wearing dark glasses. More important was our mind set; we had had two weeks of calms and light airs and, perhaps out of ignorance, associated thunderstorms with drenching rain and calm wind. I shall know better for the future. Fortunately, the only damage was to the sail, because that sort of experience really tests the seaworthiness of a yacht – not only the rigging, but how well things have been secured above and below decks after weeks when the most extreme motion we had experienced was the wash of passing trawlers.

This alarming experience is again notable for the sudden arrival in thundery weather of storm force wind accompanied by unusually heavy rain. It was noteworthy that *Matawa* was out of control and being turned by the wind like a top.

Sandy Gilbert, with *Magnum Opus* in the Mediterranean, sailing between Majorca and Minorca, tells a story of how, with a distant thunderstorm in sight, his boat was hit by a squall of tremendous violence, later accompanied by hail, which ripped to shreds the only sail that was left set. The boat would not respond to the helm and was circling. A catamaran's crew in the same situation not far away reported that they had also spun round and round. In one yacht nearby a man went overboard, and in another the mainsheet would not release under its load and the fabric of the mainsail had to be cut to prevent a capsize. Of the quite large number of yachts in the area, almost all reported an initial severe knockdown.

The event is similar to Harry Franks' tornado, in that the wind arrived with remarkable suddenness and strength, boats were spun round, and it was all over in half an hour. The forecast of easterly force 4 would not have accounted for such strong winds, estimated to

A waterspout 3 miles out of Newport Harbour, California. It formed after a tremendous thundery storm front had passed. *Photo: Blake Dragonlord*

have been force 12, and the explanation seems to have been that the thunderstorm brought about a precipitation downdraft, a microburst, which turned into a tornado.

Finally, there is another account of a large US cruising yacht in the Bahamas torn from her berth when hit by a waterspout, breaking off two marina piles in the process. The owner, who said the noise was like an undergound train at speed, saw a motor bicycle lifted into the air from the jetty, and when last seen it was ascending at an angle of 45°. His steel foredeck ventilator weighing 200lb (91kg) was found half a mile away.

Accounts of vessels being hit by waterspouts, which can be between 50ft and 150ft (15–46m) in diameter, are rare, though waterspouts are known to have caused great damage when they have come ashore.

Clearly, thunderstorms (even when distant), tornadoes and waterspouts at sea can be dangerous and should be avoided if possible. The noise of thunder, anvil-shaped clouds combined with dark low-level cloud, or an actual waterspout may be as much warning as one may ever have. The good seaman should adopt practices that will withstand sudden adverse weather and be ready for an intense squall whenever thunder is about.

The events described in this chapter, in most cases, were not particularly to be expected and the crews were operating from their normal level of preparation.

The harrowing story of the JOG Tasman Cup is, perhaps, the most instructive. The yachts that sank were close to land, close to other yachts, and experiencing rather less heavy weather than in most of the accounts in this book. A succession of chances to save the situation were missed. It has to be said that accidents often result when insufficiently strong action is taken in the early stages of an adverse situation. We need to remember Admiral Nimitz's words about precautions at the beginning of Chapter 5.

We need to ask ourselves whether we can be sure that, in the same circumstances, our own standards of seamanship would have prevented loss of life. For example, why was it that other yachts did not respond to the distress flares from the *Montego Bay*? Aboard *Montego Bay*, in the rush of activity, would we have had the presence of mind to say firmly 'it's time for lifejackets, boys' before it was too late? Would we, in *Waikikamukau*, have insisted upon washboards in the companionway?

Assuming some fundamental error has occurred, will our remedies that are required as a consequence do the job? As Chay Blyth so rightly says: 'Hope for the best: but prepare for the worst.'

CHAPTER
16 Extreme weather south of Iceland

JOHN WILSON

This account was chosen for inclusion because several storm tactics were employed, the nominally strong crew was taken to somewhere near the limit of endurance, and the vulnerability of small craft in the open ocean, such as the north Atlantic, is apparent. This yacht and crew were perilously close to being 'lost at sea'.

In May 1979 I crewed on a UFO34, *Windrift of Clyde*, from Scotland to Iceland, in the process encountering fairly severe weather – estimated at a sustained 60 knots plus for over 24 hours. The UFO34 is a deep-fin spade-rudder IOR-style ¾-tonner with tiller steering. This particular boat was built from new, as a customized cruiser, and both hull and rig were stronger than the standard boat. She also had a 40hp diesel driving a fixed three-bladed prop. We had a crew of six, of whom four – including myself – were yachtmaster qualified. The lady owner/skipper was a yachtmaster examiner.

Figure 16.1 (right)
The course of *Windrift of Clyde* from Scotland to Iceland in May 1979.

Below Aboard *Windrift of Clyde* before the storm. *Photo: John Wilson*

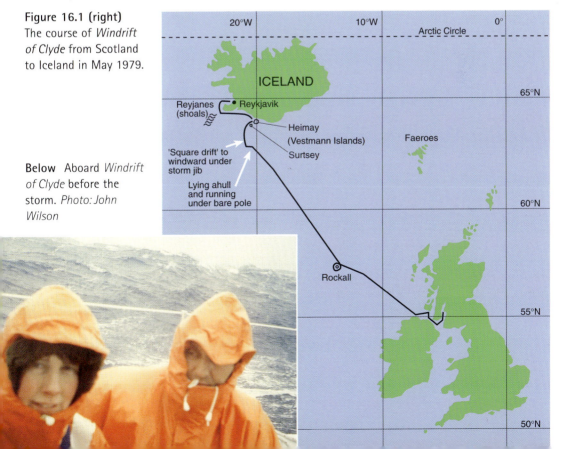

The wind built up steadily from the east, over a two-day period, during which time we broad-reached north-west from Rockall under progressively reduced sail. After two days without a fix, and a substantial potential error in our DR (which put us about 100 miles south of the southern tip of Iceland), we were concerned about closing the coast or crossing the Reyjanes shoals in heavy weather, so we decided to lie a'hull to await a reduction in the wind, which we were logging as force 7–8. The yacht did not have an anemometer, so our logged winds were estimations. We subsequently found that we were probably underestimating – we were told that the nearest Icelandic weather station at Heimay in the Vestmann Islands recorded winds over 60 knots mean for 48 hours. Their big steel trawlers were harbour-bound for four days, and a container ship near our position lost containers from the deck.

Lying a'hull was quite comfortable for around six hours, but eventually the seas built to a point where the hull was being surfed sideways in the crests, and the gunwale was starting to dig in and 'trip' the boat over onto her side. We felt that if nothing was done being rolled would sooner or later be inevitable.

We then ran off under bare pole, and for another few hours this seemed safe, although steering was hard work and the motion was very unpleasant. Then, however, the narrow bows dug in and we were inverted. Crew opinions still differ upon the exact mechanics of the inversion. I was at the chart table at the time, trying to average 12 RDF bearing readings that differed by up to 30°. I believe we pitch-poled. The boat stabilized for a short while, completely inverted, with one smashed coachroof window. One of my most enduring memories is of how springy the coachroof headlining was to stand on, and of the water from the broken window pouring in over my legs.

When we rolled upright again the two crew who had been on deck were in the water alongside, on lifelines, one quite seriously injured. After retrieving them, we started the diesel and turned to head into the seas under power. A lot of throttle was needed just to get the bows into the wind, but for the short time the engine ran the boat coped well with the conditions. Although we came to a complete stop or even made sternway when hitting breaking crests, the strong prop-wash over the rudder helped to keep control. Unfortunately, the engine then died.

We then ran off again under bare pole, while we attempted to send a radio message, without success, and discovered that the engine had stopped because a woollen scarf, among the assorted debris washing around below, had caught in the prop shaft coupling and had flailed around until it ripped out the main diesel fuel feed pipe. The seas had become substantially steeper and there was a definite cross-swell, causing breaking crests to appear suddenly from an angle to the main run of the seas. Over the next two hours or so we were knocked down twice more, these being exaggerated broaches, starting with the forward sidedecks submerging, and ending up with the hull at about 120° from the vertical, with the crew on deck swimming alongside the hull, waiting to pull themselves back in along their lifelines as she righted.

It was clear that running under bare pole was not a safe option. Although we had a large drum of heavy warp carried specifically to use as a drogue, we did not try to use this. I do not believe it would have helped. I set the storm jib, initially with the hope that more speed might give the ability to surf away from the nastier breaking seas, which looked and felt much like seas breaking in shallow water. In fact, at one point I turned on the echo sounder, even though we should have been in about 600–900 fathoms.

A few seconds after reaching the cockpit after setting the storm jib I found myself swimming again, seeing the bottom of the keel in the air. I took the helm as we righted, beam-on to the seas, and the boat accelerated fast on a broad-reach on the 'downhill' side of a sea. Instinctively I put the helm down as the next crest arrived, to bring the bow into the sea.

Force 12 in the Atlantic. *Photo: Dag Pike*

Although the conditions remained unchanged for nearly another 24 hours, we were never again in danger of a knockdown. By broad-reaching fast on the backs of the seas, and luffing almost head-to-wind to each crest, we achieved what was probably a square drift sideways, northwards towards the Vestmann Islands. Luffing into the bigger breakers would sometimes throw the whole yacht bodily astern, snatching the tiller from the helm's hand and slamming the rudder against its end stops, as green water washed those in the cockpit back against the pushpit. Despite this, the tactic worked, although hull damage was later found around the rudder stock. The storm jib was a very small one – certainly smaller than that carried by most racing yachts of the same size.

With the engine and all electronics out of action, we sailed into Heimay two days later. I wrote an account of the events, which was published in *Yachting Monthly* later that year. This was, however, a quite carefully edited version of the events, downplaying certain factors, including crew response (to save people's feelings) and the amount of damage done to the yacht (as the owner wanted to sell her!). The account also gave a different name for the yacht, for the same reasons. At this distance from the event I feel a more detailed account might be of value.

The three elements of the experience that I believe may be of significance are:

1 **Using the engine in very severe weather in deep water** Given sufficient engine power and fuel this is an option I would definitely try again in almost any hull type. In a narrow-bowed boat it would definitely be my first choice, if feasible.

2 **Actively sailing in very severe weather using a (very small) storm jib** While this would be unlikely to be feasible in a long-keeled or much heavier boat, the sheer size of deep-water waves gives you time to accelerate a responsive boat enough between crests to be able to meet each breaker exactly as you want – about 10–20° on the weather bow. This lets you punch through the smaller crests, and even if a big one does throw the boat astern, the combination of the angle of hitting the wave, the lee helm from the un-balanced rig, and having the helm down to luff into the breaker, means that the resultant sternway on the rudder slews you back onto a reaching course, ready to accelerate again.

Lying a'hull in the early stages of the storm. *Photo: John Wilson*

3 **Crew response**   I have not until now discussed this point. Of the six crew, we ended up with one genuinely badly hurt during the first inversion (broken collarbone, ribs, and internal injuries). A second, a cruiser owner and yachtmaster, and nominally one of the more experienced, became totally non-functional, more from fear than anything physical. It seems that his 30 years of experience was really 'one year's experience repeated thirty times'. I have met this syndrome several times since. A third, though fit and willing, lacked the experience to helm or navigate in the conditions. A fourth, certainly the strongest and fittest on board, was slightly injured and lost confidence, though he later, as conditions improved, did sterling work trying to get the engine going again.

For about 48 hours, the lady owner/skipper and I sailed the boat virtually on our own, and she was clearly running out of strength and stamina. I ended up so tired and cold that I was hallucinating while helming, steering for hours through brick railway arches as well as the breaking seas. I knew at the time this was a hallucination, but it didn't make it go away. The curious thing was that it didn't seem to affect my effectiveness as a helm. Much later, as the conditions improved, we sailed past a barren near-conical island which then disappeared in a sudden mist. To this day I do not know if this island was real, though there were uninhabited volcanic islands in the area. At that point we had had no fix for four days, our DR had a circle of possible error exceeding 100 miles, and the only item of functioning electronics on the boat was the plastic Casio watch on my wrist. As we finally identified Heimay and made our way into harbour, we made horrendous and quite elementary pilotage errors, and were lucky not to lose the boat among the rocks inshore.

COMMENT

This horrifying account of a crew stretched to the ragged edge of survival is reminiscent of the 1979 Fastnet storm, which took place only three months later, though by then the sea water temperature would have been somewhat warmer. Apart from fear, fatigue and hunger, hypothermia may have been another factor affecting crew response.

The popular Holman & Pye-designed UFO34 was a non-extreme yacht by the standards of her day, of moderate to heavy displacement. Apart from being a little weighty on the helm through having a rating-influenced pinched stern, they had few vices. That the UFO34

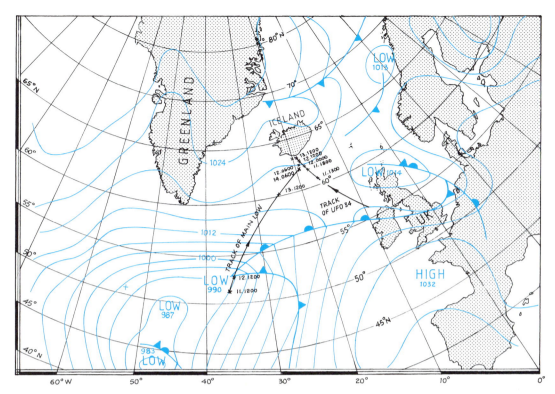

Figure 16.2 (above) The complex depression that brought storm force winds to *Windrift of Clyde* on her passage to Iceland in May 1979. Richard Ebling gives a meteorologist's explanation in Chapter 7.

Right *Windrift* hoisted out in Iceland after the voyage. *Photo: John Wilson*

was thrown about like a dinghy, therefore, is more a reflection upon the prevailing sea state than her design. Note, for example, how quickly she returned to the upright after her total inversion. The different tactics used are instructional, not that her crew would have cared much about this at the time.

There are occasions when yachts are rolled through 360° without warning. However, usually the action of the waves gives a good indication beforehand. By continuing to lie a'hull, a roll would have been inevitable sooner or later so, wisely enough, another tactic was adopted. Logically this was to steer the boat down the seas but, after some hours, it ended in disaster. John Wilson is fairly certain the boat was pitch-poled the first time she was rolled, but the fact that it was such hard work to steer could have been a factor in allowing the boat's stern to be displaced more than 20° from the stern-on position as a wave broke in the subsequent capsizes. Though John Wilson thought otherwise, perhaps the warp would have helped the steering. But if the boat was simply pitch-poled as he surmised, the warp would have made no significant difference if *Silver Shadow*'s comparable accident is anything to go by (Chapter 23). It should be noted that the strengthened rig survived the inversion without damage, as rig failure is common when a vessel turns right over.

Motoring was the next tactic employed and was the most successful, but only relatively so. A 40hp diesel driving a fixed three-bladed propeller is a lot of propulsive power for a yacht of 34ft (10.4m), yet it was insufficient to keep forward way on through the waves, a point worthy of note for those whose sole 'storm plan' is to use this technique. The engine having started, a small miracle in itself after an inversion, one's mind may concentrate on other matters, but if only someone had found the energy to give the engine a quick check over before starting or while running, the problem could have been remedied before the thrashing scarf broke the diesel supply pipe. For example, one should be tempted to check the oil level after a 360° roll.

John Wilson's splendid square-drift or shark-fin shaped course is a most original and seemingly effective variation on the traditional tactic of luffing over the crest of the wave. It is clear that his brain was still working when it might understandably have been traumatized. The rest of the crew were lucky that they had someone who, driven by a burning determination to survive, came into his own. Perhaps the lesson from John Wilson's praiseworthy conduct is that one must try to remain flexible as there is no knowing what will happen in hurricane force winds, and be ready to adopt a new tactic when the orthodox one fails. People who can do this are admirable.

One is reminded of the greater difficulties of navigation in past times when an area of uncertainty of 100 miles was quite possible, as those who have experienced this additional dimension of worry in bad weather will well remember.

It hardly needs to be said, but the broken window is a reminder that windows are vulnerable. Windows are often made of Perspex (acrylic), especially if curvature is involved, toughened glass especially when no curvature is involved or, these days, a polycarbonate such as Lexan. Polycarbonate is incredibly strong, but it does scratch. It seems preferable to use polycarbonate and to be prepared to replace the windows from time to time if it becomes scuffed.

After a very stressful voyage the mind can become so numb that easy pilotage and boat handling become unaccountably difficult. It is not surprising that the crew of the UFO34 had trouble finding their way into Heimay. Given an opportunity in such circumstances one should not be too proud to accept a tow, but there was no response from two trawlers on their way out of Heimay to 12 red parachutes and 4 red hand flares. Both the ship's VHF radio and a supposedly waterproof emergency VHF radio had succumbed to salt water.

With hindsight and modern options, what could have been done to improve the situation in the storm? Could the yacht have been hove-to? Possibly, but many fin-keeled yachts tend to be too lively to heave-to well. Would a drogue have worked? It may have done. Would a parachute sea anchor have worked? The UFO34 would seem to be a boat that prefers to have her bows into the sea, so – probably – yes. Would modern one-piece survival suits have been useful? Yes. Though *Windrift*'s crew had good foul weather gear and Helly Hansen polar suits, one-piece suits with neck and wrist seals are the only way to stay dry in really severe weather. GPS? Yes, of course.

17 The 1979 Fastnet

PETER BRUCE

The Fastnet storm of 14–15 August 1979 is still regarded as the standard by which other yachtsmen's storms are judged. This seems reasonable as, though short-lived, at between force 10 and 11 it was a very severe storm. Three hundred yachts were involved and, with 15 lives lost plus the crew of 4 from a trimaran following the race, it became a major international news item.

In order to gain a perspective on its severity, it is useful to have been given the actual wave heights by Sheldon Bacon (whose chapter on waves – Chapter 8 – gives more details on wave measurement). He says that the closest scientific instrument was installed on the Seven Stones lightvessel, 130nm south-east of the Fastnet Rock. Although the lightvessel was not under the worst of the storm, the readings show some hefty wave heights for summertime. The table (Fig 17.1) shows monthly maximum values of significant wave height taken every three hours recorded between 1962 and 1986. It can be seen from these values that a typical winter maximum lies in the range 5–9m (16–30ft) with a few extreme values up to 11m (36ft); and that a typical summer maximum lies in the range 2–6m (7–20ft), with a few values up to 9m (30ft), mostly in the April and September months. Within this pattern, the measured maximum during the 1979 Fastnet at the Seven Stones lightvessel was 7.8m (26ft); the height of an ordinary severe winter storm, but an unusually severe summer storm. As all the reports suggest that wave heights farther north were rather higher than those experienced at the Seven Stones, there can be no doubt that the 1979 Fastnet storm was of rare intensity for the time of year.

There was some controversy over the extent to which the storm had been forecast. It was known that a low had formed over Canada before the start of the race. This was correctly predicted to arrive over the race area during the Tuesday or Wednesday of the race. As the low approached the British Isles it appeared innocuous, as lows go, with a central pressure of 1006mb. The shipping forecast at 0630 on 13 August, 12 hours before the storm struck, was south-west force 3 or 4 becoming force 5, locally 6, hardly much to write home about. The first shipping forecast to mention a gale was at 1750 on 13 August. This gave south-west force 5 to 6, increasing force 6 to 8, becoming north-west later. At this time the actual wind speed was a good force 8 and rising, so the information was too late to be called a forecast. At 0030 on 14 August, by when the depression had deepened to 980mb, the shipping forecast was south-west veering west force 7 to 9, locally 10, but by this time the wind strength was all of force 10 and some yachts were already in serious trouble.

It was not admitted, but clearly the depression had caught out the meteorological office, though the weather information from the Scilly Isles and Valentia hardly suggested a storm of such ferocity. Unfortunately the extreme conditions occurred precisely in the area where the bulk of the racing fleet were gathered. (See Chapter 7, explosive deepening, for more details on the meteorology of the Fastnet storm.)

Year	Monthly maximum Hs (m) Month											
	1	2	3	4	5	6	7	8	9	10	11	12
1962	(4.06)	7.77	7.17	8.95	6.11	3.48	3.86	4.44	6.47	6.03	7.66	7.55
1963	5.18	–	–	–	–	–	–	–	–	–	–	–
1968	7.07	4.53	6.18	4.99	4.45	3.08	2.79	4.98	6.81	5.47	5.27	8.24
1969	7.81	5.70	3.63	5.52	3.46	4.57*	3.69	3.18	3.40	5.08	8.03	6.98
1971	–	–	–	–	–	–	2.36	3.60	4.28	5.72	6.32	7.70
1972	7.97	7.59	9.36	7.56	6.85	4.16	3.40	4.01	2.61	5.37	6.89	7.00
1973	7.12	7.66	5.59	5.05*	5.00	3.43	3.80	4.32	5.35	3.83	5.06	6.39
1974	9.84	8.67	5.48	3.57	5.20	4.01	–	–	–	–	–	–
1975	–	–	–	6.30	3.33	2.70	3.58	3.72	6.90	4.74	6.00	6.03
1976	7.30	6.11	10.68	4.48	3.79	3.67	3.15	2.05	5.70	7.71*	6.15	9.07
1977	7.33	7.01	7.37	6.41	4.13	4.09	3.36	5.05	4.48	5.67	6.41	6.81
1978	7.44	(2.74)	–	–	–	3.09*	4.08	3.25	5.33	3.60	5.34	9.34
1979	6.71	5.38	6.50	4.99	5.33	3.32	3.34	7.80	(2.63)	5.88	5.75	10.57
1980	7.55	8.16	9.28	3.49	3.99	5.14	2.94	3.72	7.60	7.64	6.12	7.55
1981	6.11	5.57	6.53	6.39	5.56	(2.95)	–	(3.80)	(5.96)	(5.19)	4.93	8.25
1982	5.96	7.17	6.88	4.39	3.91	4.31	2.53	4.57	4.77	11.13	7.64	8.75
1983	9.19	1.49	6.27	4.54	6.13	4.23	3.53	2.71	9.01	7.93	6.55	8.67
1984	9.64	10.22	6.08	3.87	5.07*	–	–	–	–	–	–	–
1985	(6.37)	6.28	7.18	9.37	6.21	6.97	3.05	5.34	4.86	5.74	5.37	7.17
1986	8.36	5.87	7.93	5.10	(5.82)	3.70*	(2.72)	3.55*	(6.29)	(5.62)	(10.24)	8.79*

*: missing 10–20% data   (): missing >20% data

Figure 17.1 Monthly maximum significant wave heights in metres at the Seven Stones lightvessel between 1962 and 1986. There is a box around the height recorded in the Fastnet storm of August 1979.

This chapter contains descriptions of incidents aboard a number of different yachts, and a summary of the knowledge gained from experiences of the whole fleet. By way of introduction there follows my own account of the storm, written a few days after the event, as seen from the 39ft (11.9m) British Admiral's Cup Team yacht *Eclipse*. The boat in question was not far from the centre of events, and completed the course without any major mishaps. Incidentally, she finished first in her class, first of the Admiral's Cup fleet and second overall, behind Ted Turner's 61ft (18.6m) yacht *Tenacious*.

At 0900 on the morning of 13 August, *Eclipse* was 127 miles short of the Fastnet Rock in company with the similarly sized yachts *Casse Tete* and *Regardless*. The weather was dull and visibility poor; it was curious that the wind was unexpectedly from the north-east. During the forenoon the barometer dropped steadily (Fig 17.2), the wind swung falteringly to the south-west via east, and there was something of a brooding menace in the clouds. Preparations were made for bad weather and the 1355 shipping forecast was awaited with interest. This gave south-west, force 4–5, increasing force 7 and becoming west.

As the afternoon wore on, the wind freshened and some wild surfing at 15 knots caused

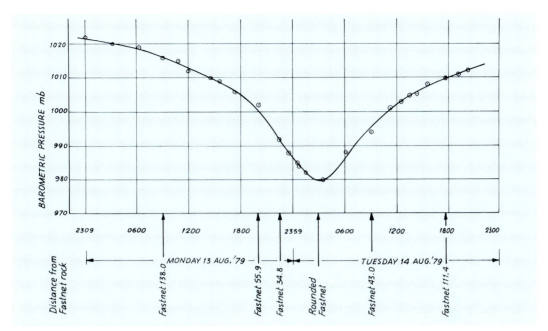

Figure 17.2 The plot of barometer readings taken in *Eclipse* by Peter Bruce.

us to lower the spinnaker. An hour after this a No 2 genoa and two slabs in the mainsail were too much, so much so that we changed right down to the storm jib. The 1750 shipping forecast gave a gale warning with south-west force 5, locally 6, increasing force 8 and veering north-west later. By 2330 the barometer had dropped to 988mb from its 2005 reading of 1002mb. We climbed a little to windward of the rhumb line so that if the wind continued to increase we could run down to the Rock. The wind strengthened steadily and the seas built up rapidly. At about 0100, 12 miles off the Rock, a curling wave top caught *Eclipse* beam-on and she was thrown over to about 70°. Evidently we had too much sail up, but though a messenger was rove to the third slab it would have been a daunting task to get it down in the normal way, so we lowered the mainsail.

There was then a discussion as to what should be done next. On the one hand, it was pointed out that it was getting very rough and the seas between the Fastnet and Cape Clear Island might be dangerous enough to warrant giving up the race. On the other hand, from the race point of view, it was important to get round the Rock before the wind went round to the north-west. Eventually the mainsail went up with three slabs, and we reached onto the Fastnet which had to be left to port. We took it a little wide, bearing in mind the shoal patches round it. Even so, when dead downwind of the Rock another curling top caught the boat beam-on, threw us over, and carried us sideways for what seemed like a long time. Nothing was said as we dropped into the trough behind the wave and carried on.

We tacked easily enough and passed comfortably to weather of the Fastnet at 0255 on Tuesday. The breaking seas, illuminated by the light, were a magnificent and awe-inspiring sight. The new course was quite comfortable and the wind was whistling less. There was even talk of hoisting the No 4 genoa, but then at 0330, with the barometer at 980mb, the wind returned with renewed strength from the west. We dropped the mainsail in haste and lashed it to the boom with a spare genoa sheet. Our speed with just the storm jib was about 7 knots, such a speed giving useful control in the wild seas. It seemed that a wave with a breaking crest would mount up from one direction, then moments later another wave would quickly follow from a different angle.

Fortunately, *Eclipse* had a good supply of skilful helmsmen who coped well with these frequently breaking and confused seas. Also she had a tiller, rather than a wheel, and though heavy work, the short response time of a tiller may have been an advantage over a low-geared wheel in this particular situation.

We all got wet and some were seasick, but an effort was made to keep things tidy, and hot soup was brewed for those who could take it. To do this, the galley stove had to be reshipped, having leapt from its mountings at some point, despite preventative dental wire. Water was finding its way down below, though operation of the electric pump with its wandering suction hose (fitted with this situation in mind) kept the amount in the bilges to a minimum.

After listening to the 0015 Tuesday forecast, which gave us south-west veering west force 7–9, locally 10 (something we had already well appreciated), both radios were turned off out of habit; but we did wonder anxiously about the smaller yachts in the race. Meanwhile, *Eclipse* continued for the rest of the night under storm jib. Things were uncomfortable, but we did not appear to be in imminent danger.

At daybreak the seas were spectacular. They had become very large, very steep and breaking awkwardly; but the boat was handling well. We could see the 46ft (14m) Hong Kong Admiral's Cup team yacht *Vanguard* running under bare poles close to starboard, and later heard that she had been nearly rolled right over while running back from the Rock with her No 4 genoa up. With this sail she had been surfing much faster than her young helmsman felt was comfortable or wise; then after a momentary lapse in his concentration, the boat turned broadside on in a trough to be rolled over by the breaking crest of the next wave. The entire watch on deck went over the side to the limit of their lifelines, and all winch handles and torches on deck were lost overboard. Fortunately, the deck crew was able to climb back on board suffering only bruising and shock, and there were more winch handles and torches stowed down below in this well-equipped yacht.

Following the capsize, the No 4 genoa was lowered and *Vanguard*'s speed dropped to a comfortable and much more manageable 6 knots, with an occasional surf to 10 knots. As luck would have it, a wave dumped heavily on board as the sail was being taken down through the companionway, bringing a huge amount of water below that filled the boat to 2ft (61cm) above her floorboards. It took a strenuous half an hour to pump out.

From *Eclipse* we saw no other yachts, apart from *Vanguard*. This was probably due to the fact that we had tended to keep to the south of track, having allowed – as it turned out – rather generously for leeway and surface drift. The many yachts that had not managed to make the Fastnet Rock would have been driven to the north-east in the night and were probably many miles distant.

The barometer had risen steadily since 0330, and though the 0625 shipping forecast was still giving force 10, the barometer was rising steadily and we felt that the wind would moderate before long. Sure enough, at midday the gaps between the gusts became longer and their strength reduced. The need for more sail met with little initial enthusiasm, but at 1220 we decided to put up the No 4 genoa. No difficulty was experienced with this much larger sail, and within a short time the watch on deck had also hoisted some mainsail. The 1355 forecast once again gave force 10 winds, but with the barometer now at 1003mb this was ignored. On the news following the forecast we heard of the havoc in the fleet behind us for the first time, but by then, there was not much we could do except sail on.

The usual Admiral's Cup team's 'roll call' by the Dutch guardship *Overijssel*, obviously busy with rescue work, did not take place, so we tried to report to Land's End radio that *Eclipse* was safe. Seemingly, this message got no further. As we rounded the Scillies under full sail the seas became much less violent and the wind went light during the night. The next morning a spanking breeze came up and we had bright sunshine. By now the reports of the disaster, to which we listened with dismay, were streaming through.

This story, when compared with the harrowing experiences of many other yachts in the race, suggests that the crew of *Eclipse* was either clever, or lucky, or both. We were certainly lucky that no one came to grief on the sharp corners of the galley stove when it parted company with its bearers. Moreover, it was only being restrained from tumbling further by a highly stretched rubber gas pipe. In the light of the thorough analyses of the race, it does seem, as was thought at the time, that having rounded the Fastnet Rock before the crew was exhausted, and run before the storm going in the right direction, concentration and enthusiasm within the top-notch Admiral's Cup crew remained high enough to keep the boat out of trouble by good steering. By this, one means working the boat over the waves to keep her on her feet, in the same way as the helmsman of a dinghy does when planing, besides paying careful attention to what might be coming from upwind. Swift helm movements were sometimes required to keep the stern on, or nearly on, to the big breaking seas, and it was helpful for a non-steering crewman to be sitting on the cockpit floor looking astern to call the whoppers that could broach the boat. It may be significant that our course brought the wind and the majority of waves about 20° off the stern.

While it was a great psychological advantage to be still in the race, confidence was not so high as to prevent the liferaft being taken from its stowage and placed in the cockpit ready for immediate use. Besides, the boat might not have come out well from a total inversion as internal lead ballast had already started to come loose after a knockdown. This could have been a most unwelcome addition to our difficulties had the boat been rolled right over. It is probable that there were some waves about that night that would have capsized a yacht of *Eclipse*'s size, regardless of her number of exceptionally able helmsmen. For example, in the case of the Class 1 yacht *Jan Pott*, due to the confused nature of the sea, it was impossible to judge the angle of the approach of the wave that went on to roll and dismast her.

In *Eclipse* we noticed the wind becoming lighter as we approached the Fastnet Rock at the very time that others were experiencing their highest wind speeds, though the wind soon became stronger again as we headed south-east. Perhaps being closer to the centre of the low may have given us a brief let-up from its full strength. The yachts in the general area of the Labadie bank had no such respite; indeed, the evidence is that many of these yachts experienced a wind field with markedly more severe conditions.

The yachting meteorologist Alan Watts calls it a 'cyclonic pool' and has gone to some lengths to work out how a 'storm within a storm' can come about. There were large boats in the cyclonic pool area that had already rounded the Fastnet Rock and, as one would expect, they generally fared better than the smaller boats. Even so, the 46ft (14m) Argentinian Admiral's Cup boat, *Red Rock*, was knocked down beyond the horizontal, and the 45ft (13.7m) German Admiral's Cup team boat *Jan Pott* was rolled through 360°.

The Fastnet inquiry report did not find sufficient evidence to indicate particular tactics to adopt in very severe conditions. It did state that 'there is a general inference that active rather than passive tactics were successful and those who were able to maintain some speed and directional control fared better'. Passive tactics generally amount to lowering sails, lashing the helm, closing the hatches, going below and hoping for the best. No yacht sank by adopting this tactic, and of the crews who felt that it was the most sensible thing to do, some found that there was as much of a need for a good lookout in bad weather as at any other time. *Sarie Marais*, a long-keeled wooden boat of traditional racing design, lay a'hull for 12 hours retaining a two-man watch on deck. With tiller lashed to leeward, this being a matter of consequence says her experienced skipper, she made 1.5 knots to leeward with few problems. The position of *Sarie Marais* was 37 miles to the north of Round Island outside the cyclonic pool area, and the skipper believed the weather he experienced was not as vicious as farther north.

Another yacht that lay a'hull successfully was Brian and Pam Saffery Cooper's 30ft (9.1m)

The Fastnet storm revealed in stunning detail through the medium of an electronically enhanced satellite cloud picture. The image was transmitted at 1637 on Monday 13 August 1979. Scotland can be seen in the extreme north-east corner and the Brest peninsula in the south-east corner, so that the Fastnet fleet lies under the cloud mass in the centre of the picture. *Photo: University of Dublin*

yacht *Green Dragon*, a newish and highly successful Doug Peterson design intended for top-class competition, but with more moderate features than some. At 2.15 am on 14 August, when 50 miles from the Fastnet Rock and therefore probably to the north of the cyclonic pool area, her crew sighted a red flare to leeward. They took down the mainsail and bore off downwind to render assistance. Under No 4 genoa alone the boat was travelling too fast, and when she fell off a wave the foremost bulkhead and ring beam broke, allowing the hull to pant. The crew made a temporary repair using floorboards, sawn-off jockey pole, a Spanish windlass and numerous drill bits. By this time they no longer felt able to render assistance and thereafter left the boat to lie a'hull with the helm lashed half-way to leeward, this being the angle at which she rode the waves best, besides protecting the damaged starboard bow.

Though 'tossed about like a shuttlecock' during the next 10 hours, the mast did not touch the water and the Saffery Coopers would use this method again to ride out such extreme conditions in a similar yacht.

Nevertheless, the accounts from within the cyclonic pool area suggest that there was a high chance of yachts lying a'hull being rolled right over, and that being rolled over could mean losing the mast, and real chaos down below with consequent crew disorientation and dramatic reduction of morale. Thus, while lying a'hull was a much wiser choice than taking to a liferaft, this manoeuvre was not necessarily more successful than the active tactics used by some of the other yachts. Such measures can be roughly divided into six categories: running before the waves with sufficient speed to steer out of trouble, much as did *Eclipse* under storm jib and *Vanguard* under bare poles; sailing into the wind under storm canvas; heaving-to under engine; lying-to a sea anchor or trailing drag devices; and lastly, heaving-to under sail.

The Fastnet inquiry report shows only 26 yachts as having hove-to under sail, clearly a less popular tactic than either lying a'hull or running off. Thirteen yachts continued under jib alone, six under reefed mainsail or trysail alone, and seven under both jib and a reefed mainsail or trysail. Reading the comments in the inquiry report it would appear that the ones that managed to keep sailing with the helmsman steering to luff to the breaking waves may have done best. This applied particularly to Contessa 32s, which are stiff boats. Their stiffness must have been an advantage, and although the Contessa 32s may not have reached the area of the strongest wind and worst seas, one Contessa 32, *Assent*, was the only yacht to finish the course in the smallest class. There is no information available on the whereabouts of the yachts that hove-to in the traditional sense, ie under mainsail/trysail with backed headsail; and without knowledge of their position, the results are not clear. In the worst area it seems probable that there was too much wind either to heave-to or sail to windward under storm canvas. It may be significant that two yachts reported that, though they used a storm jib on its own, using a trysail on its own might well have been preferable.

The French 36ft (11m) Sparkman & Stephens-designed *Lorelei*, of heavier displacement than many others, lay a'hull aided by her engine after picking up *Griffin*'s crew from their liferaft. The skipper, Alain Catherineau, had at first tried to get to the liferaft under triple-reefed mainsail, but he was travelling too fast and, after one unsuccessful rescue approach, he started his 12hp engine and lowered his mainsail. He then found he could not make into the seas under power and had great difficulty in turning through the wind to effect the rescue, but he could make across the seas to the disintegrating and unstable raft. The engine, with its automatic variable pitch propeller, gave him the vital control needed to attach a line. After being obliged to use the engine during the rescue, the skipper must have felt confident about the way the boat handled under power as he continued to use it for the duration of the storm. It is noteworthy that *Lorelei*'s skipper, who was widely acclaimed for his most opportune rescue, modestly attributes his success to the good design of the boat for heavy weather.

While engaged in another rescue, the crew of the Nicholson 55, *Dasher*, found that their boat would fore-reach under bare poles at 1.5 knots. This gives credence to the view that the addition of engine power can enable the yacht to manoeuvre quite effectively across the sea in high winds. Fore-reaching under bare poles seems to be a useful characteristic of a modern yacht, perhaps especially those that are stiff and have keels of generous lateral area.

Most yachts regarded themselves as still racing well into the storm, and did not use their engines. This was true of Graham Laslett, a veteran of the 1956 Channel Race who was skippering *Bonaventure*, an Ohlsen 35. Stemming from his long-keel experience, he was an advocate of keeping up minimum sail, but on this occasion the boat seemed uncontrollable in the confused sea of the cyclonic pool region. At first *Bonaventure* was comfortable running under bare poles. As the seas built up, increasing numbers of warps and sailbags were towed astern, eventually including a spare mainsail in its bag to give sinkage. Nevertheless, severe knockdowns and near inversion still occurred, as the small rudder was only effective at speeds above 5 knots when the boat was charging down the front face of the waves. At other times the helmsman was helpless, particularly in the troughs, when he was unable to turn the boat to avoid being beam-on to some of the waves, different angles being a feature of this sea. Significantly, the rudder was later modified on this design.

With hindsight, Graham Laslett feels an engine might have maintained steerage way at this critical point but wonders whether the towed ropes would have remained clear of the propeller. Certainly, in the case of the yacht *Autonomy*, a warp was washed forward by the following sea and jammed between the rudder and the counter, thereby making steering impossible.

Eighty-six yachts lay a'hull and 46 yachts ran before the wind towing warps or other drag devices astern. Of particular interest was the OOD 34 *Windswept*, skippered by her owner George Tinley, who not only tried both of these actions, but a sea anchor as well. After lowering his oversize storm jib, which alone had been too much sail for the boat, he at first tried lying a'hull. This seemed comfortable until the boat was caught by a breaking wave and rolled well beyond the horizontal, sweeping the two crew on watch overboard to the limit of their harnesses. Both men had difficulty in getting back on board when the boat righted herself, and they received no immediate help from those down below, who had problems of their own, such as flying jam pots.

Not wishing for this episode to be repeated, but with continuation of the race in mind, George Tinley then tried to lie-to an improvised sea anchor led over the port bow with a view to minimizing leeway. The crew was called below and a five-minute lookout system initiated. *Windswept* lay like this for a while in relative comfort with her port side to the wind and with the helm lashed to leeward. Then a sea knocked her round so that the starboard bow faced into the wind. As the helm was now the wrong way she became very uncomfortable, and George Tinley went on deck to put her through the wind under engine to lie as before. Subsequently, a jib sheet fouled the propeller, denying the use of power. George Tinley went below again, leaving all the tapered washboards in position and the main hatch open a crack for ventilation. A little later, even from down below, the crew clearly heard a breaking wave approaching, and this rolled the boat right over with a shuddering crash. George Tinley, who had been standing in the middle of the saloon, broke his right arm. Moreover, the lower washboards were lost, the liferaft came out of its stowage, and a large amount of water came down below. As lying-to a sea anchor over the bow had not prevented another capsize, the crew brought the sea anchor round to the stern, whereupon, with careful steering, the crew felt for the first time reasonably under control and safe. Ten years later George Tinley remains convinced that his last remedy was the best of the three actions taken, and the one he would employ in the future if faced with such extremes in a similar boat.

After being rolled over twice, the situation down below in *Windswept* was really very unpleasant. In particular, the lavatory had not been pumped through fully, a common enough misdemeanour, and sewage was mingled with the sodden mass of clothing, bedding and loose equipment sloshing about at bunk level. The main pump handle, normally held by two plastic clips on the underside of the cockpit locker lid, had somehow been lost in the capsize. When a broken-off tiller extension was found to fit, the pump still would not work as the strum box was choked with tea bags. The secondary pump, incorporated with operation of the semi-submerged lavatory, did not seem a good alternative at the time. Driven by acute discomfort and fear of further capsizes, consideration was given aboard *Windswept* to abandoning the boat for the liferaft tugging on its painter beside the boat but, no doubt fortunately, the liferaft defied all attempts to make it inflate.

Incidentally, some yachts' liferafts did inflate when not called upon to do so, thereby creating a tremendous problem, overcome in the case of the US yacht *Aries* by crew members stabbing it into submission.

Above The American yacht *Ariadne* dismasted and abandoned. *Photo:* RNAS *Culdrose*

Left Rescue of three of the crew of *Trophy* by HNLMS *Overijssel*. Their sole support is the upturned ring of the liferaft, the lower ring with the topping-up pump and the canopy having broken away hours earlier. The survivors have tied themselves onto the ring with their lifelines. *Photo: Peter Webster*

Of the active tactics employed, running before the storm without any drag device was employed by 57 boats. This tactic worked well for most of the yachts with a sufficient supply of alert and skilful helmsmen, capable of maintaining the concentration necessary to sail the boat out of trouble. Even members of the Australian Admiral's Cup team, who collectively managed the storm best of the international contenders, commented upon the intense effort they found necessary to cope with the conditions while on the helm.

Andrew Cassell, skipper of the light displacement J30, *Juggernaught*, spent most of the storm on the tiller. After trying the boat at every angle to wind and wave he found favour in running with the seas on the quarter. He says:

Running dead downwind under bare pole was extremely dicey as several times the boat took off like an express train. I quickly realized that many more events like this would see us being seriously damaged in a massive broach or pitch-pole. We therefore tried to stay head-to-wind and would have streamed warps over the bow had we had enough length to justify their use. As it was, we were not at all comfortable, and once or twice we were carried astern at a rate that threatened to take the rudder off. Beam-reaching was then tried. This seemed all right for a while, but then we were knocked down twice to the point where the mast was in the water.

Finally we tried broad-reaching with the sea on the quarter, treating the J30 just like a dinghy. Steering was extremely difficult, especially at night, when one had to listen for the breaking waves and line up the hull in order to surf down the wave at an angle. When caught by a breaker the low lateral area of the keel allowed the boat to slip sideways at a speed of, possibly, up to 5 knots. The method worked and, apart from one or two extremely alarming situations brought about by breaking waves from above, we were able to maintain control. I feel that a heavier and less manoeuvrable boat than a J30 would have rounded up frequently with disastrous results. On the other hand, if we had tried to lie a'hull with tiller lashed, such a light boat would have been thrown about unacceptably.

It is worth recording that Andrew Cassell has lost both his legs, and is well known for his tenacity and the tremendous strength of his arms.

The inquiry report revealed that, in general, owners felt it was necessary to keep the helm manned during the storm. Some of those who did not do so felt, in retrospect, that they should have done so. Some 80 per cent of yachts from which information was available had someone at the helm when hove-to or lying a'hull. Obviously it can be an advantage to be able to lash the helm in this situation, and it may be a reflection upon modern yacht design that lashing the helm did not occur more widely. Incidentally, in at least one yacht there were very few members of the crew prepared to take the responsibility of steering in the severe conditions.

Of the other active tactics used, there were several reports of yachts being knocked down with warps streamed and others that had success. It appeared to be best to endeavour to have sufficient drag to give control when surfing off the tops of waves, but not so much drag as to lose steerage way in the troughs. Use of *Lorelei*'s engine clearly was an advantage in her circumstances, and it worked well for her. Lying-to a sea anchor led from the bow did not seem to work for the one boat known to have tried it, for the reason that the pull was not constant and the boat, over which there was no steering control, tended to take up an awkward angle to the seas. Besides, sudden backsliding movement would impose high loads on the steering gear.

On the other hand, there is an interesting and encouraging account from Chris Dunning, whose 45ft (13.7m) *Marionette of Wight* broke her rudder at 2.30 am on 14 August, having made 20 miles homewards from the Fastnet Rock. After lowering sails, *Marionette* lay beam-on to the sea with her crew feeling decidedly exposed to the curling breakers while they put together a very long warp – perhaps 1000ft (305m) – composed of their two anchor lines and three genoa sheets. They led the warp over the bow, whereupon *Marionette* took up a steady and comfortable angle of 20–40° to the wind, though perhaps making up to 4 knots of leeway.

Golden Apple of the Sun, a yacht representing Ireland in the Admiral's Cup, lost her rudder after the storm was through. It was still very rough and attempts to steer her proved difficult. For six hours the crew tried to find a method of steering the boat without success. Typically, their original scheme involved a blade attached to the spinnaker pole with U bolts, but the pole soon broke. Aboard *Sigmatic*, a Sigma 33, the crew decided to heave-to when the storm struck. They put their anchor, 39ft (12m) of anchor chain and 295ft (90m) of rope over the bow, and found that, although the anchor was almost brought to the surface, their drift rate was down to 2.5 knots.

If the 1979 Fastnet did not give strong pointers to the best storm tactics to adopt, many significant lessons did emerge. The storm drew attention to the fact that the range of positive stability of certain yachts was such that they could remain perilously inverted for some time after a capsize. This was an important reminder that a yacht's range of positive stability is an important criterion in deciding a vessel's seaworthiness. The race also demonstrated that, however uncomfortable a yacht might have become during extremely severe weather, she provided the best refuge as long as she remained afloat. Thus a liferaft should have been thought of only as a last resort. Seven of the 15 fatalities occurred to crew who had taken to the liferafts, and of the 24 yachts that were abandoned, 19 were recovered afloat. Incidentally, the adage that 'your ship is your best lifeboat' emerged from naval wartime experience, and seems relevant to surviving storms in the open sea.

Several shortcomings in liferaft design brought further aggravation during the proceedings. For example, entry ports being at the opposite end to the raft painter, lack of stability exacerbated by inefficient drogues, and simple lack of strength. Happily, liferaft design has unquestionably improved as a result of the Fastnet experience.

The design of safety harnesses has much improved too, though again it took many harnesses to fail in the storm, accounting for much of the other half of the loss of life, to make the point. Moreover, the need for adequate strong points to clip onto, able to withstand the 2 ton stress that the harness should be designed for, was clearly demonstrated: the inquiry report revealed that at least six people were clipped onto attachments that broke under shock load.

There were many other events from which useful conclusions can be drawn. Unproven high-tech carbon fibre rudders did not fare well in the race, nor did washboards without a form of tether, particularly those designed for a tapering type of companionway. In addition, a combination of inadequate cockpit drains with unsealed cockpit locker lids became a cause of dangerous flooding. Many participants were impressed by the speed with which solid water will enter a small submerged opening. In this respect, a frightened man with a bucket proved his worth once again as an emergency bailer, not only aboard *Windswept* while the crew was discussing the idea of abandoning ship, but also on board many other craft in the race.

Most yachts did have the necessary charts to enter ports of refuge, but in the case of *Electron 11*, when considering running for Milford Haven, the skipper found that he neither had the charts, nor did his insurance policy cover him to go there. In addition to moving ballast, others reported aerobatic batteries, which must have been equally vexing. The need to stow away or secure all movable items before going to sea, and then to keep them that way, may be difficult to implement; but it was clear from experiences in the storm that such a policy would have been well rewarded in a knockdown. In particular, the good seaman's practice of stowing away spare clothing and bedding after use, contained in a heavy-duty polythene bag and sealed with a wire closure, would have prevented many instances of acute discomfort and hypothermia.

Likewise, adequate hand rails and an absence of sharp projections would have saved several injuries. For example, it is quite common to see racing yachts with protruding bolt ends below decks, which have not been trimmed off at the building stage. After the race there were reports of capsize injuries from such halyard winch fastenings on the deckhead.

Finally, it seems wise that the Royal Ocean Racing Club now requires competing yachts to have entered shorter and less demanding races as a prelude to the Fastnet, besides having a large element of the same crew together for the preliminary and final events.

Dramatic enough though the 1979 Fastnet was for all the participants and the world at large, it does *not* seem that the lessons of the Fastnet have been adopted entirely. The stability of a number of recently designed racing yachts is questionable, and racing yacht hull design remains primarily performance orientated.

18 Sudestada off Brazil

STIG LARSEN

At sea an encounter with hurricane force winds is to be avoided at almost all costs. In this account a Danish couple found themselves badly caught out.

Tir Nan Og was a one-off long-keeled 60sq yd (50sq m) steel sloop. Dimensions 38ft × 10ft × 7ft (11.6m × 3.0m × 2.1m) and displacement 10 tons. She was designed by Van de Stadt and built by the renowned Van Dam shipyard in Holland for an English gentleman in 1962. The hull is rather full in the bow with a beautiful smooth underwater body built in $\frac{1}{8}$in (4mm) steel. The deck and coachroof was at that time wood on steel frames, the cockpit is built of aluminium with a high wooden bridge for the main traveller. This bridge adds considerably to the helmsman's safety. The engine is a 28hp Volvo 2003 with a fixed three-bladed propeller that gives a maximum speed of 9 knots.

The navigation equipment was plain: a Danforth compass, Tamaya sextant, Radiofix RDF, Brookes & Gatehouse echo sounder, Walker log, VHF radio and a small Sony receiver. A Casio wristwatch doubled as a chronometer. In short, a 'keep it simple' yacht with a good speed potential.

The crew were Dorthe Eriksen and myself, then aged 27 and 36 respectively.

I have experience of many storms in different places and in various yachts. A couple of the storms were in the Roaring Forties and the Screaming Fifties around the notorious coasts of Patagonia and Tierra del Fuego, where force 10–11 is frequent – we spent three months there. *Tir Nan Og* has a deep draft and modest rig and is able to carry sails in winds near that strength, but I have never been through anything like the following storm, neither before nor since.

In November 1984 we were some 32nm east-south-east of Cabo Frio, Brazil, en route from Bahia/Salvador to Rio de Janeiro, 900nm to the south, sailing the shorter and more risky route through the Abrolhas Banks. The well-known American yachtsman and author Hal Roth, whom we met in Gibraltar, had warned us against that route; but as the weather statistics in the *South American Pilot* informed us that there was less than 1% risk of gales of more than force 7 in the area, we went for it – and duly received our punishment. However, gale force 7–9 and big, short seas in shallow water (18ft (5.5m)) in the middle of the dangerous banks forced us to turn around in a pitch-black night and head north again under trysail.

Two days later we finally got through the banks, tired and full of bruises from the storm, but this was nothing compared with what was to come. During the night preceding the next storm we were tossed around by an increasingly confused swell, which did not help us to get much needed rest. The sea was lit up by the gasfields on the port horizon. We knew there were lots of countercurrents around Cabo Frio, but felt that the increasing swell might be the forerunner of something else.

We did not normally listen to weather forecasts because of the language problem, but before any departure we had the usual weather discussions between yachtsmen of kindred spirit, and occasionally we did ask harbour officials or call passing ships on VHF. Mostly we depended on our own judgement, barometer readings, and the general remarks in the pilot books, believing that storms do not listen to forecasts. An interesting thing on this journey was that all the way around the coast local South Americans repeatedly told us that the weather pattern that year had been most abnormal. Afterwards it struck me that El Niño on the Pacific side had been especially active during the previous year.

At 0840 an odd form of cloud began to build up behind us in the north. I did not like its appearance and decided, after giving the matter brief consideration, to wake up Dorthe, who was lying down and almost unconscious with fatigue after the tempestuous week since leaving Bahia. Together we took the sails down in order to await the outcome, the first but not the last time on the trip. I had a strange uncomfortable feeling.

Five minutes later we were struck by a mighty, roaring wind. It was instantly clear to us that this was no 'ordinary' storm. It was like a hurricane. Staring horrified at each other we secured ourselves and any loose gear in the cockpit. The wind came like a steamhammer, an ironfist right into our faces, while *Tir Nan Og* was laid flat on her side even by her naked spars.

The former messy sea state soon got whipped clean by the continuous screaming wind and also, by now, fierce rain. It was impossible to turn one's face and eyes towards this wall of painful, blinding rain. I did, however, as learned in the massive horse-latitude rainstorms, manage to scan the horizon for ships, before we were struck by this hurricane-strength wind.

It is impossible to estimate if the wind was 12, 15 or maybe 17 Beaufort, but this was far beyond any wind ever experienced by us. A tremendous force from the south-east, it roared over to the land not far beyond the horizon, now a dangerous lee shore. This made us start the engine, and by using full throttle we made way out into the ocean before the waves got too big. In this unholy weather the sea could be influenced by the bottom at 164–197ft (50–60m) depth, and we were worried that, even in deeper water, for a small yacht like *Tir Nan Og* an uneven seabed and the strong countercurrents would generate freak waves.

Three hours later the wind decreased to an estimated force 9. We stopped the engine in order to save fuel, hoisted the trysail and laid the yacht on a south-westerly course. For the next few hours the wind stabilized at force 7–9. The sea became more regular, but increased steadily in height.

By 2000 the blow restarted and soon the yacht became barely manageable. The waves looked like mountains and we no longer felt safe outside despite our specially made life-lines, which were fixed to four separate strong points and held us securely and comfortably in the cockpit. We were worn out. With difficulty I took down the trysail and put it below, secured the wooden boom down to the deck, and lashed the tiller to starboard, but not too tight, as I felt it of vital importance to allow some movement. Then we secured all the hatches and criss-crossed some rope-ends over the cockpit and between the grab-handles on the coachroof – just in case. Our specially made Lexan storm windows could not be used owing to the lack of screwholes! We found some plywood sheets and placed them inside the cockpit hatch together with hammer and nails. Then we went below.

The yacht seemed to be doing quite well lying a'hull. It was certainly calmer than when running before the hurricane. The wind screamed on from south-east, but we felt relatively safe from the coast around Rio de Janeiro, in spite of our westerly drift. However, if the wind veered or continued to blow for days, well then we would be in big trouble for lack of sea room.

At midnight we were experiencing an evil hurricane-strength storm. The waves broke frequently over the entire yacht, lifted us up, tossed the yacht off the top in freefall, landed us in the troughs, and poured hundreds of tons of ocean down on our poor wooden super-structure. *Tir Nan Og* shook under the tremendous, thundering cascades of heavy water.

We did not feel at all safe. It is impossible to judge whether the physical or the psychological stress is the worst. Even when one tries to doze in the berth, each tiny muscle-fibre in the entire body works at high pressure in order to follow the absurd movements of the boat. The brain works overtime. I felt a sudden pain in my chest, but dared not tell my equally tortured mate about it. Death. You neither talk about it, nor even allow yourself to think about a close encounter, which seems to go on, on and on.

The thought of capsize or the yacht doing a somersault did cross our minds. That would

Left *Tir Nan Og* is a 38ft (11.6m) traditional design by Van de Stadt. She was built in steel by Van Dam in 1962 and is especially suited for extreme weather. *Photo: Stig Larsen*

Below Dorthe steering through a rain squall. *Photo: Stig Larsen*

be the end of it, as the wooden coachroof probably would be crushed and we would sink as a result. But we did not talk about it. In fact, it is difficult to talk at all because one's throat seems to shrink under the influence of the overwhelming amount of stress and fear. Could one do more? Has one chosen the right tactic? Has one challenged nature once too often? All these questions ran round in circles in the brain. The almighty power one experiences in the middle of such a storm cannot be exaggerated. Time stands still between every crash. The sounds and pounding from the tumultuous seas play on one's nerves. The howling and roaring of the wind, the shaking of the rig and tumbling of the hull, all is pure torture that never seems to end.

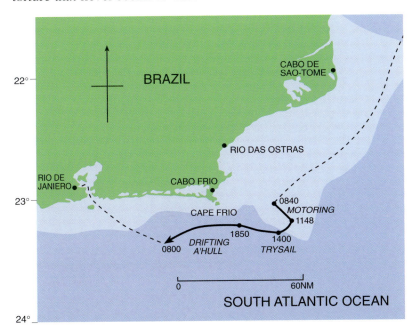

Figure 18.1 (left) The course of *Tir Nan Og* in the *Sudestada*.

Below After the *Sudestada* storm.
Photo: Stig Larsen

There comes a diabolic sizzling, a roar, one's body becomes a bundle of muscular tension – then, BANG! A freak monster falls like a gigantic iron block, while one tumbles around inside a tiny metal can in a pitch-dark wild waterworld. These monsters overtook us several times during the night. The mast 'talked' all night and seemed to be filled with tiny, babbling voodoo-devils. During this horrible time we drank half a bottle of Laphroig whisky in order to cut off the most tortured nerve-ends. In my opinion, it worked.

By dawn the wind ceased to storm and later dropped to force 6. Our worst sailing experience ever was over. Our brave little ship had fulfilled all our expectations concerning ultimate seaworthiness without a sea anchor or a parachute. I cannot think of any other way to survive 'our' storm in *Tir Nan Og* other than lying a'hull. But that certainly does not mean that it is the right tactic in all other yachts.

We reached the beautiful Baia de Guanabara at Rio de Janeiro at midnight. In the morning when we told our neighbour in a Nicholson 31 about the amazing storm, he did not believe us. In Rio there had been a slight breeze, he told us. However, in the evening this Canadian oil-engineer came to apologize. He told us that he had watched the news on television and seen the results of the storm in the Cabo Frio area. The official wind measurement over land had been 75 knots (at sea it might easily have been 85 knots according to the '10 per cent more at sea' rule). An area equal to the size of Denmark in the Cabo Frio area was declared a catastrophe area. Hundreds of houses at Rio Dos Ostros were smashed. The yacht club there was destroyed and all the yachts had been sunk. One 38ft (11.6m) yacht from Rio de Janeiro Yacht Club had disappeared with her five-man crew.

SUBSEQUENT REMARKS

There is no doubt that we received a freak blow for the area. According to the *South American Pilot* there is very little risk of prolonged gales. The common squalls from east-south-east in the north of the area are called the *Abrolhos* and in the southern region they are called *Sudestadas*, the latter formed by a cold Antarctic southerly wind replacing the warm northerly wind. According to the *South American Pilot*, the Rio de la Plata favours the development of secondary lows on a cold front and intensifies the disturbed weather. Strong *Sudestadas* occasionally reach storm force and may develop during relatively high pressure and may persist for a day or two. At the Rio de la Plata a strong south-east wind once averaged 62 knots for an hour and reached 86 knots in the gusts. However, the dreaded *Pamperos*, which come from between south and west, may be much more severe. About twenty *Pamperos* sweep the area each year against five to eight *Sudestadas*.

We had hand steered the yacht under trysail during the daytime, because our old Aries windpilot had broken its watervane in the morning before the storm. The Aries probably could have steered the yacht safely through the first five to six hours, which would have given us some much-needed rest. It would not have been safe to use the trysail with a lashed tiller, as the trysail would have been torn apart or flogged to pieces immediately in an accidental tack or gybe in the confused ocean. Under the combined forces of boat, wind and wave speed, the boat would just have broached. We therefore hand-steered until it seemed too dangerous to stay in the cockpit.

In 1982 I experienced a force 9 gale north of the Orkneys in my former yacht *Lundie*, a strong but small 26ft (8m) sloop, in which I successfully rode it out in the same way, but with a close-reefed mainsail on the mast. I would not have dared to run *Lundie* down the waves in force 9 plus owing to lack of control when she was accelerated by breaking waves. In fact, *Lundie* was laid flat in the western entrance to the Limfjord in Denmark by one such wave on the return journey.

In the same way, the extraordinary acceleration in speed from one freak, but not that big, wave, together with the inertia from the suddenly broaching hull, caused the capsize and total loss of my twin brother's 30ft (9m) trimaran in the wintry Baltic sea. We were lucky – once again – to survive.

However, my present yacht, the *Joshua*-type ketch, *Aurore*, which is a 14 ton double-ended longkeeler in steel, should not be left to lie a'hull, but be allowed to race down the waves in the same way that the renowned late Bernard Moitessier did with his *Joshua*, as described in his famous book *The Long Way*, by running down the waves at an angle. That is also my experience after nearly 10 000nm in *Aurore*, which has a 'spoon-bow', giving good dynamic and static buoyancy.

My experience in many different storms, seas and different yachts is that one carries out active measures to cope with the elements as long as one has the strength for it. Meanwhile, you try to 'read' the patterns of the elements and how your yacht behaves in these, so you can decide on the ultimate tactic for your storm, yacht and waters.

Most essential for surviving a wild storm is to be in a proper and extremely strong yacht. My personal choice for my favourite waters, which are the high latitudes, is a metal boat with a long deep keel. *Tir Nan Og* with her deep keel (7ft (2.1m) draft) and slim classic lines is well able to make to weather against an onshore gale, whereas *Aurore*'s full-bodied hull and long low keel (5ft (1.6m) draft) would have difficulty. But then she has other virtues: she is fast downwind, extremely strongly built, and second to none as an icebreaker!

We appeared to have had no damage during the *Sudestada*. However, when *Tir Nan Og* was slipped in Denmark two years later, we found a 7ft (2m) long gentle indentation in her hull and frames well below her waterline. This, we believe, must have occurred during the drops and poundings in our *Sudestada* off Brazil. Today *Tir Nan Og* has been totally rebuilt. Her deck and coachroof are now of steel and she is now cutter rigged with a small bowsprit.

COMMENT

This is an extraordinary story of two people aboard a yacht caught in hurricane-strength winds, but not many yacht owners can take comfort from their survival. *Tir Nan Og* was designed in the 1960s and has all the features of that period. She is narrow, deep, immensely strong and heavy – in fact, all the opposite characteristics to many modern yachts. She is a good example of an extremely seaworthy yacht that will look after her crew when it comes on to blow, and there are occasions, such as this unexpected hurricane-strength storm, when seaworthiness matters above all else.

Tir Nan Og's hull characteristics are those of a boat less likely to be rolled, but considering the conditions in which she lay a'hull, it is surprising that she was not. A 360° roll is not usually life-threatening, of course. Clearly, for Stig Larsen a seaworthy boat is more important than other characteristics, and his priorities are entirely vindicated in the event. Would *Tir Nan Og* have been better with a parachute? No one can be sure, but those who are familiar with their use would, no doubt, rather risk the use of a parachute than risk being rolled 360°. Besides, a lee shore was not far distant. Having not tried one, Stig Larsen is mistrustful of parachutes, but having a traditional type of extremely seaworthy yacht, he can afford to be.

What about a drogue? There has been a case of a yacht surviving a typhoon with a very, very long warp (Chapter 15) and a large quantity of oil, used together. In this case the crew had to steer for the duration and did not start in a fatigued state. The right drogue could have worked for *Tir Nan Og*, too, though she could have been frequently pooped, which could have made life difficult for anyone at the helm, and she would have been at some risk of being pitch-poled. Again we will never know for sure.

It is noteworthy that at the onset of the *Sudestada* Stig Larsen worked hard for greater sea room. To have tried to make for harbour could have been disastrous.

CHAPTER

19 *Channel storm of 1987*

PETER BRUCE

There were several small vessels at sea during the great storm of October 1987, but with massive destruction ashore, both on the north coast of France and the south coast of Britain, not much has been heard about them. The intense small depression brought winds of over 100 knots to the English Channel area, and though the wind speed was of hurricane strength, it is of course, strictly speaking, wrong to describe the event as a hurricane. It was a storm, albeit a truly violent one.

October is late in the year for leisure sailing, but the sea water temperature is still warm; so there are still a few sailors who go out for pleasure at this time. Moreover, delivery trips continue all through the year, and the Joint Service Sailing Centre yachts, based at Gosport, have a long season. Thus, with manageable conditions during the day, and without a warning of ultra-severe weather made manifest, it was not surprising that several yachts were still out at sea on the night of Thursday 15 October. A small fleet of warships from Portland naval base were also at sea for the opposite reason. In very strong winds, ships at anchor can drag onto the shore even in Portland Harbour, and as a result of a timely warning from the senior meterological officer there, Lieutenant Commander Peter Braley, who had made his own interpretation of the impending weather, the Portland fleet was ordered to sea.

Five descriptions from the sailing vessels at sea in the storm are related in this chapter, to give a wide cross-section of experiences; but before the accounts from the sea, there follows a meteorological report by Peter Braley.

METEOROLOGY

As early as the weekend of 10–11 October 1987, the Meteorological Office at Bracknell had been forecasting severe weather on the following Thursday and Friday.

At midnight on Tuesday 13 October, the depression in question was centred near 50°N 47°W, off Newfoundland, tracking east. It was expected to deepen progressively by midnight on Thursday 15 October, after which explosive deepening was predicted, with storm force winds expected in the South Western Approaches during Thursday, and moving up Channel and into the North Sea overnight. The prediction was reinforced and updated at 1545 on Wednesday 14 October, when the low had begun to move rapidly east. The storm warning suggested that the centre could be expected to be 150nm north-west of Cape Finisterre by 0600 on Thursday 15 October, with winds in its southern quadrant expected to reach storm force 10 up to 200nm from the centre. The low was then predicted to curve north-north-east to bring south-west storm force winds to the east Channel and southern North Sea areas late on 15 October.

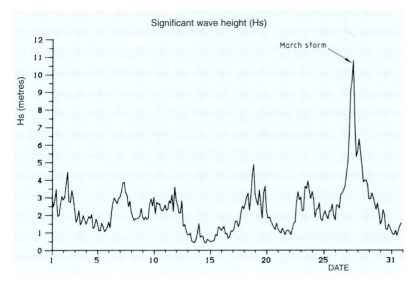

Significant wave height (Hs)

March storm

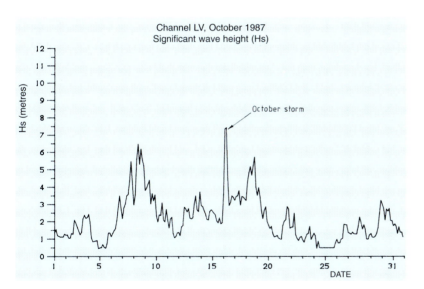

Channel LV, October 1987
Significant wave height (Hs)

October storm

Figure 19.1 The charts show two months of wave data recorded at the Channel lightvessel in 1987. This includes the very severe storm of October, and also the one in March of the same year. Though the intense, fast-moving system of October 1987 caused havoc on land, it was not around long enough to create exceptionally high waves, unlike the very large depression of the March storm.

The development became noticeable to meteorological authorities throughout Western Europe after midnight on 14–15 October. At that time, an elongated trough was located over a distance of some 500nm westwards from Cape Finisterre with two apparently distinct depression centres – one 983mb just north-west of Coruña, the other about 986mb near 43°N 19°W, some 450nm farther west. A strong pressure gradient existed on the warm southern side of the frontal trough, but with a slack gradient on the cold side. Noticeable potential temperature differences across this front were apparent from the few available observations, suggesting a sharp differential between the polar maritime and tropical maritime air masses. By midday on 15 October this broad surface trough lay from Brittany across Finisterre, and pressure in the trough was falling markedly. By 1800 the axis of the surface and upper troughs had extended north-east, bringing the frontal feature across the Channel and into southern England. The two centres were still apparent, one over Ushant, and the other now more vigorous centre of 963mb near 45½°N 8½°W. Surface pressure continued to fall within the trough but, more significantly, marked rises in pressure had occurred over the previous six hours both south-west of the main centre and astern of the cold front, with corresponding increases in wind speed. At about 2100, a signal was received at Portland from the forecaster in RFA *Engadine* in the north Biscay area, drawing attention to the sudden falls in pressure in his vicinity, thus suggesting explosive deepening of the Biscay centre. The signal also remarked upon the pronounced cross-sea and swell conditions. Soon afterwards the centre passed close to *Engadine* and winds rose rapidly in strength, occasionally to exceed 90 knots.

Thus by 2100 the depression centre had tightened considerably and begun to move rapidly north-east at about 40 knots to deepen to about 960mb in the extreme south of sea area Plymouth. The trend continued towards midnight when a centre was indicated just south of the Eddystone with a central pressure nearing 952mb. Notably, this feature was now a single, definable centre. A clear and fairly accurate track became discernible, making short-term forecasting and timing somewhat simpler and more certain. These, together with surface analyses, demonstrated the exceptional pressure gradients now developing in a narrow swath to the south and east of the centre, with surface gusts exceeding 100 knots in exposed locations.

During the next six hours the centre of the depression moved in a north-easterly direction across England after crossing the coast between Charmouth and Lyme Regis at about 0215. By 0500 on 16 October it had reached Lincolnshire and the occlusion had swung rapidly across southern England. Very marked rising pressure tendencies were widespread in the three hours from 0300 to 0600 as the depression filled: for example, +25.5mb at Portland. This later rise has now been established, by a comfortable margin, as the greatest three-hourly pressure change ever to be recorded in the UK.

Retrospective examination of meteorological records has been extensive, but it may be of interest to draw attention to a few facts:

1 The band of strongest gusts, with isolated maxima over 100 knots, extended across the Channel areas from north-west France in a band some 90 miles wide, parallel to the track of the depression centre.

2 Gusts of 70 knots or more were reported for a period of three to four consecutive hours, during which time the wind veered from 180° to 230°.

3 A double-peaked wind speed region apparently occurred over central southern England and the adjacent Channel coast. The first was associated with winds from 170° and 190°; the latter from a direction of around 230° – the peaks being at around 0200 and 0500 respectively.

4 A separate area of strong northerly winds affected Cornwall and North Devon from 2300 on 15 October until about 0200 on 16 October.

5 The strongest gust over the UK was recorded at Gorleston (Norfolk): 106 knots at 0424. Over 20 other gusts in excess of 90 knots were recorded between 0400 and 0715. A higher gust was estimated at 119 knots at a station near Quimper on the Biscay coast, while a gust measuring 117 knots occurred at 0030 at Granville on the south-west corner of the Cherbourg peninsula.

6 The passage of the cold front heralded the onset of the really strong winds at the surface. It was the strength of mean wind speeds that was noteworthy, rather than individual gusts.

7 The pressure falls ahead of the advancing depression were large but not remarkable, yet the subsequent rises in pressure appear to have been exceptional. Large areas of south England experienced rises in excess of 8mb per hour.

8 While very marked, short and steep seas built up in the Channel, recorders show that no remarkable storm surge followed and no pronounced swell developed due to the short duration and small size of the maximum windfield.

A Sadler 34 off Ushant

The first sea account comes from a new shoal-draft Sadler 34 called *Muddle Thru.* She had been bought by a Canadian, Allan McLaughlan, who had come over to Poole in Dorset, England, from Ontario with two other Canadians, Harry Whale and Bill Bedell, both of long sailing experience, to take delivery of his boat and sail for the Caribbean.

They set out on 13 October 1987, but progress towards Ushant was very slow due to strong head winds, and the boat was 'caught out' 60 miles to the north of Ushant in the 100–120 knot winds of 15–16 October. The persistence of *Muddle Thru*'s crew was enhanced by the fear that VAT might have to be paid on the boat if she was to return to the UK. After the great storm, another gale came, and this time the boat was rolled through 360°. The effects of the capsize, which included a broken lower shroud, caused Harry Whale, the skipper, to head back to Falmouth, where, incidentally, HM Customs took a benevolent VAT view in the circumstances. Harry Whale kept a log of events by speaking into a tape recorder, and it is his account of the storm that follows:

Winds increased to force 9 from the west-south-west during 14 October; and though close-hauled and carrying only a deep triple reefed mainsail, we made fairly good progress in almost the right direction. To keep a proper lookout was difficult because one could never be sure in the dark if we were looking towards the horizon or merely into yet another big wave. Certainly we did see many ships and made every effort to stay well clear, believing that under the prevailing conditions we were probably invisible, despite the radar reflector on the mast.

By about 0300 on 15 October the wind had abated enough for us to add some foresail to the sailplan and, after experimenting with the furling genoa, we rigged the detachable headstay and hanked on a small flat jib. The rest of the day was spent in heavy rain, crashing along into force 7 wind, heading south-west by south. In the afternoon the wind ceased quite suddenly and, after an hour or so, came in from the opposite direction, north-east. It then rapidly built up to force 7 again. Under jib only we were soon making splendid time directly towards our destination with a following wind, but meeting the waves that were still coming from south-west. Some waves we seemed to jump over and others we went through; nevertheless, it was good finally to be able to make our course at a respectable speed. Suddenly the turn at Ushant didn't seem so far away.

The run continued until 2100 when the wind died completely for half an hour. It then came in from the south, quickly built up, and veered to the south-west. By midnight we had taken off all sail and were lying a'hull. On the tape I said 'we are in a shocking blow'. Having experimented with the helm and the wind vane steering, I finally came to the conclusion that the boat took the best attitude to wind and waves when left to its own devices with the wheel lashed amidships and the wind vane disconnected. I feel sure this was largely due to the sprayhood and its considerable windage, which had the effect of keeping the bow into the weather.

Having seen several east-bound ships I was concerned about traffic in the area. We had heard the traffic controller at Ushant speaking to another vessel on VHF radio. I called to inform him that we were lying a'hull and virtually at the mercy of wind and sea, so suggested a *securité* call to vessels in the vicinity. This he did very obligingly, giving our position, estimated drift and course. He also told me that his wind gauge indicated wind speed ranging from 100 to 120, and that he was concerned for the safety of his radar. I did not think to ask if the wind speed given was in nautical miles, statute miles or kilometres per hour. It seems now that they were knots. Psychologically I think all of us on board felt better for the exchange, especially when he called an hour or so later for an update on our position. I provided this, and mentioned that we had noticed two or three west-bound ships

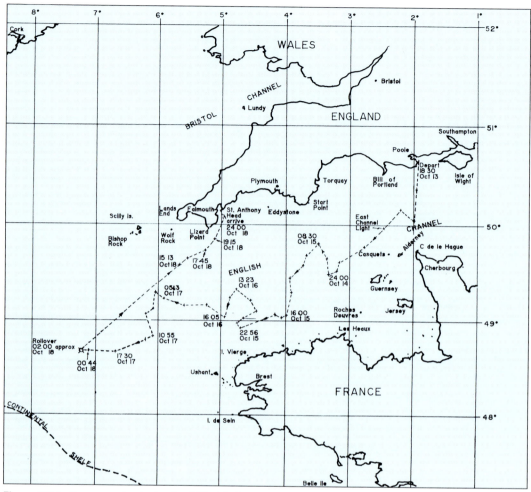

Figure 19.2 The approximate track of *Muddle Thru*, October 1987.

passing to the north of us. I was impressed by the fact that he wanted to know how our position was obtained. By now we were starting to hear parts of one-sided conversations on the VHF and realized that something pretty major was going on by the number of distress calls, including a Mayday from a yacht in a French port. Two other conversations I remember involved one vessel that had been driven hard aground, and another that had lost its steering.

Generally, our little boat seemed to be handling things very well, although the noise of the wind and the waves breaking over the vessel was extreme and the motion quite erratic. Occasionally the boat would seem to get temporarily turned broadside onto the waves and a great thumping one would hit her full on the beam. The furling jib was tightly wound about its stay, the small hank-on jib tightly lashed to the toe rail, and the mainsail lashed to the boom. A small part of the mainsail got free and proceeded to thrash so wildly that I felt sure the sail would end in tatters, and possibly even strain the rigging. Having determined that the loose part of the sail was below the second reefing point and therefore most of the sail should survive, I decided to let it flog rather than risk a man or two overboard trying to retie it to the boom, which would involve working around the sprayhood where the holding was least secure. As it turned out, the sail fared well, though the battens were lost.

The three of us remained fully dressed in foul weather gear and harnesses; we spent our time below with just a brief check on deck every 15 to 20 minutes. With so much water constantly coming onboard the boat, one had to be careful about the timing when opening and closing the main hatch.

Eventually, at about 0730 on 16 October, the wind abated sufficiently to start sailing again. We had gingerly worked our way up to a double-reefed main and small jib by 1400, and even had glorious sunshine for three hours. We were visited by some dolphins, and though still on a dead beat, we generally felt very fortunate to be in such good overall conditions as we listened to the radio telling of the damage done during the night both at sea and ashore. At 1600 more gale warnings were broadcast – force 8 going to force 9 from the south-west. For the next 13 hours we made good course of west-north-west at an average speed of $3\frac{1}{4}$ knots.

During 17 October the wind direction varied from south-west to west-south-west and we tacked accordingly, always mindful of giving Ushant a wide berth. By 2200 we were again down to bare pole in a raging gale, this time with mainsail lashed very tightly to the boom and the outboard end of the boom lowered and lashed to the toe rail. Once again I experimented with the wind vane steering and various positions of the helm, but came to the same conclusion as before – to lash the wheel amidships and allow the boat to take care of itself. From our perspective the main wave pattern was from the south-west; however, we seemed to be constantly under attack from quite unpredictable waves from the south-east and north-west. Some of these seemed to be not so much waves as just great eruptions of water, happening without rhyme or reason.

As before, we huddled below fully dressed in foul weather gear and harness trying to catnap, with a check on deck every 15 to 20 minutes. I suppose this continued for three or four hours. I was lying down in the starboard bunk and had dozed off nicely when suddenly I realized I was airborne and on my way across the cabin, easily clearing the lee cloth and table en route. I came up short against the other side of the boat on top of Bill. As I scrambled around trying to extricate myself I remember enquiring after Al, who had been using the quarter berth. He spoke up from underneath me saying that he was OK. He had given up the quarter berth and rigged himself an accommodation on top of some cans of water we had lashed into place in the U of the dinette settee and was wedged between Bill and the folding table. About this time I heard 'we're upside down, boys' from Bill in a quite conversational voice – indeed, almost a mumble.

By use of the two full-height teak pillars that the Sadler has in the vicinity of the galley and chart table, I was able to heave myself over the galley sink and, by the time the boat was completely inverted, I was standing on the deckhead holding onto a pillar with each hand, facing forward, with my back to the engine compartment and the main hatch boards.

The exact sequence of events and time involved is of course very uncertain, but I do have a vivid recollection of standing there and being aware that the noise and motion had ceased, other than the sound of water rushing in through various small openings; I was expecting at any moment to be struck from behind by the hatch boards collapsing inwards under the pressure. It was as well that Bill had insisted that the cockpit locker lids be well secured.

As the boat continued its roll-over I remained clinging to the pillars, negotiating them rather like climbing a large two-rung ladder that is being rotated. As the boat resumed its normal upright position several impressions struck me; one was the resumption of the old noise and motion, another was the additional sound of water sloshing back and forth; and the most disturbing was what I can only describe as a 'wobbly' feeling about the boat. Several explanations flashed through my mind, the first being that maybe we had sustained some sort of a longitudinal hull fracture – yet there didn't seem to be much water coming in. Then I wondered if the keel had loosened, but discounted this thought on the grounds

that surely it would have gone entirely or not at all, and since we seemed to be remaining right way up, the keel must still be in place. The only possibility was that the hull was being wrenched around by a loose rig.

My first resolve was to try the diesel engine. This would enable us to run the electric bilge and shower pumps, and also provide motive power should we need it. When we tried the switches we got the whistle of the Calor gas alarm. We waited for some time and it didn't stop. Because the alarm had acted strangely on another occasion, and because we had always been careful to turn off the supply, I felt sure this was a false alarm, at least as far as the Calor gas was concerned. We turned off the alarm and gave the engine a try. It started. Now to check the rig.

Getting on deck to investigate was no easy matter. The spray-hood, with its stainless steel framework, was crushed down over the main sliding hatch and the hatch boards. Eventually Bill and I both got through, and discovered with the help of a small torch that the port lower shroud was loose. Bill bravely went forward and took a jib halyard one turn around the mast and attached it to a stanchion base near the chain plate. He then did the same within the main hal-yard so that we now had the two halyards running from the spreader roots to the stanchion base. From the cockpit we did our best to sweat up these halyards, no easy matter without winch handles, which had left their pockets during the roll-over. Having thus more or less stabilized the rig, we proceeded to haul inboard sheets, halyards, and other odds and ends all hanging over the port side of the cockpit.

Below, Al had been doing his best to assist the bailing process by trying to pour water into the sink with a saucepan. The outlet was not very big and sometimes, because the motion was so violent, the water was flung back at him before it had a chance to drain away. However, we certainly seemed to be holding our own because the water level was not much above the cabin sole. Bearing in mind that a large part of the volume of the bilge was taken up by canned food and built-in flotation material, the actual volume of water aboard could not have been great.

We found that the shower pump was not operating, and only one of the interior lights was working. All of the electronics except the satnav had ceased to function, ie radios, windspeed and direction, log, speedometer and depth sounder. Our spectacles, charts, dividers, hand compass, torches and spare winch handles seemed to have vanished into the heap of sodden mattresses, tools, clothing and sundry other items.

I decided that the prudent course of action was to make for Falmouth. I thought of Moitessier and Vito Dumas, who advocated that the best way to survive in heavy breaking waves was to sail with them at good speed.

Because I had stared at the chart for so many hours before the incident, I knew the course was about 050°. Before shoving the gear shift into forward I tied a huge knot in the furling line of the jib, gauged to stop at the fairlead. Thus about 6ft (1.8m) of it and no more could be let out in a hurry by one man, should the engine stall and force us into taking a chance on the rig.

We were off on the wildest sleigh ride of my entire sailing career. In the cockpit it was impossible to hear the engine over the roar of the wind and water, and there were no gauges of any kind to indicate rpm or boat speed. The main compass seemed to be working, though a little sluggishly. It was strictly seat of the pants stuff, aided sometimes by the vibration of the engine and propeller through the soles of the feet. The boat was completely

In storms of extreme violence, seas can become absolutely chaotic. Note the perpendicular wave rising against the sky at the left centre. *Photo: de Lange*

overwhelmed on several occasions, leaving the helmsman spluttering and gasping for breath. It was the blackest of nights, and I remember thinking it would be so much better once daylight arrived.

When daylight did finally arrive I wished it had remained dark. It was an impressive scene, huge steep breaking waves everywhere and the air filled with water, either rain or spume. At one point some dolphins came along to join in the fun. Like young skiers on a mogul run they cavorted and frolicked around us, frequently leaping right out of the advancing face of the waves. Never did I feel so out of my element as I cowered at the wheel, tired and afraid, while admiring their wonderful performance. About the time I was beginning to worry about fatigue and hypothermia, Bill squeezed his way out of the hatch and offered to take over. This was a great relief to me, first, because I needed the break, and second, it meant that Bill was now endorsing my strategy of heading for Falmouth, albeit tacitly. I am sure he was originally not in favour.

Later, Al also came up to be initiated and join the watch roster. Time and again it would seem she was about to broach, and be rolled over in a breaking crest; yet at the last minute a little extra power would straighten her out and away we'd go, surfing down yet another huge wave, only immediately to worry that the bow could bury and cause a pitch-pole. Bill was to tell me much later that, at one point when he was steering, the boat did a complete 360° turn (horizontally this time); she seemed, he said, to sail close around a great pinnacle of water, with a cliff face on one side of the boat and a precipice on the other.

About 1900 in the failing light, the loom of the Lizard light showed 10 miles to the north-north-west. The satnav had done a splendid job for us. Now, without tidal information or depth sounder, came the task of piloting our way the remaining 20 or so miles to the harbour. As it turned out, everything went well: and the wind and waves even abated a little as we came into the lee of Manacle Point and the Manacle rocks. The limited information we had on board showed the harbour entrance and not much else. We shot through the entrance, did a sharp left turn, and suddenly all was tranquil, relatively speaking anyway.

A SWAN 46 IN THE BAY OF BISCAY

Had *Muddle Thru* made Ushant and into the Bay of Biscay, she would not have had a much easier time, as can be appreciated from another drama going on 215 miles south-south-west of Ushant. On the morning of 15 October a Swan 46 fitted with a Scheel keel, on passage to Spain, hove-to in wind speeds shown on their Brookes & Gatehouse anemometer of, at times, over 85 knots. Apart from periodic lookouts, the crew of four remained below, where it was dry. At 1800, without warning, the boat rolled quickly to port through 360°. Floorboards, and everything stored under them, flew through the boat. The yacht's owner, who was standing in the main cabin after returning from a lookout on deck, broke a shoulder. The mast broke at deck level, probably due to a lower shroud failure.

The mast remained attached to the boat by her intact rigging and, without suitable cutting devices on board to cope with rod rigging, the crew were unable to cut it free. Around 2000 the mast broke at two other points and started to pound against the hull. At this juncture the owner decided to ask for outside assistance, and an EPIRB was activated. The Swan 46 was 'localized' in 45 minutes, and a Japanese freighter appeared on the scene at 0100 in the morning of 16 October. The freighter launched a boat, but this soon capsized; so the yacht, with her engine still working, was asked to go alongside. While the crew were disembarking, the yacht was smashed several times against the freighter's hull, and at one point she surfed down a wave and struck the freighter at full speed with her bow. Though the EPIRB was heard for an hour afterwards and hatches were left closed, the yacht was never found.

A significant point in this episode was the difficulty experienced in detaching the mast. Bolt croppers will not cope with heavy rod rigging: only hydraulic cutters or other special tools will do the job.

RESCUE SEEN FROM A DESTROYER BRIDGE OFF PORTLAND BILL

But for the seamanship of the rescuers, another craft might have been lost that night. The story is a little bizarre, and is best told by the captain of HMS *Birmingham*, Commander Roy Clare, who is himself a most experienced yachtsman. The vessel is a modern gas-turbine powered destroyer, carrying a Lynx helicopter on board:

HMS *Birmingham* was operating 7 miles south-west of Portland Bill, turning endless circles on the calibration range. At about 1800 on 15 October my navigator showed me the latest Mufax weather chart, with isobars tightly packed over the Brest peninsula. I commented that I was glad we weren't farther south, and forgot about the weather. We did not see Michael Fish, the weather forecaster, on TV that evening.

At about 0115 I was nearly thrown out of my bunk by an unusually heavy roll. I called the officer of the watch on the intercom to find out what he was up to; he answered at once, saying that the weather had suddenly freshened and that he had just heard a call on VHF for help from a yacht ... would I come to the bridge?

I quickly established that the yacht was in touch with Portland Coastguard. Her position was some 18 miles south of me, about 24 miles from the Bill. Our weather conditions were wind: south-south-west force 8–9; visibility 6 miles, less in drizzle. We set off on a course of about 200° at 22 knots; this was the maximum we could do in the prevailing conditions. We pitched heavily in the steep seas, but there was only a modest swell and we did not thump at all.

Meanwhile the yacht transmitted frequently on VHF, using Channel 67, as directed by the Coastguard. I put an experienced yachtsman on the circuit to give an informed point of contact. We started an incident log book, told the naval operations room we were proceeding to assist, kept in touch with the Coastguard, established that the Royal Fleet Auxiliary tanker

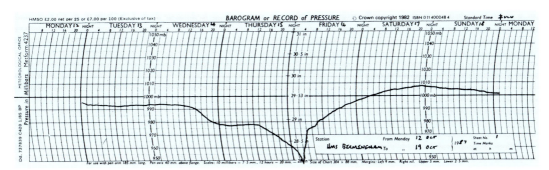

Figure 19.3 The barograph trace from HMS *Birmingham* recorded during the October 1987 storm while standing by a distressed multihull some miles south of Portland Bill.

Black Rover was also in the area, and made basic preparations on board for search and rescue. Flying was out of the question; the sea state was worsening rapidly and the wind limits for helicopter operations would have been exceeded unless we had been heading out of the wind at some speed. This was clearly undesirable; in any case, the ship's Lynx helicopter was not equipped for night search and rescue over a small object like a yacht, so it would only have been able to aid the search, not the rescue. Ashore, the coastguards decided that the Weymouth lifeboat should be called out. I do not know whether the shore-based search and rescue helicopter was considered; in my view, it would have been of very marginal value in those conditions. In the event, search was not necessary; location was straightforward, aided by a reasonable position report in the first instance, and by continuous VHF transmissions from the yacht, which were DF'd by the Coastguard stations at Portland Bill and Berry Head to give a cross bearing fix.

By 0150 we had established that the yacht was a cruising multihull of 40ft (12m) length. The vessel was in no immediate danger of foundering, had sustained no damage, and was managing to make way across the wind at about 4 knots on a westerly course apparently bound for Ushant. The crew sounded terrified; they were pleading to be taken off their craft, urging rescuers to hurry before dire things happened. It seemed that there had been a difference of opinion as to whether to continue or turn back. The yacht was said to be shaking violently in the gusts and the voice was convinced that each moment was to be his last. In the background of each transmission, it had to be admitted, there was a fearful noise of wind in rigging and crashing waves. We did our best to reassure and console the yacht, keeping the crew informed of our progress.

By 0215 we were down to about 15 knots. The sea state was rising high, the wind gusting 75 knots. Visibility was down to a mile or two. *Black Rover* and *Birmingham* arrived on the scene at about the same time – 0245 approximately. Between us we manoeuvred to windward of the yacht, whose lights were clearly visible in the driving spray.

Black Rover kept pace with the catamaran and provided a solid breakwater; I manoeuvred *Birmingham* between the two, pumping light oil from my bilges to take the edge off the sea. The yacht crew reported that our combined efforts gave them an easier ride; how much of this was due to oil and how much simply to our lee I don't know. Derek Sergeant, the lifeboat coxswain, said he thought the oil helped, but none of us felt it was a conclusively valuable contribution. I believe that the yacht was moving too fast to make maximum use of my slick; with hindsight it might have been more effective if laid to leeward and ahead of the yacht, to allow the craft to pass through the relative calm. That the oil calmed the water was not in doubt as we could see its effectiveness in the searchlight beams: placing it where the yacht (and, subsequently, the lifeboat) could benefit was more tricky.

The craft continued to make progress to the west-north-west as the wind increased to 90 knots. My anemometer would not register above this speed, but it was clear from the roar in my own masts and aerials that the wind was still rising. There were long periods, while I lay virtually a'hull, rolling violently, keeping pace with the yacht, when the anemometer needle lay hard against the stops, and the note in the wind continued to rise steadily and unbelievably higher. On the bridge of *Birmingham* I think most of us were too busy to marvel at the strength of the storm. The ship rolled nearly 45° at times, her stabilizers unable to operate as designed at these very low speeds. I used the bridge throttle controls myself as if they were Morse controls on a speed boat, using high power on each shaft, alternately ahead and astern, keeping the ship close – but not too close – to the yacht. This seamanship was as nothing compared with that in *Black Rover*; she had a single shaft, variable pitch screw, and has a generally heavier and more ponderous hull. Yet she stayed in position and coped very well indeed.

Shortly after 0320, with no warning whatsoever, the wind swung from 180–190°, 95 knots plus, to 270–280°, 95 knots plus. This was remarkable for all sorts of reasons, not least of which was that the sea flattened out for a while. 'Confused' is too elementary a word; the sea was gob-smacked, as one of my sailors put it! The catamaran at this point began to head north-north-east, maintaining a beam wind and a speed of about 4 knots. The crew of the yacht continued to plead periodically with me to take them off. I pointed out that since they were in no immediate danger they were better off where they were. I was about 4800 tons of crushing death if I closed with them in those conditions, and I was not about to put my rigid-hulled inflatable in the water in those seas.

Meanwhile, the Weymouth lifeboat approached steadily from the north-north-east. They had a heavy time of it, and it was to their undying credit that they arrived so quickly, at about 0420, to set about rescuing the crew of the catamaran. For the ensuing hour we in *Birmingham* had the privilege to be spectators as the Arun class vessel manoeuvred repeatedly alongside the yacht. We closed in to about 200yd (183m) from the scene to provide the best lee. The sea was beginning to build steadily from the west. The dramatic wind shift was followed by two hours of unabated fury: the sea became very angry indeed by 0530 when the lifeboat completed her last approach, with, incidentally, no damage on either side. By then the wind was 260°, 80–100 knots, with possibly stronger gusts. The seas were confused and steep with a very heavy Atlantic swell. The female member of the yacht crew had been invited to cross to the Arun first, but she was in fact the last to go, showing some courage. The skipper elected to stay on board and drove his yacht to shelter in Weymouth with resolution, though nearly coming to grief on the Shambles in the process. Once in the lee of Portland Bill, at about 0800, I used the rigid-hulled inflatable to transfer an experienced yachtsman to assist the yacht into harbour.

A CONTESSA 32 IN THE SOLENT

Meanwhile, not far away, a Joint Services Sailing Centre Contessa 32 called *Explorer* was on passage from Poole, Dorset, to Gosport in Hampshire on the last day of an RYA coastal skippers' course. The instructor and skipper was Ray Williams, but the story is told by one of the crew, Martin Bowdler, due to take his examination the next day:

We intended to make this a lazy passage, adding a few night hours to our week's trip. Therefore when we heard the shipping forecast at 1750, we knew we would have a lively sail. The general synopsis gave gale warnings for most sea areas, and for Wight it was cyclonic, becoming west to south-west force 7 to the severe gale force 9, decreasing to 6 later.

We cast off from the Town Quay at Poole around 1845. Our course had already been planned and plotted on the charts. All the sails were sorted out for quick access, in case the conditions strengthened. Anything that could crash around was secured or put away and our harnesses were fitted once more. Though in the week we had many a soaking, we all still had at least one dry shirt at the ready to don if we were to have another wet trip. All other clothes were stowed away. One important aspect that we did not remember was to fill our thermos and make lots of sandwiches for the passage.

When we cast off, the sea and sky gave no indication of the waves and wind to come. The sky was watery; dark – yes; forbidding – no. The course planned was a very simple one: from Poole Fairway across Christchurch Bay to Bridge Buoy, through the Needles Channel to the Solent and thence to Gosport.

At Poole fairway we had one slab in the main and the No 1 genoa set. The weather sharpened to force 6 from the west-south-west, and a well-rehearsed sail change to the working jib was executed. Our thoughts of this passage had not been to push ourselves, therefore our sail changes were always one step ahead.

By the time we were crossing Christchurch Ledge this routine was overtaken by events. The wind picked up to what we imagined to be around force 8 or more, which caused the crests of the waves to froth up and turn into heavy spume. By then we had three slabs in the main and the storm jib set. We were surprised how suddenly it had become very dark; this was not your average cloudy sky at night. The wind continued to pick up; and as a result the sea was gathering strength and height. We had been able to pick out the lights of Bournemouth and Highcliffe continuously, but this became more difficult with the spume and the deepening of the troughs.

Our navigation became an increasingly odious task. As the seas increased so, too, did the emergence of a pattern of rogue waves. These would hit us on our quarter and happily break on the cockpit and coachroof. Every so often, one of these would be much larger than the others. We had the hatch shut and the washboards in except for the top one, but these larger rogues had enough force to slide the hatch forward and completely drench the navigator and chart table. I had just finished my stint at the helm and, as part of the rotation of crewing, found myself down below navigating. At last I had a chance to change my sodden shirt. This done, I felt so much better. However, the first of the larger rogues swamped the boat. I know this because much of it came down my drier and warmer neck and the chart table was awash. As I appeared in the hatch this caused much amusement to the crew, who had already taken the brunt of the wave.

We found that we could be prepared for the normal series of waves by continually weaving along them to avoid the breaking crests. We could feel the normal pattern, as the boat began to lift, and whoever was at the helm would play the waves, riding through them as they broke at their crests. A Contessa may be a most forgiving boat, but in these waters we had to play her firmly, constantly dumping and tightening the main. The motion gave us the overall effect of cork-screwing through the water.

However, the rogues were different, in so much as we could not see them coming until the last possible moment – too late. One of the crew, armed with a torch, was detailed to watch for these rogues. Not a very satisfactory task as he would be certain for a head-on soaking. This was one of the jobs no one really enjoyed, but certainly amused the rest of the crew.

Our crew rotation proved valuable in these conditions, due to the various physical tasks on the boat. No one person could continue on a particular job for a long stretch, as certain jobs required more exertion or concentration than others.

The most spectacular seas were off the Shingles where the large waves piled up on meeting the shallows. White waves resulting from this could be made out, although the visibility was limited, while the crashing noise was almost deafening. We had the impression that we were much nearer to the Shingles than we actually were. The seas around us were very steep, broken, erratic and white. This made steering difficult, as our rudder would be as much out of the water as in. We did notice we were being blown down towards the Shingles, and had to harden up to allow for our considerable leeway. For about the next hour the heel of the boat was such that her cabin windows were almost constantly under water. When we bore away there was a moment when *Explorer* would drunkenly come upright, only to fall over again in the next gust. One of the crew found it all a bit overwhelming and he had to retire to the cabin, where he spent the rest of the trip. I cannot say that we were all scared, because there was so much to check on. Having said that, we were apprehensive off the Shingles.

The sails and rigging were being put under a great deal of strain, so the general appearance of the sails, hanks, reefing lines and sheets had to be checked so as to pre-empt any sort of accident. This was a hazardous job, but one that was enjoyable.

Explorer was fairly bucking around and very wet at the bow. But with a lifeline to prevent one being lost overboard, the job felt like a fairground ride.

By the time we had passed Hurst Castle, the wind became increasingly local under the lee shore of the island. The seas had lessened, so while navigating I tried to take the opportunity to make a sandwich for the crew. However, odd omnidirectional gusts threw *Explorer* around; the same can be said of my attempts below – but we were all grateful for something to eat, even if crude, wet and very salty. Past Yarmouth this freak condition lessened. The wind had not yet reached its full force, even though it was screaming through the rigging. The barometer was still falling at an extraordinary rate.

People have often asked why we did not make for shelter to somewhere like Yarmouth; the simple answer being that we seemed to be safer on the water than making for land, and we had our appointment with the examiners the next day at Gosport. However, passing close by Cowes, we did have a small twinge as we could see all the various lights on. The thought of a whisky in the warm, talking about the storm, was not lost upon me.

Past Prince Consort buoy we put our final slab in the main. This did little to affect our speed, some 6½ knots. At just before midnight we came out of the lee of the island and were once again in the full force of the storm. This was an interesting experience as the change of conditions was so quick. From the very loud wind we had experienced in the lee of the island, the wind now roared. *Explorer* could be felt groaning under the strain, while rapid easing of all the sheets did little to improve the slamming of the boat. We fairly hurtled towards Gilkicker Point.

The 0030 shipping forecast was now nearer the mark. Wight was 'south-westerly gale force 8 to storm force 10, decreasing force 6 to gale force 8'. The storm force 10 surprised us, but accounted for the noise and strong conditions.

Normally we might have taken the inshore small boat channel between Gilkicker Point and Portsmouth, but to give a greater margin for error we took the Swashway route. When the moment came to turn towards the harbour entrance we tacked rather than gybed as far to windward as possible. On the new course our angle of heel was markedly increased, such that the cabin windows were constantly awash, and we noticed that we were making a good deal of leeway towards the beach. We were able to make a large allowance in our course for the leeway and, thankfully, no extra tacks were needed to get inside the harbour entrance.

Once we came within the protection of Fort Blockhouse, *Explorer* immediately came upright and we seemed to stop. Our handkerchief representation of sails was dropped and secured. It was just after 0100 and we had made our destination in good time, though, ironically, when day dawned our examiners had to call off the tests due to the weather, being blocked in their homes by fallen trees.

A HALLBERG RASSY 42 IN THE NORTH SEA

At much the same time some more heavy weather sailing was being experienced in the North Sea. In this case the account is by Jeff Taylor who, with two crew, was delivering a new Hallberg Rassy 42 from her builders in Sweden to Southampton. This was a trip he had done many times before in all weather conditions:

After a trouble-free trip across the North Sea, we called into Lowestoft on the morning of Thursday 15 October to fill up with diesel. With a forecast of south to south-west force 4–5 for Thames and Dover, but a wind from the east to south-east of 5 to 10 knots, we departed at approximately 1400 and made good progress motorsailing at 7 knots for the first three to four hours. The 1750 shipping forecast was the first indication that there might be a strong south or south-west wind on the way. At this time we were just north of east from Harwich, with a light south-east wind, making good progress motorsailing with full sail. I looked at all the options and decided to carry on, with the intention of going in to Ramsgate should the wind pick up later, as forecast. After all, even if the wind should increase to force 8 from the south-south-west, it was nothing that we could not cope with, as we were in a well-found boat in which I had utmost confidence.

The wind gradually increased from the south and by midnight was approximately 20 to 25 knots. We were by now motorsailing with no genoa and one reef in the main. Our position at the time was 8 miles west-south-west of the Galloper light buoy and the tide was about to turn with us. The sea was starting to build up from the south. I heard a gale warning on the VHF just before midnight; the forecast was for gale force 9 from the south-west, imminent. I was firming up my plans to make for Ramsgate as we were only 21 miles away, and obviously something was going to happen. The wind steadily increased up to south-west 30 to 35 knots, with the sea becoming quite rough and uncomfortable. It was

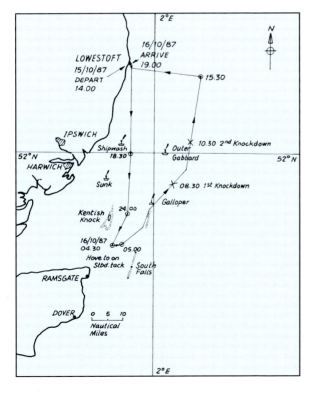

Figure 19.4 The track chart of the Hallberg Rassy 42 during the October 1987 storm.

enhanced by the now south-going tide. There was a lot of water over the decks at this stage, and our boat speed was down to 4 knots.

At about 0130 on Friday morning I was on watch when George popped his head out of the hatch; he told me there had just been a storm force 10 given for Thames and Dover. By this time I was starting to get nervous about the situation, so I asked George to make sure everything down below was well stowed and to prepare for some very heavy weather. The next gale warning came at about 0330 and forecast south-west violent storm 11, imminent.

The wind was still only 35 knots and we were making about 4 knots towards Ramsgate; but it was obvious that we were not going to arrive before the gale.

At 0430 the wind suddenly increased to 60 knots. I decided to heave-to on the starboard tack and stand out to sea. This presented me with a bit of a problem as we had no storm jib or trysail on board. In the end I found that with no sail up, the helm lashed to weather and the engine running ahead at about 1200rpm, the yacht lay with the wind about 60° off the starboard bow and was reasonably comfortable in the circumstances. We were 12 miles north-east of Ramsgate at this stage. The seas were getting very big with breaking crests and spray everywhere; we started to get laid over on our beam ends as the boat rose up the face of the waves and over the tops. Visibility was down to about half a mile.

At 0500 the wind had increased further and we were approximately 14 miles north-east from Ramsgate. Our radar, which worked well throughout, showed a lot of shipping in the vicinity; so I was very keen to get outside the North Falls banks, and decided to run off into deeper water. We were running downwind in generally a north-easterly direction, using our faithful Decca for navigation. The sea continued to rise and became very steep, with every crest breaking. Flying spume filled the air, reducing visibility to nil.

It became increasingly difficult to steer, due to our speed; but it was essential to keep the boat dead down the face of the waves in order to avoid a broach. I felt we really should have had a sea anchor out, but we had nothing suitable on board to rig one with, and I thought it too dangerous to let anyone out of the cockpit.

We suffered our first knockdown at approximately 0830. As we surfed down a very steep wave the boat started shearing off to port, and I was unable to correct this. The wave then broke on top of us knocking the boat down to about 90°. The boat righted herself very quickly, and the only problem left was a cockpit full of water; but this drained away quickly. The seas were continuing to get worse. I had sailed in winds as high as we were experiencing, but I had never encountered seas as severe and dangerous. Previously I had always been in very deep water which made the seas long, unlike these very steep short waves that were being caused by the shallow waters of the North Sea.

The storm was at its peak around 1030, which was when we suffered our second knock-down. This happened in the same way as the first one, but was far more severe. We were covered by a solid wall of water that seemed to pin us down below the horizontal with a suddenness that was quite alarming. When we came upright we noticed the liferaft, complete with its stainless steel cradle which had been attached to the deck, had been washed over the side. The liferaft, having by now inflated itself, was being towed astern by the painter. Our sprayhood had been turned inside out and the lifebuoy washed over the side. The water in the cockpit had seeped through the sides of the washboards, soaking the VHF radio and rendering it inoperable. Then the liferaft broke adrift and I started to feel very vulnerable, as without a liferaft or VHF radio, I realized that we were very much alone.

The storm started to abate around midday when the average wind speed dropped to approximately 40 knots; but there was still a very fierce sea running. In comparison to the average wind speed of 70 knots that we had sustained over a period of about half an hour, with gusts up to 95 knots (as recorded on the Brookes & Gatehouse equipment), it was rel-atively quiet. The sea had died down enough by 1530 for us to set some sail and confidently turn the boat beam-on to the seas. We headed in a westerly direction for Lowestoft, from whence we had come. We were approximately 25 miles east of the port, and arrived at 1900 where three very tired and relieved yachtsmen were glad to get ashore.

As a professional delivery skipper, sailing approximately 15 000 miles a year offshore, it is easy to become complacent. I felt that I had a lot of experience interpreting the UK shipping forecasts, with the time delays that one normally gets prior to a severe gale.

In this case I was wrong about the weather, and perhaps could have got some shelter in Harwich. In retrospect, this may not have been a good idea, as there was much damage to yachts in this part of England. Certainly I feel that when we turned and ran, this was the only and correct decision to make.

An experience such as we had brings home the fact that we are all human and that one must always have utmost respect for the sea. There was no doubt in my mind that if I had been in a less seaworthy boat we could have been in serious trouble.

COMMENT

Peter Braley modestly describes the meteorology of the Great Channel storm of October 1987 as seen from the old naval base at Portland. As a result of his recommendation to the Portland Admiral (which put his professional reputation at risk, as his view was not supported in other meteorological quarters, cf Michael Fish), the Portland naval fleet was ordered to sea. This must have been an unpopular action just before the weekend, but evidently the Admiral did not ignore the bringer of bad news. No doubt he found Peter Braley's case logical, and consequently made a tough, but – as it turned out – correct decision. In this case a potential disaster was averted.

Muddle Thru's brave story provides much interest. First, one has to say that mid-October is getting rather late in the sailing season to embark upon Atlantic crossings via the Bay of Biscay. Having elected to go, one would urge caution to those planning to leave in strong head winds. One should try to look beyond the pressure of tight schedules when making a decision to sail in unsettled weather.

In the worst part of the storm, *Muddle Thru* was left to lie a'hull with the windage of her sprayhood pushing her bow into the wind. We can be sure that the wind speed was over 100 knots, and yet she survived. Only later was she rolled through 360° while lying a'hull in the next gale. Apparently the sprayhood was not enough to keep her bow to wind. Of course it is not the high wind speed, as such, that is dangerous to yachts that lie a'hull, it is the breaking waves that develop as a result. Sooner or later, it seems, a yacht lying a'hull in breaking seas will be inverted.

The wisdom of keeping cockpit locker lids firmly closed is apparent from this account. Should one open when a yacht is badly knocked down, she will fill and sink rapidly.

The matter of the lost winch handles bears comment. Both cockpit winch handles were lost when *Muddle Thru* capsized, and in case of this eventuality spares should always be kept below (see Chapter 17).

With *Muddle Thru*'s mast damaged by the roll, it was necessary to use the engine, and it was noteworthy that by increasing power, and therefore the water flow over the rudder blade, broaching was avoided.

The Swan 46 story shows that 360° rolls are not confined to yachts of under 40ft (12m). The Swan is described as having been hove-to, but it is not known what sails she had hoisted and at what angle she was lying to the wind. It seems possible that she was caught beam-on, or nearly so, just as a wave broke. The situation was aggravated by a severe injury to the skipper and the fact that the floorboards were not secured and everything stored under them 'flew through the boat'. It is a time-honoured practice to stow tins of food under the cabin sole, but owners of ocean-going yachts have to weigh the consequences should their boat be unlucky enough to be rolled. The solution may be to assemble groups of tins that constitute a meal, tape them together and mark them, make a stowage plan so that each meal's whereabouts is known, and screw down the floorboards or use special fastenings, so that the floorboards will stay in place in an inversion, yet can easily be removed.

The rescue by the Japanese container ship sounds most alarming, and underlines the difficulty that ships experience when trying to rescue yacht crews (see Chapter 22).

The catamaran rescue is more revealing of human qualities than anything. The skipper was clearly a determined man and may have been right in considering his multihull to be in little danger. However, when the wind increased to hurricane strength he must have had some special reason for not choosing to go to a safe refuge, especially when Weymouth was at hand. Heavy weather is something a crew should work up to by going out in successively stronger winds and bigger waves. Whatever was going on in this case, it does not look as if the crew was familiar enough with rough conditions to warrant an overnight passage in October in fierce storm conditions.

The story of the bold participants of the coastal skipper's course in their Contessa 32 reinforces the reputation that this design has for good sea-keeping qualities. To have navigated the dangerous Needles Passage at night in such conditions calls for a good deal of luck and skill. Generally it seems that the crew was keen, strong and cheerful. With such a crew, a good skipper can work miracles. Some would say that Ray Williams did just that, though perhaps the seas had not had time to build up to be really dangerous, when the Needles Passage could have become impassable.

Jeff Taylor's courageous account of his delivery trip with a new Hallberg Rassy 42 is an example of how quickly conditions can change. It must have been difficult to imagine in a light south-easterly that the wind would be blowing like fury in a few hours. As luck would have it, his chosen port of refuge was to windward, ie the worst case.

At least Jeff Taylor had a sound engine and did not have to make to windward to avoid a lee shore. Without a trysail, storm jib and then VHF, he would have been in worse trouble. He does not say whether he was carrying flares.

Regarding his liferaft, this is yet one more instance of a raft lost overboard from its deck stowage, as frequently seems to happen. It has taken too long for designers to plan for integral storage of liferafts. There may be an occasional eventuality when a deck-stowed liferaft is an advantage, as for example in Chapter 5, but more often than not it may suffer from exposure and not inflate when required or, as happened in this case, be driven overboard by the force of a breaking wave. On balance, it does seem best to stow liferafts in a dry dedicated cockpit storage, or below.

20 *Rolled near home in Morning Sky*

OLIVER ROOME

UK sailors would regard sailing off Dartmouth in early September in a Nicholson 32 a very ordinary thing to be doing. The passage would have remained so if it had not been for one unusual wave.

Morning Sky is a Nicholson 32 built in 1964. She is long-keeled, of moderate to heavy displacement, and traditional design.

At about 2300 on Wednesday 8 September 1993 *Morning Sky*, with a crew of four, on passage from the Isles of Scilly to Yarmouth, Isle of Wight, was about 10 miles east-south-east of Dartmouth sailing on a course of 075° (True), bound for a point 5 miles south of St Alban's Head about 50 miles on. The wind had been blowing fresh to strong from the south-east for some days, and had veered to south force 5 at about 0500 that morning and freshened steadily to about force 8. A synoptic chart for 2300Z shows winds in the west Channel generally force 4 to 6, but force 8 off Dartmouth where the isobars were pinched. The boat was reaching at 5 to 6 knots on the starboard tack under the genoa, rolled in to about the size of a storm jib. The sea was considerable but in no way dangerous; we were

Morning Sky, a Nicholson 32, built in 1964. This venerable design has proved to be a good sea boat and a highly successful cruising yacht. *Photo: Christopher Thornhill*

taking a certain amount of spray down the starboard side and an occasional small dollop into the cockpit. The cabin door was in and the hatch closed, but the top flap of the door, about 5in (13cm) deep, was open.

James and Jo were in the cockpit with their harnesses clipped onto the lifeline running round the deck, James to starboard and Jo to port. James was on the helm. Amy was below in the pilot berth on the port side and I was in the port saloon berth below and inboard of her. Jo heard the hiss of a large sea approaching and shouted to James. They saw a sea astern towering vertically above them which they both subsequently described as 'as high as a two-storey house'. The top was curling and about to break. A moment later it broke over the boat and they were completely engulfed, and James was aware of being pushed out of the cockpit. Jo also was washed over the port forward edge of the cockpit. Moments later the boat was upright again and they were in the cockpit. James had felt his hand on a guard rail and he clung on (getting an electric shock), but neither of them took any action to get themselves aboard again – they simply found themselves back in the cockpit.

The scene on deck was fairly chaotic. The cockpit was full of water, which drained slowly away. The genoa was still there and the boat was hove-to on the port tack. We left her so while we cleared up. There was a tangle of ropes and lines everywhere. The Autohelm leads were wrapped round the backstay, and the instrument was hanging overboard astern. It was recovered and was still winking away, and later found to be in working order. The lifebelts and their holders had gone from the pushpit, but were caught on board by their lines. The danbuoy was towing astern, and the lifebelt light was hanging over the taffrail flashing, which Jo mistook for a thunderstorm on top of everything else. The cover of the outboard, on the after rail, had come off, but its elastic was caught on the engine and it was recovered. The outboard was of course later found to be drowned. The port dodger had split in two, and on both sides the guard rail stanchions were bent over inboard, worse on the port side onto which we had fallen, distorting two of the pushpit stanchions also. The PVC cover of the hood had disintegrated, but the metal frame appeared to be all right. Aloft, the burgee stick had bent through 70° and the masthead light cover and VHF aerial had come adrift and were dangling on their leads. Forward of the hood the deck appeared hardly touched – the deflated dinghy had not shifted although quite loosely lashed down, and the lines remained coiled at the foot of the mast.

Below, Amy, half asleep, heard the hiss of the sea and felt the boat going over and herself being pushed against the deckhead. She shot to the hatch like a rocket thinking we were going to be filled, and she reached the hatch as we came upright again. I shouted to the cockpit, 'Are you both in the cockpit?' and the reply came back, 'Yes', relayed by Amy. I had remained in my bunk during the roll, trying to picture how far we were going over, and which way we would come up. When we first went over the water from the breaking sea poured through the top of the hatch straight into the two leeward bunks – the ones occupied by the watch below. Most of the gear in the open starboard lockers ended up on the port side one level higher; gear from the tool and winch handle lockers were on top of the stove, with the galley floor mat on top of them all; the books in the bookshelf were on the port saloon bunk, except for two books in the pilot berth and two on the table; the washing gear was on the ledge by the port side window, while the heads floorboards had jumped over the heads. A saloon floorboard had also jumped into the saloon port bunk and all the small tins of screws, drills, etc in the tool box had burst open and spread their contents everywhere. I have since measured these various journeys through space, and have concluded that, on the basis purely of gravity (as opposed to projection), we probably went over 120–130°. Not as far as we thought at the time.

Amy checked the leeward windows, which were undamaged, and then tried the galley light and got an electric shock. However, most of the lights worked, including the remaining lights on the mast and deck. Amy quickly cleared the mess below into lockers so that we could look into the bilge – a job of about 10 minutes. By that time Jo had pumped the bilge virtually dry. I doubt whether the water in the bilge ever reached the batteries (below the floorboards), and had we been fully closed down I doubt whether we would have had any measurable quantity of water below.

We spent about an hour clearing up the mess and taking stock of our situation and then resumed our course and sailed on. We reached Yarmouth 15 hours later and the engine started at the first turn.

SUMMARY

We appear to have been rolled to 120–130° by an exceptional sea, caused possibly by a convergence of south-easterly and southerly swells. Subsequent examination revealed no damage to the essential structure of the boat, rigging, engine, engine mounting or sails. Some damage was done to peripheral equipment such as guard rails and masthead fittings, and in general any gear not firmly secured or in enclosed lockers was thrown out and down to leeward. None of this in any way affected the integrity or safety of the boat herself. The heaviest items on board, two 12 volt batteries and three anchors, including a 56lb (25kg) plough in the forepeak, were all firmly secured and did not shift. No great quantity of water came below, and had we been fully closed down we would probably have remained virtually dry below. Nothing was lost overboard, but the two crew members in the cockpit each had a good bruise to show from the incident.

COMMENT

Morning Sky is a widely travelled Nicholson 32, a traditional yacht with good stability. The English Channel off Dartmouth would be considered by her crew as virtually home waters. The sea that knocked the boat down to 120–130° came as a surprise. Some would describe it as a rogue wave, but Sheldon Bacon (Chapter 9) would call it an extreme wave, and would say that such waves are predictable in those circumstances. If an extreme wave happens to break just as it reaches a yacht, she is in danger of being either pitch-poled or rolled through 360°. Clearly, the boat was prepared for the eventuality. The companionway was closed but for 5in (13cm), and all heavy weights were secure. The incident did not turn into a disaster.

Could the knockdown have been avoided? If a wave that is about to break over a yacht is identified early enough in a big ocean sea it is sometimes possible to steer away from it. For example, modern fast lifeboats can accelerate away from waves that are about to break. In the shorter-wavelength seas of the English Channel, by trying to steer away from the wave the helmsman of a 32ft (9.8m) yacht runs the risk of presenting more of the ship's side to the breaking wave, and therefore exacerbating the chances of being rolled through 360°.

On the other hand, by steering to keep the stern 'square on' to the breaking wave a yacht will not be rolled, but there is a chance that she will be pooped, and a much lesser chance that she will be pitch-poled. All other things being equal, the consequences of being pooped are far less than being rolled. If the sea is big enough to cause the yacht to be pitch-poled, and this is only likely in hurricane-strength winds, there is nothing immediate that the helmsman can do except keep the stern square to the wave and hope it won't happen.

Yachts that have an angle of vanishing stability of less than 120–130° could be inverted by a similar wave to the one described. Since *Morning Sky*'s wave was isolated, a fully capsized yacht would most likely remain fully capsized because there would probably not have been any waves about to heel her back to within her range of stability. Eventually, sufficient of her interior would flood to the point when she would self-right. If she was floating before she righted herself then she would be floating afterwards, though perhaps rather low in the water.

CHAPTER

21 A Pacific storm to remember

ERNEST & VAL HAIGH

Pacific means 'peaceful' but there are times when the Pacific Ocean, like anywhere else, can become very rough. Ernest and Val Haigh, an experienced cruising couple, planned to avoid bad weather but had prepared for the possibility. Their account of an unexpected storm provides an interesting comparison between lying a'hull and streaming warps, and the experiences of another yacht, not far distant.

At the end of a long passage, we are often asked: 'Were you in any bad storms?' For years Ernest and I had answered truthfully, and to the disappointment of our hearers, 'No, not really.' We have met our fair share of dirty weather, even though we have always tried to plan our passages to avoid it. This was true of our voyages both aboard *Truce*, our 36ft (11m) Hohmann cutter, and before that (with our daughters aboard) on *Tryste II*, our 40ft (12.2m) trimaran. But we had to sail 130 000 miles before we could finally answer, 'Yes, we have been in a really bad storm.'

Having decided in New Zealand that we wanted to be back in British Columbia for the summer, we planned a voyage with only two stops, Tahiti and Hawaii, and left Whangarei at the beginning of April for the 2500 mile passage to Tahiti. Two days of sunshine, moderate north-west winds, and noon-to-noon runs of 137 and 138 miles, gave us our easiest-ever start to a passage. We wondered if we should have to pay for it.

On the fourth day out a fresh gale had come in from the north-north-east which soon had us shortened down to staysail and deep-reefed main. It was to be a rough unpleasant day with water breaking over the boat and (something we had not expected) finding small leaks around several ports. Ernest had had the forward hatch open a crack over the bunk, as we often did when the weather was quiet since the hatch was

Truce in home waters. *Photo: E & V Haigh*

Figure 21.1 The course of *Truce* during the Pacific storm, April 1993.

under the dinghy, but he had forgotten to close this as the weather worsened, and now all our bedding was seawater soggy. More serious than this was a hard to trace leak of diesel from the starboard tank.

By nightfall the wind was force 7. The log at 2200 read, 'Continuous rain, filthy night.' We considered heaving-to, but as the wind seemed to have peaked around 40 knots we decided to keep going. 'Never seen such rain', Ernest had added to the log entry. Around 0500 next morning the last squall blew through at force 8 and two hours later the wind had gone, leaving a wild, undisciplined sea. The barometer rose for a few hours.

With the wind down, we hastened to take off the soaking wet mainsail and push and pull it below to mend a triangular tear in one of the lower panels. Once we had bent it back on, we celebrated with a large bacon and egg breakfast.

By afternoon, the barometer, now standing at 29.88, was once more falling steadily. The wind rose again from the north-north-east and the combers started re-building. Below, the boat was a mess of wet clothes, towels and bedding. Ernest had mopped out the bilge four times and patched the diesel tank, but still it continued to ooze.

At midnight the wind was back up at force 7–8 while the barometer had sunk to 29.66 and was beginning to nose-dive.

We had rolled up the furling jib and were hove-to under the deep-reefed main. Continuous steady rain became torrential as raucous squalls thundered through, their noise making it hard to think, while a violently uncomfortable sea made us lurch about below like drunkards. It was even darker and more miserable than the night before. The idea of keeping watch for shipping in such conditions was ludicrous. Feeling that we had done all we could for the boat's safety we both tried to get some sleep.

Next morning, conditions were even worse. The wind had increased and veered into the east and the barometer was now down to 29.02. We handed the main and lay a'hull. To prepare for whatever was coming we lashed an extra line around the mainsail from end to end, furled the jib as tightly as we could, and hardened in its sheets on the cockpit winches. Then we went below to consider what was vulnerable there.

We had given some thought to these dangers before we left home on this, *Truce's* second voyage to New Zealand, and the ship's batteries were well restrained with wooden bars, while the lids over the diesel tanks, under the aft saloon seats, were screwed down. Now we also fastened down the lids of the lockers at the forward ends of the seats, under which the dry stores like flour and pasta were kept, and tied up the removable slats behind the backs of the seats that kept the canned goods corralled.

Around breakfast time the barometer bottomed out at 28.98in (982mb). In the last seven hours it had plummeted from 29.63. We waited for catastrophe to arrive, but instead the wind moderated a little and veered more into the south-east. We brought *Truce* around on the other tack with the motor, and optimistically set the storm jib.

Although the glass had now started rising (29.14) we felt sure that the gales we had experienced so far were not enough to explain the barometer's horrendous drop. We waited.

Less than an hour later Ernest, who was standing near the chart table looking out of the big port, said, 'Come and look at the rain, Val!' The horizon had disappeared and a white wall was approaching, a wall of rain and spray and hurricane force wind. *Truce* went over on her beam-ends. Ernest knew that the storm jib would have to come down immediately and he knew who was going to have to do it. With trembling fingers he fastened his oilskins, wrenched open the hatch and, without waiting to put on a safety harness, scrambled out on deck.

When he had crawled out to the bow he found the boat laid right over so that he was standing almost upright, lying on the deck, his bare feet braced against the port bulwarks, as he struggled to free the halyard from the flogging sail; he expected to go overboard. Somehow he managed to attach the snapshackle to the deck fitting. Leaving the sail flattened by the wind, he crawled back into the cockpit and jumped below out of the rain and the terrifying noise.

Some time during the next hour *Truce* turned around so that when our first-ever knockdown came, it was to starboard. Our preparations had been good, but not foolproof. I had forgotten the plastic egg box in a side locker beside the quarter berth. This now flew over to the foot of the chart table together with the bunk's pillow and the contents of the icebox (pots of butter, cheese and meat). Luckily, only a single egg escaped to spread itself over the pillow. The only potentially lethal thing that we had missed was the heavy 5in (13cm) deep lid of the icebox which leapt across to join the mess on the cabin sole, landing between Ernest and me and yet not hitting either of us.

Out on deck the self-steering gear was blowing apart. The fabric cover ripped and the vane pulled out of its stainless tubing and turned upside down over the stern, attached only by a narrow, twisted bar of stainless steel. The boarding ladder had also come free from its on-passage perch and was hanging overboard, banging against the rudder, while the fat Apelco GPS aerial had been knocked sideways.

The noise of the wind was a solid, continuous tone, a single note that encompassed us, *Truce*, and an ocean gone mad. The seas had built steeply and quickly to create a breathtaking display: the whole blowing white surface in motion; combers rolling over with their crests tearing off; the sea a blue-green maelstrom overlaid with spray. We had gone past 'rough' in the logbook, past 'rougher', and had reached 'extreme'.

When the wind eased to storm force Ernest went back up on the foredeck, with his safety harness on this time, and unhanked the sopping wet storm jib, struggling it along to the cockpit where we wrestled it below and onto the head grating to drip and drain.

A little later, while the wind was still as strong, he went out into the cockpit and this time hauled back aboard the boarding ladder and two pieces of the steering gear and passed them down to me to stow on the quarter berth. It was while he was doing this that luckily he came across both the jib winch handles sloshing around in the cockpit well.

Cresting waves continued to break over us and the galley port was sometimes blue with sea. Ernest began to worry that we were going to be rolled and wanted me to put on a lifejacket. We had two on board, but they were kept hooked up awkwardly in the wildly gyrating forepeak. With difficulty I managed to get them both out.

Our second knockdown came less than four hours later. This time Ernest was sitting on the starboard side and was conscious of a tremendous bang as we went over. I was standing by the companionway, holding on tight, and saw the quarter berth porthole completely underwater as the seas overwhelmed us for a long, slow knockdown.

This one was much more dangerous. Later we would find evidence of how far we had gone, such as the dodger torn on the starboard side where it must have hit the water, the cutlery from three other sections all crammed in the starboard one and, when we reached Tahiti, the anchor chain completely inverted so that it could not run out, since it was feeding from the bottom.

But none of this was obvious at the time. Half the books from the port bookshelf did hurdle their restraining bar and fly across to join Ernest on the starboard settee, and the ice box pots (which I had put in a bag and replaced about five minutes before) leapt out again, but luckily we had not replaced the lid; it was firmly wedged on the quarter berth with the boarding ladder and the wind vane.

Earlier Ernest had been considering towing warps. He blamed himself for this second knockdown, because he had not done so. Now he went out in the cockpit and tied together 600ft (183m) of our heaviest lines and fastened them to the two mooring bitts on *Truce*'s sidedecks to form a large bight astern. The improvement was immediate as *Truce* now kept her stern to the seas and ran off almost dead downwind. No more portholes filled with blue water.

By suppertime the wind was down to gale force west-south-west, but the seas still threatened and we were still trailing warps and running under bare poles. It was too dangerous to cook anything hot in such a wild motion, as *Truce* rolled from side to side and huge breakers thumped us on the port quarter. With the wind down a little Ernest took the helm for an hour or two to try to help keep her stern-on to the waves, but when I asked him if he was ready to eat he left her to it and came below. I went to get him a glass out of the port locker, forgetting for a moment to hold on. The boat gave a bound and I was flung across the saloon, hitting my head with a nasty-sounding crack on the opposite locker door. My head sounded worse than it was, but I also hit my elbow, hard, and that was a bruised and bloodied mess. At least no bones were broken. That night we were so emotionally and physically drained that, in spite of the noise and discomfort, we managed to sleep intermittently, me on the lee settee and Ernest on a mattress on the cabin sole beside me. The gale continued all night without let-up.

At 0600 next morning, we finally decided it was safe enough to boil a kettle. A bottle of paint thinner had spilt in the bosun's locker and leaked into the bilge, so that at first our 'sniffer' there kept sounding the alarm and we could not persuade the propane stove to light. Eventually we ventilated under the sole enough to light the burner and had our best-ever cup of early morning tea. As we updated the logbook Ernest said, 'Today's task is to mend the self-steering gear.' With a large hammer, brute strength and persistence, we did. Replacing it was dangerous in the big seas running (we still had a full gale), with Ernest hanging over the stern and me doing my best to keep *Truce* dead downwind, but by 0900 even the vane itself was repaired and *Truce*, still under bare pole and still trailing warps, was once more steering herself. In all we were 28 hours under bare pole after handing the storm jib, and for 22 of these hours we were towing warps.

We had suffered two knockdowns, experienced hurricane force winds, lost the cups off the anemometer, and watched the self-steering gear and the boarding ladder try to batter the rudder to death; but we were not injured, at least not badly, and the boat was still in one piece. We were well aware that we had been fortunate.

When we reached Tahiti, 19 days out from Whangarei, we learned that a Valiant 40 called *Windsong* had left Whangarei the day before we did and had been caught in the same storm. She had been pitch-poled and lost her rig, and one crew member had been so badly hurt that New Zealand had sent a frigate 800 miles to the rescue. The comment from the New Zealand weather office was: 'A major depression which had its genesis in the tropics had deepened rapidly as it moved quickly south-east. It was not analysed as a tropical cyclone and was therefore not named. It appeared not to have had true tropical cyclone characteristics, but was a major depression and one that could be called a "bomb", ie it exhibited rapid deepening and rapid movement. Winds were estimated to be 40–50 knots close to the centre, but with gusts to 60–65 knots.' '*At least*,' we would say, and *Windsong's* crew might want to put it more strongly.

ERNEST'S NOTES

I hesitate to draw any positive conclusions from this experience since a lot of luck is involved. If you hit the wrong wave at the wrong time in the wrong way it can be bad news.

It was very rough and many waves were breaking.
Photo: E & V Haigh

We certainly did not do anything brilliant when the front came in. We just lay a'hull and waited for it to go away. The sea was far too confused and erratic to have done anything else before the first knockdown. But had we streamed warps sooner as the seas became more uniform with the new wind direction after that, we could probably have avoided the second knockdown.

The main lesson we learnt from this experience is that everything must be contained. Nothing (and on some yachts this will include loose floorboards) must be free to fly and do damage. Looking at the dent in the chart table drawer-face made by the ice-box lid makes me grateful that it was not one of us that took the blow. People too must be contained, and have plenty of solid handholds and use them.

Although both Val and I tried to recollect just what happened when, and to write it down soon after the storm, there remains an element of fuzziness. This disorientation would seem to result from the sort of hurricane force wind that we experienced. When it hit we were heading east so we were laid over to port, and yet when we were knocked down we were thrown over onto our starboard side. When and how we were turned around we have no idea.

We were luckier than *Windsong* in that we were not pitch-poled and we did not lose our rig. But I consider that is what it was – luck. *Windsong* suffered far worse than *Truce* did in this storm, and yet (given the Valiant's 40ft (12.2m) compared to *Truce*'s 36ft (11m)) the two yachts bear a strong resemblance in dimensions, hull form, rig, displacement and ballast ratio. I would hope that our strong rig would withstand being rolled or pitch-poled, but I would prefer not to put it to the test.

Luck notwithstanding, *Truce* proved she was a fine sea boat. How would our old trimaran *Tryste II* have fared? Multihull design has come a long way since we built *Tryste*, and her moderate beam-to-length ratio (20ft 6in to 40ft (6.2m to 12.2m)) would not have served her well in the conditions that we experienced. She would have been lucky to survive the right way up.

COMMENT

Was the wind speed more than that assessed by the New Zealand Met Office? Sources of actual weather information in the middle of the ocean are scarce and, even with satellites and huge computers, actual weather can be very different from that assessed. For example, a depression 'dart board' can be more complex than it appears to be, with areas of more and less wind. It seems probable that *Truce* and *Windsong* encountered the former.

Haigh refers to the 'disorientation' and 'element of fuzziness' that both he and Val experienced during the storm, making it difficult to remember everything that had happened. I believe that the mental and physical stress of extremely bad weather and the uncertainty as to what may happen next makes this condition predictable. It may be necessary to make an effort to remain calm, and to logically assess priorities.

Ernest Haigh stresses the importance of securing all movable objects at sea, and the importance of this action is borne out time after time. Their major rogue object was the icebox lid; and not for the first time in this book. Ice box and freezer lids are often square, heavy and deep with insulation, and with nothing to hold them down except gravity. Not only do such lids make dangerous projectiles, but so also do the contents of the locker. Earlier we have seen the effects of frozen chickens on the loose. Owners commissioning new yachts should specify that the lid should be hinged and latched. Existing owners should employ sliding bolts if a hinge and latch is not practical.

It appears that *Truce* was indeed a good sea boat and looked after her crew well, but her knockdowns were worrying. Left to lie a'hull as she was, *Truce* could easily have been rolled through 360° had one of those breaking waves just caught her at the critical moment. It seems that the yacht was much more comfortable with the 600ft (183m) of lines in a bight over the stern, and it was a nice reflection on *Truce*'s design that this length of warp alone was sufficient to keep the stern into the seas and no helmsman was necessary. But keeping the stern into the seas, it seems, did not stop *Windsong* being pitch-poled. It could have been safer for both yachts to heave-to, as Ernest Haigh had at one time considered, or to adopt another bows-into-the-seas tactic.

Val Haigh struck her head and was lucky not to have suffered worse injury. Given proper lee cloths, the safest place to be down below is in one's bunk. It was interesting, but not surprising, that the Haighs covered 130 000 miles before they encountered a bad storm. Some have managed to cruise all their lives and have never done so. On the other hand, the consequences of not being prepared for a storm are too severe to be left to chance.

22 The Queen's Birthday storm of 1994

PETER BRUCE

Every year between November and April some 500 cruising boats avoid the south-west Pacific cyclone season by sailing to New Zealand for the summer. As it is customary to return to the tropical Pacific islands from New Zealand after the cyclone season, and before the New Zealand winter, the Island Cruising Association organizes a cruise in company starting around the end of May, an event called the Auckland–Tonga Regatta. It was widely believed that the date finally selected in 1994 coincided with a perfect weather window. About 80 yachts were heading happily north-east at this time, either as part of the regatta, or on independent passages with a similar strategy in mind.

After the bulk of the fleet had left, a number of late starters were caught in the path of an unexpected storm of extraordinary ferocity and duration. Large breaking seas overwhelmed many of these yachts. One yacht was lost with her crew of three, two people aboard other yachts received severe injuries, and seven yachts were abandoned. Another yacht suffered a fire when electrical circuits shorted after a knockdown.

This storm is often called the Queen's Birthday storm, as it started during the annual New Zealand holiday to mark this event. Alternatively it is also called the June 'Bomb' in recognition of the meteorological term used to describe the explosive manner in which some depressions can develop. It has some parallels with another fierce storm that had occurred at the same time of year in 1983, when some yachts were returning to Auckland after a race to Suva. On that occasion eight lives were lost. The situation was also similar in some respects to the 1979 Fastnet Race in that a group of yachts was caught out in unforecast hurricane force winds, although the 1994 Pacific storm lasted rather longer and most of the yachts were larger. A notable difference was, of course, that in the Fastnet the fleet was composed of racing yachts with racing crews, whereas in the Pacific storm the fleet was mainly cruising yachts with cruising crews and, in some cases, children.

The rescues have been well recorded and make dramatic reading. Much can be learnt from Kim Taylor's *1994 Pacific Storm Survey*; from Tony Farrington's *Rogue Storm*; from Commander Larry Robbins' report as seen from the bridge of the principal rescue ship, HMNZS *Monowai*; from a television documentary; and from the New Zealand Maritime Safety Authority's report. An especially valuable feature of Kim Taylor's *Pacific Storm Survey* was his inclusion of the yachts that were in the direct path of the storm, but which did not seek outside assistance. Media attention leans heavily towards casualties, yet we can probably learn more from those who did not need help.

The fact that a number of different craft were caught out in the same storm has allowed comparisons to be made that might not otherwise be so reliable, and this chapter endeavours to recount the strengths and weaknesses exposed by the storm and any lessons that can be gleaned. The emphasis in *Heavy Weather Sailing* is on prevention rather than cure, and little attempt will be made to comment upon rescue or matters of legislation that arose as a result of the storm. The aim is to identify those actions that will give justifiable confidence to a crew, rather than have them look to making a Mayday call on the SSB radio or the activation of the EPIRB, notwithstanding that these appliances are well worth their place aboard as a last resort.

The yachts, in the order mentioned in the text, are as follows:

Silver Shadow	42ft (12.8m) Craddock-designed sloop, 4 crew
Pilot	32ft (9.8m) Colin Archer cutter, 2 crew
Arosa	32ft (9.8m) Lotus sloop, 4 crew
Sabre	34ft (10.4m) Ganley steel cutter, 2 crew
Destiny	45ft (13.7m) Norseman 447, 2 crew
Ramtha	38ft (11.6m) Simpson catamaran sloop, 2 crew
St Leger	41ft (12.5m) GRP cutter, 2 crew
Sophia	32ft (9.8m) Thistle cutter, 2 crew
Quartermaster	40ft (12.2m) Paul Whiting sloop, 3 crew
Mary T	40ft (12.2m) Cheoy Lee yawl, 4 crew
Waikiwi II	40ft (12.2m) Les Rolfe sloop, 4 crew
Heartlight	40ft (12.2m) Catalac catamaran sloop, 4 crew
Sula II	45ft (13.7m) Clark-designed cutter, 5 crew
Por Vida	43ft (13.1m) Westsail ketch, 2 crew
Hippo's Camp	43ft (13.1m) Morgan cutter, 2 crew, 2 children
Kiwi Dream	35ft (10.7m) Ganley sloop, 2 crew
Swanhaven	48ft (14.6m) Roberts ketch

PREPARATION

This storm showed that there is no substitute for knowing how one's boat will react in really bad weather when using a variety of tactics. For example, one owner said that 'he lacked familiarity with how to heave the boat to. That's the one area where I don't know whether I did her justice.' If an owner knows that his boat will lie comfortably hove-to, he will save a lot of energy by having found this out beforehand. Alternatively, if an owner knows that his boat always takes on volumes of water from somewhere or other in rough weather, then although there would be no reduction in pumping, there will be significant reduction in *stress*. However, a survival storm is not the time to experiment with heavy weather tactics. It is too dangerous, exhausting and stressful.

When *Silver Shadow* had the misfortune to be knocked down and then rolled, her crew was able to note that few items had broken loose. They attributed this to the double latches that they had fitted to lockers and the care with which everything had been stowed before leaving harbour. The instrument sensor plug that was blown out of its tube into the inside of the boat illustrated the force in the wave that caused their first knockdown. When she came to be rolled through 360°, her floorboards and floor locker tops came out, but that was a lot less than might have happened. When the rescue aircraft asked how serious their predicament was on a scale of 1 to 5, the answer was 2. Overall, one gets the impression of a well-prepared boat, and a competent, courageous and resourceful crew.

It has to be said that not all the yachts that suffered heavy knockdowns or rolls gave the impression of being as well secured for sea as *Silver Shadow*. In particular, the frozen contents of freezers were a common hazard. Being struck by 'aerobatic frozen chickens' rather than the 'aerobatic batteries' encountered in the 1979 Fastnet might be regarded as an improvement, but this too may probably be avoided by spending 20 minutes putting a

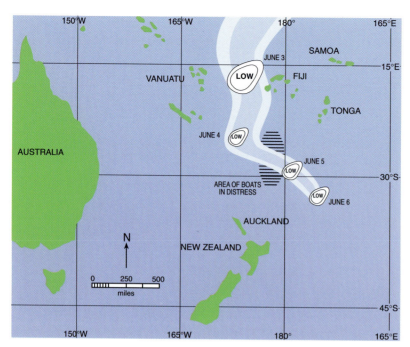

Figure 22.1 The path of the Queen's Birthday storm cut across the route of yachts taking part in the Auckland–Tonga Regatta, and forecasts were not entirely helpful as to both the strength of wind and the direction the storm was to take. The predicted 40–50 knots became 75 knots in the event, and instead of taking the anticipated south-easterly course, the storm first veered to the south.

sliding bolt, or whatever, on the freezer door. There was a 24 volt battery in one yacht that came loose, releasing battery acid and breaking a portlight. The same boat, which had been prepared for a five-year cruise, also had to contend with the spillage of diesel fuel and a two-year supply of flour. One yacht suffered from flying pot plants. When one's boat is one's home, it is understandable that such items come on board, but it might be suggested that such items as pot plants must have a proper sea stowage made for them if they are to come to sea – for example, a bracket within a locker with a restraining arrangement to prevent the plant escaping from the pot even if the boat is inverted. The same applies to another yacht's vagrant sewing machine.

Chaos resulting from a 360° roll is dramatically reduced if a yacht has been systematically prepared for this eventuality before departure. At one time the Royal Navy and other navies made a religion of 'securing for sea', the practice of fastening or enclosing every object that could possibly break loose in a heavy sea before leaving harbour. They probably still do. However, those who have been brought up properly in this respect may agree that teaching a crew, especially those who operate the galley, to secure for sea is difficult without the heavy hand of naval discipline. Nor does the average human seem to learn quickly by experience, especially the slightly reluctant sailor.

Few yachts are built with 360° rolls in mind. It must be appreciated that standard production craft are seldom, if ever, 'ocean-passage' seaworthy when new. For example, positive locking arrangements are required for horizontal locker doors, chart table lids and floorboards; in short, anything kept in place by the force of gravity. It behoves owners contemplating ocean voyages to spend considerable resources in preparing a vessel properly in order to warrant the expression 'roll-over ready'. As it is time-consuming to make proper brackets for pot plants, sewing machines and all other potentially hazardous items of equipment, one should take advantage of any suitable purpose-made brackets.

Seasickness was a problem for some, though with all the high drama not much about it was reported. One yacht's crew tried seasickness pills in the Queen's Birthday storm for the first time in the storm. The pills apparently caused an adverse reaction worse than the illness, suggesting that the best time to try out new remedies is ashore.

CREW EXPERIENCE

There has been no suggestion that difficulties arose because crews lacked seagoing experience. Very severe storms are, thankfully, rare in the sailing seasons, which raises the question as to whether the crews who requested help were experienced enough to cope in such conditions – a different matter to sailing even 50 000 miles in normal weather. One skipper who lost his yacht said, 'We certainly had enough experience on board for normal sailing, but we didn't have experienced people for those extreme storm conditions; if we'd had three people who could steer in 46ft (14m) seas, maybe it would be a different story now.' There is little information on this question, and anyhow a survey on this matter would be hard to quantify. However, it could be argued that those who have great skills in avoiding bad weather may sometimes be the least prepared for it if caught out.

Some crews comprised simply a couple, and others had six or seven on board. There were examples of tremendous feats of endurance, as in the 1979 Fastnet, when boats had only one helmsperson confident and strong enough for the conditions. In this particular storm it would have needed super-human endurance to carry on steering for two or three days. The skipper of *Pilot* said, 'If we'd had just one other strong healthy crew member, I don't think that we would have abandoned.' One of the yachts that came through the storm unscathed, but not without difficulty, the 35ft (10.7m) Lotus sloop *Arosa*, was steered by hand for the duration. *Arosa* was one of the smaller and lighter yachts in the storm, so she could be expected to be lively. Such yachts do not tend to heave-to comfortably, and clearly the owners felt that four capable crew were essential for them to cope with drogues and, no doubt, steering in heavy weather. Aboard one boat the crew had never hand steered at sea, and had to learn when their autopilot gave up. Thus, bearing in mind that autopilots and self-steering gear often become unequal to the task sooner or later, one may conclude that one should have a crew strong enough to continue to hand steer a boat competently in all weather conditions, unless one has been able to prove that the vessel can be left in some way so that she will look after herself.

Ideally one should have a second-in-command on board who is ready, willing and competent enough to take over should the skipper be incapacitated, as happened to *Destiny*. When the crew consists of only a man and his wife they should exchange roles from time to time so both are familiar with all aspects of handling the boat. Practising for 'man overboard' is more important than for 'woman overboard' as, generally speaking, a man is the more likely to fall over the side and a woman is less practised in recovery.

CREW ENDURANCE

Fatigue is one of the biggest enemies of the small-boat sailor. Thus one of the fundamentals of coping with storms is the conservation of energy. There is little doubt that some of the yachts were abandoned simply because their crews were over-stressed and utterly exhausted. After the first 24 hours of storm conditions, few of these crews, understandably, were able to do much to help themselves. Yet the 34ft (10.4m) Ganley steel cutter *Sabre*, with a crew of only two on board, encountered as severe weather as any, and passed through the eye of the storm without any serious problems, hove-to under deep-reefed main. Comments made by the crew after the storm, drawn from Kim Taylor's report, are illuminating: 'The confidence of previous heavy weather experience tended to reduce stress. Practise well beforehand to identify any weakness. We lay on the floor and attempted to rest. Consumption of liquids and high-energy foods is important. Our small opening ports are modified to take an outside storm window. Our boat is prepared with very rough weather conditions in mind and, lying hove-to, has proved herself on many occasions.' One has the impression of sailors who were mentally and physically prepared for whatever the sea could do. They did not need to experiment to try to find the most comfortable way to ride the storm and, owing to confidence in their preparations and their robust craft, they could conserve their energy and cope for as long as was necessary.

Less confident and less heavy-weather conditioned crews may have used up energy dealing with matters that should have been dealt with before going to sea. It is important to make a careful selection of priorities. Certain irritating things should have been dealt with at another time. They were not and everyone has to force their minds to ignore them. It can be more important to avoid the risk of injury and husband one's strength for life-threatening situations that usually have to be dealt with straightaway. Not only does the workload sometimes have to be kept to essentials for survival, it also may have to be spread evenly, rather than have one over-motivated person do it all.

Even when all the crew is in their bunks, for example, a crew should stay in watches if possible, so they take it in turns to worry about what might be going on up top. In dire straits, notwithstanding collision risks, a skipper should be prepared to order his crew to stay in their bunks with as much force as he may use on other occasions to have them leave their bunks.

DESIGN ISSUES

A fundamental of coping with heavy weather might be thought to be the size and design of the craft. In this respect, all the hulls stood up pretty well. One catamaran suffered a cracked hull and there were broken windows of all sizes; otherwise, there were very few structural problems. In terms of length, beam, stability and displacement there did not seem to be any particular reason why some boats were rolled and others not. Factors such as a vessel's aspect to the breaking waves and luck seemed to be more relevant. Yachts that were lying a'hull were prone to join the '360° Club' as one might expect, but not in the case of the Robert Perry-designed 45ft (13.7m) Norseman 447 cutter *Destiny*. She seemed to have been overtaken by an extreme wave that pitch-poled her, and it is hard to see what her crew could have done to avoid their predicament. Likewise *Pilot*, a 32ft (9.8m) Colin Archer cutter, was running under control with bare pole when she was pooped by a wave that carried away her heavy-section mast. One can only pity the plight of the crews of the dismasted yachts. Without the windage of mast and rigging it was found that the boats simply did not lie-to drag devices, rigged either from the bow or stern, and thus they adopted disastrous beam-on-to-the-seas attitudes. Only aboard *Pilot* was the broken mast cleared away and then the boat steered by hand down the seas. Again, without a mast this could be done only with difficulty, but she experienced no knockdowns, and running before the seas seemed infinitely preferable to lying a'hull. One must not forget, though, that yachts seldom seem to sink if left to their own devices. Of the eight or nine yachts abandoned, four (*Destiny, Ramtha, Silver Shadow* and *Sophia*) were found later either afloat or aground somewhere.

Only one vessel appears to have sunk as a direct result of the storm, and her family crew was tragically lost too. This was *Quartermaster*, a 40ft (12.2m) Paul Whiting sloop, advertised as being designed for serious cruising, but of lighter displacement than most offshore cruising yachts of her size. During the onset of the storm the owner had been in regular contact with the Kerikeri shore radio station, and from just before midnight on 4 June he reported the first of a series of bad knockdowns and the fact that his wife had been injured. Two hours and 18 minutes later the third 'hard knockdown' was reported. The boat and her crew appeared to be in serious trouble, though no flooding was mentioned. This was the last call that was heard. *Quartermaster*'s EPIRB was activated another two hours and 36 minutes after that, and at 1745 on 6 June, a day and a half later, *Quartermaster*'s transmitting EPIRB was found lashed to her eight-man liferaft. Examination showed that the liferaft canister had been smashed, probably by the mast, and some or all of the crew had been aboard the liferaft until a wave had, presumably, washed the occupants out. One can only speculate what might have happened after the owner's last radio message. *Quartermaster* could, for example, just possibly have been sunk by a whale-strike, or collision with a semi-submerged container; however, the most likely explanation is that she was sunk by breaking waves.

Apart from this awful and harrowing misfortune, no other yacht was abandoned because she was actually sinking. One of the yachts, thought by her crew to be in immediate danger of foundering due to the battering of the hull by a section of her broken mast, was spotted afloat some months later and then found after yet more months high and dry on a distant reef. In all cases, with the possible exception of *Quartermaster*, the boats' hulls appeared to withstand the conditions better than the crew.

Standing rigging did not break, but mast tubes did not usually withstand a full 360° roll, as they also had not in the 1979 Fastnet. There is a case for looking again at the derided 'tree trunks' of the past, bearing in mind that mast failure is catastrophic for a sailing boat. Apart from the additional strength, a heavier mast section will bring about an increase in inertia that will reduce the chances of being rolled in the first place.

Steering arrangements were another weak point, as they were in the 1979 Fastnet. *Ramtha*, a 38ft (11.6m) sloop-rigged catamaran designed by Roger Simpson, had a steering failure before the storm and again during the storm. Her crew was not new to stormy weather but, apart from severe discomfort, they were having control problems, as well as near-capsizes. With the survey ship HMNZS *Monowai* close by, they had talked about being taken off, but when their steering failed again at the height of the storm the decision was made to abandon ship. *Mary T*, a 40ft (12.2m) Cheoy Lee offshore yawl, also reported steering problems at one time, and the 42ft (12.8m) Craddock-designed sloop *Silver Shadow* was found to have an uncontrollable rudder when the crew tried to motor her. In the 1979 Fastnet the numbers of steering failures were increased by the fact that many rudders from a particular designer had been changed to an inadequate carbon-fibre construction. Others failed by simply not being strong enough. One has the feeling that owing to the additional complication of having two rudders to operate from one wheel, catamarans' steering systems need to be particularly well engineered. This seems obvious, but one does not know the extent to which, in order to keep prices competitive, someone has thought in terms of the average yacht that, arguably, will never encounter a survival storm. It may not be relevant to say so here, but there are brilliant naval architects who are not such good engineers. Design and construction of the steering gear of ocean-going yachts should allow generous safety margins.

A notable similarity with the Fastnet was leakage from cockpit locker hatches after the cockpit had been filled. At one point *Mary T*'s crew found that water was coming in faster than it could be pumped out. It was some time before it was realized that the leak was from the cockpit locker lids. Builders seldom fit watertight seals to cockpit locker lids; indeed, sometimes glassfibre mouldings are constructed so that making a watertight seal can be very difficult. Nonetheless, as cockpits can be filled frequently in heavy weather and remain filled owing to small-diameter drains, it is important that locker lids can be positively clipped in the closed position and adapted, as necessary, to make a watertight seal when closed. Undersized cockpit drains were a problem for *Destiny* as well as for *Mary T*. Pumps also gave problems in at least two yachts. *Mary T* had three pumps operable from on deck, but her crew regretted that they did not have a manual pump that could be worked from down below.

Cabin windows are often a risk to watertight integrity and, through breakage or deformation, became matters of concern in this particular storm. The leeward windows of the 44ft (13.4m) Les Rolfe-designed sloop *Waikiwi II* did not have storm boards and were broken. Big windows, such as those of many catamarans, caused big worries. An anonymous catamaran owner cited his big windows as the principal danger during the storm. To

Ramtha and her crew before the rescue. Wind speed at this time was 55 knots average, gusting to 70 or more according to HMNZS *Monowai*s instruments. Significant wave height was 33ft (10m).
Photo: Lindsay Turvey (RNZN)

make a series of large windows requires much of the sides of the coachroof to be cut out. This action can normally be expected to reduce the strength of the coachroof and hence its ability to withstand a plunging wave. It may be relevant to note that *Quartermaster*, built as a dedicated cruising yacht, had four comparatively large windows on each side of the coachroof, and her skipper had registered concern about them before contact was lost, though there is no evidence that they caused the loss of the yacht. *Ramtha*, a 38ft (11.6m) sloop-rigged catamaran designed by Roger Simpson, sensibly had storm covers for her large windows. So did *Heartlight*, a 41ft (12.5m) Catalac sloop-rigged catamaran designed by Tom Lack, but one of them was ripped off by a wave. Moreover, the smaller portlight windows let in water when they flexed.

It is significant that none of the three catamarans in the storm area capsized, even though two of them lay a'hull for periods. However, two of the catamaran crews abandoned their vessels. Their accounts did not lend much confidence to the seaworthiness of catamarans, as opposed to monohulls, in the extreme conditions they experienced. One catamaran crew was at one moment standing on the side windows. Capsize, with its dire consequences for non-self-righting craft, came very close to both *Ramtha* and *Heartlight*.

A serious problem, and not a new one, was injuries sustained when crew were flung out of their bunks. Coming out of one's bunk in this Pacific storm, either intentionally or unintentionally, increased the risk of bodily injury acutely. For example, Peter O'Neil, owner of *Silver Shadow*, was brewing up at the galley when his shoulder was broken. In *Mary T*, sailbags were brought into the saloon and successfully used as buffers. Thus for one not importantly occupied, a bunk is a very sensible place to be and good lee cloths become of tremendous consequence.

Of all the interior appurtenances ever supplied to a yacht, few need as much careful thought as the lee cloths. *Destiny's* lee cloths failed before she was pitch-poled, and one therefore assumes they were not strong enough. If the maximum possible forces at work in a storm are taken into account it will probably be found that few standard lee cloths are strong enough for the job. When told that people fell out of their bunks, one is curious to know how strong and deep the lee cloths were – probably not strong enough or deep enough. It is possible to design a lee cloth that is held down at the outboard side of the bunk, which is next to impossible to come out of unintentionally. In so doing it may be necessary to provide additional handholds around the bunk, a quick release system for the upper body end, and greater material strength than the norm. The skipper of *Sula II* suggested that strongpoints should be fitted down below and safety harnesses worn in bunks.

Australians Bill and Robyn Forbes, both aged 53, being hauled aboard HMNZS *Monowai* from their 38ft (11.6m) catamaran *Ramtha*. Photo: CPO AHS Lindsay Turvey (RNZN)

TACTICS

Regarding tactics and drag devices, as in the 1979 Fastnet, there was no obvious procedure that could be guaranteed to work for everyone. Two yachts were rolled when lying a'hull, and most – it would seem wisely – did their best to avoid this situation.

It is noteworthy that more boats found comfort and safety heading into the seas than the more popular tactic of running before them. Heaving-to under sail or engine was success-ful for all the yachts that tried it. A fourth reefing slab in the mainsail and an inner forestay was often an advantage when hove-to. *Sabre*, as we have already seen, remained hove-to under deep-reefed mainsail for the duration of the storm without any significant problems. *Por Vida*, a 43ft (13.1m) Westsail ketch, went through the worst of the storm by motoring straight into the wind and sea at two-thirds throttle. She lost her storm jib and anchor from the pulpit, which carried away the hawse pipe leaving a hole to be plugged. Otherwise she had no problems. The 43ft (13.1m) Morgan-designed cutter *Hippo's Camp* spent part of the storm hove-to under storm jib, with her helm lashed to steer to weather. She used her engine in the windless eye of the storm to motor 'around' the waves, but later found the wind blew the boat flat under her storm jib. Then she lay successfully to a plastic drogue, though it is not clear whether this was led over the bow or the stern. *Kiwi Dream*, a 35ft (10.7m) steel Ganley sloop, successfully hove-to under a backed scrap of headsail and deep-reefed main, and *Swanhaven*, a 48ft (14.6m) Roberts ketch, hove-to successfully with-in the area of the strongest wind. Finally, *Sula II*, a 45ft (13.7m) Clark-designed cutter of 12 tons, was sailed close-hauled under trysail and her speed maintained at 3 or 4 knots by feathering into the wind. The effect of feathering got the speed down to a comfortable level and brought the bow closer into the wind than would have been achieved by heaving-to. She experienced no rolls or knockdowns, but might be considered outside the strongest wind area. Kim Taylor points out, interestingly, that all these vessels were in the moderate or heavy displacement category.

It was disappointing to an analyst that the two yachts carrying parachute anchors did not deploy them, but their reasons were understandable. By the time they had come to realize that it was parachute anchor time, conditions had become very risky for working on deck.

In the moderate conditions just prior to the storm, *Ramtha*, the catamaran, had spent a night lying to a sea anchor on a 300ft (91m) warp from her bows, but in the morning the sea anchor was found hanging vertically rather than holding her into the wind and sea. For some reason the sea anchor could not be tripped and, as there was only a twosome on board, winching it in proved very heavy work. Consequently, it was cut loose and abandoned. The catamaran *Heartlight* did have an 18ft (5.5m) Paratech parachute on board, but the skipper felt that a drogue was more suitable in the extreme conditions prevailing due to varying angles of the seas. Only when the drogue line fouled his propellers was the parachute deployed. Not finding it an advantage, had not the skipper been intent in remaining in one place to be rescued, he said he would have cut it adrift.

After *Silver Shadow* had been dismasted and later rolled, her crew managed, much to their credit, to release their broken mast and, following various experiments, lay from the bow a sea anchor made from a No 4 genoa. Then they rigged a jury mizzen sail which was enough to hold the yacht into the seas some of the time, and which seemed to help to prevent further capsizes.

A variety of drag devices was used over the stern, either warps, warps and chains, or drogues. Six yachts were either rolled or knocked down when trailing drag devices, two of them while being hand steered and four when not. The 41ft (12.5m) cutter *St Leger* was the most successful. Her crew deployed a Galerider on 250ft (76m) polypropylene while under vane steering. Though the boat steered well and the speed was comfortable, the line went slack when the boat was in the troughs and it was found necessary to shorten the line to 80–90ft (24–27m). For the next 60 hours with winds over 60 knots the drogue remained stable and effective. *Destiny* towed a Sea Squid drogue using 200ft (61m) of line and 12ft (3.7m) of $\frac{3}{8}$ in (10mm) chain that proved to be very satisfactory at first. With hand steering dead downwind, the drogue kept *Destiny* at a 'comfortable' speed of 3–8 knots, but as conditions became worse the drogue broke out from the surface on two occasions, allowing the boat speed to become dangerously fast. They felt with hindsight that a longer line was necessary, but one could also imagine that more weight of chain could have helped. As it happened, *Destiny* was pitch-poled in spite of her drogue. *Quartermaster* was probably towing drogues, and was under engine and autopilot when she was last heard of in an attempt 'to get seas to come in over the back quarter' which 'seemed to be working'. *Silver Shadow* was running under storm jib and autohelm when she was struck by a breaking wave, 30° more towards the port beam than the usual seas, and this brought down her mast. At least four yachts were neither rolled nor knocked down when on autohelm or vane steering.

These records, once again, may not indicate anything very strongly, but there seems to be more than a tendency in favour of hand steering. For example, *Pilot's* skipper felt that he would have been able to avoid the 360° roll if he had been hand steering, and *Waikiwi II's* skipper wished he'd had more storm-skilled helmsmen. *St Leger's* skipper felt that the quick reaction of a helmsman was essential to avoid a broach. An experienced sailor at the helm is influenced by what he can see or hear coming at him. He is influenced by speed, acceleration, angle of heel and waveform. On the other hand, the automatic helm has no anticipation and is merely influenced by the angle off course, which may occur too quickly to make any difference at critical times. Thus it could well be that the hand-steered yacht is safest, provided that the helmsman is alert, strong and competent for the task. This was a finding from the 1979 Fastnet.

A useful point made by several skippers was that, when lightly crewed, only one tactic might be feasible. Once a severe storm has developed, one may be stuck with whatever tactic was chosen first. This point underlines the case for experimentation in moderate conditions.

One wonders how much crews are influenced when choosing their tactics by the direction that they happen to be already going in. It is easier to carry on along roughly the course one had originally intended than not. It requires a very definite decision to change course from going into it to running away from it, and a yet more bold and confident decision to turn into the wind and sea having been running away from it. In this storm the quickest route out of it was the same direction as the fleet was heading. Thus those on the western side of the storm track tended to run with the wind astern and those on the eastern side were more inclined to head into it. Another subject to ponder is the use of oil in instances where the drift rate is low, either through lying to a parachute anchor, or when a yacht has been dismasted and is unsteerable.

As noted above, perhaps one of the most significant aspects of the storm was the surprisingly high number of problems encountered by yachts running before the sea compared to those heading into it. On the face of it, the time-honoured technique of 'heaving-to' under sail appeared to have been the safest tactic for moderate- or heavy-displacement yachts. On the other hand, modern, lightly constructed yachts do not always heave-to comfortably under sail, as *Arosa*'s crew decided. Many are too lively, make too much leeway, and do not 'look after themselves' as traditional yachts do, so an alternative has to be found. Running before the seas under hand control and drogue or heaving-to under engine and helmsman may be the solution if a strong crew is carried. Alternatively, one has to consider lying to a parachute anchor.

LIFERAFTS

During rescues, hand-held VHFs were useful on board. One would imagine that a hand-held VHF could be even more useful if forced into a liferaft. Several crews were tempted to inflate their liferaft as a precautionary action. *Waikiwi II* had two on board, and one of these was inflated in case of immediate need. After four hours it was 'blown to bits' and eventually was torn away. *Destiny*'s only liferaft was also inflated and lost when the painter parted. Two other liferafts were ripped from their deck mountings and were later found inflated and, presumably, some considerable distance from where they had been lost.

These events suggest that one should keep the liferaft in its container, stowed until required in a purpose-made deck locker or down below in an easily accessible position, and rely on regular maintenance to ensure it does inflate when really needed. One should note that *Quartermaster* carried an eight-man liferaft and a crew of only three. Liferafts are designed to perform best with their full complement weighing them down, and it could be that the *Quartermaster* crew was lost because of this. Having said that, it is inevitable that an owner will have a liferaft for the maximum normal number of crew he is likely to have on board. Short of hiring a liferaft for the appropriate number each time crew size changes (an unlikely solution), the owner is left in an unfortunate dilemma. Larger craft often have two four-man or two six-man liferafts; this is a tidy, if rather expensive, solution to the problem. Alternatively one supposes, if at all possible, an oversize liferaft should be ballasted with whatever sensible means comes to hand. A point well made by Kim Taylor in his *Storm Survey* is that the crews who asked to be taken off were in more danger during the transfer than at any other time. Moreover, they were putting other lives at risk. Another point worth considering is that, once abandoned, the boat may be considered a hazard and deliberately sunk. So, as in the past, everything points to staying with the boat and keeping her afloat.

USEFUL EQUIPMENT

Useful miscellaneous items of equipment cited were: strobe lights, ski goggles, cyclume sticks, hot water bottles, wetsuits and cyclists' helmets. Commander Larry Robbins, commanding officer of HMNZS *Monowai*, mentioned that *Mary T*'s strobe light was very, very effective. He makes the point that the strobe is much more visible than standard navigation lights and, as it can't be mistaken for prescribed lights, the strobe could become a useful safety aid, as with aircraft. Pilots say that the powerful strobes of commercial aircraft can be seen at distances up to 40 miles, and they have to switch them off on the ground to avoid dazzling everyone. Perhaps when the entire crew is stormbound down below would be a good time to switch on a strobe. Anyone who has tried to look to windward from a small craft in force 10, both with or without goggles, will vouch for their value. Goggles have become standard equipment in the BT Global Challenge, the race around the world the wrong way. As Alby Burgin said after Cyclone Emily (Chapter 15), 'If I'd held my head up the wind and water would have cut my eyes out.' Cyclume sticks provide a source of light when everything electrical has failed. Could this ever happen? Given bad enough conditions and the hostility of salt water to all things electrical, the answer has to be yes.

Even in the relatively warm waters in which the storm originated, hypothermia was a problem. Dampness works its way into the insulating layers, reducing their efficiency, and forced inaction does nothing to keep the body warm. One can become uncomfortably cold even on the equator if one has no protection from heavy rain. *Pilot* had a hot water bottle on board, and this came in handy when Greg Forbes started suffering from hypothermia. *Mary T's* crew found space blankets good for keeping warm in the damp conditions. A wetsuit can often be worth a place on board. For example, Bill and Robyn Forbes wore wetsuits when they were hauled aboard HMNZS *Monowai*. Apart from using a wetsuit for diving for pleasure, it can be used, for example, when clearing a fouled propeller.

A wetsuit's survival capabilities are illustrated by a story of many years ago, when a fishing boat capsized at night in a winter storm some miles off Iceland. No one else realized what had happened until one of the crew, who was wearing a wetsuit top, fetched up alive on the beach. He was the only survivor. Drysuits have now become cheaper, easier to put on, and can be made of breathable fabric. Consequently, they are worthy of consideration but, probably more worthy, are the survival suits that are coming onto the market. Sailing people are not likely to invest in clothing that may only be used once, so survival suits that have a dual purpose are the ones likely to be best value.

As for cyclists' helmets, one can see the virtue of head protection in almost any sport. The 'Boombanger Club' can be even more disastrous than the '360° Club' and a helmet could be a major benefit. However, most people feel self-conscious about wearing helmets aboard a boat, so not everybody will be seen wearing one, but this attitude could change in time.

Silver Shadow from HMNZS *Monowai* as her four crew were taken off. *Photo: PO AHS Lindsay Turvey (RNZN)*

EXTERNAL SUPPORT

Nine yachts, which ranged from 32–45ft (9.8–13.7m), put out Mayday calls. All except one of these was fully equipped with safety equipment, and all had either reasonably experienced or very experienced crews. Most of the crews that were rescued had actuated their EPIRBs. Not only can a 406MHz EPIRB alert shore authorities of a Mayday, it will identify the boat and give its position. Then when rescuers are within a few miles they can home in on the EPIRB's transmissions. This equipment, *from a rescue point of view*, could be called the outstanding device of the event. New Zealanders will remember the story of *Rose Noelle*, a catamaran bound for Tonga in 1979 at exactly the same time of year. She capsized in a storm, eluded the search, and drifted with her crew for five months before going ashore on Great Barrier Island. The event makes a good case for the 406MHz EPIRB, though it has to be said that *Rose Noelle* was carrying an older-type EPIRB, but this was not heard.

Judging by the recordings of the radio conversations, many boats used Kerikeri shore radio – incidentally now closed down – for meteorological advice. As the storm developed some leaned heavily on the radio station for comfort and the general support that was readily given. Indeed, Jon and Maureen Cullen, who used to provide their service as a hobby, managed to stay on the air for the duration of the storm. While SSB is a superb product of the technological age, and the Cullens provide a wonderful service – especially during this storm – ideally one will not want to depend too much upon advice from someone who is not present and therefore cannot be expected to appraise the situation fully. It can be argued that the ability to talk to those ashore, and the existence of an EPIRB on board, could possibly divert attention from the primary task in severe weather and to give a false sense of security. One cannot pass responsibility on to someone else over the radio. Nor, equally, should one give up trying to take control of the situation just because the EPIRB has been activated. On the arrival of a rescuer it must require a lot of courage to announce that help is no longer required. Such decisions need finely balanced judgement, not easily found in an overtired, over-stressed mind. Nevertheless, assuming one does decide to do without help and lives to tell the tale, it should be remembered that one can always show one's gratitude properly and explain the circumstances to the would-be rescuer at a later date. A good seaman will understand entirely and may be glad not to have to attempt a difficult rescue.

Another form of a false sense of security can be given by the presence of other friendly yachts in the vicinity. While there are circumstances where this situation can be of advantage, in a storm of this violence, there is little chance of assistance from other small craft. Crews have to cultivate a sensible level of self-reliance.

FINALE

One might be disappointed, but one should not be surprised to find that, once again, there was no obvious panacea, no one piece of equipment or single tactic identifiable that would have enabled all the yachts to lie quietly for the duration of this storm while their crews slept. If only a bow-led parachute anchor had been deployed we would have learnt a lot more about the capabilities of this device compared to other techniques, but none were used.

So we are left with the conclusion that to survive a rare and tremendous storm like the tropical depression of June 1994 one must have some fundamentals right, such as tactics proven for each individual yacht as a result of experiments with a strong crew on a daysail. One must also put into effect many detailed preparations for prolonged bad weather. Once caught out in a severe storm one must avoid becoming over-tired and over-stressed, and ruthlessly separate 'nice-to-have' actions from those upon which survival is likely to depend. Even then, a measure of luck may be necessary to avoid extreme breaking waves, perhaps coming from an unexpected quarter.

23 North Atlantic weather seen from a family catamaran

RICHARD HERBERT

Though there are those who believe that the open ocean is no place for small children in a short-handed small boat, Richard Herbert set off with his Austrian wife and six week old daughter on a cruise to the Caribbean. In typical Atlantic storms he came to appreciate the power of the sea and the good qualities of his catamaran.

We left England at the end of July 1990 with little experience of sailing catamarans offshore. I was a yachtmaster instructor and a voluntary skipper for Ocean Youth Club, so had plenty of experience of monohulls up to 66ft (20m) but, as was pointed out to me, I had no experience of ocean sailing. My wife, Ingrid, had virtually no experience beyond an RYA shore-based course, and my daughter Kristina, at six weeks old, had no experience of anything at all.

Our catamaran, a Derek Kelsall-designed Kelly 32 built in balsa polyester sandwich construction, was 32ft 8in (10m) long and 18ft 4in (5.6m) wide, high volume with a lot of freeboard, and with very buoyant hulls. I had made storm shutters for all windows in $\frac{1}{2}$in (12mm) ply that could be bolted in position or quickly fitted using strongbacks in an emergency. The door to the cockpit was a sliding patio door constructed in aluminium and $\frac{1}{4}$in (6mm) Perspex, a weak structure for which I had also prepared a shutter in $\frac{1}{2}$in (12mm) ply. Bow and stern cleats were massively attached and oversized to take sea anchors, and for this purpose I was carrying three car tyres wrapped in duct tape which also doubled as additional fenders. Our rig was a standard masthead Bermudan sloop with roller reefing No 2 genoa. We also carried a fluorescent orange trysail and a storm jib that could be set on the inner forestay. We carried all normal emergency equipment.

Our first test came in crossing Biscay in unpleasantly rough conditions when the motion of the catamaran, so different from a monohull, made me anxious and uneasy for the entire passage. While remaining level at all times, the lightweight craft, just 4 tons, had a jerky motion that I can only describe as being like an old London underground train taking a sharp bend at speed. Exactly the sort of motion that on a monohull presages disaster, a knockdown or worse. I adopted my usual 'storm' tactic of storm jib to steady the motion and motoring slowly. If nothing else, the sound of the engine, a noisy but reliable Perkins 27hp, masks the noise of the wind and makes me feel better, I have full control of the yacht, and the very small sail is not going to cause any problems.

For the rest of the passage from La Coruña to Lisbon I was continually on edge. I admit it, I had no confidence in *Anna Louise*. She was too light, the windows and patio door to the cockpit were far too weak for a serious yacht, she could capsize at any moment; she just didn't feel 'right'. We were too weakly crewed; I was effectively singlehanding most of the time as my wife cared for our new-born child. We decided to head for the Med.

In Lisbon, however, a perfect weather forecast for a passage to Madeira, supplied by the UK Met Office, stiffened our spirits and we set off for the Atlantic, only to be met by a south-westerly gale. We learned a lot in this gale. A passing Russian weather ship gave the wind strength as force 10 and wave height as 33ft (10m). Our very light-weight and extremely buoyant hulls meant that we were very much a surface craft. Although we were bouncing around a lot, waves were not breaking over us, the 'weak' windows were staying pretty dry, and the 'patio' door was not even taking spray. Because we had virtually no grip in the water, two long, low-aspect keels and a draft of just 1ft 7in (0.5m), we rode with the waves instead of standing up to them.

We were pretty manoeuvrable under engine and could make progress in virtually any direction. Although we could surf downwind at up to 14 knots and tack upwind under power, plugging over the waves at a steady pace, we couldn't really make any progress towards Madeira, so we hove-to, storm jib set on the inner forestay

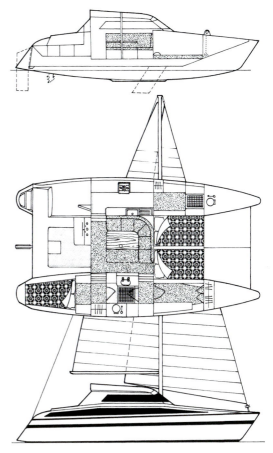

Side views and accommodation plan of *Anna Louise*, the 32ft (10m) Kelly 32 Derek Kelsall-designed catamaran.

and wheel fixed hard to windward. We sat like that for four days, fairly comfortably. Life went on. We were always able to cook hot food and eat with a knife and fork sitting at the table. One night we even drew the curtains, turned the ghetto blaster to full volume, had hot showers, and tried to pretend that we were somewhere else, preferably onshore. Although we were getting knocked around, staying upright at all times meant that every-thing stayed in place and a reasonably normal life was still possible.

We were, naturally, pretty scared the whole time. An Atlantic gale is awesome, and it just went on for such a long time. We became more and more tired, but our confidence in *Anna Louise* grew.

Lying hove-to under storm jib felt relatively good and safe. We lay at an angle of about 30° to the approaching waves and so presented virtually our maximum diagonal length while fore-reaching at 1 to 1.5 knots. When struck by waves, far from feeling that we might be capsized, we found that the wave would raise the windward hull quickly but steadily, pass underneath the bridgedeck, and strike the leeward hull just as the windward hull was passing into the back of the wave, causing us to drop more violently into the back of the wave. In other words, instead of experiencing a motion that felt as though we could 'flip over', it was quite the reverse – and the strongest movements were always into the back of the wave.

Breaking seas were mainly felt as a lack of buoyancy in the water/air mix of foam at the crest. Seas just about to break were the ones that struck hard, but these had the effect of knocking the bows away. We would speed up for a short while before resuming our previous attitude, and this acted as a safety valve. We only rarely took a hard knock, and never had any green water on deck or any water in the cockpit.

When we finally arrived in Madeira our confidence in *Anna Louise* was 100 per cent. As far as we were concerned we had come through just about the worst that the sea could throw at us, unscathed, scared but comfortable, with no damage to yacht or crew. What was particularly important for us, considering our crew strength, was that she could be left to look after herself virtually indefinitely and that life onboard was still 'liveable', even in what we then considered extreme conditions.

Sails prepared for the storm.
Photo: Richard Herbert

By the following May our Atlantic circuit had taken us to Bermuda, from where we set off for the Azores on Tuesday 21 May. It is 1800 miles from Bermuda to the Azores; we had fuel for one-third of that distance and we expected to complete the passage in about two weeks at our normal cruising speed of about 120 miles a day. For the next week we crept slowly north to 38°N, hoping to pick up some steady westerlies.

On Tuesday 28 May the barometer started to fall, from 1025mb in the morning to 1017mb by midnight. The wind became south-east force 3–4, at first nothing to worry about, but tending to continue to push us farther north. During the course of the night conditions continued to deteriorate, the wind veered to south 7–8, and we reduced sail to our storm rig of trysail, storm jib and a little bit of roller genoa, but still continued to make good progress eastwards. We felt pretty fed up. After months of tropical cruising once again it was cold, wet and windy and overall pretty miserable. By lunchtime on Wednesday 29 May we had decided to heave-to (by then in about 39°N, 51°W), winds were southerly force 9, and the barometer had dropped to 1006mb.

Hove-to we were fairly comfortable. Our previous experience had given us a lot of confidence so we settled back to wait for the weather to blow through. We had plenty of food and water, and although a deck ventilator over our bunk leaked, wetting our bedclothes, conditions on board were fairly normal. Our motion was much the same as between Lisbon and Madeira, bouncing around on the top of the waves, riding up the face of them as though in a lift, and dropping into the back with a bit of a thump as they rolled underneath.

At 1800 as I went off watch, the barometer had dropped to 1000mb and Ingrid called 'all ships', our usual, surprisingly effective, technique to get a weather forecast, and got a reply from the *Bangkok Panda*. There were two approaching lows, and we were right in the middle. Still, they were very friendly and helpful, and it was nice to talk to someone.

As I was dozing in the saloon off watch at 2000, I heard Ingrid, who is Austrian, talking in German to a vessel called the *Heidlberg Express*. The words 'trog orkan' floated over the VHF causing a reaction in me that can best be described as panic, although Ingrid showed no reaction at all. A fuller explanation was that the low to the north of us was deepening

Running with warps trailing was not satisfactory as the pull was not steady.
Photo: Richard Herbert

and expected to produce winds of hurricane strength, but that we should not worry as it should pass to the north of us! The barometer had now dropped to 998mb, but the winds had also dropped to force 6–7 and were slowly veering westerly. So we decided to head south-easterly away from the storm centre with all dispatch.

By 0500 on Thursday 30 May the barometer had dropped to 992mb. The winds were north-westerly force 9 and I was hand steering downwind under storm jib alone, surfing down the waves at speeds of up to 17 knots, far too fast for us, and well beyond the capabilities of our simple autopilot. We wanted to press on southerly, but in the increasing seas we were surfing ever faster and it was becoming increasingly difficult to hold the bows straight as we reached the bottoms of the troughs. I was worried that if we yawed the whole weight of the boat would be taken on one bow, it could then dig in, and we would pitchpole or broach. Bearing in mind our previous experience of lying hove-to for four days, it was also clear that I could not hand steer for that long, and Ingrid was fully occupied caring for Kristina, who needed constant attention. In any case, Ingrid probably did not have sufficient experience to steer in these conditions.

The obvious tactic at this point was to stream some form of drogue to slow us down. I was carrying car tyres for this purpose, a tactic suggested by catamaran designer and builder Pat Patterson. The theory was to deploy them on the beam to hold the cat in a comfortable hove-to position in the middle of a long bight of rope streamed from the bows to the stern. Unfortunately, it was at this stage I discovered that the tyres, which normally lived on deck and had been getting in the way during the last nine months, had been swept away by the seas.

I improvised a drogue with a 6lb (2.5kg) folding grapnel dinghy anchor and a length of $\frac{1}{2}$in (12mm) line, streamed from a cleat and fairlead fitted towards the centre of the aft beam. This worked perfectly. The anchor sank deep into the face of the waves and at the end of only about 66ft (20m) of line; it slowed us to a steady 7 knots. We rode the waves comfortably. Now they rolled underneath us – slowly and steadily – we sailed in a straight line, and the autopilot had no difficulty steering as we jogged along with the waves. We were not so firmly held by the drogue that the stern(s) could not rise easily to the sea and there was never the slightest suggestion of seas climbing into the cockpit. Our sterns were relatively wide, but also buoyant, so that we surfed easily. The wave fronts were moving at a relative speed to us of maybe 10 knots, and overall everything felt stable, steady and safe. The pull of the storm jib was balanced by the drag of the drogue and the autopilot had virtually nothing to do.

At this point I estimated that the wind speed was 50 knots plus (our handheld anemometer was hard on the end of the scale at 56 knots in gusts) and the waves were in excess of 39ft (12m) in height.

Unfortunately the drogue line started to chafe as it passed through the fairlead and I couldn't recover the anchor, or fit padding around the line, as it was under too much strain. I normally protect lines with a short length of thick polythene tubing where they pass deck fittings, but on this occasion I had omitted to do this. After an hour or so the line parted and our speed immediately climbed back to 15 knots plus. I streamed several hundred metres of warp with anything heavy and spare that came to hand – the outboard bracket, gas cylinders – but nothing slowed us down as effectively as the grapnel anchor had. It had bitten into the sea about 33ft (10m) astern and maintained a steady drag. The long lines, on the other hand, let us run fast down the face of the waves, as they were in the back of the wave behind the crest, before pulling us up at the bottom. By not being in the same part of the wave as we were, they just couldn't maintain a steady pull as they were being affected by a different part of the wave's rotary motion. They also tended to be pulled out of the water because they were not biting deeply.

The motion at this point was unsteady and just didn't feel safe. I was worried about both ends at this point, burying a bow or being pooped. I was very aware of the high volume of our cockpit and the very large opening of the patio door. We hove-to under storm jib as before and things steadied down, although now the seas were bigger than anything we had previously experienced. By 1000 the barometer had started to rise slowly to 994mb, but the winds continued to increase.

There was a crash and the rig started to shake violently. The storm jib had carried away and was flying to leeward still attached to the inner forestay that had broken away from the deck fitting. I was able to get the sail down and stuff it under the dinghy, and attached its halyard to the deck fitting to take the place of the stay. We now had to motor slowly to hold the right attitude to the seas. By now we had only about 10 gallons of diesel in the fuel tank, enough for only 24 hours' running, and although we carried another 30 gallons in jerry cans there was no way that I could refill the tank in these conditions.

I decided to try Pat Patterson's method of putting a drogue on the beam. The theory is that as well as holding the cat at a good attitude to the seas, any tendency to capsize would be prevented by the pull of the drogue on the windward hull. I streamed 330ft (100m) of $\frac{5}{8}$in (16mm) nylon line with a sailbag one-third of the way from the front from the bow and stern cleats. This was certainly effective in holding the cat in the right position, but now we were held firmly to the seas and started to feel the full violence of the waves as they crashed into us, putting a tremendous strain on the structure.

At least I was now able to repair the inner forestay – the shackle holding the stay to the deck U bolt had parted – but I could not reset the storm jib as the wind was simply too strong. *Anna Louise* really felt as though she was taking a pounding, her big buoyant hulls were now being forced to work against the seas instead of riding with them. Also I could imagine the cleats, bolted through heavy glassfibre reinforcement into massive metal backing pads, being ripped from the decks. I restarted the engine and recovered the line. Immediately the motion was easier, being bounced out of the way by the waves rather than being held hard against them. Like a boxer our lightweight buoyancy and lack of grip in the water let us ride with the blows. The seas were pushing us around and not crashing into us.

The seas had now built up to the point where I could no longer consider running before them, even with a drogue. Using a drogue on the beam meant that the seas crashed violently into us instead of just pushing us along. A drogue from the bows would mean our point of least buoyancy facing the steep breaking crests.

I sent a Pan Pan message. We were desperate for weather information. Was this the height of the storm; how much longer was it expected to last? Miraculously we received a reply. The deep-sea fishing vessel *Seneca* was about 8 miles to leeward of us and slowly jogging along with the storm. They had a weatherfax on board and also were in contact with the US Coast Guard via short-wave radio. The storm was expected to continue and increase. Our situation did not seem good. At the moment we were OK, but everything seemed to depend on our engine. If the engine failed for any reason, the bows would swing downwind and we would be surfing wildly; a drogue would hold us too firmly to the seas. Although we were safe and fairly comfortable, everything depended on a single diesel engine.

I asked *Seneca* if they could come to us and stand by. Initially they refused, inviting us instead to sail downwind and join them. I explained the problem with surfing and they eventually agreed to come up to us, no small matter for them as it took them nine hours to reach us against the wind and seas. While talking on Channel 16 with *Seneca* another yacht called *Good Results*, a Macwester 32 that we had met in Bermuda, heard us and decided to try and join us. They had been running before the weather for about 24 hours, hand steering under bare pole.

By evening both *Seneca* and *Good Results* were with us. It was clear that there was absolutely no chance of transferring from one vessel to another and indeed, seeing the waves breaking right over the top of *Seneca*, an aluminium deep-sea fishing boat of about 82ft (25m), I am not at all sure that they were better off than us!

There was nothing to do now but wait and worry. The wave height was about 49ft (15m), wavelength seemed to be about 660ft (200m), and they were travelling past faster than we had ever sailed, in excess of 17 knots. The front of the waves had an angle of about 17°, measured against the horizon using a protractor. Only the top 5–6ft (1.5–2m) of the waves got steeper and broke. Wind strength was in excess of 56 knots.

The engine was rumbling away slowly and we were moving forward at about 1 knot, just enough steerage that we could hold our bows at an angle of 30° to the wave front. We rode up the front of the waves, they rolled underneath us, and we dropped into the back of them with a thump. The breaking crests hissed and frothed under us and we could feel ourselves sinking into them. Occasional bad waves hit us hard, smashing against the hull as though we were being rammed by a lorry, knocking the bows to the side and making us speed up for a moment before resuming our previous angle to the waves; our safety valve. One wave in particular knocked up the windward hull and pushed us along in front of it before letting us go.

The night of 30–31 May was a bad one. *Seneca* was standing by us (we could see their lights), and giving us weather information, which was not encouraging. The wind was incredibly strong and gusty and now we couldn't see the waves as they thundered down on us. Every window and hatch was leaking, everything had flown around inside and was soaking wet, and we were shocked and exhausted. We were all wearing oilskins and life-jackets. I did not consider using the liferaft. I didn't believe it would be possible to inflate and board it in those conditions.

Waves pounded into us continuously. We received a tremendous blow and I felt the motion change. I later discovered that the seas had spun the rudders and driven the engine outdrive leg to one side through failure of the support structure. I hand steered riding up

The day after the storm with *Seneca*, the deep-sea fishing boat nearby. *Photo: Richard Herbert*

into the waves and gently over the back. Everything still worked. I could see nothing but spray, which was driving so hard that the pain on any bare area of skin was unbearable. At the tops of the waves it was possible to make out a complete flat landscape of driven spray.

This, thank God, was the height of the storm.

During the course of Friday 31 May the winds slowly moderated and the barometer climbed back up to 1008mb. At dawn on Saturday morning *Seneca* advised us to head south, as the lull would not last. They came over to say goodbye and we saw them clearly for the first time. They had saved our sanity if not our lives. *Good Results* joined us and we set off, still in heavy seas but, thankfully, no more than a gale, heading south away from it all as fast as we could. By motoring and sailing, we reached Horta in the Azores on 9 June.

COMMENT

The first serious point of anxiety was when the catamaran was surfing down the waves far too fast and, out of necessity, under hand control. This predicament is common, and short-handed yachtsmen know that they cannot continue for long in these circumstances. The plan was to use car tyres as drogues but, after 'getting in the way for the last nine months', at the time they were needed they had been swept overboard. Even if they had not been, car tyres do not act very well as drogues, especially if the annular space where the wheel goes has been wrapped with duct tape. The next improvisation worked surprisingly well as the grapnel dinghy anchor on the end of 66ft (20m) of $\frac{1}{2}$in (12mm) line seemingly had enough weight and the necessary shape to 'dig in'. If the line had not chafed through, the story might have gone no further. As it was, Richard Herbert was soon looking for materials for further improvisation, but the outboard bracket and gas bottles were evidently too buoyant and gave neither a sufficient nor steady enough load.

Writing after these events in the Atlantic, Richard Herbert said that his next yacht would be better prepared for extreme conditions with heavy items, such as tanks, better bonded in. It is interesting to hear that his next yacht would certainly be a catamaran.

24 An autumn Biscay storm

JAMES BURDETT

Three yachts set out for home to the north from La Coruña at about the same time. This is the account of the smallest and oldest.

La Coruña in late summer resembles something of a motorway service station on the main route to a holiday resort. Some boats are at the end of a summer cruise and are provisioning for the passage home, while others are heading south to warmer waters and have barely started their adventures. My cousin, Tom Hasler, and I were heading home after a six-week cruise of north-west Spain in my Laurent Giles-designed 25ft (7.6m) Vertue *Mary*, built in 1939.

I had bought *Mary* two years earlier and she is the first 'big boat' I have owned. She was built just before the war and had been owned for most of her life by the couple who sold her to me. When I bought her she had been laid up for 12 years in a yard on the Tamar River. Her surveyor reported that there wasn't a spot of rot in her pitch-pine planks or oak frames and was, in most respects, a thoroughly sound boat.

By Friday 10 September 1992 we had been sitting in La Coruña for nearly a week and, despite the many attractions of the town, we were both sick of *tapas* and were getting itchy feet.

The day before I had telephoned my parents to get a long-range Met Office forecast. This was uncharacteristically vague and spoke only of a low-pressure system moving in from the west and creating gales over North Biscay. We had already sat through the first of the autumn gales earlier in the week, and knew only too well that the longer we stayed in Spain the more likely we were to get stuck there. So when on Friday a Danish skipper gave us a synopsis from the Danish Met Office, which totally contradicted the British one, we latched on to it. The Danes predicted that the weak high-pressure ridge over South Biscay would fill and push any depressions farther north and out of the way. One of the forecasts had to be wrong. After lengthy debate between us, forever the optimists, we decided it had to be the British one.

So at lunchtime on Friday we weighed anchor, sailed round the massive Digue Abrigo breakwater, and headed north-eastwards on a beeline to the Raz de Sein, Brittany, 360 miles away.

The outward passage had taken us 62 hours and now, with a force 4–5 behind us, we expected a repeat performance on the homeward leg. After 24 hours at sea we had covered 120 miles and could almost smell the freshly baked croissants that awaited our arrival in France. We were brought sharply down to size, though, by the 1800 shipping forecast on Saturday, the first we had tuned into since our departure: '...Biscay, North Finisterre, southerly violent storm 11 imminent...' The announcer read it out with the same emotion as the talking clock. I wondered if he could imagine the sense of disbelief and acute apprehension that had suddenly gripped me when I heard those words. Tom and I stared at each other in amazement. How could we have been so foolhardy as to ignore the long-range British forecast, scant as it was? And why on earth were we in the middle of the Bay of Biscay in a boat that was older than our combined ages waiting to be hit by a near hurricane? All those questions flew around my head. Still, it was too late to try to come up with answers.

We were undoubtedly too far from land to make a dash to shelter. The Spanish coast was 120 miles to windward and the French coast 270 miles to the north-east. There was nothing for it but to ride it out as best we could.

We had to act fast and make use of what little fair weather we had left. The first priority was to get as much sea room as possible. By heading north-west we came onto a broad reach and began to make valuable miles out into the Atlantic and farther away from land. The two prime dangers were the lee shore of south Brittany and, close at hand, the line of the Continental Shelf. This runs roughly from Ushant in a south-easterly direction to the French–Spanish border, and the depth of water rises from over 656ft (200m) to less than 328ft (100m) in the space of 15 miles or so. It has the potential for creating huge and confused seas as the deep-water swell piles up over the shelf.

We handed the sails and lashed the main tightly along the boom. I put extra lashings over the pram dinghy that stowed on the cabin roof. I had brought along two 150ft (46m) heavy warps for trailing astern, as a more manageable alternative to a sea anchor, and placed them in the cockpit in readiness for deployment.

By dusk on Saturday, *Mary*, Tom and I were as ready as we could be for what lay ahead. The wind was rising steadily and by midnight had reached an estimated force 6 (we did not have an anemometer). We streamed the warps in two large bights, one from both the sheet winches and one from the large bronze cleats on each quarter. The warps undoubtedly held the stern up to windward and slowed us down. They weren't as effective at checking our speed as a drogue would have been, as we were still moving through the water at 3–4 knots.

By dawn, the true scale of what we were in for became apparent. The wind by now was a steady force 10 from the south. It was extremely difficult to look to windward to see where the next wave was coming from as the spume and spray hit you full-on like a sandblaster. The waves had built up overnight. It was difficult to gauge the wave height, but when we were in a trough the crests would tower well above mast height and create an unnerving lull in the wind. These lulls were short-lived though, as the next wave would arrive from astern, carrying us up like a piece of flotsam back into the teeth of the storm.

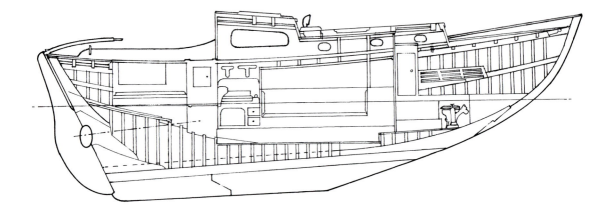

Figure 24.1 Side elevation showing *Mary*'s underwater shape.

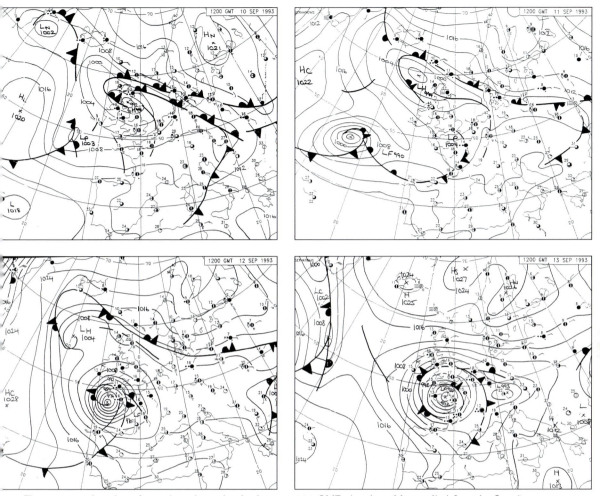

Figure 24.2 A series of weather charts beginning at 1200 GMT, the time *Mary* sailed from La Coruña on Friday 10 September 1993, and 1200 GMT on Saturday, Sunday and Monday 11–13 September.

Shortly after daybreak on Sunday, while I was in the cabin – the motion was too violent to sleep – Tom shouted down to me for a white flare. It had to mean only one thing. I shot up the companionway and looked round behind me to see the outline of a ship emerging out of the mist and spray. She was headed straight at us and no more than a quarter of a mile away. Luckily, after Tom had set off the flare, she altered course and passed a couple of hundred metres to port of us. I managed to raise them on the VHF; she was called *Triton*, and I got an accurate GPS fix from them. Encouragingly, we were only 10 miles out on our dead reckoning since La Coruña. They asked if we were OK. I answered, 'Yes.' Although our situation was far from pleasant, I still felt in control and expected the centre of the low pressure system to move through quickly, taking the strong winds with it. In any case, there was little that they could have done for us even if we had needed assistance. The seas were so short and steep as to rule out completely any sort of rescue attempt. I discovered later that *Triton* had reported us to the French coastguard.

By now the wind had veered to the south-west and our original hope of being blown northwards far enough to be clear of Ushant was no longer realistic. The south Brittany shore was now directly downwind and about 150 miles away. Although that was well over

Mary, the Laurent Giles-designed 25ft (7.6m) Vertue, built in 1939.

a day away at our speed, the 328ft (100m) seabed contour change was less than 75 miles away, and this posed the most imminent danger.

The waves gradually grew larger and more menacing. Where before there had been smooth crests, many were by now breaking. It was virtually impossible to avoid a breaker when it came down on you, you simply had to try to align the boat to minimize the damage. We started by steering directly down the front of each wave in the belief that this was the best way to avoid broaching or rolling. In theory it makes sense because you are presenting the smallest surface area to the wave, but it only works up to a point. Naturally the course directly down the wave is the steepest and fastest route, and when each wave is a good 60ft (18m) high, a 5 ton boat can reach quite a speed down its face, even with warps trailing. We learned this the hard way and had spectacular sleigh rides down the face of some waves. *Mary*, though, was as forgiving as ever and her long keel tracked so perfectly that one barely had to exert pressure on the tiller to prevent her from screwing round at the bottom.

Mary has no self-steering (not that it would have been much use in these conditions), so when on watch one was constantly on the helm. This took a lot out of me and by midday on Sunday fatigue was setting in. We were both soaked to the skin and unable to keep warm, despite having the cooker burning constantly in the cabin.

The wind showed no signs of letting up; instead it grew stronger and stronger. Just when we thought it couldn't possibly get any fiercer it did, and with each passing hour the seas became steeper and more unpredictable. Virtually every wave crest was breaking and we couldn't see for the spray and spume on the surface of the sea. Breakers regularly swamped the entire boat, filling the cockpit instantly. After each swamping it took a good 10 minutes to pump the boat dry, as inevitably a large amount of water found its way down below through the cabin doors and cockpit locker lids.

With the now dreaded 328ft (100m) contour getting closer and closer it was only a matter of time before we would be unable to keep pace with the onslaught of the seas. It was decision time. We had a stark choice: attempt to continue into what was a rapidly deteriorating situation, or swallow our pride and call for help. I was acutely aware of the fact that *Mary* might not be able to stand up to the punishment we were putting her through for much longer. When I eventually sent a Mayday, no one responded. Realistically, though, I shouldn't have expected anyone to hear, as my handheld VHF probably had a range of no more than 10 miles in these conditions. In retrospect, we were extremely fortunate that no one did hear us, since any attempt to abandon *Mary* and scramble up the side of a heaving merchant vessel would have been suicidal.

The Mayday was a turning point since we now realized that we were totally alone and entirely dependent on our own resources. Our only hope was to keep *Mary* afloat at all costs. The liferaft wasn't an option. Even if we had managed to go forward to cut its lashings, the chances of launching it, getting in and keeping it upright were close to zero.

As night fell on Sunday, all hell let loose. The night was pitch black and the only warning of the next wave was the glowing phosphorescence churning up in its breaking crest. There was spume and spray everywhere. We both had stinging and bloodshot eyes from looking into the wind. We both remained in the cockpit harnessed in, as I was convinced that if *Mary* did go down she would go down fast.

Thankfully, Tom had discovered that the best way to tackle the unrelenting onslaught of breaking seas was to steer so as to take them on the quarter. This meant that the line of descent down the face of the wave was not at its steepest. Although it did not prevent *Mary* from being completely swamped, it did reduce the amazing acceleration and speed we had encountered when going straight down the waves. This 'Tom Hasler Oblique Storm Steering System' also meant that we could put more east in our course and avoid heading for the nearest part of the French coast.

By midnight on Sunday, the storm had been raging for 24 hours. It had been blowing a constant force 11 and gusting stronger for at least 12 hours. Neither of us had had any sleep for over 30 hours. We were soaked through, tired, hungry and becoming more and more despondent. I found myself thinking that it might be altogether simpler if the next wave took us to the bottom. It was all too easy to huddle in the corner of the cockpit and doze off into semi-consciousness, although this could never last for long since a shout from Tom on the helm would alert me to the next swamping and then what seemed like hours of pumping to empty the boat.

We had a go at singing and stamping our feet to boost morale and keep alert, but even Tom, the doyen of singers, had forgotten all his tunes.

The waves had totally lost any pattern and were coming at us from all directions; we needed to pump almost continuously to have any chance of preventing the boat from filling. The louvred companionway doors were woefully inadequate at keeping the water out of the cabin and it regularly filled up to the level of the bunks.

During one of my spells on the helm I looked back and saw high above and behind me something that seemed like a cloud. I was mistaken only for a second – the next moment it plummeted down towards us and hit *Mary* full on from above with enormous force. We were both pinned down into the cockpit, green water above our heads, and then with the most almighty acceleration we took off down the face of the wave, completely out of control. The force of the breaking water gave *Mary* a tremendous buffeting as she flew down the face like a bobsleigh. It seemed that something had to go, and it would only have taken one plank to spring or the coachroof to stove in for the whole lot of us to go down. Somehow we survived it.

Sometime in the early hours of Monday morning I was again on the helm battling to

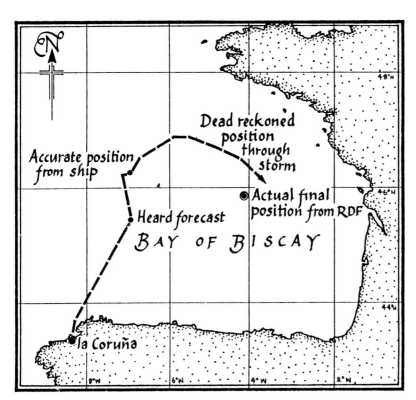

Fig 24.3 Track chart for *Mary*, September 1993.

control her. Almost by accident I discovered that the most effective way of slowing us down was to hold the tiller hard over to port and effectively lie a'hull. The warps still kept the stern into the wind to a certain extent, but it meant that the wind and the majority of the waves were coming from just aft of the beam. This seemed to reduce the frequency of swamping, as the waves tended to wash over the coachroof rather than fill the cockpit from astern. Although it increased the risk of rolling we were both too tired to care and, because pumping was reduced to once every 20 minutes or so, we decided to lash the helm to port and turn in.

I crashed out on the leeward bunk and slept, and woke to find that Tom had resurrected the primus cooker (which had jumped out of its gimbals) and was warming up the cabin.

By daylight the wind had dropped to force 9–10 and we spent the rest of the day lying in our oilskins, soaked to the skin, hoping that the worst was now over. By Tuesday morning the wind had moderated enough to consider sailing, although the seas were still big and occasionally breaking over the coachroof. I got an RDF fix at 1000 which put us 70 miles west of La Rochelle. We had been blown over 200 miles in the previous 50 hours under bare pole.

Before setting sail we assessed the damage. The only breakage was the topping lift that had been cut through at the top of the mast by the radar reflector (which had merrily spun its way up the backstay during the storm). The rigging and mast were intact. Ironically this may have been thanks to the lightness of construction (the mast is hollow spruce) and the small surface area of the spars that would have presented less resistance to the waves than something more heavily built.

We set sail and headed north-east towards Isle d'Yeu, only to find some hours later that I hadn't brought any charts of the island. When I discovered this, and after a serious humour failure on both our parts, we headed for the next closest landfall, Belle Isle, about 40 miles farther along the coast. Eventually we entered La Pallice at 1200 on Wednesday 15 September, but not before being pooped twice in the tide race off the southern tip of the island – a final reminder from the Biscay of our mortality.

I later discovered through the Coastguard that a Danish yacht and another British yacht had left La Coruña shortly after us. Both were lost.

COMMENT

The Vertue yacht has always been considered a wonderfully seaworthy yacht for her size, and this fearsome autumn Biscay storm confirms this opinion. The situation that faced the crew of *Mary* is a familiar one. Weather-bound for a week and anxious to be home, there was a very human tendency to take the most favourable forecast. After making the decision to leave it would have been wise to have listened to shipping forecasts between midday on Friday, when *Mary* sailed, and Saturday evening, by which time she was well into the Bay of Biscay. Out in the Atlantic the innocuous-looking low with a central pressure of 1003mb (visible on the Friday chart) deepened sharply, but not explosively, in this period. By Sunday the central pressure was 970mb and the isobars had become sufficiently tightly packed to justify the very strong winds experienced.

A successful outcome to the voyage was finely balanced and required considerable courage, toughness and determination. That nothing of consequence broke is a good reflection on the nature of the boat and her preparation.

Having made the fateful decision to sail, what else could the crew have done had they had the means to do it? Would a parachute sea anchor have helped? Perhaps, James Burdett says. He would have had to tie the parachute line to the keel-stepped mast to take the load. Would a drogue have helped? Definitely, he says. The two warps brought *Mary*'s speed down to 3–4 knots when the wind speed was estimated to be force 6. Later, when the wind really got up, we read of spectacular (and hairy) sleigh rides down the huge seas, and one that was 'completely out of control'. A steering mistake, had there been one, would have meant an instant broach. A good drogue would have provided much more drag than the two 150ft (46m) warps carried on board *Mary*. It would have reduced the stress of steering, improved control and steadied up the boat, but too much drag would have only increased the number of poopings.

The 'Tom Hasler Oblique Storm Steering System' is a method of steering down waves at an angle to prevent excessive speed and is used by many eminent sailors. For example, Bernard Moitessier, influenced by Vito Dumas, and Alan Webb describe their use of the technique in Chapter 15. The method undoubtedly works as long as there are helmsmen able to employ it. When *Mary*'s helmsmen understandably ran out of steam she ended up in an unusual position lying a'hull by the stern, a position that was found to be comfortable. Though the warps prevented her from lying broadside-on to the seas, which would have been yet more dangerous, this tactic was still probably more comfortable than safe, as was no doubt well appreciated by both of *Mary*'s crew. It was lucky they were not rolled, though at that stage it is difficult to see what they could have done better.

In extreme weather, ordinary two-piece oilskins do not provide sufficient protection, and cannot be expected to. A one-piece drysuit or a survival suit becomes of high value in survival conditions ... 'Awesomely good', says Mike Golding in Chapter 10. Goggles or eye protection would have been valuable, too. James Burdett would have been glad of a proper yacht heater. Noting how much water was coming down below, one is reminded that a lot of it often comes through cockpit locker lids when the cockpit is flooded. By putting sealant on the lid and grease on the land of the locker while the sealant is setting – or the other way round – a permanent watertight seal can usually be made.

Tom Hasler displaying the ensign after the storm. (It was full size before leaving La Coruña.)
Photo: James Burdett

Given what they had, there is only one particular oversight that James Burdett regrets. Seemingly there was no lanyard on the only bilge pump handle and, had this been lost, *Mary*'s survival would have been yet more in doubt. This points to the wisdom of the Offshore Racing Council's 'Special Regulations', which are obligatory for racing boats. Among many very sensible items listed in these regulations, there is a requirement that bilge pump handles be secured by a lanyard.

25 A winter storm off the south-west coast of Australia

DEBORAH SCHUTZ

A letter to the Australian magazine Cruising Helmsman, *seeking accounts of the use of parachute sea anchors in severe storms, led to Deborah Schutz's description of how* Prisana II *rode out sustained winds of hurricane strength off Perth. The story shows whether a parachute sea anchor is capable of doing its business when it really comes on to blow.*

Prisana II is a 45ft (13.7m) glassfibre ketch. She is a Tayana Surprise 45 with two equal-height masts, both with in-mast furling. Her draft is 7ft (2.1m), displacement 13 tons, beam 13.5ft (4.1m), and her ballast 5 tons. She has a fin keel, a skeg rudder and a hydraulic autopilot-to-quadrant-wheel cable steering.

We departed from Adelaide, South Australia, in early July 1996 with six people on board. These were Steve (the skipper and my partner), myself and our son Ben (7 years old at the time), and our long-time friends Trevor, Sam and Patrick. Steve has sailed for most of his life. Ben and I have been sailing for the six years since Steve and his father purchased *Prisana II*. Trev had considerable sailing experience and was mechanically minded (like Steve). Sam had sailed previously, but Patrick had no previous sailing experience. Our plan was to cruise the Western Australian coastline and offshore islands for six months. We expected the Great Australian Bight would test us – especially as it was the middle of a southern winter. I had visited the Bureau of Meteorology a couple of weeks before we left and was warned by a gentleman there that we were about to cross one of the worst seas in the world for storms.

With this in mind, we decided to set up our 18ft (5.5m) Para-Tech parachute anchor before we left port. The parachute anchor – with a $\frac{3}{4}$in (18mm) stainless steel swivel – was shackled to the rode which was 410ft (125m) of $\frac{3}{4}$in (18mm), three-strand nylon contained in a deployment bag. The other end of the rode was shackled to a $\frac{1}{2}$in (12mm) chain link welded to the ship's main anchor that is stowed on the bow in a custom-made stem fitting. To give added security, the anchor was held by a $\frac{3}{8}$in (10mm) Ronstan rigging screw, secured to a $\frac{3}{8}$in (10mm) stainless steel plate bolted under the windlass. Winch and plate were fastened by six $\frac{3}{8}$in (10mm) stainless steel studs. Both the fixing point to the anchor and to the plate were backed up by secondary systems. A slack chain from the nylon rode was attached to a $\frac{5}{8}$in (16mm) stainless steel bolt passing through the anchor cheeks, and another short length of chain was secured between the anchor shackle and the $\frac{3}{8}$in (10mm) plate bolted under the windlass. We used a partial trip line – two floats and two 49ft (15m) lines with swivels (see Fig 25.1).

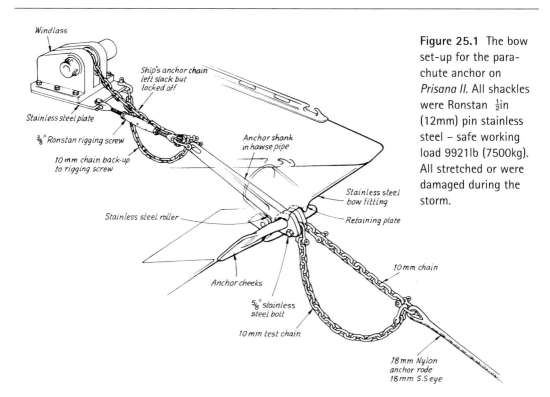

Windlass

Ship's anchor chain
left slack but
locked off

Stainless steel plate

3/8" Ronstan rigging screw

10 mm chain back-up
to rigging screw

Anchor shank
in hawse pipe

Stainless steel roller

Stainless steel
bow fitting

Retaining plate

Stainless steel roller

Anchor cheeks

5/8" stainless
steel bolt

10 mm test chain

10 mm chain

18 mm Nylon
anchor rode
18 mm S.S eye

Figure 25.1 The bow set-up for the parachute anchor on *Prisana II*. All shackles were Ronstan ½in (12mm) pin stainless steel – safe working load 9921lb (7500kg). All stretched or were damaged during the storm.

Fortunately we crossed the Bight within a high-pressure system. After eight days, we sighted Cape Leeuwin, the south-western-most point of mainland Australia and one of the world's great navigational landmarks. A wide berth is required to round the Cape, as immediately west and north of the lighthouse lies an extensive area of reefs. The area is known for rogue breaking waves and strong tides. We encountered choppy seas, much large shipping and a falling barometer. Winds increased up to 30 knots from the north. As the day progressed we headed farther out to sea while the weather deteriorated. During the night, gusts reached 40–45 knots as we beat into a westerly, by now 80 miles out from Cape Leeuwin.

Near nightfall on Sunday 14 July we were almost abeam of Cape Naturaliste. Our weatherfax showed a complex low was fast approaching. Growing darkness, our position, the unfamiliar coastline and the wind direction (a 40 knot north-north-east) meant that it was inadvisable to look for an anchorage. We had already considered using our sea anchor, but owing to the number of ships in the vicinity we decided to keep going. We reduced sail, expecting the winds to swing south-west with the approaching front, which we would use to get us to Fremantle. We were wrong! Throughout the night, Mother Nature unleashed a storm of unrelenting fury, with the wind increasing to 50 knots from the north-north-east with large seas, leaving us little choice but to head out to sea.

At first light on Monday 15 July we came about. Perth Radio issued another gale warning. The barometer read 996mb and was falling rapidly. By evening, the wind had become a strong westerly, the barometer now read 990mb, though the sea had moderated. As the night progressed, squalls reached 60 knots and lightning could be seen behind us as we sailed in a northerly direction. Eventually the anemometer was off the scale at over 65 knots and the seas were rising dramatically. At approximately 0300 a huge wall of white water knocked us over to starboard. The helmsman (thankfully harnessed) was chest-height in water, and our masts were horizontal in the sea. Ben and I were asleep below and we were both flung out of our bunks.

Steve, Sam and Trevor deployed the sea anchor, using a flying set. Even in the dark, this was relatively easy. Deployment simply involved reaching from the safety of the cockpit to the rode deployment bag, unlacing the top, removing the end of the rode, and shackling it to the parachute anchor. Trip line and float buoys were fed overboard, followed by the parachute anchor in its deployment bag. Within about 30 seconds, we had taken up all the rode and were gently pulled head-to-wind, allowing us to furl the sails entirely. They were to remain furled for the rest of the storm. Then we put an ¾in (18mm) bridle line on the rode, with a view to lying to the parachute at an angle in the manner described by Larry and Lin Pardey, but the bridle broke almost as soon as it was tensioned. So we gave up that idea and contented ourselves with leaving the rode to lead straight out over the bow. After that it was all crew below with hatches battened. At this point we were 30nm to the west of Rottnest Island.

During the morning of Tuesday 16 July I ventured into the cockpit and was immediately awestruck. The seas were incredibly huge. I soon retreated below, after taking a couple of photos. I later found out the seas were reported to be 36ft (11m) on top of a 30ft (9m) swell – a total of around 64ft (20m). When the parachute rode emerged as it spanned a trough, it sliced through the water like a knife, and one could see massive tension come on it as *Prisana* surged forward and back with the waves. A lot of white water was being swept from the tops of the swell, with large rolling crests of white water underneath. *Prisana* took many loads of white water across the deck, and even some green water. The conditions were such that it would have been foolhardy to be anywhere on deck. We used a safety harness when visiting the cockpit, otherwise almost all of our time was spent down below.

At that time we felt that we had plenty of sea room as we drifted in a southerly direction in the Leeuwin current on a west wind for 24 hours. This current runs southward down the Continental Shelf from Indonesia, bringing masses of warm water. It begins flowing around April each year through until October, and seldom moves faster than 1 knot in a band approximately 31 miles (50km) wide. Throughout the storm our drift rate averaged 0.9 knots. The parachute anchor held us while the winds screamed at over 70 knots. The noise was incredible! We rolled heavily from gunwale to gunwale and it appeared that we yawed about 45° on one side to 35° on the other. Occasionally, we felt the rode become slack as the bow paid off somewhere over 45°, then there would be a tremendous jerk as the rode became taut again. This may have been due to rogue waves coming in on a different angle, but we believed that it was because the boat yawed a lot and surged on the huge swell. It was hard to tell from down below.

Steve awoke at dawn on Wednesday 17 July to see a ship on our stern, only 0.8 miles away. We tried to make contact using VHF, and an Australian boat promptly answered, but he was 6 miles away. He informed us that the other vessel was a foreign ship, along with mentioning that he didn't envy us one bit. For 15 long minutes, we tried to make contact. We were losing sight of the whole ship (approximately 400ft (125m) long with an extensive bridge structure) behind the seas. Finally, a man's voice responded in broken English causing us a minor panic. He didn't seem eager to alter his course, telling us he had no ballast and that he couldn't even see us. We managed to persuade him to alter course a little and, after ensuring that he could see our spotlight, we saw him pass 0.4nm away on our radar.

We had drifted as far south as Bunbury when we began to drift east and believed we were in an eddy of the Leeuwin current. We appeared to have been caught up in a typical anticlockwise flow that took us inshore and then northwards along the coast.

The weather remained unchanged. All day long the winds continued to blow over 70 knots. We heard that a large cargo ship had just lost 30 containers off Cape Leeuwin. The Adelaide media reported that a cyclone had hit Perth.

By Thursday 18 July conditions were moderating, the wind was now down to 50 knots and the barometer slowly began to rise; the seas were still large and getting steeper with shallowing depth as we crept closer to the coast. Concerned about running out of sea room late in the afternoon, we decided to retrieve the parachute anchor. This wasn't easy. Noise from the wind and sea made it difficult to hear the skipper's instructions from the helm to the bow. Trying to use the engine to pick up the recovery float, we fouled the rode on the propeller. When we finally retrieved the parachute anchor, we found two large well-frayed holes in two separate panels between the vent hole and the skirt. We have no doubts about the manufacture or design of the parachute, nor do we believe that it was snagged during recovery, so it is probable that the holes were caused by flotsam. By the time we set a course for Rottnest Island the wind was down to 30–40 knots, which felt like a gentle breeze.

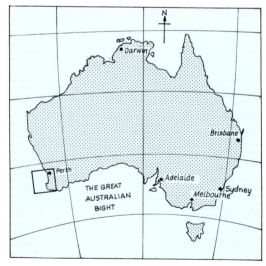

Figure 25.2 Track of *Prisana II* during the storm, July 1996.

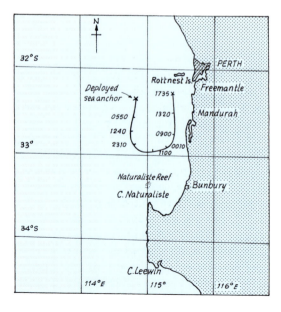

Around 1030 on Friday 19 July we motored into the Fremantle Sailing Club, grateful that we had decided to buy a parachute anchor. With it we were able to ride out and survive the storm with our bow held into the seas. During the storm, Bunbury and Fremantle Harbours were closed and the harbourmaster at Fremantle said they were the largest seas he could ever remember. Rottnest Island, 12 miles off the coast of Fremantle, had holiday-makers stranded there for three days as the ferries were unable to make the crossing. When he docked at Fremantle on 19 July the captain of the ship that had lost 30 containers off Cape Leeuwin said, 'In all my time, I've never seen seas like those.' In addition to the unusually strong winds, what the weather bureau in Perth described as a rare winter tornado, which had formed at high altitude somewhere around where *Prisana* was on the night of 15 July, had struck south Perth with 200km/h (108 knot) winds.

We spent the following three to four weeks in Fremantle repairing *Prisana*. She had suffered quite some damage. The rudder shaft had been twisted, the forward bulkhead damaged, and four stanchions had been ripped from the deck, to name but a few of her problems.

During the storm both our primary systems to take the load of the rode at the bow had failed. The Ronstan rigging screw had broken, stripping eight turns of thread, and the chain/link welded to the ship's anchor had torn off. Thankfully, in both systems, the back-up held but, when the rigging screw broke, the anchor was free to smash around, which caused some damage to our stainless steel bow fitting. We also found that our 410ft (125m) of ¾in (18mm) rope had stretched an extra 66ft (20m).

Prisana's rudder shaft had about a 15° twist in the 2in (50mm) diameter 316-grade stainless steel shaft at the point where the quadrant is fixed. It definitely wasn't twisted before the deployment of the parachute anchor. The rudder lashings holding the rudder on the centreline at the quadrant had broken twice during the storm. We managed to hold it, third time lucky, on spare ¾in (18mm) nylon anchor rode. The forward bulkhead was damaged, mostly due to a design fault rather than the conditions.

To the question, 'Did the sea anchor save the boat?' the answer is, 'Absolutely!' In the conditions we were caught in, we believe that having the parachute anchor set up before departure was crucial to its safe and easy deployment. Had we not had it (an awful thought) we would probably have tried to find shelter behind Rottnest Island by sailing on a broad-

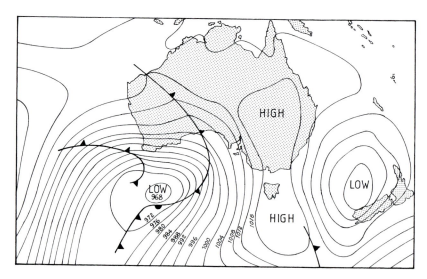

Figure 25.3
Weatherfax chart for 17 July 1996 showing the deep low south of Cape Leeuwin and the packed isobars between the two.

reach, possibly dragging warps as we were not carrying a drogue. I believe our chances of surviving had we done so would have been extremely slim.

Comment

It seems that *Prisana II* must have experienced hurricane strength winds for about 48 hours. That she survived in the way she did brings credit to her crew and their parachute sea anchor. It is one of the most testing accounts of a parachute sea anchor deployment, and goes to show that a parachute can work in very extreme weather. It is significant that the parachute sea anchor was set up before the yacht left harbour, in anticipation of bad weather.

The parachute system appears to have been taken to its limit. The canopy was damaged, the rode stretched, and the primary method of securing the parachute line at the boat end failed, showing that the minimum recommendations for size of parachute and rode are just that.

The parachute did not give a comfortable ride: *Prisana* rolled from gunwale to gunwale and yawed about 80°. Then there was the time when the parachute line would become slack and then take up with a jerk. Having two masts, *Prisana* had more windage aft than a sloop and therefore just about managed without a riding sail at the stern. It is probable that she would not have yawed as much, nor would the parachute line have snatched, had one been used. The Pardey method of lying-to a parachute, which was conceived to improve comfort, was tried without success in that the bridle line broke.

It was noteworthy to find that *Prisana* was in danger from other shipping. A lookout in a yacht in storm conditions cannot easily look to windward without eye protection. Even then, spume can obscure visibility almost entirely. Looking from most enclosed bridges of ships in a storm does not improve visible range by much. The windows are continuously spattered with spray that blurs the view entirely between sweeps of the wiper. Only just after the wiper has passed is there a split second of good vision before the window blurs over again. This allows a brief view in one narrow direction. Radar is not much help either, as a yacht's echo may well be completely lost in the wave returns. Thus there is no better chance that a yacht will see a ship than vice versa. Salvation comes in the form of VHF, and it is wise to make a regular Sécurité call, giving position and circumstances.

Did the parachute save the boat? We don't know what would have happened if the crew had been forced to adopt other storm tactics, but at least we do know that by using the parachute the crew of *Prisana II* survived to tell the tale.

CHAPTER

26 *Orca's last cruise*

MAGGI & ROBIN ANSELL

Any account of a yacht caught in a cyclone has to be of interest. This one especially so, as a parachute sea anchor was used, and for the first time by her owners.

S/V Orca was a New Zealand-designed Hartley Tahitian ketch, LOA 55ft (16.8m), waterline 47ft (14.3m), and beam 13ft 6in (4.1m). She was totally of ferro-cement construction, and built, we believe, in the Isle of Wight in 1976. She had a full keel with 7ft (2.1m) draft, displaced 80 000lb (36 288kg), and was equipped with a 165hp engine. There were two of us on board, myself and my husband Robin.

Queensland to the Solomon Islands was the first leg of the second half of our Pacific circumnavigation via Japan, Korea, Russia and the Aleutians to reach Alaska by August to over-winter, before returning to Canada. We knew we had to risk bad weather somewhere en route. Having just spent 15 months living in the Philippines experiencing at first-hand the ferocity and frequency of the typhoons there, and bearing in mind the past few years' cyclone history for northern Queensland, early March 1997 was chosen as our least-risk departure date.

Our assessment of low cyclone risk at that time was shared. The largest combined military exercise since D-Day, the US/Australian 'Operation Tandem Thrust', was in full swing off the Queensland coast, involving 250 aircraft, 50 warships and 23 000 personnel, all of which were subsequently evacuated.

For a week prior to our 4 March departure, we had been watching our weatherfaxes indicating a normal monsoonal trough with embedded lows, and set off with a steady 20 knot south-east wind flow, motorsailing south to the entrance of the 60 mile Hydrographer's Passage, through the Great Barrier Reef. We hove-to for a few hours before entering the passage, to ensure that we negotiated the most difficult outer section in daylight and at slack tide.

In the early hours of 6 March, we set course for Lihou Reef, our first waypoint in the Coral Sea. The usual Pacific swell didn't prevent *Orca* from making good progress in the 20 knot-plus south-east winds under double-reefed main, single-reefed mizzen and half-furled genoa. During the day the wind increased steadily and the barometer started falling. By nightfall we had reefed down again and had only a small portion of genoa set. Possibly because of our proximity to the reef, seas were agitated, superimposed on the swell. Overnight the barometer continued downward and the 6 am weather forecast on 7 March reported that a low in the Coral Sea had deepened to become Cyclone Justin with a central pressure of 976mb, approximate position 17.5°S 151.1°E, which was directly in our path. Historically, the cyclones move west towards the coast, or run south and recurve east to the Tasman Sea. We hove-to under a storm jib to await developments, so that we could set a tangential course. Conditions deteriorated rapidly. We were tossed and rolled about on the increasingly turbulent seas, and a mid-morning cyclone update alerted us that justin was intensifying, but remaining stationary.

We didn't feel happy waiting any longer for indication of movement, so at about 10 am we decided to try to motor east to gain sea room while it was still possible. Some peaks had breaking crests as we motored across the seas. I hand steered, trying to prevent broaching, and was surprised that we kept rising up over each wave. Robin lurched round the pitching deck checking rigging, fittings and lashings, and removed the storm jib that by now was in shreds. After about two hours under power Robin went below to check the GPS, which showed that *Orca* was being driven north-west faster than we were motoring east. Although we were making boat speed we were not making easterly progress over the ground. We decided to take the engine out of gear and to set our 24ft (7.3m) diameter Cape Hatteras parachute sea anchor. Thus we found ourselves heading north-west at about 5 knots under bare poles in sustained winds exceeding 50 knots.

It was impossible to maintain a foothold on the deck due to the pitching and rolling. With harnesses clipped onto the jackline running from the bow to the stern, we crept forwards on all fours, grabbing handholds, and dragging the flotation buoys and the parachute anchor in its deployable stowage bag. On occasions the seas sluiced us with gallons of water which raced over the deck. Fortunately, the 500ft (152m) 1in (25mm) diameter nylon line for the parachute was stowed up forward in a bag in the chain locker, and by reaching into the hawse pipe we withdrew the thimbles on both ends. Lying face down on the deck, Robin threaded the line over the starboard bow roller and under the bowsprit sidestay and back onto deck, so we could then shackle the assembly together, using a ¾in (18mm) stainless steel swivel and shackles, and wire them closed. We knew we had just one chance. With only two of us, we couldn't afford a mistake or an injury.

When the line and parachute bag were connected and the flotation buoys attached, we pulled out 50ft (15m) of the line, and belayed it. The ensemble was then forced under the sidestay. It only took seconds for it to sink under the weight of the stainless steel gear, before the bag popped off. The chute must have opened almost instantly for we were suddenly jerked as the chute filled and the line snubbed up. It then became a matter of urgency to pay out the rest of the line, as with only the initial 50ft (15m) of line out, the full parachute felt like a dead weight preventing the bow from rising freely. I hauled the remaining line through the hawse pipe and Robin eased the belay round the large mooring bitts. Finally, with the full 500ft (152m) out, *Orca* was free to rise and move with the waves and the stretching component of the nylon line acted as a shock absorber.

Orca's underwater body showing her long keel.
Photo: Maggi Ansell

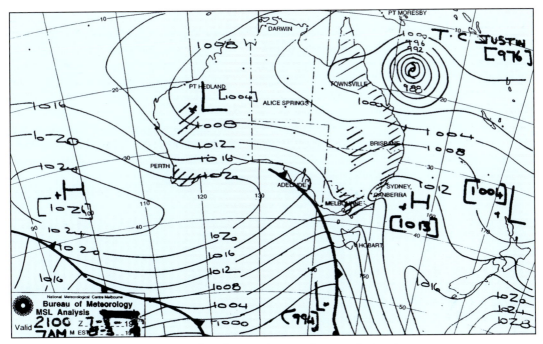

Fig 26.1 Meteorological chart at the time the parachute anchor was deployed.

When all the line was out, Robin tried to place the chafe-guard between the line and the bow roller, but it was impossible. The rode under constant tension was like a steel cable welded to the roller. This was not good. We then attempted to use a pendant line to control our angle from the wind (as suggested in Lin and Larry Pardey's *Storm Tactics Handbook*). The block, however, continually ran up against the hull, so we gave up. In total it took us about two hours to set the parachute. We frequently had to wait and just hang on to prevent us from being washed through the safety lines. To add to our problems, thoughout the deployment, sea water and rain had soaked the pristine nylon line of the parachute anchor. As it stretched tight passing round the mooring bitts, a mist emanated from it, and sprayed over us. It tasted acrid and stung our eyes, noses and throats.

Finally, at about 4 pm, it was almost dark as we clawed our way back and went below, battening down securely. By now, my eyes were burning. I could no longer read the instrument dials, and the radar was a green blur. I tried flushing them clean. Robin admitted that his eyes felt as if he had a case of welder's 'arc-eye'. However, unbeknown to me, he went outside again. He knew our most pressing problem was to arrange chafe-protection for the line. It wouldn't take long to abrade and break. He removed the 10ft (3m) of $\frac{5}{8}$in (16mm) anchor chain attached to our stern anchor, and dragged it forward to the bow. By some superhuman effort, he attached one end of the chain to the thimble in the end of the nylon line, the other to a length of $1\frac{1}{8}$in (28mm) diameter three-strand nylon rode secured around the port mooring bitts. He then eased the whole assembly inch by inch round the starboard mooring bitts until the chain lay over the bow roller. This single feat probably saved our lives.

With nothing worse than a dislocated finger and a severely bruised ankle from being trapped between chain and toe rail, he had relieved us of the need to venture forth hourly to check chafe, not that we could have done much about it.

Conditions inside were uncomfortable. I had long since given up boiling kettles, following a scalding earlier when the kettle flew from the gimballed stove, which was our most vulnerable point. We were pleased, however, that during our last refit we had secured every locker, seat and floor section; all batteries, toolboxes and possible projectiles were strapped down. Nevertheless, we were pitched bodily against the fixtures, gathering multiple contusions as *Orca* continued her manic dance on the end of the lifeline.

The parachute was holding us between 10° and 60° from the wind, but green water regularly broke over the deck. This had the effect of lifting hatches, and compressing hatch seals, resulting in some severe seepage. Even our brand-new $700 galley hatch was no match for the water pressure. We pumped bilges and constantly wrung out the towels we'd placed on the floor to prevent slipping. After 12 hours, the pain in our eyes subsided, and after a further 12 we could begin to see with hazy vision.

On 8 March, weather reports and weatherfaxes confirmed that Justin had reached Category II and remained stalled. We could now read the wind speed indicator again and the sustained wind was exceeding 60 knots. With the GPS connected to the radar, we watched ourselves drifting towards Justin's forecast centre, and the isolated Malay Reef that lay directly in our path. Our rate of drift, however, had been reduced from 5 to about 1.5 knots by the parachute anchor. Occasionally, by looking through the cockpit window when at the bottom of a trough, we saw the rode leading away, but visibility was too poor to see the flotation buoys.

Ever fearful of an electrical fire, we had covered our breaker panels and electronic gear with a large polythene drop cloth. Electric bilge pumps were handling the water well so far, but a large dry bilge in the forward cabin had several inches of water in it. The chain locker must also have been full of water by this time, and I didn't like to think of our possible nose-down attitude. For 41 hours we did not leave the cabin, nor did we sleep. We just worked from one end of the vessel to the other, coping with the ingress of water.

During that time we experienced some exceptional waves, which approached from the starboard quarter. They were audible above the constant noise of the cyclone, and were heralded by a roaring rumble culminating in an ear-numbing bang as they hit. With a great shudder *Orca* was slammed over and propelled sideways, but the masts never hit the water. Perhaps our full heavy keel prevented us from being rolled. In a 24 hour period we think we suffered about four of these waves. We have no idea of their size, as we didn't see them, but only felt their effect. At 9.30 am on 9 March the loudest rumble yet resulted in tons of water hitting us with massive force, and seemed to squash us down into the water. I was braced in the galley and saw the small 12in × 5in (30cm × 13cm) galley portlight fly past my face ahead of a cataract of water. We scrambled around in the water on the floor and retrieved the window pane and wedged it back in the splintered frame. Robin made a temporary repair by drilling and screwing heavy battens across. Nails would probably have been punched out again. He then struggled outside to lash a folded, heavy waxed cotton tarpaulin across the outside, to buffer the impact of the waves.

Orca's engine was still running, and it had been since we motored from the reef two days earlier. It made me feel safer that way, not that it would have been any use if the anchor line had broken. Noon weather reports on 9 March brought no comfort. There was no change in Justin's position and the cyclone was still intensifying. Our barometer read 965mb. The wind direction was constant and we were still drifting towards Malay Reef. We kept hoping for a tiny wind shift.

At 2.30 pm another roar grew above the sounds of the storm. When the wave struck, the crack was so loud we felt certain we had hit something like a submerged container from a ship, at full velocity. We were dashed against the cabin walls as *Orca* recoiled and slammed over on her side before righting. A quick check of all the cabins revealed that hull and windows were intact, but the noise was different from the other times we were side-swiped. Robin peered through the forward facing cockpit windows, and for a moment was puzzled. He could see clear across the deck, but he hadn't been able to before. Then it dawned on him that the starboard Dorade boxes had been cleanly sliced off at deck level. We rushed to check the starboard and forward cabins beneath the Dorades, and looking up we could see the sky through four dribbling 3in (7.6cm) holes in the hull. With large bungs and sailcloth Robin went outside to effect a temporary repair. I clipped my harness inside the companionway to put my head out and keep an eye on him, while checking for further rogue waves.

As I watched him struggling, I glanced beyond, and noticed two safety-line stanchions swaying from the slack line. Although Robin was clipped onto the jackline, he often braced himself against the stanchions as the boat rolled. He lifted his head for a second, so I gesticulated and yelled 'STANCHIONS GONE – NO SAFETY LINE'. He couldn't possibly hear me, he was 20ft (6m) upwind. However, he glanced over his shoulder and understood.

When he returned below and had secured the hatch, we took stock. We were battered, bruised and scalded, but had no incapacitating injuries. We were taking water in through all hatches, the galley portlight and the four holes in the deck, but the electric bilge pumps were coping – so far. If the electrics failed, we had our big hand pump ready. Masts and rigging were intact, the parachute anchor was holding firm and the engine was running. The latest weather reports had given Justin as 500nm across, intensifying and still stationary. We were getting ever nearer the centre but, worse by far, we were moving unswervingly towards Malay Reef.

At 3 pm Robin called Townsville Radio to update them on our situation. After a discussion the operator asked if we were declaring a Mayday. We were stunned, as we had never considered the possibility. He calmly explained that 'abandoning' the yacht would not only mean abandoning her physically, but also abandoning certain rights to her. He added that a rescue would not be possible in the dark, and conditions were worsening.

We could hope there would be no more damaging rogue waves. Our large area of unprotected windows had been spared so far, but if one succumbed, it wouldn't take long for *Orca* to fill. Yet that still wasn't the prime consideration. The one thing we couldn't do was alter course to avoid Malay Reef. At our current rate of drift, we would founder before the end of the day. It was not an easy decision. We had to fight denial, but reluctantly admitted we were in a life-threatening situation and agreed to abandon our home of seven years. Townsville Radio reported a Mayday situation to the Maritime Rescue Coordination Centre in Canberra. At 3.45 pm Robin talked direct to MRCC and passed on details. There were no promises that anything could be done in the atrocious conditions and at that late time of day. We continued with our routine.

Our rescue was effected within three hours. A US Navy Hercules in the area was diverted to locate us via our 406 EPIRB signal, so they could guide the Queensland Emergency Services (QES) helicopter that was fitting long-range tanks to reach us. A Royal Flying Doctor Services Beechcraft Super King Air flew in tandem at 17 000ft (5181m) ready to drop additional liferafts if needed. On standby as back-up were an Australian Army Blackhawk helicopter and an Australian Navy warship, being the only platform left if the QES helicopter was unsuccessful. Fortunately, the latter two were not needed. When the QES helicopter arrived it had just 20 minutes' fuel time to assess hovering capabilities and effect the rescue. As we were unable to safely dismast, we had been instructed to prepare our dinghy for streaming astern. At the given signal we launched the dinghy and Robin held it close while I jumped in, but then he had to let go and leap. He somersaulted in, but as the line came up tight he continued his journey into the water. As he was free-floating he was picked up first by the rescue swimmer on the wire, and by the time the rescuer returned, I too was in the water since the dinghy had capsized almost immediately, but I was clipped onto the dinghy and still had the EPIRB attached to me. The rescue was completed with two minutes to spare and we were flying towards Townsville before the winch boom was retracted and the side door was closed. The crew then congratulated us on not

Building seas outside the Great Barrier Reef.
Photo: Maggi Ansell

panicking, and doing only what we were told, thus allowing them to do their job and make possible an almost impossible rescue.

We subsequently learned from the helicopter crew that gusts to 85 knots were experienced, and in order to maintain station off *Orca*'s stern the pilot had at times to go astern at 12 knots plus, during passage of the larger waves. Some waves gave the appearance of being double-crested, so *Orca* would rise up the face of the first wave, and then roll over the top straight into the advancing wall of the second. It is possibly this phenomenon that caused our damage. The crew of the helicopter told us they had never experienced conditions like it before. Hovering 100ft (30m) above a moving datum, they lost sight of yacht and mast behind the swells. They reported the masts 'whipsawing' through the air, rolling 60° either side of vertical, with a roll rate of about one per second, which made it very difficult and dangerous to approach the vessel, jeopardizing the safety of the crew. Down in the belly of the boat, it hadn't felt that dramatic. The Hercules crew described 'giant swells', estimated at 50–80ft (15–24m), behind which they lost *Orca* after an initial sighting. They recorded winds between 50 and 70 knots with blowing rain and occasional cloud decks to the surface. Visibility ranged from zero to $\frac{1}{2}$ mile.

The three-man QES rescue crew received commendations for bravery in Australia, and in the USA in February 1998 were awarded the Helicopter Association International's (Salute to Excellence) Golden Hour Award for the most outstanding rescue worldwide during 1997. The Hercules crew was decorated for their extraordinary skill and professionalism.

It wasn't until much later that we fully realized how fortunate we had been. According to the MRCC data, we were picked up only 5nm from the reef. Even if the reef had not been there, Justin turned out to be the largest (although not the strongest) cyclone for 20 years, measuring 500nm across, but most remarkable was its duration. It remained virtually stationary from 7 March for 15 days. During that time it weakened slightly before gaining strength again and finally coming ashore, hitting Cairns and Townsville on 22 March.

There has never been any sighting of *Orca* or a single piece of debris found from her.

A few isolated observations:
- We never once felt seasick. We had started our voyage with a Travacalm seasickness pill, and continued taking a couple a day.
- The ferro-cement hull and superstructure, the masts and galvanized rigging must have been very strong.
- Our almost fanatical securing inside paid off.

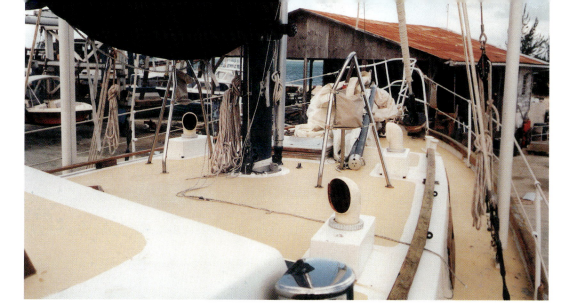

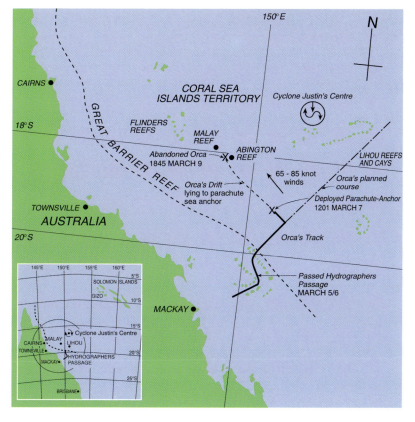

Above *Orca*'s upper deck showing three of the four Dorade ventilator boxes which were stripped off by the sea. *Photo: Maggi Ansell*

Figure 26.2 (left) Track of *Orca* during Cyclone Justin, March 1997.

- We didn't stow anything on deck apart from the dinghy on the cockpit roof, and the outboard motor at the stern.
- Being shorthanded we always tried to sail conservatively. Even in good weather we never went on deck without harnesses clipped on. With the exception of Robin going outside to attach the chain to prevent chafe, we never went outside without telling the other what we were doing.
- We should have had storm covers to screw over all exposed windows, although the logistics of manhandling and attaching them in a severe storm would be interesting. (Our next vessel, in the planning, is looking remarkably like a submarine!)

- Removing the plastic air scoops and screwing in the metal plates doesn't help a lot when the Dorade boxes are sliced off at deck level.
- It was not possible to insure an ocean-crossing ferro-cement yacht – perhaps with good reason, although had *Orca* been made of less stern stuff, she might have broken up.
- But for the proximity of Malay Reef we would never have agreed to abandon *Orca*.

COMMENT

This story of an experienced ocean cruising couple's encounter with a seasonal cyclone shows that such crews have but few options in a cyclone, especially in a 55ft (16.8m) yacht when the gear has to be proportionately heavy.

On the basis that tropical revolving storms do usually move, though they do dither too, it might seem eminently sensible for the parachute sea anchor to have been deployed when it was. After all, there have been situations when a parachute was carried but not used because its deployment had been left too late. As it was, it was a good effort to deploy it from *Orca* in the circumstances. Handling 500ft (152m) of wet 1in (25mm) diameter line is not easy in harbour, let alone at sea in 50 knots of wind. A bowsprit does make the task more complicated, and it would have been almost impossible to manage without a parachute deployment bag. The blinding acrid chemical was hardly to be expected and would have been extremely unwelcome at any time. Yet it helps to make the case for trying out a parachute sea anchor in non-life threatening circumstances.

A length of chain in the parachute line where it passes over the bows is vital, otherwise chafe will soon cause it to part. No doubt Robin Ansell wished several times that he had put the chain in the system on an earlier occasion. Nonetheless, it was a great achievement to insert 10ft (3m) of $\frac{5}{8}$in (16mm) chain into the system in the prevailing conditions.

One of the most noteworthy aspects of the whole episode is how well the parachute performed and, following their experience, the Ansells recommend a parachute as a first line of defence in extreme bad weather. With the 24ft (7.3m) diameter parachute sea anchor set, *Orca* drifted at 1.5 knots. This is rather more than would be hoped for, but the wind strength, *Orca*'s size and the windage of her high superstructure aft has to be taken into account. It is interesting to compare *Prisana*'s drift rate of under 1 knot, a 45ft (14m) yacht with an 18ft (5.5m) parachute in roughly similar conditions (Chapter 13). The mizzen mast and the superstructure will have prevented much yaw and the need for a riding sail. The variation in apparent wind angle suggested that she might have yawed from 10° through to 60°, remaining on one tack as it were, and this could probably have been reduced further with a scrap of mizzen set. *Orca* lay at an angle to the wind and waves taking up a position much like the Ansells had been trying to achieve with a pendant line. Though relatively safe, riding to her parachute anchor, *Orca*'s movement was far from comfortable. Robin Ansell estimated the roll rate to be 60° per second and, together with all the other movement described, the situation below must have been hellish.

If one has no practical experience, accounts such as this one give an indication of just how much load there is on the parachute line. Deploying a parachute sea anchor is, of course, a very committing step to take. It will not be possible to recover the parachute until the weather has moderated and, in addition to the cost of replacement, to cut the line or let it go loses one of the best heavy weather options – unless one happens to have more than one parachute and line on board.

The account of the abandonment of *Orca* illustrates the fickle nature of tropical revolving storms, and the importance of sea room. Perhaps a numerically stronger crew could have saved the yacht, though probably not without grave risk. Maggi Ansell does not think so.

27 An experience with a sea anchor

TIM TRAFFORD

Ardevora is a 55ft (16.8m) aluminium ketch with a long fin-keel with centreplate and a spade rudder, weighing 50 000lb (22 680kg). She was designed by Steve Dalzell and built by Whisstocks in 1989.

On 6 September 1997 we were close-reaching at 40°S and some 30 miles off the west coast of Chile, having just crossed onto the Continental Shelf, on passage from Easter Island to Valdivia. There were three of us on board: myself, as skipper, Sophie, my wife, and a surveyor friend, Bruce Burton. It had been blowing a northerly gale since 0900 and gusting to 47 knots. The forecast was north or north-west 30–40 knots gusting to 50. For two days we had been racing a depression (on the weatherfax) and it was now clear that we would not make the shelter of Corral before the blow.

At about 1600 we decided to heave-to. We had done this twice in force 8 in the previous 10 days and had spent 50 hours hove-to off Easter Island, as the anchorages were untenable. Our usual drill was staysail and reefed mizzen. Although the trysail, of 25 per cent of mainsail area, was bent on and ready to hoist, I was reluctant to use it as it is just too big. Shortly after setting the mizzen three seams started to part. It was immediately handed and Sophie offered to make a running repair, but it would have been very difficult in the prevailing conditions. With the staysail sheeted flat and hard on the wind we were making significant leeway towards the coast, so we switched to storm staysail and fore-reached at 3 knots with a course made good of 120–140°. By 1700 it was clear we were still closing the land too fast. Tacking was a possibility, but we would have ended up far downwind of our destination. I was keen to try out a new weapon in our armoury: a Para-Tech sea anchor.

I had become intrigued by Lin and Larry Pardey's *Storm Tactics Handbook* and acquired an 18ft (5.5m) diameter parachute anchor suitable for boats up to 50ft (15.2m). Although perhaps on the small side (according to the literature), the next size up was 24ft (7.3m) diameter and suitable for boats up to 90ft (27.4m) – I felt that was just too big for us. I rather hoped that this blow would be no more than a gale – like the previous two – and therefore good conditions to experiment with the beast.

SET-UP

Some 600ft (183m) of 1in (25mm) diameter plaited nylon line acted as rode. It was attached to the sea anchor without a swivel (which was awaiting our arrival in Valdivia). In the event, the lack of a swivel did not seem to be a problem. The rode was led through a closed fairlead 2ft 6in (76cm) aft of the stemhead fitting (which could not be closed), through a snatch block on the starboard toe rail and directly onto the starboard primary yankee sheet winch and across the cockpit onto the port winch – both Lewmar 65s. The rode was paid out from a drum mounted on the stern. A 3ft (1m) section of reinforced plastic hose served as anti-chafe through the fairlead. A fender attached to 30ft (9m) of polypropylene acted as pick-up. The sea anchor self-deploys from its bag once in the water.

DEPLOYMENT

While lying a'hull and with the storm staysail handed, the pick-up buoy and line were fed out over the weather rail followed by the bag containing the sea anchor. An extremely anxious minute followed: the trip line, rode and partly deployed sea anchor washed along the weather side of the boat. Until the whole lot cleared the keel, prop and rudder, my heart was in my mouth. Once opened, the sea anchor dragged the bow head-to-wind and the rode was fed out from the safety of the cockpit.

LYING TO THE SEA ANCHOR

By 1900 the sea anchor was fully deployed. The motion was appalling. *Ardevora* was pitching heavily: chafe marks seen later on the stem indicated up to 45° above and below horizontal. She was also rolling her gunnels under and yawing up to 30–40° either side of the wind. I had hoped that leading the rode through the starboard fairlead would ensure that we lay on the starboard tack. When the bow veered to starboard the rode rubbed all the way down the stem and around and over the top of the stemhead fitting. In an attempt to rectify this, the mizzen boom (with the sail lowered) was backed to push the stern round,

Ardevora.
Photo: Sophie Trafford

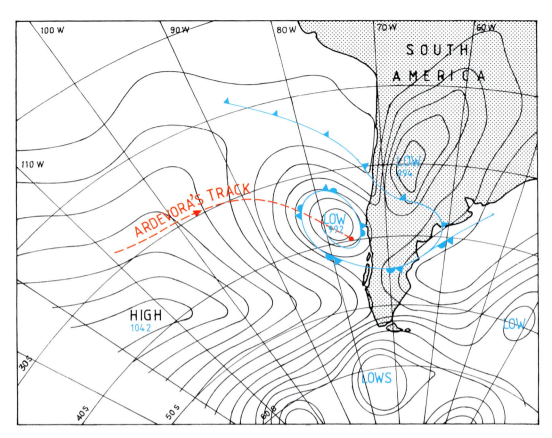

Figure 27.2 Weather chart at 1800 VTC (1300 local) on 6 September 1997. The depression on the west side of the tip of South America pursued *Ardevora* across the Pacific and force 9 was experienced 10 hours after this time.

but with little effect. Turning the wheel a few degrees to starboard improved matters, but I felt this tactic could damage the stock so it was lashed amidships. As a final resort, a pendant was rigged through a closed fairlead amidships on the starboard side and attached onto the rode with a rolling hitch. Despite easing the rode with strain on the pendant, we couldn't get the bridle arrangement to work. In the dark, and barely able to crawl along the sidedeck, this had been a dangerous operation. We therefore decided to sit the blow out riding to the sea anchor, and change the nip on the rode every half hour – in itself a hazardous exercise.

The strain on the rode was so great that I seriously thought the starboard winch would tear out of its mountings. By 2300 it was blowing a steady 45 knots and gusting to 59.9 knots (the highest gust spotted on the damped Brookes & Gatehouse anemometer). Our average GPS-derived speed over the ground was 1.9–2.0 knots. The *Admiralty Pilot* indicates that the Humboldt Current runs to the north at up to 2 knots, so average speed through the water may have been much higher. This may also have contributed to big seas and therefore extreme pitching. On large breaking crests we were surging sternwards at some speed. I was so concerned about damage to the rudder that I considered cutting the rode.

To our alarm, on the crests of the waves, Bruce spotted a navigation light to weather. The knife was readied, the deck lights switched on, and Sophie contacted the vessel on VHF. We warned her (in Spanish) of our parachute line and she quickly passed to weather, perhaps half a mile away. She was a large trawler on her way to seek shelter in Corral.

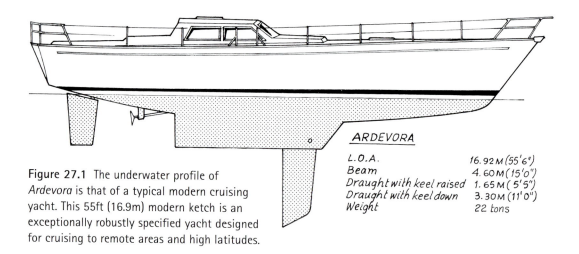

Figure 27.1 The underwater profile of *Ardevora* is that of a typical modern cruising yacht. This 55ft (16.9m) modern ketch is an exceptionally robustly specified yacht designed for cruising to remote areas and high latitudes.

ARDEVORA

L.O.A.	16.92 M (55'6")
Beam	4.60 M (15'0")
Draught with keel raised	1.65 M (5'5")
Draught with keel down	3.30 M (11'0")
Weight	22 tons

CHAFED THROUGH AND LYING A'HULL

Shortly after 2300, and almost four hours after deployment, the rode parted. The decklog entry at 0020 records: 'The relief that it had gone was just – I don't know what – but like throwing off a huge weight, stress just went. We immediately lay a'hull and it was as if the wind had died, gone were the dreadful yawing and rolling ... I was initially keen to set the storm stays and fore-reach to get more offing, but to my surprise we're so comfortable lying a'hull we'll stick with it. The breeze is now only a steady 40–45 knots...'

Lying a'hull *Ardevora* heeled over at between 20–30° and with the helm hard over she lay 70–75° off the wind. She was so comfortable that we took turns to sleep – something that had not been possible while lying to the sea anchor. Leeway was about 2.5 knots over the ground. In the first hour after the rode parted three large breaking waves crashed into the turn of the bilge. By 0400 the breeze had eased to 28–32 knots and we were beginning to roll. Sail was set at 0700, and when we arrived at Corral we found it crowded with about 30 ocean-sized fishing boats and other assorted shipping sheltering from the weather.

CONCLUSIONS

1 **Deployment**   It took two exhausting hours to rig and set the sea anchor. Lying a'hull to deploy the sea anchor the boat tended to fore-reach slowly. It may have been worth going slow astern under power to ensure the sea anchor could not snag the keel, rudder or propeller.

2 **Chafe**   I grossly underestimated yawing and pitching. If we had been able to control yawing by holding the boat on starboard tack, then chafe would have been far less of a problem. Despite changing the nip, edges on the stemhead fitting cut through the rode in less than 30 minutes.

3 **Motion**   Extreme and violent movement was experienced while lying-to the sea anchor. Doubtless the windage of the rolled-up headsails did not help the yawing. If we had been able to rig a bridle it might have been a little better. Lying a'hull was relatively peaceful, but heaving-to under backed headsail and mizzen would have been better still.

4 **Strain**   The strain on the rode can only be described as alarming. Two Lewmar 65s were used in tandem to adjust the rode, but I was doubtful that they were up to it. I was grateful that the building owners had oversized the sheet winches. No anchor winch or deck cleat would have survived the load. I do not believe that any foredeck fitting on a mod-

ern production yacht is man enough to take the load imposed by a sea anchor in a real blow. Properly installed bitts through-mounted to the forefoot may suffice.

5 **Leeway**   Lying to the sea anchor in 45 knots gusting to 60 knots, leeway was 1.9–2.0 knots. Lying a'hull in a steady 35–45 knots, leeway was 0.5 knots more – a surprisingly small difference. Doubtless it is arguable whether an 18ft (5.5m) diameter sea anchor was large enough for *Ardevora*, but to be held even more securely with a 24ft (7.3m) diameter sea anchor would only have increased the already large loads.

6 **Heaving-to v sea anchor v lying a'hull in force 9**   I made mistakes and miscalculations, and so lying to our sea anchor was an unpleasant experience. However, I believe that even if a sea anchor is perfectly set up, lying to it would not be as comfortable as heaving-to. It may be the case that for smaller modern boats in true open ocean gale conditions, lying to a sea anchor offers a tactical alternative to heaving-to, provided the deck gear is strong enough. For *Ardevora*, heaving-to will always be the preferred technique for riding out strong winds. Instinct suggests that lying a'hull is inviting damage/disaster. I was surprised how well she lay a'hull, but she is a very strongly built boat. On a future voyage I would only contemplate deploying a sea anchor if rig or rudder had been lost and an unfriendly shore was close to leeward. For me, the sea anchor has become a tool of the very last resort.

COMMENT

The yacht was subjected to force 9, a severe gale, which provides a worthy test of storm tactics. That the drift rate was unacceptably high, as Tim Trafford appreciates, was because an 18ft (5.5m) parachute is too small for a 55ft (16.8m) yacht. As stated in Chapter 6, it is better to go up a size rather than down a size, and an 18ft (5.5m) parachute is only recommended for yachts up to 50ft (15.2m).

Orca's drift rate, described in Chapter 26, bears comparison. Both yachts were of the same length, but *Orca* was much heavier and had much more windage. *Orca* was probably experiencing quite a lot more wind too. These are all factors that should increase her drift rate compared with *Ardevora*. We do not know what *Ardevora*'s drift rate was because of the effect of the Humboldt Current. It is probably safe to assume it to have been 2.5 knots through the water and, combined with the surge resulting from the stretch of the parachute line, enough to cause serious concern for the rudder. Aboard *Orca*, with her drift rate of only 1.5 knots through the water, the rudder does not appear to have been of any concern. It can be concluded that if *Ardevora* had used a 24ft (7.3m) parachute, her drift rate would have been reduced to an acceptable level.

Tim Trafford's description of the wild ride lying to a parachute sea anchor corresponds with that of both *Orca* and *Prisana* (Chapter 25), but would have been considerably aggravated by the Humboldt Current running against the wind. In these two latter cases the unpleasantness of the extreme movement of the yachts was considered preferable to other options.

It is noteworthy that it took two hours to prepare the parachute sea anchor system aboard both *Ardevora* and *Orca*, but aboard *Prisana* the parachute was set up and ready so that all the crew had to do was to release the lashings. Clearly a parachute sea anchor should be made ready before a storm, if at all possible.

Lack of a swivel can cause the parachute rigging line to twist if laid rather than plaited parachute line is used, lowering the cross-sectional area. Some parachutes can rotate too, but Para-Tech parachutes do not tend to turn. Anyhow, it is not certain how well swivels work under heavy load. As Tim Trafford suggests, the lack of a swivel probably made no difference.

Tim Trafford's account bears out some disadvantages of a parachute sea anchor. Had the parachute been of 24ft (7.3m) diameter it seems possible that the winches used to secure the parachute line might have been torn out of the deck. One has to remember that the parachute line has to be secured to something that will take not far short of the weight of the whole boat. It is doubtful whether the structure to which some primary winches are secured will take this kind of load. When yachts have been built with sturdy toe rails, the fastenings of which join the deck to the hull moulding, the load will be spread through the length of the boat.

Yawing would have been reduced with part of the mizzen set, had it been available, making the ride more comfortable besides reducing chafe. Nevertheless, one has to accept that chafe will always be a problem and, unless one is able to lead the parachute line over the stem, the parachute line will cut across the bow at times. Even when the parachute line is led through an ordinary stem fitting, chafe will remain high as the rope is unlikely to stay on the roller and will abrade against the vertical plates of the stem fitting, but there is less chance that there will be abrasion against the hull. In the case of larger yachts, such as *Ardevora*, trying to protect the parachute line with plastic hose will not do the job. Anchor chain is really the best answer.

Lowering the centreplate might have reduced yaw. However, Victor Shane in his *Drag Device Data Base* recommends that, as a rule, centreplates should be raised to reduce the possibility of the yacht 'tripping over her keel'.

Lying to a parachute head-on is a very uncomfortable way of riding out a storm, hence the development of the Pardey method of lying at an angle to the waves, but I have not heard of this method being successful for a yacht as large as *Ardevora*. The strain on the pendant line would be enormous.

It was interesting to read that the 600ft (183m) 1in (25mm) parachute line was stowed on a reel. This kind of length of heavy rope needs a dedicated stowage. Tim Trafford will not be alone in believing that the most worrying moment is when the parachute line is being deployed. If the load were to come on the parachute line after it had been caught around the rudder or propeller shaft, the damage could be catastrophic.

The comment that the trysail area at 25 per cent of the mainsail area was 'just too big' is interesting. The Offshore Racing Council's special regulations require that trysails are no larger than 17.5 per cent mainsail luff length × mainsail foot length. These criteria usually lead to a trysail of about 30 per cent mainsail area, so *Ardevora*'s trysail would appear to be about the correct size. If trysails are not trimmed hard aft they are apt to generate excessive drive and heeling moment.

It seems to be significant that in three out of four cases of yachts lying-to parachute sea anchors in this book, collision with other vessels became a cause of concern. In these cases VHF radio was used to good effect, and clearly when lying to a sea anchor it is wise to make an 'All ships' call at regular intervals. Bruce, by the way, should be congratulated on keeping an eye open to windward, as this can be rather unpleasant in force 9.

Tim Trafford's conclusion that it is better to heave-to rather than lie to a parachute anchor could be attributed to the inadequate size of his parachute. However, if a yacht will heave-to reliably and comfortably, and there is sea room to do so, this tactic is almost always preferable. *Ardevora* has a long keel and can be expected to heave-to well, and indeed she does. As it happened in this case, after the parachute line broke heaving-to was not adopted because of the mizzen problem, and she was allowed to lie a'hull which can, of course, be a risky tactic. My preference would have been to heave-to under a well-sheeted trysail.

We are left with the conclusion that for many non-extreme yachts in heavy weather, heaving-to should be the preferred primary tactic, but skippers should be fully prepared to employ other tactics if the time comes when lying hove-to is not sustainable. One of these should be a drag device.

Bibliography

1994 Pacific Storm Survey. Kim Taylor. Quarry Publishing. 1996.

All Weather Yachtsman. Peter Haward. Dobbs Ferry NY: Sheridan House, 1994.

Alone Through the Roaring Forties. Vito Dumas. London: Adlard Coles, 1960.

Around the World with Ridgeway. John Ridgeway and Marie Christine Ridgeway. Heinemann, 1978.

Because the Horn Is There. Miles Smeeton. London: Nautical Publishing Company, in association with Harrap, 1970.

DDTB: Drag Device Data Base: Using Parachutes, Sea Anchors, and Drogues to Cope with Heavy Weather—Seventy Documented Case Histories. Victor Shane. Para-Anchors International, 1998, currently out of print.

Deep Sea Sailing. Erroll Bruce. Stanley Paul, 1953, currently out of print.

Desirable and Undesirable Characteristics of Offshore Yachts. John Rousmaniere. New York: W. W. Norton, 1987.

Drogues: A Study to Improve the Safety of Sailing Yachts. Carol Hervey and Donald Jordan. Washington DC: Marine Technology, 1988.

Eight Sailing/Mountain-Expedition Books. H. W. Tilman. Seattle WA: Mountaineers Books, 1987.

Fastnet, Force 10. John Rousmaniere. New York: W. W. Norton, 1993.

Fastnet Race Enquiry Report. RORC & RYA. 1979.

Halsey's Typhoons: A Firsthand Account of How Two Typhoons, More Powerful than the Japanese, Dealt Death and Destruction to Admiral Halsey's Third Fleet. Hans Christian Adamson and George Francis Kosco. New York: Crown Publishers, 1967.

Handling Small Boats in Heavy Weather. Frank Robb. London: Adlard Coles, 1976.

Heavy Weather Cruising, 2nd ed. Tom Cunliffe. Fernhurst Books, distributed by State Mutual Book & Periodical Service Ltd., New York, 1998.

Heavy Weather Guide. William J. Kotsch and Richard Henderson. Annapolis MD: U.S. Naval Institute Press, 1984.

How to Cope with Storms. Dietrich von Haefton. Dobbs Ferry NY: Sheridan House, 1997

My Lively Lady. Sir Alec Rose. Dobbs Ferry NY: Sheridan House, 1988.

North Atlantic. K. Adlard Coles. Robert Ross, 1950.

Offshore. Captain J. Illingworth. London: Adlard Coles, 1963.

Offshore Racing Council Special Regulations. Offshore Racing Council.

The Parachute Anchoring System and Other Tactics. J. Casanova, V. Shane, D. C. Shewmon, and G. Macmillan. Boston: Chiodi Publishing, 1985.

Rescue in the Pacific. Tony Farrington. Camden ME: International Marine, 1998.

The Sea Anchor & Drogue Handbook. Daniel C. Shewmon. Safety Harbor FL: Shewmon, Inc., 1995.

Seaworthiness: The Forgotten Factor. 2nd ed. C. A. Marchaj. St. Michaels MD: Tiller Publishing, 1996.

Storm Tactics Handbook: Modern Methods of Heaving-to for Survival in Extreme Conditions. Lin and Larry Pardey. Arcata CA: Paradise Cay Publications, 1999.

This is Rough Weather Cruising. Erroll Bruce. Nautical Books, 1987, currently out of print.

Venturesome Voyages of Captain Voss. John Claus Voss. Sidney BC: Gray's Publishing, 1976.

Yachting Casualties 3–8 June 1994. Maritime Safety Authority.

Acknowledgments

As I wrote in the previous edition, *Heavy Weather Sailing* has become such a cornerstone of yachting information that it would have been a formidable task for any normal person to carry out the task singlehanded. I have sought the most eminent and wise counsel that I could find to help me with the task, and have had the script read by as many yachtsmen of scholarship and long experience as possible. Once again, I owe much to others in the compilation of the thirtieth anniversary edition of *Heavy Weather Sailing*.

Again both Sandy Watson and Leonard Wesson, both members of the Royal Cruising Club, have given up much of their time to read the script, and I have almost invariably adopted their numerous suggestions. Other readers who have been of great help are Patrick Croker, David Scaife and Richard Head. I have leant on Simon Forbes for advice in the multihull sector, and received gallant all-weather support from Paul Gelder, James Beattie, Richard Clifford, Bill Carlyle, Robert Burdett, Tim Jeffreys, and a legion of others in respect of the drag device trials.

Lin and Larry Pardey's careful advice, also, has been tremendously helpful regarding parachute sea anchors and more general matters. Kim Taylor undertook some especially useful work on the Queen's Birthday storm. I have also to thank Ross Coles, Adlard Coles's son, for his sensible advice and last, but by no means least, Janet Murphy, Director of Adlard Coles Nautical, for her encouragement and support.

The first part of the book has benefited magnificently from the wealth of knowledge provided by contributions from:

Olin J Stephens II, who must rate among the most admired yacht designers of the century and whose yachts are famous for their sea-keeping qualities.
Andrew Claughton from the Wolfson Unit for Marine Technology, Southampton, whose chapter enables comparisons to be made between design characteristics of yachts in a way that was previously only achieved by subjective means.
Matthew Sheahan, a very experienced yachtsman who currently writes for *Yachting World*, and previously worked for a leading British mast manufacturer. His book *Sailing Rigs and Spars* is a rare and perceptive written contribution to the subject.
Richard Ebling, who has been a meteorologist for 40 years. For the past 12 years he has been providing the Royal Ocean Racing Club with weather information for all its major events.
Mike Golding, whose success as a yacht-racing skipper with a large crew seems to be matched by his skill sailing solo. He won every leg but one of the last BT Challenge Round the World Race, and holds the record for sailing round the world 'the wrong way'.
Dr Sheldon Bacon from the Southampton Oceanography Centre, who has put a new angle on the subject of waves that is likely to be understood by people who, like him, enjoy small-boat sailing.
Dag Pike, one of the greatest exponents of power boating and author of numerous books.
Professor Noël Dilly, a professor of medicine, who writes on the subject of seasickness in the most comprehensive manner, but who also has been a source of valuable information on the subject of drogues which he has researched from his own small yacht.

Cathy Foster, a dinghy champion turned coach, who has discovered some interesting information regarding the important basic matters of food and sleep at sea.

Dr Gavin LeSueur, whose credentials as a heavy weather multihull sailor were reinforced by an encounter with Cyclone Bola, writes a chapter on multihull heavy tactics that complements his book *Multihull Seamanship*.

I must also thank those who have enlivened and enriched the text by a contribution from their own experiences or who have helped in some other useful way. Among these are:

David Alan-Williams, Robin and Maggie Ansell, Bugs Baer, Martin Bowdler, Peter Braley, Warren Brown, James Burdett, Alby Burgin, Robert Burns, Andrew Cassell, John Channon, Roy Clare, Richard Clifford, Bill Cooper, Mike Collins, Richard Crockett, Cheri and Richard Crowe, Barry Deakin, Steven Dixon, Alan Dooley, Chris Dunning, Steve Edwards, Carole Edwards, Peter Farthing, Bob Fisher, Geoffrey Francis, Harry Franks, Tony and Coryn Gooch, Alan Green, Ernest and Val Haigh, Mary Harper, Mike Harris, Richard Herbert, Timothy Hobson, Ted Howe, Bugs Hughes, Bruce Hyde, Nigel Irens, John Irving, Roy and Tee Jennings, Stanley Jewson, Willy Kerr, John Kettlewell, S Kirby, Robin Knox-Johnston, Marilyn Lange, Stig Larsen, Graham Laslett, Stephane Leveel, Cyril Lyon, Brian Macnamara, Alan McLaughlan, Dudley Norman, John Pennefather, Timothy Pickering, Jérôme Poncet, Stuart Quarrie, Skip Raymond, Michael Richey, Alan Roach, Larry Robbins, Jonathan Rogers, Oliver Roome, Bob Ross, John Rousmaniere, Niel Rusch, Brian and Pam Saffery Cooper, Dave Saunders, Deborah Schutz, Mike Seal, Greville Selby-Lowndes, Victor Shane, Daniel Shewmon, Skip Spitzer, Jeff Taylor, George Tinley, Tim Trafford, Charles Watson, Alan and Kathy Webb, Harry Whale, John Wilson, Peter Wykeham-Martin.

I should also thank all those who sent in material for which space has not been found. Much of this material has, nevertheless, been valuable in shaping conclusions.

International Marine
A Division of The McGraw-Hill Companies

First published in Great Britain in 1967. First published in the USA in 1968. Reprinted 1969, 1970, 1971, 1972; Revised and enlarged Edition 1975; Reprinted 1976; Third Revised Edition 1981 (three printings); Fourth Edition 1992 (paperback edition 1996); Thirtieth Anniversary Edition 1999

2   4   8   10   9   7   5   3   1

Copyright © K Adlard Coles 1967, 1975, 1980, 1991
Copyright © Peter Bruce 1991, 1999

A CIP catalog record for this book is available from the Library of Congress.

ISBN 0-07-135323-2

Questions regarding the ordering of this book should be addressed to
The McGraw-Hill Companies
Customer Service Department
P.O. Box 547
Blacklick, OH 43004
Retail customers: 1-800-262-4729
Bookstores: 1-800-722-4726
www.internationalmarine.com

Printed in Hong Kong

Frontispiece: Peter Bruce sails *Owl* to victory in heavy weather. *Photo: Tim Wright*

Index